The World Is Not Enough

A Biography of Ian Fleming

Oliver Buckton

FOREWORD BY JEREMY BLACK

ROWMAN & LITTLEFIELD
Lanham • Boulder • New York • London

Rowman & Littlefield
Bloomsbury Publishing Inc, 1385 Broadway, New York, NY 10018, USA
Bloomsbury Publishing Plc, 50 Bedford Square, London, WC1B 3DP, UK
Bloomsbury Publishing Ireland, 29 Earlsfort Terrace, Dublin 2, D02 AY28, Ireland
www.bloomsbury.com

First paperback edition 2025.

British Library Cataloguing in Publication Information available

A catalog record for this book is available from the Library of Congress.

For product safety related questions contact productsafety@bloomsbury.com.

♾™ The paper used in this publication meets the minimum requirements of American National Standard for Information Sciences—Permanence of Paper for Printed Library Materials, ANSI/NISO Z39.48-1992.

I dedicate this book to Laurice Campbell Buckton
who has shared the journey

Contents

Acknowledgments

I would like to acknowledge the following individuals and organizations for permission to quote from copyrighted materials:

Emily Russell, for permission to use photographs of Maud Russell and unpublished excerpts from her private diaries

Margy Kinmouth, and the Estate of Admiral John Godfrey, for permission to reproduce excerpts from Admiral John Godfrey's Naval Memoirs

The Ian Fleming Estate, for permission to quote extracts from unpublished letters and other materials by Ian Fleming

The Random House Group, for permission to quote from unpublished materials in the Jonathan Cape Archive, University of Reading Special Collections

I am grateful to the Lilly Library at Indiana University, Bloomington, for awarding me the Everett Helm Visiting Fellowship and granting me access to the Ian Fleming manuscripts and the John Pearson papers in their collection.

I am grateful to the director and staff of the Churchill Archive Center, Cambridge, for granting me access to the archive and their support of my research.

I would like to thank my colleagues and friends in the Department of English and Dorothy F. Schmidt College of Arts and Letters at Florida Atlantic University for providing a supportive and stimulating intellectual environment in which to work on this project. I am grateful to Florida Atlantic

University for awarding me a sabbatical term in spring 2019, which allowed time to write several of the chapters of this biography.

I would like to thank my literary agent, Thomas Cull of Cull & Company, for believing in this project and for working with me to find the best publisher for the book.

My thanks to Susan McEachern, Katelyn Turner, and Janice Braunstein at Rowman & Littlefield for their work on the editing and production of the book.

For ongoing conversations about Fleming and Bond, and for their encouragement and feedback about various stages of the project as it progressed, thanks go to Nick Anikitou, Eric Berlatsky, Chris Buckton, James Chapman, Matthew Chernov, John Cork, Steve Engle, Fergus Fleming, Mark David Kaufman, Ian Kinane, Timothy Melley, Jay Parini, John Pearson, Matthew B. Sherman, and Stephen Watt.

I dedicate this book to my wife, Laurice Campbell Buckton, who has been there with love, support, and extraordinary patience for the entire journey and shared many of its adventures.

List of Photos

Author's Note

This biography of Ian Fleming is a work of nonfiction based on substantial research in the Fleming archive. The narrative of Fleming's life also draws on research in other archives of military history, intelligence history, and literary culture. In a few cases, I have developed scenes featuring speculative dialogue that represent what I believe may have taken place between Ian Fleming and other key figures in his life. I have attempted to make this dialogue consistent with my understanding of Ian Fleming's character, history, and relationships.

Foreword

Ian Fleming is one of those authors who gives more than it at first appears. His character as the sportsman about town and womanizer is not one that suggests hard work, and his style is not that of the scholar. James Bond, whether Fleming's alter ego or not, is not noted for reading books. But in Fleming's case, we only need go to Bloomington, Indiana, and, in the Lilly Library, see the books he collected. Even more so, his drafts of the Bond novels, with the frequent crossings out and additions, mean that any author will recognize him and say, "I see you." Fleming's is writing as work and therefore purpose, hard purpose.

> Soldiers were forbidden to take cover when attacked. . . . They had to face the approaching enemy standing erect and with naked torso. . . . Spirit soldiers took up positions and, as ordered by the spirit, began to sing pious songs for 10, 15, or 20 minutes. Then the time-keeper blew a whistle. On this sign, the troops began marching forward in a long line, shouting at the tops of their voices: "James Bond! James Bond! James Bond!"

More Flashman than Bond, this description of the battle tactics of the Ugandan Holy Spirit Movement is an unusual tribute to the global fame of Ian Fleming's noted alter ego, as, more conventionally, was the opening celebration of the 2012 London Olympics. Oliver Buckton's *The World Is Not Enough* is an excellent guide to Fleming's life, one—stuffed full of character and characters—that also throws light on a tranche of British life. Fleming's lifetime, 1908–1964, was one in which Britain was still an imperial power, and his creation provides a way to understand aspects of the collective imagination of the era. Thus, as Buckton points out, "Bondmania" took off in the 1960s, the decade of the sexual revolution: "Bond . . . has 'licence' to violate the taboos and norms of bourgeois life. . . . While his conservative background and establishment role seem to disqualify Bond as a countercultural hero, his uninhibited lifestyle and enjoyment of sex struck a chord with a new generation."

Indeed, it is the frequent and interesting, although sometimes allusive, resonances between Fleming's multiple contexts, such as the work of the Austrian psychoanalyst Alfred Adler, and Bond that provide part of the interest of this gripping work. The shifting physical environments are also teased out, as with the dynamic counterpointing of Kitzbühel and Jamaica in his skillful short story "Octopussy" (1962). To Buckton, Kitzbühel, which also shows up in *On Her Majesty's Secret Service*, is important as the scene of the deaths of two of the people most important to Bond: his surrogate father and his wife, both brutal gun murders committed by selfish villains whom Buckton indeed suggests have resemblances to Fleming.

Sex, violence, setting, and people of interest, all are woven with skill by Buckton, and the people backlit in particular settings, for example, Maud Russell, a wealthy lover with whom he had "a rabid political talk" in Chelsea on July 28, 1939, serve to offer occasion for more wide-reaching passages, as on Fleming's political views at the time of Appeasement. Again, the theme is one of complexity, and there is a careful reading of the evidence, both themes of Buckton's book, which is, at once, impressive and sprightly.

Fleming's somewhat aimless course of life was transformed by World War II, and, as with Bond and the Cold War, conflict gave him purpose. Both men had a "good war," and seeking success through force characterized the adventure heroism that is the setting for their espionage. There is a degree of sophistication in Fleming's work lacking in Herman McNeile's "Bulldog" Drummond, one that reflects contrasts in experience as well as imagination, but, at the same time, there is an ability to draw on a shared sense of danger.

In his generally unsympathetic *Snobbery with Violence* (1971), Colin Watson presented Fleming as important in the development of "a secret police literature," but that is an off-center view of both Fleming and Bond. Each were really romantic heroes of a dark type, men who were troubled and whose lives, real and fictional, reflected this in spades. Buckton, indeed, is very good on the shadowing effects of Ian Fleming's elder brother Peter Fleming's achievements and is very interested in bringing through Ian's troubles both into the novelist's life and into Bond, who, in *Casino Royale*—

his very first outing—considers the very worth of his career and, therefore, life. Indeed, the secret policeman is not an apt description of an adventure hero who considers abandoning his career and, eventually, in *Man with the Golden Gun*, tries to kill his boss, M.

Shifting contexts—pre-, during, and postwar—are also ably captured by Buckton in his energetic book. In the case of Bond, a postwar figure with many echoes of the prewar and wartime worlds, Fleming gives him a wealth of life and comfort in adventure that was particularly attractive to a Britain coming out of rationing and struggling for purpose. Fleming could play the role better than most, as with his letter to Claude Taittinger, the champagne producer, thanking the latter for sending Bond some of his champagne. There is indeed a drollness to both author and creation, one at times verging, for each, on self-destructive somberness but one that also makes a fascinating subject for a book of excitement and cast: cast of people, cast of place, and cast of adventure.

Providing exotic dreams to lift British spirits from postwar misery, Fleming was a key writer for the New Elizabethan Age. His was a Cold War of meaning, and if he could not maintain quality or always end his stories well, the same could be said of many more famous writers, such as Dickens. To appreciate his skill as a writer, see the female perspective in *The Spy Who Loved Me* or the dramatic energy of *Moonraker*. And always, Fleming's work displays an edginess of the dark romantic hero. The power and the spirit survive.

Jeremy Black, author, *The World of James Bond*

Prologue

A Fateful Meeting

In May 1939, Ian Fleming was recruited to serve as the assistant to the director of Naval Intelligence, Admiral John Godfrey. The decisive meeting between the two men took place over lunch at the Carlton Hotel Grill in London and may well have unfolded as described here.

It is noon on May 24, 1939. London. At a table inside the Carlton Hotel Grill, on the corner of Haymarket and Pall Mall, a distinguished-looking gentleman in his fifties, wearing a carefully pressed naval uniform with four gold bands around the sleeve, is seated at a table near the back of the restaurant. The setting is traditional, complete with white tablecloths and formally attired waiters, yet it evokes a former style and glamor that has now faded. The *Manchester Guardian* would write, in 1942, of this famous restaurant of the Carlton Hotel, "the grill room looked very old fashioned and glum in latter years, but still Mr. Andrew Mellon and other major millionaires thought it the only satisfactory place in London."[1] The present gentleman certainly does not have the appearance of a major millionaire but rather of an overworked member of the Admiralty, which is located just around the corner in The Mall. Judging by the reverent way this man is greeted by the waiters, however, he is a highly respected guest in the restaurant. And as a matter of course, he has been shown to his usual table, away from the hubbub and nowhere near the windows. Perhaps he does not wish to be recognized.

The man is Admiral John Godfrey, and for the last three months, he has been the director of Britain's Naval Intelligence Division (NID). His luncheon here today is for a specific purpose. After Godfrey's appointment, one of his predecessors in the post, Admiral Sir Reginald "Blinker" Hall—who was at the helm of NID during World War I—advised him that he would need an assistant: an able and accomplished administrator who could help coordinate with other branches of government and intelligence. "You'll need someone to be your eyes and ears in Whitehall, John. It can be a treacherous place," Hall had cautioned. Most urgently, Godfrey needed a capable man who could liaise with other branches of the secret services and help manage Room 39, the hub of the naval intelligence-gathering operation, where the sheer volume of incoming intelligence traffic could be overwhelming.

Following Hall's advice, Godfrey had reached out to two old friends, Sir Montagu Norman, the governor of the Bank of England, and Sir Edward Peacock. To Godfrey' s surprise, Norman —himself a very busy man—had offered to come see him at the Admiralty and arrived promptly in his office at ten o'clock one morning. He already had the name of his proposed candidate for Godfrey's assistant on his lips.

And now Godfrey is waiting to meet the recommended candidate for lunch. He orders a cocktail—a dry martini—and lights his pipe. He does not need to look at the menu, for he always orders the same dish—grilled lamb cutlets with roast potatoes—when he lunches at the Carlton. But he is on a tight schedule now, and his guests are late. He looks impatiently at his watch, an old Rolex, shiny with use.

Suddenly two men enter the grill room together, and Godfrey raises a hand of salutation. They join him at the table, the two being Admiral Aubrey Hugh-Smith and Angus MacDonnell, both friends of Godfrey. An experienced naval officer and former assistant director of Naval Intelligence under Admiral "Blinker" Hall, Rear Admiral Hugh-Smith would, a couple of months later, host a dinner party at his Marylebone home that Godfrey would attend. Also in attendance at this dinner was Count Gerhard von Schwerin, who had come to warn the British of Hitler's plan to invade Poland. Among other recommendations, von Schwerin would urge that Neville Chamberlain be replaced by Winston Churchill as prime minister.[2] MacDonnell is a successful city businessman with long-standing ties to the intelligence service.

Both men also order martinis from the waiter. MacDonnell, who has asked for his martini to be shaken not stirred, looks critically around the grill room.

"This place is rather suggestive of faded grandeur, wouldn't you say?" he comments to his companions.

"It's certainly not the fashionable hub it used to be when Ritz and Escoffier ran the place at the turn of the century," agrees Hugh-Smith. "My wife and I came here for our wedding lunch in 1899, just after the hotel opened. It was the talk of the town in those days, stealing customers away from the Savoy, if you please!" Hugh-Smith is starting to drift into reminiscences, but Godfrey—who knows these signs of distraction only too well—wants to stay focused on the present.

"Well, the food and cocktails are good enough for our purposes," he says tersely. Their martinis arrive, and the two guests raise their glasses in a toast with Godfrey.

"So, where *is* our man?" asks MacDonnell with a trace of anxiety in his voice.

"Good question," replies Godfrey irritably. "Sir Montagu assured me he had passed on the time and place."

"He'll be here. Who was it that said, 'punctuality is the thief of time'?" remarks MacDonnell with a chuckle. Godfrey frowns.

"Whoever it was, he obviously didn't have a naval intelligence department to run with a war looming," replies Godfrey. A sense of humor, it is apparent, is not his chief quality.

"I can't imagine what's happened. He's usually very punctual," says MacDonnell. He had been one of those to recommend the candidate and feels his own reputation is at stake.

"Are you sure he's a solid, reliable type?" asks Godfrey, puffing contemplatively on his pipe.

"Absolutely! First-rate chap," Hugh-Smith assures him. "I've known the family for years. He comes from the best stock."

There is a stir as another man enters the restaurant, looking slightly flurried. He is tall, with his brown hair carefully combed into a parting on the left, its natural waviness subdued by hair cream. He wears a dark pinstriped suit—he is currently working in the City as a stockbroker, and the dark formality of his clothes seems fitting. But there is also a flourish of color and exuberance in the polka-dot bow tie he sports. He is strikingly lithe and handsome, his features standing out from the crowd despite—or perhaps because of—a broken nose, the result of a football accident when he was at Eton College. He has the power to change the atmosphere of a room when he walks into it, and several of the female customers turn to look at him. He has dark, somewhat intense eyes that glance eagerly around the restaurant. His facial expression is serious, even anxious. But as he sees Godfrey's party and approaches the table at the back of the room, the new arrival breaks into a captivating smile and extends his hand warmly to Admiral Godfrey.

"Sorry I'm a bit late, Admiral. Got held up in a stockholders meeting. They do prattle on, you know. The name is Fleming . . . Ian Fleming."

"Yes, of course. A pleasure to meet you," replies Godfrey, standing. He is immediately impressed by the firmness of Fleming's grip and the prolonged handshake. What one of his female friends would later describe as "Ian's charm offensive" has begun, and its target is Godfrey. The table of four now complete, they all sit down, and the waiter arrives to take the new arrival's drink order.

"What are you all having?" Fleming asks deferentially.

"Martinis," says Godfrey.

"Splendid! I think I'll join you." Ian often has martinis at lunchtime but wanted to take his cue from his potential employer.

"I recommend you have it shaken not stirred," suggests MacDonnell. "It's the only way to make sure it's really cold!"

"I agree. Only please have the barman make mine with Russian vodka—with a slice of lemon peel," Fleming instructs the waiter politely. The man nods and departs. The new arrival has not noticed Godfrey looking at him slightly askance. Martinis, as far as he is concerned, are made with gin. This introduction of the Russian spirit is not appreciated.

"Whatever do you want vodka for?" asks MacDonnell.

Fleming raises his eyebrows. "Oh, it's just a quirk of mine. I spent some time in Moscow a few years ago and picked up a taste for the stuff."

Godfrey decides to overlook this peccadillo in the interests of national security. "I've heard a great deal about you, Fleming," he says, getting down to business. "You have some good friends in high places."

"Well, it's comforting to know that someone thinks well of me," replies Fleming modestly. Yet one might suspect, by the confident smile he gives, that he thinks rather well of himself too.

"I suppose Sir Montagu has explained the purpose of this meeting?" continues Godfrey.

"Yes," says Fleming with a disarming directness. "He told me you are looking for an assistant."

Godfrey raises his eyebrows at this blunt description of the post. "Yes—but you must realize, this is a position of national importance? The successful candidate will assist me as director of Naval Intelligence. He will have to be my 'eyes and ears' in Whitehall," Godfrey explains, quoting Admiral Hall.

Fleming nods with enthusiasm. "Of course. I believe I'm ready for this challenging opportunity, sir."

Godfrey likes being called "sir." Even Sir Montagu Norman had addressed him thus at their meeting in the Admiralty. "I suppose you agree that war with Germany is now inevitable?" he asks.

Fleming looks thoughtful. "At this stage of the game, yes, sir. Hitler has just gone too far. His intentions can't be concealed any longer by honeyed words. He is determined to have war with Britain."

Godfrey nods with satisfaction. Unless there is war, his own appointment will be meaningless. "And what is your opinion of Mr. Chamberlain?" he asks bluntly. This question is a test—not of the candidate's political views but of his discretion.

The younger man realizes this immediately. Fleming's cocktail arrives. He looks at it critically, is apparently satisfied, and takes a large draft from the glass before answering. "I think his is not a position to be envied by anyone, sir," he replies diplomatically.

"Do you think Mr. Churchill would make a better leader?" asks Godfrey abruptly.

"In wartime? Quite possibly. But, of course, Winston is a friend of my family, so I'm slightly biased." Ian is pleased to have got in this personal reference to Churchill.

"And you realize that, once war breaks out, Naval Intelligence will be of vital importance in gathering the intelligence we need to protect our shores from enemy invasion—as well as to launch successful attacks on the Hun?" Godfrey has resorted to the derogatory term used in World War I.

"Absolutely," replies Fleming eagerly. The other two men drink their cocktails and look closely but surreptitiously at Fleming. Fleming has realized, with his quick instincts, that they are part of the interview team as well.

"It hasn't escaped my attention that you don't have any naval background or experience," notes Godfrey.

Fleming looks a bit sheepish but sips his martini to conceal the awkwardness. "I'm afraid not. But I come from a military family. My father, Valentine Fleming, served in the Oxford Royal Hussars during —"

Godfrey interrupts him. "Yes, I know—as we all do—about your father's distinguished service for his country—and his ultimate sacrifice."

"Well . . . then I also went to Royal Sandhurst."

"But you didn't graduate," states Hugh-Smith abruptly. His role—previously assigned by Godfrey—is to point out possible shortcomings in Fleming's background, not that he wishes him ill.

"No . . . I decided the army wasn't for me. I'd much prefer the navy." Fleming smiles graciously at Godfrey, who has heard some unpleasant rumors about Fleming's sexual exploits at Sandhurst but decides not to pursue this line.

"How old are you, Mr. Fleming?" asks Godfrey.

"I'm just thirty. Actually, my thirty-first birthday is in four days." Fleming smiles at the thought of the birthday trip by car he has planned with his current girlfriend.

"What makes you think that you, still a young man, are the right person for this great responsibility?" asks Godfrey almost severely.

The cold, potent liquor gives Fleming confidence. "Well, I'd like the opportunity to serve my country during the war. I've worked in journalism, so I have the ability to communicate effectively and write quickly. I know all about high-pressure deadlines too," he adds, smiling.

"Very well," says Godfrey. Apparently, he isn't entirely satisfied with this answer.

"And then . . . well, as you know, I lost my father at a young age, Admiral. I think about him often and want to live up to his example. I think what this country needs now is leadership at a time of great peril. I believe you can provide that leadership, as director of the Naval Intelligence Division, and I will strain every nerve and muscle in my body to help you."

"Are you a good manager of men?" asks Godfrey.

Fleming doesn't hesitate. "I believe I can handle the office effectively and leave you to deal with the higher-ups in government," he says modestly.

Godfrey smiles. "Mr. Fleming, you seem to me eminently the right sort of chap. But it's probably best if we proceed on a probationary basis at first. Does that suit you?"

Fleming is visibly disappointed. He had hoped to be offered the job outright. "Well, of course, sir—what did you have in mind?"

Godfrey relights his pipe. The other men have begun a conversation about cricket, leaving Godfrey and Fleming to talk business.

"Well, I'd like you to come into the office for a few hours several days a week to familiarize yourself with the routine and the personnel and to get the feel of the job."

"Excellent," replies Fleming, pleased to have a more definite offer. It is the best news he has received in a long time.

"Are you free in July?" asks Godfrey. Fleming looks puzzled. Is he being asked about his holiday plans? He was looking forward to a summer visit to his beloved Kitzbühel, but of course that could wait.

"Of course, sir."

"That's fine, then. We'll expect you in the Admiralty starting in July."

"But . . . won 't you need me before that, sir? I mean, with war on the horizon?" Fleming 's need for action, familiar to his friends, is now revealing itself.

Godfrey glances at Hugh-Smith, who stops talking to MacDonnell and gives an imperceptible nod. "Well, I daresay we could move it forward to June, a couple of weeks from now. Would that give you enough notice to inform your current employer?"

This is MacDonnell's cue, and he doesn't miss it. "Oh, I think I can vouch for Rowe and Pittman that they won't object to our man's being seconded—on urgent matters of national security, that is."

Godfrey nods. "Very good. That's all settled." He gestures to the waiter for another round of drinks.

"Excuse me, sir, but will I have a uniform?" asks Fleming, now all eagerness.

Godfrey seems nonplussed for a moment. "Ah, of course . . . we haven't discussed your naval rank. I propose we draft you into the Royal Naval Volunteer Reserve."

"What rank, sir?" asks Fleming. These things matter to him. His older brother, Peter, is already a reserve officer in the Grenadier Guards, and Ian wants to match him.

"I was thinking that lieutenant would be a good entry-level rank to start off with," Godfrey replies. Fleming's face does not exactly light up. "Only during the probationary period, of course. I believe your promotion to lieutenant commander would be a matter of course."

Fleming is smiling again. He thinks that "Commander Fleming" would sound more impressive. "Thank you, sir. I'm looking forward to working with you."

"Likewise, I'm sure. Now that's all settled, let's order lunch. I have another meeting at two o'clock, and I missed breakfast today!" The second round of cocktails arrives, and the men toast the recruitment of Ian Fleming.

Recognizing their moment has come, a trio of waiters descend and take the food and wine orders. Everyone selects oysters to start. The three older men all order lamb cutlets and mint sauce, but Fleming requests beef tournedos with béarnaise sauce and sautéed potatoes. MacDonnell looks at him with amusement.

"Very sophisticated, Ian. Roast lamb not to your taste, then?"

"Oh, I like lamb all right. But I acquired a taste for this dish in the south of France. Making the sauce properly is an art. In fact, if I were ever to marry, one of my requirements would be that my wife know how to make béarnaise sauce." Now that he is secure in his appointment, Ian is allowing his more raffish side to show.

"You may have trouble finding such a wife in England," Godfrey remarks bluntly.

"Oh, I remain hopeful," replies Ian deferentially.

"Are you still running around with that model—what's her name?" asks MacDonnell. He is enjoying making Ian a bit uncomfortable. But if he hopes to see the young man squirm, he is disappointed.

"Yes . . . Muriel Wright. A splendid girl all around. But she's more of an athlete than a model. Wonderful polo player. And she skis like a dream. Much better than I do, in fact." The second martini has loosened his tongue.

"Does she have any security clearance?" asks Godfrey warily.

"I'm afraid not," says Hugh-Smith.

"I should remind you, Fleming, that this appointment is top secret, and any information you disclose about your activities will be strictly on a need-to-know basis. Is that understood?" Godfrey's tone is severe, and Ian looks suddenly uncomfortable.

"Yes, of course, Admiral Godfrey. My lips are sealed, sir."

"And, moreover, most of the documents that will cross your desk will be classified—for your eyes only. Is that clear?"

"Absolutely. I am the soul of discretion," replies Ian with suitable gravity. The food arrives, and the topic of conversation changes to a comparison of the merits of claret from Mouton Rothschild versus Pichon Longueville Baron.

* * *

Two o'clock. Lunch now over, the three interviewers have all departed, Godfrey having placed the bill on his account before rushing off to a meeting in Whitehall. Ian, though, has lingered at the table to enjoy a luxurious cigarette, which he extracts from a gunmetal cigarette case. Thoughtful, he smokes for several minutes, leaning back luxuriously to exhale the smoke. Eventually, he extinguishes the cigarette in an ashtray, gets up from the table, and exits the grill room. Inside the hotel lobby, he spots a public telephone near the toilets. He walks up to it, lifts the receiver, and places a local call. When it is answered, he says, "Miss Muriel Wright, please." There is a pause, then a pleasantly low, slightly husky female voice comes on the line.

"Hello?"

"Moo? Is that you? It's Ian. I have wonderful news. I got the job!"

"That's marvelous, Ian. You must be thrilled." Her enthusiasm is evident, and she clearly knew all about the prospect.

"I start in June. I'm afraid it means that Kitz is off this year."

"Never mind, darling. We still have Royal Sandwich to look forward to for your birthday. There'll be other times for the Tyrol. Congratulations, Ian! Eve will be so proud of you."

Ian's elated voice suddenly loses some of its enthusiasm. "M? Of course she will. But I was thinking of Father."

"How do you mean?" asks Moo, puzzled.

"Now I can make peace with him. You see, this is the first time I've ever felt worthy to be called his son."

Chapter One

Spyway

The Early Life of Ian Fleming

Ian Fleming's position as the child of privilege was established from the day of his birth, May 28, 1908. Ian was the second son of Valentine and Eve Fleming, born at 27 Green Street, Mayfair, the exclusive and wealthy area of London where his parents resided. Green Street runs from Park Lane to North Audley Street and is part of the Grosvenor estate owned by the Duke of Westminster—one of Britain's wealthiest landowners. The street underwent extensive redevelopment in the 1910s and 1920s, by which time the Flemings had moved to Hampstead. Distinguished former residents of Green Street include the Romantic poet William Blake, while later—in the 1960s—the Beatles, newly arrived in London, would share a flat at number 57. Ian's birthplace landed him at the center of cultural, social, and business elites in London.

Fleming's mother, born Evelyn Sainte Croix Rose, was a beautiful socialite from a distinguished Berkshire family. Her father, George Alfred Sainte Croix Rose, was a captain in the Royal Buckinghamshire Militia and a justice of the peace for Berkshire. Eve's physical beauty was celebrated by all who knew her, and Tom Pellat—the headmaster of Durnford School, a preparatory school that Ian and his older brother, Peter, attended from 1914—referred to her "striking beauty" and "lovely face," which he recalled many years afterward.[1]

Ian's father, Valentine, was the oldest son of Robert Fleming, the Scottish banker and financier. From humble origins in Dundee, Robert Fleming had become a millionaire, largely through shrewd investments in American railroads. Robert had founded the Scottish American Investment Trust in 1873, which established the basis of his fortune. He represented a Victorian ideal, the self-made millionaire who rose from a position of low birth to occupy a high place in the business and banking worlds. He later donated large sums to the University of Dundee and to improve workers' housing in the city. The Flemings' influential connections in banking and finance would play an important role in Ian Fleming's future.

Valentine was educated at Eton—as were his younger brother Philip and Valentine's four sons—and Magdalen College, Oxford. He gained his commission to the Queens Own Oxfordshire Hussars in June 1908, the month after Ian's birth. The family spent most of their time at Braziers Park, in Oxfordshire, where Val (as he was known by his family) had bought a large estate to which he made substantial renovations. However, following his election as Member of Parliament for Henley in Oxfordshire in 1910, Val, needing to spend more time in London, purchased Pitt House, an impressive building on Hampstead Heath. The family thereafter divided its time between Oxfordshire and London, giving Ian Fleming plenty of idyllic time exploring in the country as well as deeper roots and an extended presence in an exclusive area of the capital city.

As was the case for many of his generation, Val's ascent through the ranks of his profession was harshly interrupted by the outbreak of the First World War. He was seen as a promising rising star of the Conservative Party when war broke out. Val was captain in his regiment and was sent to France in September 1914. From the western front, Val wrote harrowing letters to friends back in Britain—including his friend and political ally Winston Churchill, later the British prime minister—in which he described the carnage on the battlefields. "First and most impressive," Fleming wrote,

> the absolutely indescribable ravages of modern artillery fire, not only upon all men, animals and buildings within its zone, but upon the very face of nature itself. Imagine a broad belt, ten miles or so in width, stretching from the Channel to the German frontier near Basle, which is positively littered with the bodies of men; . . . in which farms, villages, and cottages are shapeless heaps of blackened masonry; in which fields, roads and trees are pinned and torn and twisted by shells and disfigured by dead horses, cattle, sheep and goats, scattered in every attitude of repulsive distortion and dismemberment.[2]

Along this "terrain of death" were lines of trenches in which, Fleming explained, "crouch lines of men, in brown or grey or blue, coated with mud, unshaven hollow-eyed with the continual strain, unable to reply to the ever-lasting run of shells hurled at them from three, four, five or more miles away." Fleming concluded by writing, "It's going to be a long war in spite of the fact that on both sides every single man in it wants it stopped at once."[3]

Val's prediction of an enduring war proved correct, for despite optimistic views that the First World War would be "over by Christmas," it would last four long years and result in millions of dead and wounded on both sides.[4] Tragically, Val Fleming himself became a casualty of this terrible conflict on May 20, 1917, when he was killed by German shellfire at Somme, France, while trying to hold a position, Gillemont Farm, against enemy attack. He was posthumously awarded the Distinguished Service Order. In his will, Val Fleming left Pitt House and its effects to his wife and left his fortune in trust for his four sons and their future families. Eve would receive a generous income from the trust, provided she did not remarry. In the event of her remarriage, Eve would receive a reduced income of £3,000 per annum. Thus, the chances of Ian and his brothers inheriting their father's fortune were very slim and almost certainly deferred until the end of Eve's life. According to Alaric Jacob, who worked with Ian at Reuters,

> This will is of vital importance, because it altered the lives of the entire family, right up until the end. All the money was left in trust with the use available to Mrs Fleming provided she didn't marry again. So she couldn't marry and the boys were kept dependent on her.[5]

Indeed, the likelihood of Eve providing her young sons with a new father figure was also remote, for there was a powerful financial incentive for her to remain single in her widowed state. And, in fact, she never remarried.[6]

* * *

Where you are born matters. Edmund Gosse, the famous Victorian critic, once wrote lamenting his friend Robert Louis Stevenson's decision to move permanently to Samoa in the South Sea Islands: "The fact seems to me that it is very nice to live in Samoa, but not healthy to write there. Within a three-mile radius of Charing Cross is the literary atmosphere, I suspect."[7] If Gosse was correct, then Ian Fleming spent most of his life within that "literary atmosphere," whether as a journalist, a spy, or a novelist. Although few writers have been more closely associated with exotic locations and global travel than Ian Fleming—due to the legacy of James Bond—the fact is he remained firmly rooted in the exclusive area of London in which he was born. Fleming's stay in Kitzbühel was essential to his development, and his winter sojourns in Jamaica were necessary to his literary creativity. However, the majority of the professional, publishing, and business aspects of his literary life were conducted in London.

Similarly, Fleming's famous character James Bond has become synonymous with globetrotting, luxurious travel, missions in exotic locations, and exciting foreign adventures. But throughout the novels, Bond's overseas missions are short-lived interludes set against the constant background of his life in London. Like Fleming, Bond enjoys his flat in an exclusive area of the capital—Chelsea—and his daily routine involves going to the office each day and spending his evenings gambling or socializing.

Fleming would also write a successful travelogue, *Thrilling Cities*, that cemented his reputation as an international jetsetter devoted to pleasure seeking, luxury, and thrills. Because the James Bond novels were written each winter at Fleming's Jamaica home, Goldeneye, the tropical Caribbean surroundings in which Fleming created and developed his character have become part of the Bond (and Fleming) mythology. Yet Fleming was born, and essentially remained, a Londoner. As Gary Giblin writes, "Well-known hotels, restaurants, museums, theatres, auction houses, jewelers, golf courses, public schools, train stations, bus routes, news agencies, tobacco manufacturers and more turn up with remarkable frequency in the pages of his novels."[8] His writings are replete with geographical detail, and a high proportion of these references are to places in London. His birth in Mayfair, childhood in Hampstead, and adult residences in areas such as Sloane Square and Belgravia imprinted the city in his blood and formed the privileged orbit to which Ian would remain bound for his entire life.

Ian's education at Eton (at Windsor) and Royal Sandhurst, both in Berkshire, did not remove him far from the capital city. After the war, Fleming continued to live in the capital, purchasing an elegant Regency house at 16 Victoria Square in 1953, just before he published his first novel, *Casino Royale*. This remained his main home in England until he and his wife, Ann, moved to Sevenhampton, Wiltshire, in 1963. Thus Victoria Square was the location of Fleming's most productive years as a novelist, and "here, on the top floor, the author retreated from the incessant, and frequently annoying, parties given by his wife for their many rich friends."[9]

Throughout his adult life, most of Fleming's work and social connections were in London. Fleming's ties with the city were strengthened in 1932 when he worked for the merchant bankers Cull and Company, moving to the stockbroking firm Rowe & Pitman the following year. He lived in an unusual apartment at Ebury Street from 1934 to 1945, during which time his wartime service in Naval Intelligence took him to the Admiralty in The Mall. However, Ian left the flat after the Blitz began and moved to the Carlton Hotel: another exclusive landmark of London society. After the war, Fleming was appointed foreign manager at Kemsley Newspapers, working from the Kemsley House offices in London's Gray's Inn Road, in Bloomsbury.[10] In 1959, after Kemsley sold his newspaper business to Roy Thomson, Fleming took an office in Old Mitre Court, at Serjeants Inn. Here he wrote or dictated his correspondence with publishers, friends, and readers and worked on revising the typescripts of his novels. Fleming would go over the proofs of the novels from his publisher, Jonathan Cape, located in nearby Bedford Square, from his Mitre Court workspace.

Not only was London Fleming's workplace throughout his life, but it was also his social center. In the 1930s, while at Ebury Street, Fleming formed a group of friends called Le Cercle Gastronomique et des Jeux de Hasard, composed of other Old Etonians, businessmen, and professionals. On weeknights, the Cercle would dine at each other's homes, or at exclusive London clubs such as Whites, and spend the evenings playing bridge. On weekends, they would gallivant off to golf courses such as Huntercombe, Royal St George's (at Sandwich), or, more adventurously, Le Touquet on the Normandy coast. Fleming also carried on affairs with various women in his London apartment at Ebury Street, including Muriel Wright and Ann O'Neill, who eventually became his wife. During the war, Ann—whose husband, Shane O'Neill, was in active service with the North Irish Horse, Royal Armoured Corps—lived at the Dorchester Hotel, where Fleming was a frequent visitor.

Fleming's sphere of professional and social activity occurred within a surprisingly small section of the capital city. Whether as an author, newspaper man, banker, stockbroker, publisher, friend, or lover, Fleming's identity was deeply enmeshed with the area of his birth. In writing the James Bond novels, the readership Fleming had in mind was the upper-class milieu he was familiar with and that he referred to as the "A class" of readers. Only later—with the paperback publication of Bond by Pan Books—did Fleming aspire to reach the "B and C classes," making Bond a phenomenon of mass culture.

Fleming's London base and orbit were also transferred to James Bond. Bond lives in Chelsea, London (where Fleming's mother lived in Cheyne Walk), and he travels to work in his Bentley to the Secret Intelligence Service headquarters, which is located (in the novels) near Regents Park. Though Bond's missions take him to far-flung, exotic places, Fleming reminds us in *Moonraker* that these missions are the exception rather than the rule: "It was only two or three times a year that an assignment came along requiring his particular abilities. For the rest of the year he had the duties of an easy-going civil servant."[11] Bond's "evenings spent playing cards with a few close friends" and "weekends playing golf for high stakes at one of the clubs near London" are the mirror image of Fleming's existence, at least before the war.[12]

It is important to understand this context of London to grasp the effect on Ian of being uprooted from it at a tender age. Yet, as a young boy of only eight, in September 1916, Ian was sent away from home to attend Durnford Preparatory School on the Isle of Purbeck, Dorset. This was a remote location for a small boy leaving home for the first time. Going off to boarding school at such a young age can be traumatic for many children, and Ian's situation was not helped by the austerity of the school itself. According to previous Fleming biographers, Durnford School was Dickensian in its Spartan arrangements, bad food, and abusive schoolmasters. The headmaster, Thomas Pellatt, is often portrayed as an Edwardian version of Wackford Squeers at Dickens's grim Dotheboys Hall, who "presided over a harsh and often cruel establishment."[13]

The image of Durnford as a sadistic environment has been reinforced by Fleming's biographers. Ben Macintyre, for example, writes that Durnford was "the traditionally brutal prep school . . . which epitomized the strange British faith in bad food, plenty of Latin and beating from an early age."[14] Even the website of the current establishment on the Durnford estate, Spyway School, informs readers that Thomas Pellatt—or "TP," as he was known—"was a violent bully and could not abide sensitive boys or those who were homesick or did not excel at sport."[15] Clearly, Fleming would fall into the first two categories, and even his athletic excellence did not emerge until he went to Eton after leaving Durnford.

Yet there is evidence that Durnford was actually a nurturing and inspiring school to Ian Fleming in a variety of ways. Peter Fleming, who attended

Durnford at the same time as Ian, described Tom Pellatt as "a great man . . . a most original man. In some ways the school was run more like a country house than a conventional school."[16] It is known that TP insisted that the boys strip naked and plunge into the icy waters of the swimming pool each morning: "strip and swim" being the name for this ritual. As TP's daughter, Hester Chapman, later recalled, "My father blasted a natural pool in the rocks for the boys to swim in, and during the summer every morning they used to run down past the Home Farm to swim. From the start they did this without bathing dresses."[17] The pool had been blasted out of the rock at Dancing Ledge near the sea, on the Jurassic coast of Dorset, allowing the pool to be filled with frigid seawater. Yet this practice was a sign not of cruelty but rather of TP's conviction that boys benefited from sea bathing and should spend as much of their time in the "great outdoors" as possible. In his 1936 memoir, *Boys in the Making*, TP writes poignantly of how he shared in the natural beauties of the Dorset coast with his pupils, "I used to go about my daily round with the children, when we took their lunch down to the sea at Dancing Ledge on some lovely spring morning, or went with them to help build their 'houses' in the woods," when he experienced a "bucolic sort of longing to write a suitable and touching bit of poetry."[18] Far from practicing the harsh philosophy of "spare the rod and spoil the child," TP was highly critical of the "brutal methods" of much formal education.[19]

Although it is, of course, possible that TP didn't always practice what he preached at the school, he declares in his memoir that "one conviction that has impressed itself upon me above all others is, that sympathy, affection, forgiveness, patience and tolerance are the only really effective instruments to work with."[20] Hester wrote, "My father . . . had . . . the completely novel idea for those days that boys should be happy at school and, as he was something of a schoolboy himself, was quite amazingly successful at this."[21] Far from despising weakness in his boys, TP expresses sympathy for boys who were backward in intelligence or suffered from health problems. He insisted that although "the range from the backward boy to the precocious one seems infinite," eventually (using a favorite horticultural analogy) "the forward plants ceased growing at a certain point, and the others have caught them up."[22] One pupil who suffered glandular problems was sent to Durnford "as an experiment (the London specialist being as great an enthusiast as I was for sea-bathing)."[23]

Pellatt and his wife lived in the Manor House, which he had bought in 1893, and he converted the outbuildings at Durnford into the preparatory school. Hester describes it as "the most beautiful spot imaginable. The house was Jacobean, and this part of Dorset was just the place to appeal to any boy with a sense of beauty and adventure. I am sure it did to Ian. It had been a great place for smugglers."[24] TP saw the school as a business venture, taking a financial risk by giving up his post at Marlborough College, but also as an outlet for his progressive educational philosophy. In particular, he also had a strong desire to provide a supportive environment for young boys that would bring out the best of their abilities. As he wrote, "In countless numbers of cases, when you find a kink in a child's character it is lack of sympathy that has caused it."[25]

This is not to accept Hester's quite rosy portrait of Durnford without scrutiny. Pearson believes "the school must have been very tough, and this seems to have been partly Pellatt's intention. The food was rough, the dormitories unheated, and Peter's story of the boy who died of whooping cough is probably true."[26] Pearson believes Ian had been bullied there, and Peter Fleming recalled "there was a lot of bullying there, although I wouldn't say that Ian came in for more than anyone else."[27]

However, be that as it may, the Durnford experiences recounted in *Boys in the Making* are significantly different from the accounts offered in biographies of Ian. For example, TP writes that when he established the school with his wife, Elinor, "the plan which my wife and I had thought out for the school was based on one word: FREEDOM. Our policy was not to suppress anything in a child."[28] Indeed, rather than conforming to the draconian image of the "traditional prep school," Durnford under TP was the ideal preparation for Ian's later experiences of adventure and freedom.[29] TP's philosophy was intended to prepare the boy for future liberty:

> Our policy of freedom resulted, as far as he was concerned, in the following way: when the time came for his going on to Eton he had had his fling; he had had his measles. It was the old plan of letting the child employed in a sweet factory eat as many sweets as it likes to begin with. . . . The secret of success in education is, that while the boy gets the advantage of being thrown into the pack you treat his case individually.[30]

Was Fleming indeed beaten by the Durnford masters for failing to do his work properly and for infractions of the disciplinary code? This seems unlikely given TP's sympathy for boys who were educationally backward. He dubs one such boy "Ernest" and reveals various "howlers" in Ernest's responses to questions about the Bible and history. But, TP insists, "Ernest was no fool, and I knew that as soon as he had got over his terribly late start he would be able to hold his own." TP made a special case on Ernest's behalf for entry to Eton and "implored them to take him in spite of his backwardness." The result was "Ernest did excellently at Eton, and before he left was managing the whole of the field telephone service for their O.T.C."[31] While "Ernest" was clearly not Ian Fleming, their cases are comparable. Ian could not be described as one of the brighter students, yet he gained entrance to Eton with TP's recommendation.

Intriguingly, *Boys in the Making* makes no reference to Ian Fleming. By contrast, TP sings the praises of Peter, calling him a "brilliantly clever child" and describing him as "not only precocious but very full of that mixture of the Old Adam which caused Nelson to put his blind eye to the telescope." In other words, Peter was not a goody-goody, and the matron noted that "Peter breaks all the dormitory rules every night . . . but I can never catch him." The matron evidently noted Peter's cleverness and duplicity, anticipating his later role as the "Master of Deception" in World War II (as the title of the biography of Peter calls him). TP was impressed rather than dismayed by these signs of rebellion, and TP predicted a glowing future for the young prodigy: "When Peter was with me, I felt 'in my bones' that he would distinguish himself quite early in life."[32]

Of course, this may be an example of hindsight being twenty-twenty, for by 1936 Peter was a successful, famous author of travel books such as *Brazilian Adventure*. Peter distinguished himself at school with the brilliance of his précis exercises, and TP states, "I have got one of these reproductions by Peter Fleming of the passage with which 'Le Peau de Chagrin' begins. This précis illustrates what these clever boys could tackle with perfect ease." Peter's early literary promise would be reflected in his books, but TP also traces their success back to his rebellious instincts: "He has apparently only gone on just the same, breaking all the rules of every outlandish country he visits (where the penalty is not just a smacking, but death), and not as yet being found out."[33] Could TP but have known it, the stakes would be even higher for Peter while working in intelligence in India during World War II.

On the other hand, Ian's rebellious propensities are not mentioned, nor are any academic strengths or even shortcomings. Even Ian's athletic ability, his chief area of success at Eton, goes unmentioned, despite that TP was an enthusiast of football and other sports. Ian is a complete blank in Pellatt's memoir, as though he were not one of the "boys" that TP had a hand in the "making" of. Instead, TP dwells on "the striking beauty of Peter's mother

(Mrs Val Fleming)" with such rapture that one suspects the headmaster was a little in love with her. He describes her beauty "immortalized by Augustus John" (who was Eve's lover). Yet even while praising John's painting, TP suggests that previous artists such as Reynolds or Gainsborough might have "provide[d] for us a more spiritual reflection of that lovely face."[34] With TP's lavish praise for both Eve and Peter, it is as though Ian had never attended the school. However, Hester Chapman remembers things differently, describing Ian as "a great favorite with my parents who, between you and me, thought he was worth six of Peter."[35]

According to Peter, "It was very uncomfortable. And the food was terrible. Ian always objected to that. . . . He always made his feelings very clear about bad food even as a boy."[36] Ian wrote to his mother wistfully from school, "I am afraid I do not like school very much. I do not know what form I'm in, in so many. I'm afraid I have not made many friends, they are so dirty and unreverent."[37] Ian also complained about a "whoping coff" (whooping cough, presumably) but asked his mother "not to tell Mister Pellat [*sic*], cause just this morning he said that nun of us had coffs."[38] Ian's five years at Durnford instilled in him a dislike of institutional authority and bullying that never left him. The words written years later by one of his closest friends, Maud Russell, in her wartime diary might sum up Ian's personal code: "The more I see of life, the more I hate cruelty and the more struck I am by fine, generous, noble behavior."[39]

Yet the Dorset influences were not all negative. It was while at Durnford that Ian also imbibed a love of nature and the environment. Even much later, in the 1940s, according to one former pupil, Durnford "had some good things about it as it was extraordinarily advanced in its understanding of ecological issues, being green and natural, way before its time."[40] This seems a continuation of TP's approach to education, which included midday trips down to the swimming pool at Dancing Ledge, bracing rambles in the Dorset countryside, and building "houses" in the woods, as Hester recalls.[41] Lycett—who portrays TP as a "looming and threatening presence" at the school—does admit that "Ian's abiding love of the sea and its creatures was spawned on Dancing Ledge."[42]

It was not just a love of the sea that was born in Ian at Durnford but also a passion for the beauties of nature on land, including the birdlife and wildflowers so enjoyed by TP. Hester recalls meeting Ian much later, at Saint Margaret's, Kent, and being impressed how "he knew about birds and had studied them so much."[43] This passion for birdlife was nurtured at Durnford.

Pellatt recalls in his memoir visiting "a farm where wild daffodils and narcissi grew in a meadow" and writes rapturously of "the common wild flowers in an upland pasture, which, on one never-forgotten morning, were to let me share the echo of their everlasting message."[44]

TP is full of praise for "the clear and varied landscape without" while lamenting the damage done to the natural environment by the "greedy trowel of the tripper." In his own schooldays at Lancing, TP reminisced he would "wander . . . far and wide over that lovely country round the school, spoilt, alas, now forever by aerodromes, chicken farms . . . and all the hideous cockneyfied paraphernalia of the pylon and the Green Line bus."[45] Despite TP's antipopulist sentiments, his message to his young charges was clearly to feel and express reverence and joy in the natural world. The location of Durnford on the idyllic Isle of Purbeck on the Dorset coast was advantageous for this purpose. The seed of ecological passion was planted in young Ian's mind, and he would immortalize this protective and celebratory outlook on the natural world in his James Bond novels.

Ian also developed another passion, for thrilling stories, while at Durnford. As Hester recalls, "Every Sunday night, as a regular institution, my mother would read an adventure story to the whole school. For several years it was *Moonfleet* and then about the time when Ian arrived she changed over to the Bulldog Drummond books."[46] Nell, as Mrs. Pellatt was known, also included John Buchan's Richard Hannay novels (*The Thirty-Nine Steps* and *Greenmantle*, both popular while Ian was at Durnford) in her reading list. These riveting adventures not only offered a temporary escape from any hardships Ian suffered but also planted a seed of inspiration in his young mind. Many years later, he would draw on the influence of Buchan and "Sapper" in creating his own spy hero, James Bond. But rather than simply recycling the past, Ian would update the model of the "clubland hero" devised by his predecessors, bringing the spy into the modern age.

Durnford established the pattern of Ian's resistance to strict discipline and authority. Amaryllis, Ian's half sister, attributed Ian's rebellious streak to his relationship with his mother: "the powerful domineering personality trying to impose its slightly dotty will on the sensitive small boy."[47] Throughout his life, Ian would be happiest and most productive in less disciplined, more relaxed environments, where he was free to work at his own pace without intrusive supervision. These would include institutions such as Am Tennerhof at Kitzbühel and Kemsley Newspapers under Lord Kemsley, where Ian enjoyed a relatively relaxed schedule. Of course, the environment most conducive to Ian's literary work was Goldeneye, the home he would build on the coast at Oracabessa in Jamaica. The obvious exception to this pattern was his time working in Naval Intelligence during World War II, a period of intense work in a disciplined environment. But in this case, the rigors and pressures of the job were made acceptable by the fact that Ian was working under a man he respected and admired, Admiral John Godfrey. At Durnford, Ian had no special place in the school's hierarchy, whereas in the Naval Intelligence Division, he had a prestigious job that gave him a great deal of freedom in running Room 39 and ceded him the authority to plan his own missions.

At Durnford, Ian was often lonely and homesick, while Peter seemed more at home in these Spartan surroundings and excelled academically. The boys had arrived at school the same year, 1916, as Peter was considered too physically fragile to attend the previous year. The challenging experience of going to a new school was compounded by the tragic loss of their father, Valentine, killed at Somme on May 20, 1917. The fact that this traumatic event happened while Ian and Peter were at Durnford etched the school in his mind as a place of misery and grief. With the death of their father, Peter would step into the role of male head of the family and accept this responsibility with relative equanimity. But for Ian, the loss was more devastating; he had lost the most important anchor and guide in his life.

Lycett writes that, "like true Flemings confronted with a hostile world, the two boys stuck together."[48] But for Ian, the "hostile world" was more troubling than for his elder sibling. Ian had been favored by Valentine, who called him "Johnny"—to the boys, Val was known as "Mokie"—and the loss of Val's paternal affection and guidance severely affected him. Both brothers idolized their father and struggled, in their different ways, to live up to his example. Both of them would serve in intelligence during World War II, and both would later display copies of Val's obituary in *The Times*, written by Winston Churchill, in their homes. When Peter asked Churchill to sign his copy, Ian inevitably followed suit.

Already feeling displaced and isolated, the death of his father forced Ian into an emotional shell from which it would take him years to emerge. It is interesting to speculate about the impact this traumatic news had on the two young Fleming boys. On the morning of Monday, May 21, the brothers were unexpectedly pulled out of their lessons (German for Ian, English for Peter) and called to the office of the eccentric headmaster. His reputation of being disdainful toward sensitive boys did not make him the ideal person to relay sad news. But it had been left to him to inform the Fleming brothers of the information that had arrived at his desk that morning.

Peter and Ian stood anxiously in the hallway outside the headmaster's office. Though a year younger than Peter, Ian was already several inches taller, yet he still looked to his older sibling for strength and support. Had he been called in to see TP on his own, Ian might have assumed his poor academic performance was about to earn him yet another reprimand from the headmaster. But Peter's presence, a "brilliant boy" and star pupil at Durnford, would have quashed such a fear. This left the puzzle of why the brothers had been brought to this intimidating place.

Peter looked typically calm and composed. Ian always felt safer and happier in his brother's company and confided to his mother that Peter was "a great help to me" at school.[49] He only wished they could have spent more time together at the school—perhaps this would protect him from the bullies who were tormenting the younger Fleming brother for his eccentric behavior.

A photograph of the four Fleming brothers from around this time shows Peter standing confidently alone, hands in pockets, with Richard and Michael—the two younger sons—standing between him and Eve. Ian, by contrast, stands on his mother's left in the picture, almost as tall as her, his arm hooked through hers, a picture of filial devotion. Perhaps surprisingly, it was the seemingly fragile Peter who showed the greater emotional independence at this crisis in their young lives. This is how the scene might have unfolded.

After what seems an eternity, the door to TP's office opens, and the man himself appears. Dressed in a dark suit with academic gown, glasses perched on the end of his nose, he is a rather stern man. However, his hair stands up on end, which together with a bushy moustache and somewhat bizarre garb makes him an eccentric rather than frightening figure. More like Mr. Pickwick than Wackford Squeers.

"Come in, boys, come in," he says with typical bluster.

Dutifully, the Fleming brothers troop into the headmaster's office, which has a large bay window overlooking the school grounds on the Durnford estate, looking toward the village of Langton Maltravers. The room is furnished in rather austere style, though there is a small, colorful Turkish rug in the middle of the wooden floor. The walls are lined with bookshelves filled with classical literature, sporting volumes, and English novels. TP sits behind his large mahogany desk and fiddles awkwardly with his pen.

"Sit down, boys, please," he invites them with a hand gesture.

Ian and Peter sit in two uncomfortable wooden chairs facing the desk. Many years later, when he was furnishing Goldeneye, Ian would remember these chairs and try to replicate their rough-hewn ricketiness—chairs designed to discourage visitors from extending their stay too long. Unusually, on this occasion, TP seems lost for words.

"Would you like some tea?" offers the headmaster. Ian can scarcely believe his ears, and a small gasp of amazement escapes him. This is unprecedented. Boys called in to see the headmaster are never offered tea. They are more likely to emerge rubbing their backsides after a caning. This offer reassures Ian that they are not in any trouble.

"No, thank you, sir," replies Peter respectfully.

"Yes, please, sir," replies Ian, almost simultaneously. Ian, always hungry, is hoping that the tea will be accompanied by biscuits. Peter looks at his brother with irritation—he wants to get the meeting over with, not cozy up to the head. There is a delay while TP prepares a pot of tea and pours them each a cup, ignoring Peter's previous refusal. On each saucer is placed a Creola biscuit, which Ian immediately dunks into his tea and eats. When they have settled down, TP begins.

"Now . . . how are you boys today?"

"Fine, thank you, sir," says Peter, speaking for both.

"That's good. Very good. You're both happy at the school?"

"Very much so, sir," replies Peter eagerly, again speaking for Ian, whose facial expression suggests he feels otherwise.

TP looks as though he expected no less than this enthusiasm. "I'm pleased to hear that. You know, my philosophy is that boys do their best work when they are happy and free."

"I agree, sir," said Peter, still obviously unsure why they are there.

"I'm afraid, though, I have some very bad news to deliver." TP pauses awkwardly and stirs his tea. "I wish it wasn't my duty to inform you . . ."

Without knowing the news, Ian already feels the tears springing into his eyes. "Is it about Mother?" he asks faintly. Peter again looks with irritation at Ian.

"No, it's your father. I'm terribly sorry to inform you that he was killed yesterday in action in Somme, France."

Peter merely blinks. Ian's tears start to flow.

"Please, sir, how did it happen?" Peter asks calmly.

TP seems relieved to be able to answer the question. "His battalion had occupied a farmhouse at Somme in France, apparently taking shelter from

German shelling. But regrettably the farmhouse took a direct hit, and your father was struck and killed by a shell fragment. Terribly bad luck. But you should be proud of him. He died a hero, fighting to protect us all from the Hun. He was a great man." At this praise of their father, Ian finally bursts into tears, and TP, despite his sympathetic demeanor, cannot conceal his disdain for such displays of overwhelming emotion. He believes in freedom for boys, but he also takes pride in a "stiff upper lip." His face shows admiration of Peter's reserve, just as he looks askance at Ian for his weakness.

"How awful," Peter says. "How could they do such an awful thing?"

Several minutes later, the boys are standing outside in the corridor again. Due to Ian's teary face, they receive curious glances from other boys passing by, who assume they must've been caned for some unknown offense. To their surprise, they have been excused from lessons for the rest of the day. This would normally be a blessing—especially to Ian—but under these circumstances, the unexpected freedom is stressful. Under the circumstances, both brothers would prefer the comfortingly familiar surroundings of other boys and the distraction of schoolwork.

"What are we to do now?" asks Ian disconsolately.

"I don't know. We could go for a walk?" says Peter vaguely.

"I'd like that," says Ian, flattered by his brother's wish to spend time with him.

"Shall we go to the Robbers Walk?" suggests Peter.

Ian's expression shows that he likes this idea. There is a beautiful old gazebo at the end of the pathway, with a spectacular view of the rolling downs. Here they could be alone, knowing the other boys were occupied with their lessons in school. The two boys agree, and they set off down the graveled pathway toward the gazebo. Ian's mind is elsewhere, but Peter suddenly stops abruptly and places a hand on Ian's arm.

"Blast it!" he says irritably. Ian looks at his brother, confused.

"What's the matter?"

"TP is already there. In the gazebo, with a lady."

Ian, who has remarkably sharp vision, looks into the distance and sees their headmaster engaged in deep conversation with a beautiful woman in her midthirties, dressed in elegant fashion.

"He got there quickly!" exclaims Ian.

"Do you recognize his companion?" asks Peter, peering into the distance.

"It's Mrs. Wilcox," says Ian matter-of-factly.

"Who?" asks Peter, whose eyesight is not quite as acute as his brother's.

"You know, Arthur's mother. She's a beauty. A widow!" He says this as though the attractive Mrs. Wilcox were available as a romantic interest for the nine-year-old!

"What do you suppose they're talking about?" asks Peter.

"I think it's about the facts of life," Ian suggests.

Peter looks perplexed. "Isn't she a bit old to be learning about that?" he asks.

Ian guffaws, briefly forgetting their tragedy. "No, silly. I mean, they're discussing how to go about telling *Arthur* about the facts of life. He still doesn't know."

Peter shrugs as though the facts of life were a matter of supreme indifference to him. "Well, anyway, that rules out our visit to the gazebo. They might be there for ages. How about the Dancing Ledge instead?"

Ian gives an involuntary shudder at this suggestion. Though situated on a beautiful rocky promontory on the coast, near Langton Maltravers, the Dancing Ledge has the unfortunate association of early-morning ice-cold compulsory bathing sessions in the rock pool, under the eagle-eyed supervision of TP himself. He cannot shake the unpleasant thought of these frigid dips.

"I'd rather not. Let's go to Spy Hill."

"It's a bit far," objects Peter.

"Not really. It's a lovely warm day. And we have the whole afternoon!"

Peter shrugs, feeling responsible now and wanting to cheer up his brother, so the two boys walk out of the school grounds onto Langford High Street. Though they have been given official leave, they still look furtively around them, half expecting to be hailed by some sharp-eyed master and accused of playing truant.

They walk side by side along a narrow lane until they reach Durnford Drove, the thoroughfare that leads to Spy Hill. Because of this destination, the drove is known locally as Spy Way. As they leave the school behind them, the two brothers become visibly relaxed, even playful. They encounter a stray collie dog—probably belonging to one of the local farmers—and Ian amuses himself by throwing sticks for it to chase, patting its head fondly when it returns to him. Eventually they reach Spy Hill and climb to the top along a steep rutted track carved out of the limestone soil by generations of smugglers, villagers, and schoolboys. From the top of the hill, Ian and Peter enjoy a magnificent panorama of the local countryside, a view of the downs on one side and on the other the fields stretching all the way down to the sea.

They can see the cliff path that runs from Saint Aldhelm's Head and even the lighthouse at Swanage several miles away.

"I wish we had a telescope," Ian muses sadly.

"You don't need one. You can see for miles with the naked eye."

"I bet the smugglers had a telescope," Ian insists.

Peter nods. "This is where they looked out for the excisemen when those fellows were rum running down by the sea," Peter rehearses. "They'd have a lantern that they could use to send a signal to their fellows as a warning."

"I'd like to be a smuggler," says Ian thoughtfully.

"Why?"

"I've heard that there's a smuggler's tunnel running between here and Corfe Castle. It would be fun to escape through that tunnel. And smuggling's a good way to make a fortune without paying taxes."

"But it's illegal. You'd be put in prison. Or strung up on the gallows," Peter explains ominously.

Ian flinches at this grisly prospect. "Then I'd like to be a soldier, like Mokie," he declares, and at the memory of their loss the tears well in his eyes again.

"That's a better idea. But let's hope there will be no more wars after this one, because people will have learned their lesson, so we won't need any soldiers."

Ian thinks about this for a while. "In that case, I'd like to be a spy."

"Why's that?" asks Peter.

"Well . . . we're on Spy Hill, aren't we? And they'll always need spies."

Peter has no reply, and the two brothers fling themselves down on the soft grass and gaze out to sea.

Years later, Thomas Pellatt would build a new school to be run by his daughter, Hester, and call it Spyway House. The name "Spyway" was in local use for a farm, and its name originated from nearby Spy Hill. This name had clear echoes of Stevenson's *Treasure Island*, one of Fleming's favorite books as a boy, with its plot of treasure hunting, pirates, and smuggling. In Stevenson's novel, the juvenile hero, Jim Hawkins, first meets John Silver at the "sign of the spy-glass," and later there is a location marked "Spy-glass Hill" on the map of Treasure Island that Jim takes from Billy Bones's chest. In Durnford, Spy Hill had indeed been used by smugglers as a lookout post in the late eighteenth and nineteenth centuries at a time when smugglers were rife on the Dorset coast, as at other coastal locations in the West Country. Spyway School was not established until 1927, years after Fleming left

Durnford. It was run by Hester and her husband, Nigel Chapman, and after their marriage collapsed, she would later achieve fame as a historical novelist specializing in fiction set during the reigns of the Tudors and Stuarts.[50]

But the place known as Spyway was certainly a fitting location for the creator of the most famous fictional spy in history. It was here that Ian found his own "spyway," envisaging himself as the author of spy thrillers set in exciting coastal locations. It was also here that Ian first encountered the family name "Bond." The school was also next to the estate of John Bond, an Elizabethan spy, the Latin motto of whose family was "Non Sufficit Orbis"—the English translation of which is "The World Is Not Enough." This motto, of course, would be assigned by Fleming to James Bond's family, as revealed when Bond visits the College of Arms in London to investigate Ernst Stavro Blofeld in *On Her Majesty's Secret Service*. Bond—who is not especially interested in learning his distinguished family's history—nonetheless does concede that "it is an excellent motto that I shall certainly adopt."[51]

Quite fittingly—given Ian Fleming's penchant for using names of people and places in his novels, often without asking permission—John Bond originally stole the motto "Non Sufficit Orbis" from King Philip of Spain, perhaps as a joke at the foreign monarch's expense. John Bond, who assisted Sir Francis Drake on many missions under Elizabeth I, would experience foreign escapades and dangerous missions similar to those of his more famous namesake, such as when he escaped the 1573 Bartholomew's Day massacre in France by taking a woman and her child hostage and threatening to kill them if he was not allowed to leave. While this ungallant act toward a woman is surely unworthy of 007, it does show the original Bond getting involved in scrapes overseas and somehow extracting himself. Bond was one of the great Elizabethan spies and a worthy precursor of Fleming's hero.[52]

Despite its beautiful setting and the eccentric appeal of TP, Ian was grateful and relieved to leave Durnford in 1921, following Peter to Eton that year. Although Val Fleming had been educated at Eton, Peter recalls that "in many ways it was all rather rushed and last-minute, because we suddenly found that our father hadn't put us down and there was something of a panic to get us in."[53] Fellow Etonians included Eric Blair (who later became famous under the pen name George Orwell) and Aldous Huxley, who taught French at Eton for a year in the 1920s. Peter soon became a star pupil at Eton—continuing the academic excellence he had shown at Durnford—which meant that Ian had a lot of catching up to do. TP prided himself on the strong connections he cultivated with Eton and believed that the school was based on his own principles of freedom.

According to John Pearson, "Intellectually [Ian] seemed no match for his brother Peter, who was already being tipped as a natural for an Eton scholarship."[54] Indeed, as Ian would discover, the sibling rivalry with Peter was one that he had no hope of winning. Peter's position was unassailable, having stepped into the responsibilities of male head of the family following the death of their father. Peter's academic excellence and general popularity meant that he was out of reach of Ian's abilities. Yet perhaps the competition was not as one-sided as this implies: Peter recalls, "For me a great source of angst was that I was smaller than Ian and at Eton you wore Eton jackets up to 5ft 4 inches and tails afterwards. Ian wore tails from the start."[55]

There was a strong Fleming tradition at Eton, both Val and his brother Philip having attended before going on to Magdalen College, Oxford. Peter excelled in all subjects at school and seemed a worthy successor to his father and uncle. He was also a member of Pop, the social society at the school, whereas on Ian's first attempt to join he was blackballed. Ian found ways to compensate for his academic mediocrity, finding an outlet for his energy and competitive spirit in athletics. While he played team games like football and rugby, he was more accomplished at individual sports such as sprinting and hurdling. He preferred the solo effort involved in track and field, which also allowed him precious time to himself. Ian's close friend Ivar Bryce reported that Ian felt he needed at least three-quarters of an hour of solitude each day. Perhaps Ian was not really a "team player," a preference that was reinforced by the collision with Henry Douglas-Home (younger brother of the prime minister who was in office at the time of Ian's death in 1964) in a football match that left him with a broken nose. A metal plate was inserted in the bridge of his nose, which accounted for the somewhat piratical look to Ian's features. This plate would cause him severe migraines and problems with nasal congestion in later life.

It was in athletics that he achieved his major success at Eton, earning the title of "Victor Ludorem" two years in succession—a feat that had never been achieved before or bettered since. This athletic prowess gave Ian the satisfaction of excelling in an area of physical endeavor where his older brother was not superior. The emphasis on physical action, toughness, and mobility was deeply influential on the kind of masculinity Ian valued and that he would develop in the persona of James Bond. Ian's athletic success also revealed his deeply competitive personality, which had been somewhat thwarted in his rivalry with Peter.

Ian was successful at his second attempt to join Pop, thanks to Peter's active sponsorship, and this membership improved his social standing at the school. Yet though he became more popular, Ian's preference was to spend time with a few close friends, preferably out of school bounds. Chief among these was Ivar Bryce, who would remain Ian's closest lifelong friend. The boys had originally met on the beach at Bude in Cornwall in 1914—not long before Ian went to Durnford in Dorset. Ivar recalls in his memoir, *You Only Live Once*, the rather intimidating presence of the Fleming brothers on this occasion. He remembers "four strong, handsome, black-haired, blue-eyed boys, from my age down," recalling "the leaders were Ian and Peter and I gladly carried out their exact and exacting orders." Later, at Eton, the friendship was cemented, and it was based on their shared disdain for institutional authority, love of pranks, and willingness to flout the rules of the school. Ivar

Figure 1.1. Ian Fleming winning the 1924 Junior mile race with a time of four minutes, 54.2 seconds. P. L. Bickersteth took second, and F. W. Lowndes Stone Norton took third. ***Courtesy of Ian Fleming Images/The Provost and Fellows of Eton College.***

recalls their friendship was forged "especially in one or two escapades that were never forgotten, and references to these adventures were used in clear code between us a third of a century afterwards."[56]

In fact, the two would continue to go on exciting escapades together throughout their lives, including their trip to Jamaica in 1944, when Ian fell in love with the island. On an earlier occasion, in the summer of 1938, Ian sent a cable to Bryce demanding that he join him in a journey through Europe, concluding "do not fail." Ian's youthful dominance over his friend would ensure that Bryce complied with this cable. On arrival in Boulogne, however, he discovered that Ian was accompanied by an American girlfriend, Phyllis, and unfortunately was driving a two-seater sports car. This meant Bryce had to sit perched uncomfortably between them. Soon, however, Ian's preference for his old friend's company triumphed, as Phyllis complains, "He was nothing but a brute, but [I] was really in love with him." Ian then decided to jettison Phyllis in order to go off with Bryce, for which Bryce apologizes that he can't take her home before Ian pushes her off the car! This symbolic act, choosing the male companion and carelessly dumping the woman, would become familiar in Fleming's later life. Although Bryce claims he was "distressed and embarrassed by this ruthless behavior," he clearly cherished his preferential status in Ian's life and notes of this trip that "after the bad beginning, everything went well."[57]

History does not record whether affairs with young women were among the "escapades" that Bryce refers to during their time at Eton. Bryce claims in his memoir, "Neither Ian nor I had the slightest notion of the world of girls which was soon to become so important to us and many of our friends, until our twentieth birthdays were behind us."[58] However, it seems likely that Ian did have sexual experiences at school, though perhaps without Bryce being involved. In *The Spy Who Loved Me*—perhaps Ian's most autobiographical novel, despite being written in the guise of a female protagonist—Viv Michel recalls losing her virginity to an Eton student, Derek, on the floor of a local cinema in Windsor. Fleming got in trouble with publishers and critics for the fairly graphic (for the time) description of Derek and Viv's lovemaking in the box of the Royalty Kinema, but the episode is so vivid as to be clearly drawn from Ian's memories. As Andrew Lycett notes, "Ian later told his friend Robert Harling this was where and how he first made love to a woman."[59] The tryst ends in disaster, as they are discovered by the cinema owner, who declares, "What the hell do you think you're doing in my cinema? Get up, you filthy little swine!"[60] Significantly, in *You Only Live Twice*, we learn that James Bond was removed from Eton after some scandal involving the school's maids, possibly based on Ian's sexual escapades at the school.[61]

Ian's aspirations of becoming a writer found some encouragement at Eton when he edited and contributed to an issue of *The Wyvern*, the Eton literary magazine. With help from distinguished contributors including Augustus John and Vita Sackville-West, who contributed a poem, the issue—timed for the Eton-Winchester cricket match in 1925—sold very well. With the proceeds from this publication and Ivar's earlier literary venture—a one-off magazine called *Snapdragon*—Ian and Ivar were able to purchase a second-hand Douglas motorcycle, on which they rode to London on various adventures. On one occasion, they were discovered by a "beak" (the schoolboy slang for schoolmaster) riding back from Great Wembley Exhibition in London. Fortunately, this teacher—the German master, ominously nicknamed "Satan" Ford—did not have them expelled, and Bryce notes, "We owe a lot to Satan Ford's heavily concealed kind heart."[62]

Ian's literary dreams were not confined to this early publishing venture. Bryce records that even at school, Ian had visions of a literary life. Bryce later recalls Ian's youthful vision of the writer's profession as a "wonderful way of life" with "the advantages and pleasures of writing thrillers while traveling about the world."[63] In his interview with John Pearson, Bryce recalled that "Ian had wanted to write thrillers for almost as long as I knew him."[64] Yet, in the meantime, Ian needed a practical profession to support himself. His mother had already formed a plan: as Bryce reports, "Ian's famous mother, Eve, respected by all and loved by Augustus John, had, rather oddly, chosen Sandhurst for him as a stepping stone to the Foreign Office where she envisaged his early promotion to ambassador at Paris or Washington as a routine certainty."[65]

Bryce here suggests the unrealistic expectations Eve had of her second son and mocks the foolish idea that he would easily achieve the status of ambassador. But her ambitions for Ian's great success in the "diplomatic" are less probable than her relief at finding some settled course in life for him. Sandhurst would not have seemed "odd" to the family given his father's military career and posthumous medal, though perhaps Bryce knew his friend was unlikely to take to military discipline. Unfortunately, however, the choice of Sandhurst meant further academic humiliation for Ian. He was removed from the university track at Eton (in which Peter had thrived before heading off to further academic glory at Christ Church, Oxford) and instead placed in the military class. Ian was being branded as an intellectual failure, further denting his dreams of literary achievement.

According to Alfred Adler—the Viennese psychologist whose disciples included Phyllis Bottome and Ernan Forbes Dennis, the English couple that ran Am Tennerhof school in Kitzbühel—each young child forms at an early stage a "life plan." This plan is based on the materials, influences, and experiences to hand and is therefore limited by the shortcomings, incomplete knowledge, and problems encountered in early life. Adler writes,

> The gradations in the powers inherent in the constitution of an individual, the child's evaluation of them and the experiences obtained from the environment, influence both the goal set and the lifeline. As soon as both are definitely fixed, character and instincts will be seen to fit into them exactly.[66]

Even from the earliest experiences, such as Ian had at Durnford School, a "life plan" had emerged in order to make sense of those experiences and to compensate for their disappointments.

For Adler, whether the experiences are positive or negative, they only take on meaning for the child with reference to a "goal" or purpose that the child sets. Adler insists that

> nobody really permits experiences as such to form, without their possessing some purpose. Indeed, experiences are moulded by him. That simply means that he gives them a definite character, being guided by the way in which he thinks they are going to aid or hinder him in the attainment of his final goal. What is active within our experiences and continuously at work, is the life-plan with its goal.[67]

Ian Fleming's "life plan" was formed at Durnford under the pressure of isolation and persecution, compounded by the trauma of the death of his father. The motto "The World Is Not Enough"—which he discovered while at Durnford—was an ideal launch pad for this overcompensation characterized by a quest for superiority and striving for dominance and power. Ian's life plan of imaginary dominance was consolidated at Eton, where his inferiority complex regarding Peter was deepened by academic failure and social exclusion, particularly after being placed in the "military class" and thus branded an intellectual mediocrity. Ian's later public diffidence and self-denigration about his novels may have derived from this inferiority complex. However, it concealed a fierce ambition for success in the fiction market.

From his early years, Ian's life plan was based on a fantasy of success and superiority that would raise him to a position of dominance over both Peter and his peers. In this life plan, Ian would realize his fantasy of becoming a spy, after the fashion of the heroes he read about in John Buchan, "Sapper," and Anthony Hope. But Ian's related goal was to become a writer of thrillers and thereby to achieve fame and fortune while vicariously pursuing the exciting path of espionage. Durnford provided some of the materials for this life plan, with the "Spyway" farm and Spy Hill prompting thoughts of espionage. The neighboring estate of the Bonds inspired Fleming with the deeds of the Elizabethan spy John Bond and planted the idea for the future secret agent hero in his imagination. James Bond—the code name 007 was also used by John Bond to sign his secret messages—would embody the dream of omnipotence that Ian had formed as a boy. Even as he absorbed and found inspiration in the beautiful natural surroundings of Durnford School, this dream of power was nursed during Ian's setbacks and sufferings as a young pupil at the school.

For Adler, the response to an inferiority complex in a child—male or female—was what he termed "masculine protest," or an aggressive assertion of "masculine" traits in order to "be a man." Likewise, a rejection of perceived "feminine" experiences such as suffering, waiting, and weakness was necessary in order to give precedence to the masculine role. The fantasy of becoming a masculine "hero" or "father" would be realized in the creation of James Bond.

Peter's superiority to Ian was not, of course, due only to his academic excellence, popularity, and approval from their mother. It was also caused by his assuming the role of male head of the family, or "father," thus usurping Ian from his desired masculine role. After being moved to the military class at Eton, Ian had an opportunity to assume the masculine role and gain ascendency by going to Sandhurst. Valentine's heroism had been defined in World War I; thus, a military career offered Ian a chance to emulate him. Ian still idolized his father, the dead war hero killed in his prime, and the prospect of following in Val's footsteps was in some ways enticing. Perhaps Ian could become another war hero in the family and thereby gain an advantage over Peter, who had followed the academic path to Oxford. Ian had passed the Sandhurst entrance exam with ease, finishing eleventh out of 120 candidates. But dealing with the realities of the parade ground, military discipline, and relative lack of personal freedom was another matter.

Ian went to Sandhurst in September 1926, joining Number 5 Company, whose commander was Major the Lord Alwyn. Unfortunately, Ian did not take to life at Britain's premier military academy. Its strict regime and discipline reminded him unpleasantly of the Spartan aspects of Durnford School, only by this time—at age eighteen—he had grown used to the comparative freedom at Eton. Life for Sandhurst cadets was organized down to the last minute. The early rising (reveille at 7:00 a.m.), obsessive attention to details of one's uniform, and the necessity to follow orders all grated on Ian's sense of independence. The first part of the Sandhurst course was dedicated to intensive drill exercise, or "square bashing."[68] In the second term, more emphasis was placed on academic work, such as military history and international affairs as well as foreign languages. Despite the emphasis given to organized sports—at which Ian had excelled at Eton—Ian was turned off by the strict discipline and lack of social life, which was largely limited to the college itself.

Geographically, Sandhurst was close to Eton, but it was poles apart in terms of the amount of liberty Ian could enjoy there. It was especially galling for Ian to know that Peter was basking in the academic prestige, freedom, and comfort of Oxford, while he was shouldering the brunt of military training. The course at Sandhurst was supposed to last eighteen months, but Ian left after one year without receiving a commission. He was more interested in practicing the Hawaiian guitar or going on dates with girls like Peggy Barnard, who herself came from a military background—and Ian would later fictionalize some of their trips together in the journeys of Viv Michel and Derek in *The Spy Who Loved Me*. Yet, despite the youthful passion of this relationship, Ian still sought sexual solace elsewhere. It has been alleged that Ian visited a prostitute in London—perhaps to avenge Peggy's decision to attend a ball with another man—and later discovered to his shame and embarrassment that he had contracted gonorrhea. Ian's friend Cyril Connolly recalled, "Ian said that if she did [attend the dance with another man] he would go to London and have a tart. He did and caught gonorrhoea. Somehow this led . . . to Ian leaving Sandhurst."[69] This was not only a dangerous disease but also a potential scandal for Ian's future career. Eve quickly decided to remove him from Sandhurst on temporary medical leave. However, Ian made it clear to his mother that he did not see his future in military life and had no intention of returning to the esteemed academy.

Despite recognizing that Sandhurst was not fulfilling its role as a refining fire for her errant son, Eve had by no means abandoned the plan for Ian to join the Foreign Office (FO). Eve therefore convinced Ian to write a letter resigning his cadetship at Sandhurst, and a letter from Charles Lewis of the War Office to the Civil Service Commission confirms that "this gentleman served as a Cadet at the Royal Military College, Sandhurst from 3rd September, 1926, to 31st August, 1927, when he resigned his Cadetship."[70] Fortunately, there was no whisper of the embarrassing circumstances leading to Ian's removal from Sandhurst. His record was not besmirched, and his 1928 application for the FO was endorsed by the headmaster of Eton as well as Ian's house tutor E. V. Shaw. Ian also had impressive letters of recommendation from the archdeacon of Saint Paul's Cathedral and Viscount D'Abernon, the British ambassador to Germany.[71]

But both Ian and Eve recognized that, without a university degree or a commission from Sandhurst, Ian needed additional skills to achieve success in his chosen path. He passed the first interview stage of the application for the FO with flying colors. But he still faced the daunting challenge of the notoriously difficult FO exam, only the most outstanding candidates for which would be selected. Eve decided that Ian needed to improve his language skills, and fortuitously foreign languages were Ian's best academic subject at Eton. He had impressed the German master at the school, who had not pushed to have Ian and Ivar expelled after their illicit motorcycle trip to London in part because of Ian's language skills. He also had some fluency in French. Eve therefore decided that Ian should return to Kitzbühel to study languages under Ernan Forbes Dennis and Phyllis Bottome.

Ian had spent several months there with Peter in the summer of 1926, both brothers improving their German before going off to Sandhurst and Oxford, respectively. Ian had enjoyed his time in the Tyrol and was keen on returning there for further study. Eve's initial idea of sending Ian much farther afield, to Australia—often the chosen destination for "black sheep" of British families—was abandoned, and the more congenial environment of Am Tennerhof was agreed on.

What lessons can we learn from Ian's early years and education before his transformative period at Kitzbühel? His performances in academic institutions were not impressive, either at Durnford or at Eton. While TP lavished praise on Peter's "brilliance" in his memoir, Ian did not even merit a mention. At Eton, Ian distinguished himself as a top athlete but was overshadowed by his brother Peter's stellar academic success and social popularity and daunted by Peter's assumption of the role of male head of the Fleming family. The confidence in his physical prowess through his athletic successes at Eton was hardly compensation for academic mediocrity. It certainly did not redress the imbalance between the brothers' standings in the family or indeed in wider society. Peter was the "golden boy," a credit to his father's memory and recognized as one of the most promising young men of his generation. Ian, by contrast—as Eve often reminded him—was in danger of disgracing his father's memory by his scholastic ineptitude, ungentlemanly conduct, and scandal. The special attention Ian would receive at Kitzbühel and the chance of entering the FO offered the prospect of a fresh start for this errant son, but there were already several black marks against him.

Despite the conservative nature of some of his values in later life, Ian would remain (at a deep level) a rebel against conformity, repression, and authority. Ian's much-publicized sexual exploits and womanizing may have been in part the expression of a hedonistic personality, but they were more than this. For Ian, sexual conquest was a form of "masculine protest" against "the possibility of his being forced to play an inferior, painful and feminine role."[72] Sexual promiscuity was also Ian's way of rebelling against the oppressive Victorian fear and dislike of sex and the hypocrisy of Victorians who preached abstinence while indulging their lustful desires.

In discussing the sexual desires of one of his patients suffering from an inferiority complex, Adler made a telling remark that his "love becomes strong *only when a rival made his appearance*, i.e. when love came to be connected with the masculine characteristic of robbing and fighting."[73] For Ian, love—or sexuality—would be a way of gaining an advantage in his rivalry with Peter. Later in life, Ian would pursue women who were attached to other, more powerful, men. By stealing Ann Charteris away from two wealthy noblemen—first Lord O'Neill, then Lord Rothermere—Ian would assert his masculine dominance and compensate for feelings of inferiority. Notably, James Bond also chooses women who are claimed by dominant men—usually the powerful villain—and his ability to "steal" these women from the villain is a measure of his masculine success. It is also a measure of how Bond represented Ian's "masculine protest."

Bond was at once a fantasy of omnipotence—a way for Ian to find recompense for others' (especially Peter's) superiority in real life—and a dream of sexual freedom and defiance of repressive morals. Bond, above all, has "license" to violate the taboos and norms of bourgeois life—the taboo against killing, of course, but also the interdiction against sexual promiscuity. This is one reason that "Bondmania" took off in the 1960s, the decade of the sexual revolution. While his conservative background and establishment role seem to disqualify Bond as a countercultural hero, his uninhibited lifestyle and enjoyment of sex struck a chord with a new generation.

It would be a long journey indeed from the unhappy, lonely, bullied, and bereaved schoolboy at Durnford Prep to the international celebrity and creator of a popular icon and spy hero. But that journey had already begun in Dorset, and Ian Fleming had set his life goal. He was on the road to his objective of becoming a spy and spy novelist, and the local stories about the Elizabethan spy John Bond were fuel for Ian's dream. Another influential name derived from the landscape around Durnford was the road known locally as Spy Way. Unknown to all those around him, Ian Fleming had already found his own spy way, and it would eventually lead him to create the most famous fictional spy in history, James Bond.

Chapter Two

Escape in the Alps

Ian Fleming and James Bond in Kitzbühel

Fleming's experience at some of the most prestigious educational institutions in Britain had left him feeling both despondent and rejected, his self-confidence and sense of direction in tatters after ignominious exits from Eton and Sandhurst. Having been branded an academic mediocrity at Eton—unlike his brother Peter, who was off to Christ Church, Oxford, and a glittering career as a journalist and writer—Ian nonetheless had a powerful sense of ambition. His life plan formed while at Durnford Prep School was still in effect—the plan to forge a new identity as a spy and to find success as a writer. Perhaps Ian had contributed to his own humiliating departure from Eton with his escapades with Ivar Bryce and his liaisons with young women in Windsor and its environs. When Ian left Sandhurst under a cloud and without graduating, his mother, Eve, was understandably anxious about her troubled second son's future career. What was she to do with Ian, who seemed to have suffered most among her sons from the absence of a father?

Her solution, as it turned out, would be one of the most inspired decisions she made concerning her son's future. This choice altered the history not only of Ian Fleming but also, indirectly, of British literature and popular culture. Eve decided that Ian should be prepared to take the exam for the Foreign Office (FO), with the purpose of becoming a diplomat. In preparation for the FO exam, she sent him to study at the Villa Tennerhof at Kitzbühel, Austria, run by a British married couple, Ernan Forbes Dennis and Phyllis Bottome. This unusual school had a reputation for getting the best out of maladjusted young men sent to improve their language skills under the Forbes Dennises' care. The couple—who had been married since 1917—could hardly have been better chosen to bring out the potential of Ian Fleming by tapping in to his unrealized talents and ambitions.

In Ernan Forbes Dennis, Ian discovered a mentor who was also a former spy—having served as Secret Intelligence Service head of station in Vienna, with responsibility for spy networks in Austria and Hungary, under the cover of Passport Control. Forbes Dennis also had the patience and insight to break through Ian's emotional defenses and recalcitrance and coax him into trusting him and producing good work. In Phyllis Bottome, Ian found both a teacher and a mother figure. She was a successful novelist, achieving worldwide fame with her 1937 anti-Nazi novel *The Mortal Storm*. Their combined influences were crucial in shaping Ian's future as an intelligence agent who went on to write spy novels. In September 1963, after Phyllis's death, Ian wrote a letter of condolence to Ernan in which he made clear the important role of the couple during his formative years: "You were father & mother to me when I needed them most & I have always treasured the memory of those days at Kitzbühel."[1]

Another of the young men studying for the FO at Kitzbühel—Ralph Arnold, who went on to become a novelist—recalled the unusual bond that formed between Phyllis Bottome and Ian: "Her imagination gave her a world which was much more real and more colourful to her than the dull world she had never really entered. Ian walked into this imaginary world of old Phyllis's like a gift from God."[2] Like Phyllis, Ian was a fantasist who sought, in his imaginative adventures, an escape from the dullness of everyday reality.

The enduring importance of Kitzbühel and the Swiss Alps to Ian's imagination would be evident in the fact that he and Ann vacationed there in the 1950s, when Ian attempted to recapture some of the romance of his youthful sojourn in the Tyrol. No less important, Kitzbühel also figures in several of his novels and stories, including one of the most personal and reflective Bond novels, *On Her Majesty's Secret Service*: the villain, Blofeld, is lodged in the Swiss Alps, his private clinic atop Piz Gloria, and Bond's skills as an Alpine skier are called on when he makes his escape from the villain's lair. After Bond has destroyed Blofeld's Alpine base and married Tracy, the newlyweds are on their way to Kitzbühel for their honeymoon. Kitzbühel also features in "Octopussy," an important late short story by Fleming, in which Bond's motive for tracking down the dissolute Major Dexter Smythe in Jamaica is to avenge the murder of his surrogate father figure, Hans Oberhauser. Smythe had murdered Oberhauser in the mountains above Kitzbühel during World War II. Clearly, Fleming's imagination remained attached to the location many years after he left it as a young man. His memory was also haunted by the trauma of his own youthful affair and broken engagement to a young Swiss woman, Monique Panchaud de Bottomes. Although Fleming dwelled on Kitzbühel with nostalgic affection, there is also a darker side to his recollections of the Alpine setting and even some ambivalence in his fiction about the Forbes Dennises.

THE HOUSE OF ADLER: AM TENNERHOF

By the time Ian Fleming arrived at Am Tennerhof, located in Kitzbühel, the Austrian Alpine region of the Tyrol, the Forbes Dennises were already committed adherents to the individual psychology theories of Austrian psychoanalyst Alfred Adler. One of the key concepts of Adlerian psychology is that the individual's family position, beginning from infancy, is the most important factor for the formation of identity. For Adler, the young child chose (consciously or unconsciously) a "*gegenspieler*"—that is, a rival in the family against whom she or he would compete for superiority, dominance, and parental approval. This *gegenspieler* might in some cases be a parent, but it was more likely to be a sibling with whom the child competed for parental approbation and rewards. However, in some cases the child found it could not match up to the *gegenspieler*, resulting in wounds to the ego that left an enduring sense of inferiority. Phyllis Bottome had herself developed an inferiority complex toward her older sister, Mary—a beautiful, socially successful girl with whom the less obviously attractive and physically ailing Phyllis could not compete.

Because Peter and Ian Fleming both spent time at Am Tennerhof—though separately, not together—the Forbes Dennises had an excellent opportunity to observe them and compare the personalities and demeanors of the brothers. Through the Adlerian lens, they soon realized they had on hand a classic example of this sibling rivalry and consequent inferiority complex in the younger sibling. Ernan also recognized how demoralized Ian had been by his educational failures: "I soon saw that Ian was immensely frustrated, and that he was caught between burning ambition and discouragement."[3]

Peter, Ernan believed, was the "thoroughbred" horse that arrived shining and well disciplined, set to win the race. Ian, by contrast, was the carthorse, a rebellious and intractable animal who resisted and resented any attempts to discipline and train him. In her biography of Phyllis Bottome, Pam Hirsch includes Ernan's memories of his young charge: "My first impression of Ian was that he was very good-looking, very arrogant, very Etonian and very prickly. What the French call *difficile*. It was almost impossible to get through his defences, and he showed no great inclination to work."[4] Ian had formed an inferiority complex due to Peter's role as male head of household and superiority in all activities (except athletics) at Eton. Ian therefore had, in reaction, retreated into a shell of diffidence, resistant behavior, and rebellion against authority.

Ernan and Phyllis quickly took Ian under their wing, seeking to help him find a new "life plan" that focused on his areas of strength, guiding him toward the chance for excellence rather than dwelling on his inferiority to Peter. As Phyllis wrote,

> Adler thought that every child forms his own life-plan unconsciously, from the examples and materials that he finds around him at birth; and since this pattern is already fixed at a time when the child is still ignorant of life and his reason is undeveloped, it is generally a faulty life-plan.

By contrast, Adler's individual psychology "gives him the opportunity to change a faulty life-plan for a more reasonable goal."[5] Phyllis—who would title her autobiography *The Goal*—took on herself the task of helping Ian find a better goal, which would determine his lifeline.

Phyllis also encouraged Ian to write fiction, seeing this activity as a means by which Ian could develop his talents and form a new life plan. One of his earliest stories, called "A Poor Man Escapes," was written at her prompting, and Ian later expressed his gratitude to Ernan and Phyllis, admitting that without Phyllis's mentoring, he would not have become a successful writer. In 1962, when Phyllis was about to reach the milestone age of eighty years old, Fleming asked Leonard Russell at *The Sunday Times* to publish a paragraph about her to "cheer her up," explaining the important role she had played at Kitzbühel in his development as a writer:

> It was our first contact with a "famous writer," and it may be that by a process of osmosis we imbibed some of Phyllis's undoubted talent, because of the very few boys who stayed with them in Kitzbühel three, myself, Ralph Arnold . . . and Nigel Dennis have ended up successful writers. . . . So far as I am concerned I wrote my first story at Phyllis Bottome's behest when I was about nineteen, and I remember my pleasure at her kindly criticisms of it.[6]

This assessment of Phyllis Bottome's influence on Fleming's writing is supported by Bottome's biographer, Pam Hirsch:

> Having a working writer in the house spurred several of the boys to try their own hand at the art, and Phyllis would always read and critique stories that they had written for her. In this way, at Kitzbühel, she mentored the apprenticeship writings of Ian Fleming, Nigel Dennis, and Ralph Arnold.[7]

There was another source of increased self-confidence for Ian at Am Tennerhof. He came to discover his attractiveness to women, having various affairs with local young women at Kitzbühel. Such activities were obviously extracurricular but important nonetheless to his self-esteem. Ian seems to have carefully cultivated the role of a young, Byronic antihero, somewhat mournful and melancholy in bearing, his dramatic good looks rendered still more striking by his broken nose. According to Ralph Arnold, in Kitzbühel Ian was "completely and utterly irresistible to women."[8]

Phyllis, it must be said, was somewhat disturbed by Fleming's cavalier treatment of young women in and around Kitzbühel. Pam Hirsch argues that a novel she wrote during this period, *Wind in His Fists*, incorporates a critical portrayal of her womanizing young charge: "Her rogue male character, the amoral Max von Ulm, takes some of the personality facets she had observed in Ian Fleming: the love of risk-taking, the love of fast cars, the careless use of women."[9] Bottome's critical view of Fleming's philandering surfaced years later, when Ian's affair with Ann Rothermere caught the headlines. Phyllis seemed to almost gloat about his getting his comeuppance in the complicated divorce and remarriage proceedings with Ann:

> Perhaps you will have seen that our poor Ian, who must now be forty-five and has never stopped having love affairs which were all catastrophic, has now at last got himself—in the direction to which they all pointed—well into the Divorce Court. He is cited as correspondent in the Rothermere case. He introduced us to Lady Rothermere once, and I thought her as hard as nails; so I very much doubt—even if he wanted to marry her—whether such a marriage would not be the end of him.[10]

Phyllis here suggests that the divorce scandal, and Ian's proposed marriage to Ann Rothermere (née Charteris), was somehow Ian's comeuppance for his youthful philandering. However, I will argue that Ian's relationship with Ann represented a new stage in his maturing views of, and emotional involvement with, women.

Phyllis was a very different kind of writer than those whom Ian had admired and wished to emulate. Unlike the spy yarns of John Buchan and "Sapper," Phyllis's novels were often characterized by melodrama, domestic drama, political conflict, and propaganda about the threats of Nazism. They usually featured a strong-willed, independent, and talented female protagonist who faces a crisis or challenge of an extreme kind. Phyllis's gifts at creating complex characters, however, always prevented her work from descending to simple diatribe. Her novels were all informed by Adler's principles of individual psychology, and some of her characters were clearly surrogates of Adler or embodied his psychological ideas, such as Professor Roth, the heroine's father in her most successful work, *The Mortal Storm* (1937). However, Bottome did also pen a thriller with Dorothy Thompson in the 1920s and would write a spy novel—*The Life Line*—in 1946, so her writing overlapped in some ways with the genre that Ian chose to pursue.[11]

There is no doubt that Bottome had an enduring impact on Fleming's writing and that he remained grateful to her for her encouragement and support. In the early 1960s, Ian wrote Phyllis in praise of her recent autobiography, *The Goal*, acknowledging the role she had played in his development as a writer:

> Looking back, I am sure that your influence had a great deal to do with the fact that, at any rate, three of us [from the Kitzbühel school] later became successful authors, and I remember clearly writing a rather bizarre short story for you which you criticized kindly and which was in fact the first thing I ever wrote.[12]

Significantly, this letter to Bottome was written in January 1962—just before Fleming's fame as the author of Bond was about to reach new heights with the release of *Dr. No*, the first EON Bond film. At the time *Dr. No* was being filmed in Jamaica, he was writing *On Her Majesty's Secret Service* at Goldeneye—this being the novel in which Kitzbühel and the Alpine scenery play a crucial role.[13]

Despite the kindly and sensitive mentoring of Phyllis Bottome, there was an obvious obstacle to Ian's writing as a source of self-confidence and superiority—namely, that his older brother was also a successful literary editor at *The Spectator* and would become a famous author in 1933, with *Brazilian Adventure*, a popular travelogue based on Peter's journey into the Amazon in search of the lost British explorer Colonel Fawcett. This was followed by other successful travelogues, like *News from Tartary*. Peter's success in literature would "block" Ian's path; hence he delayed writing his first book until much later, after World War II. However, by creating James Bond, Ian would eventually far outstrip his brother's success, becoming one of the most famous novelists in the world.

For Fleming, Kitzbühel represented a new world of personal independence: his time there offered his first real taste of freedom from the demands, conflicts, and rivalries of family. He got into some serious scrapes, including a car crash where his vehicle was hit by a train. Ian also embraced danger in the Alps, including one ski slope that was off-limits because of the threat of avalanches. Ernan recalled, "Of course this was an irresistible thing for Ian. It acted as a sort of challenge, and he was buried by snow."[14]

Episodes such as these would later provide material for dramatic events in Ian's novels, such as *Casino Royale*, *Moonraker*, and *On Her Majesty's Secret Service*. It was his first escape from the domineering influence of a mother whose ambitions and expectations burdened Ian with a sense of inadequacy and inferiority. In Kitzbühel, Ian found not one but two sympathetic surrogate parent figures who encouraged him to pursue his own interests and impulses. Ian's evident appeal as a handsome, worldly, yet melancholic Englishman in this small Alpine community undoubtedly boosted his self-esteem.

The separation from his all-conquering brother also proved crucial for Ian's new development. Peter, as Phyllis Bottome soon realized, was Ian's *gegenspieler*, "a person to compete with at all costs in an endless neurotic duel."[15] In her own book on Adler, Bottome wrote, "The Gegenspieler is a contemporary brother or sister by whom the child has felt dethroned or otherwise outdistanced. . . . In almost any intimate relationship that follows, the child as he develops into the man will build up the same perpetual antagonism between himself and any beloved person."[16] His time in Kitzbühel helped Fleming escape, if temporarily, from the suffocating pressure of rivalry with Peter.

How had the Forbes Dennises become such aficionados of Adler's work? It began with Ernan, who had visited Adler in Vienna in order to learn more about the psychologist's theories. Adler, frankly, asked Ernan how many of his books he had read and, on being told that the neophyte had read none of the master's works, told Ernan to go away and read his books and return in a year. Ernan did so, and his wife—Phyllis Bottome—also began to avidly read his opus. Eventually, Phyllis would become an even more fervent disciple of the Viennese psychologist than her husband, and she later wrote an important biography of Adler.

Armed with Adler's theories of the inferiority complex and *gegenspieler*, the Forbes Dennises decided to focus on strengthening Ian's self-esteem. They did this by identifying and nurturing talents of his, areas in which he could achieve success and feelings of superiority. The first of these strengths was foreign languages—the improvement of which, of course, was the main reason Eve sent Ian to Kitzbühel. Ian became fluent in German during his stay in Austria. He had a skilled tutor in Forbes Dennis, who was also cultivated, charming, and patient with difficult, temperamental young men. Perhaps he had attained this through his long friendship with the famous songwriter and actor Ivor Novello. Ian probably didn't know that Ernan had for years been part of the homosexual and artsy circle gravitating around Novello and another charismatic gay friend, Frank Lascelles, whom Ernan helped arrange spectacular pageants, first in Canada, then in Britain. Ernan was spellbound by the charismatic and dominant personalities of Novello and Lascelles and had at first been somewhat evasive when Phyllis expressed her interest in him.

Phyllis had sometimes doubted that Ernan could manage to detach himself from his artistic gay circle and commit himself to her. Perhaps, in Ian Fleming, Ernan recognized another talented and attractive young man who needed his nurturing attention and affection to blossom. In any case, Ernan was living proof that a career in the FO was not a dull desk job in a bureaucracy but involved active fieldwork, espionage, and intrigue.

Ian's gift at literary composition would, for many years, find an outlet in journalism rather than fiction. Yet, it is clear that Phyllis had planted the seed of literary ambition in the young Ian and that he only needed the right subject—and suitable materials and opportunity—in order to produce something creditable, even special. For Ralph Arnold, "all the plots and fantasies of his later books were all there, even in those days."[17] The journalistic experience Fleming obtained—after his plan of joining the Foreign Office had collapsed—would also develop and hone his writing skills, especially his powers of taut description and keen sense of place. These skills would also prove valuable when he turned to fiction.

THE KITZBÜHEL CASANOVA: FLEMING IN THE TYROL

Ian's discovery of his attractiveness to the young women of the Tyrol—after the years spent in the all-male environments of Durnford, Eton, and Sandhurst—came as a revelation. In fact, though, Ian was not simply playing the field or sowing wild oats but falling in love. At a ball in Geneva, he had met Monique Panchaud de Bottomes, the attractive young daughter of a local Swiss landowner. She was renowned as a beauty, and the two young people became inseparable. In the summer of 1931, Ian even moved homes to be closer to her, finding lodgings along the shore of Lake Geneva during his time studying at the University of Geneva. Ian and Monique became unofficially engaged at this time, with the blessing of her parents. For despite Ian's reputation as a Lothario, he was handsome and educated and came from a highly respectable British family.

Unfortunately, Ian's mother was less enthusiastic about the match. Worried that Monique was distracting her son from his studies for the FO, Eve disapproved of the relationship and, when Monique visited the Flemings in London, did her utmost to break up the couple. Monique herself later wrote that every time she attempted to be alone with her fiancé, Eve would come between them: "She did her best to try to separate us. When I dared to go into Ian's room, she threw a fit. . . . She was simply jealous."[18] Although Ian had become seriously attached to Monique, their semiofficial bond was no match for Eve's determined opposition, and she even pressured Ian's new boss—Bernard Rickatson-Hatt, chief editor at Reuters—to prevent the marriage. Rickatson-Hatt refused, knowing only too well that if he broached the subject with Ian, "he would be perfectly entitled to tell me to go to hell."[19] Eve, however, was convinced that Monique was not worthy of her son and that she was not from a distinguished enough family.

Ian was heartbroken by the enforced separation and end of their affair. It became clear that, if he persisted in the relationship, there would be financial repercussions, including the termination of his allowance from his mother. A mutual friend of Ian and Monique's from their Geneva days, William Martin Hill, believed "the breaking off with Monique ended the chance for him of a normal life."[20] For years afterward, Ian held a bitter grudge toward his mother for having thwarted his early romantic desires and vowed to become hard-hearted in his treatment of women in future. He told Ralph Arnold, "I'm going to be quite bloody-minded fr[om] now on. . . . I'm just going to get what I want without any scruples."[21] Despite this resolution, the special place

Figure 2.1. Ian and Monique Panchaud de Bottomes beside Lake Geneva, 1932. ***Courtesy of Ian Fleming Images/Private Collection.***

that Monique had found in his heart reemerged, many years later, when Fleming chose the name Monique for James Bond's Swiss mother. However, her maiden name of Delacroix also linked Monique Bond to Eve, whose maiden name was Sainte Croix Rose.

Despite the unhappy end to this relationship with Monique, his affairs with various women during his time in Kitzbühel had been a boost to Fleming's self-esteem. Had this period of intensive study combined with rigorous outdoor exercise and enjoyable relationships produced the outcome Ian wished for—securing a place in the Foreign Office—the time in the Tyrol might have counted as the foundation for a new "superiority" and helped him overcome his inferiority complex regarding Peter. However, Ian's failure to pass the exam—or to score highly enough on it to gain admission to the FO, coming twenty-fifth out of sixty-two applicants—was yet another traumatic fiasco in young Ian's life. His dreams of becoming the kind of master spy he had read about in the thrillers of William Le Queux or John Buchan—a combination of diplomat and secret agent and gentleman, which Ernan Forbes Dennis so appealingly embodied—were dashed.

Acting quickly on the heels of this setback, Eve leapt into action, using her contacts to secure Ian a position at the Reuters news agency on a renewable contract. His career was launched, but it was to be in journalism—still a dubious profession in many eyes—rather than the prestigious field of international diplomacy. Of course, Reuters was a respectable organization, and Ian had nothing to be ashamed of in failing the FO exam, one of the most difficult tests in British government. But the failure left another blot on his record—at least in his own mind—and deepened the inferiority complex.

As though to make things harder for Ian, Peter had completed a bold and exciting expedition in the Amazon jungle and was busy writing his account of it. Published in 1933, *Brazilian Adventure* would quickly become a best seller as well as garner critical acclaim and launch Peter's career as a successful travel writer. This achievement and recognition cast Ian's failure to enter the FO into even deeper shadow. Where Ian was fortunate to gain a short-term appointment at Reuters, Peter actually gave up the editorship at *The Spectator* to pursue Amazonian adventures leading to literary celebrity.

Ultimately, Ian would have to create a fictional, idealized "superman" version of himself in James Bond. Only this alter ego could provide proof of his superiority, his capacity as a spy, virility as a hero, and importance to his nation's security. With many similarities to Ian's own background and tastes, Bond had the key advantage of being needed by his country. Insofar as Bond was—or resembled—Ian, he enabled the author to impose his will on the world to transform inferiority into superiority (the first of Adler's tenets). By giving Bond so many of his own traits—the brooding good looks and dashing style, Eton education, mode of dressing (a mixture of class and casual, with Sea Island cotton shirts, etc.), heavy consumption of cigarettes and alcohol, enjoyment of fast cars, and pursuit of beautiful women—Fleming was claiming Bond as his own *gegenspieler*.

Yet nagging doubts persisted that Bond, after all, had qualities Ian lacked—most notably extreme physical courage, firsthand experience of military action, and a position in the intelligence world that reflected a professional career rather than a wartime interlude. Fleming, when all was said and done, was a desk man, a bureaucrat closer to M than to Bond. By contrast, 007 was always a field agent and man of action.

The importance of Kitzbühel in Ian's life is reflected in the role it played in his later years, long after he had left the tutelary supervision of the Forbes Dennises. In 1958, the Flemings went on a holiday to Kitz, about which Ann Fleming wrote to her close friend Evelyn Waugh concerning the strange rituals it involved her in:

> Twice a week there are confetti battles in the town and a band plays, it usually rains and the confetti is thrown with great violence. . . . These confetti orgies have great significance for Ian, he spent his nineteenth and twentieth years here being coached for the Foreign Office, they remind him of his youth and though he insists on my accompanying him I am invariably in disgrace.[22]

In Ann's account, Ian's youthful sojourn in Kitzbühel is a sensitive topic that he takes very seriously. His touchiness about her behavior in Kitz derives from the fact that it is a sacred place for him, a site of treasured memories when he was young and single, for which she lacks reverence. Ann seems to enjoy the discomfiture of "Thunderbird"—the mocking name she used for Ian in letters to Waugh, following his purchase of a Ford Thunderbird—at his thwarted attempt to recapture his youth.

On a later visit to the Alps in the winter of 1961, the setting brought back more poignant memories for the physically ailing creator of James Bond. Ann wrote to Waugh,

> The height has affected Thunderbird's blood pressure, and at night he has to be propped up with pillows because of panting, but he clings to youth and dreams of the days when he was the Kitzbühel Casanova; he is now better because a

> German girl aged fourteen called Lilo (hun for Lolita?) fastens his skis and collects him from snowdrifts.[23]

The suggestion that Ian, by this time in his fifties, was attracted (like Nabokov's Humbert Humbert) to a teenage girl seems malicious, but the idea that Ian wishes to recapture his own youth by revisiting the Alps is very plausible.

If Ian was frustrated in reality in his attempts to return to the (nostalgically) blissful years of Kitz, it was a different matter in his fiction. As was so often the case, Ian's fiction was a way to compensate for the shortcomings, the disappointments, and the failures of actual life: to provide a more colorful, satisfying, and triumphant outcome to his imaginary visits to this vital place in his development. An important clue to the importance of this venue can be found in the 1962 short story "Octopussy," in which James Bond avenges the wartime murder of his mentor and surrogate father, Hans Oberhauser. This murder, which took place during World War II in the mountains above Kitzbühel, was carried out by Major Dexter Smythe, a fictionalized version of Ian himself during his latter years in Jamaica.

As one critic has observed, Oberhauser is a parental figure to the orphan Bond:

> *"He taught me to ski before the war, when I was in my teens. He was a wonderful man. He was something of a father to me at a time when I happened to need one."* And he is clearly based on a father-figure of Fleming, Ernan Forbes Dennis, who tutored the teenaged, fatherless Fleming in Kitzbühel—the same town Oberhauser hails from. Fleming revisited it throughout his life.[24]

TRAGEDY IN THE TYROL: BOND AND FLEMING'S PAST

"Octopussy" was written in 1962, a time when Fleming was in declining health and reflecting with intense nostalgia about his youthful years in Kitzbühel. In the portrait of the seedy, corrupt, and ailing Major Dexter Smythe, many have detected a rather bitter self-portrait of Fleming himself. Jon Gilbert writes,

> This story also features a tragic character in the form of Major Dexter Smythe, who bears an uncanny resemblance to the ageing [*sic*] Fleming: both were formerly active military men, now residing in a Jamaican beach house and spending their time exploring the shores, and both were heavy smokers and

> drinkers in their sunset years who ignored medical advice to reduce their consumption.[25]

Gilbert also points out the resemblance between the fictional MOB A force—in which Smythe had served during the war—and Fleming's own intelligence-gathering commando unit, 30AU.

Michael Howard, who received the typescript of "Octopussy" at Jonathan Cape in autumn 1962, was complimentary about the story, though he was concerned about the relatively small role of James Bond:

> I like your story very much. I think it's rather better than the best of the stories in *For Your Eyes Only* but shares with one or two of those the disadvantage from the point of view of including it in a collection of Bond stories that Bond's appearance is fairly immaterial and the part he plays a negligible one, so that Bond fans might well react as they did to *The Spy Who Loved Me* and demand more of their hero.[26]

While Howard is, of course, correct that James Bond appears late in the story, he was wrong in claiming that his role is negligible. To understand Bond's significance in the story, we have to consider his role as an avenging angel. If Smythe is a disillusioned self-portrait of Fleming himself, and Hans Oberhauser is a father figure for Bond—as Forbes Dennis was for the young Fleming—then the murder of Oberhauser must be viewed as an especially heinous crime for which Major Smythe is eventually punished by Bond.

Artistically, Fleming had more scope for experimentation and innovation in the short stories than he did in the novels and could, for example, write a Somerset Maugham-esque portrait of a disastrous marriage in "Quantum of Solace," in which Bond is merely the listener to a cautionary tale about the consequences of matrimonial betrayal and revenge. But by the time he wrote "Octopussy," Fleming had come to terms with the fact that he could not kill off Bond—as he had attempted to do at the end of *From Russia, with Love*. When asked by an interviewer from CBS TV whether one of his Bond novels would end with his hero being killed, Fleming responded with amusement: "I couldn't possibly afford it."[27]

As Ian acknowledged, Bond was now more famous and popular than Fleming himself—with the release of the first EON film, *Dr. No*, and its successor, *From Russia with Love*, underway—so that if either of them was to die off, it seemed more likely to be the author rather than his hero. With a flourish of acerbic self-awareness, Fleming therefore appointed Bond to be the executioner of his own surrogate in "Octopussy." Bond, in effect, arrives to put Smythe—and his creator—out of their misery, though giving the despairing major the "gentleman's option" of committing suicide rather than facing a scandal and prosecution. Smythe does so by using the scorpion fish and his own beloved pet octopus, Octopussy, to end his life. However, Bond covers up the suicide by writing "found drowned" in his official report.

Though the present-day frame of the story is set in Jamaica, the crucial past events during World War II, recalled by Smythe, take place near Kitzbühel. The descriptions of Kitz in this story—especially in contrast to the disillusioned mood of the scenes in the present-day (1962) Jamaica—are nostalgic, even elegiac. When Bond first mentions Kitzbühel, it has a dramatic impact on Smythe: "One of the names he had been living with for all these years forced another harsh laugh out of Major Smythe."[28] Bond reminds Smythe that he had asked "for the best mountain guide in Kitzbühel. You were referred to Oberhauser." Smythe recalls—at Bond's prompting—where the German gold hoard was located, in the Kaiser Mountains, "that awe-inspiring range of giant stone teeth that give Kitzbühel its threatening northern horizon." Fleming introduces a sense of the danger and even terror in his description of the mountains. He had previously used the image of "snarling milk-white teeth" to describe the imposing White Cliffs on the Kent coast in *Moonraker* while, in *Diamonds Are Forever*, Ian described the "mountains, streaked with red like gums bleeding over rotten teeth."[29]

The two men drive along the bottom of the Kaiser range, with Smythe, apparently sensitive to the beauty of landscape, "making admiring comments on the peaks that were now flushed with the pink of dawn." The mountain that most interests him, however, is the one he thinks of as "the Peak of Gold." Though Smythe's suspicion of Germans is a prejudice Fleming shared, influenced by the war, his inability to distinguish Germans from Austrians counts against him: he reflects contemptuously of Oberhauser, "after all he was only a bloody Kraut. . . . What would one more or less matter?"[30]

In fact, Oberhauser's fate does matter greatly to Bond—and Fleming—both because of his role as Bond's mentor and because he is an Austrian from the Tyrol, a region that Fleming had deep attachment to. Despite the beauty of the mountains, there is a sinister tone to Fleming's descriptions of "the final crag, grey and menacing." Fleming makes it clear that Smythe's obsession with capturing the German gold has blinded him to the natural beauty around him. As occurs elsewhere in Fleming's work, the villain shows indifference to a fragile and precious environment: Smythe's "paying no heed to the beautiful panoramas of Austria and Bavaria that stretched away on either side of him" is another strike against him. Ironically, though, Smythe uses the "wonderful view up here" to entice Oberhauser into his trap and prevent the guide from building a fire—which would give their location away.[31]

Asking the guide to show him the view on the other side of the mountains, Smythe cold-bloodedly shoots Oberhauser in the back of the head from two feet away. The Austrian's body returns to nature, crashing onto the glacier below. Smythe, indifferent to the murder of Bond's mentor, is only concerned with his dreams of wealth on finding the gold, which curiously resemble Bond's consumer preferences—"his mind went orbiting through Bentleys, Monte Carlo, penthouse flats, Cartier's, champagne, caviar and, incongruously, but because he loved golf, a new set of Henry Cotton irons." By disposing of Oberhauser's corpse, Smythe also commits violence against the fragile Alpine environment: "He dragged the remains of Oberhauser to the nearest deep crevasse and toppled it in. Then he went carefully round the lip of the crevasse and kicked the snow overhang down on top of the body."[32]

It is intriguing that a place of such idyllic memories for Fleming becomes a site of trauma and tragedy in his fiction. Perhaps because Fleming associated Kitzbühel with lost youth and even blighted promise—as Ann's letters suggest—the Tyrol becomes a scene of disaster for Bond and other characters. Oberhauser is murdered there in cold blood for a hoard of gold, and this crime eventually seals Smythe's fate in a long-deferred vendetta that is accomplished in his—and Fleming's—postwar refuge of Jamaica.

The profound imprint of Kitzbühel on Ian's imagination is apparent in a far more substantial work of fiction he wrote in 1962: the tenth Bond novel, *On Her Majesty's Secret Service*. This is not only one of Ian's best novels but an unusually personal and nostalgic James Bond story. Its success was essential to Ian, for his two previous novels, *Thunderball* (1961) and *The Spy Who Loved Me* (1962), had both been controversial—in very different ways. The former had led to a damaging—both to his finances and his health—plagiarism case in a lawsuit filed by Kevin McClory, which did not reach closure until 1963. The latter book resulted in Fleming's worst-ever reception for a Bond novel, so hostile that Fleming canceled the plans to release the novel in paperback despite the advice of Aubrey Forshaw, managing director of Pan Books, that "you're sitting on a lot of cash."[33] Following these painful setbacks, in *On Her Majesty's Secret Service*, Fleming returned to the source and origin of his success—*Casino Royale*—and placed his hero back in the same fictional French seaside resort, Royale-les-Eaux (based on Le Touquet, one of Ian's frequent golf and gambling destinations), in which his career had begun.

This coastal location prompts memories of Bond's childhood seaside holidays, and Bond's mood of nostalgia is poignant and quite unusual: "It was all there, his own childhood, spread out before him to have another look at. What a long time ago they were, those spade-and-bucket days!"[34] While in Royale, Bond also visits the grave of Vesper Lynd, the woman he had loved and been betrayed by in *Casino Royale*, preparing him—and the reader—for further emotional entanglements. The meeting with Tracy di Vicenzo at Royale does not seem auspicious—the novel begins with Bond saving Tracy from drowning in the sea and then relates in a flashback the events of the night before, when he rescued her from the scandal of a "coup du déshonneur!" When she is unable to pay her debts at the casino and is refused credit, Bond comes to her rescue with a "gift" of two million francs.[35]

The nostalgic tone continues when Bond arrives in the Swiss Alps at Blofeld's base of Piz Gloria, looking down on the skiers and recalling his teenage skiing lessons in the Arlberg—located, like Kitz, in the Tyrol region of Austria. Having escaped from Blofeld's clutches with Tracy's help and destroyed the villain's Alpine clinic, Bond reveals to Marc-Ange Draco (Tracy's father) their intention to return to Fleming's youthful refuge: "Everything is arranged. We will be married within the week. At the Consulate in Munich. I have two weeks' leave, I thought we might spend the honeymoon in Kitzbühel. I love that place. So does she."[36] Bond's love for Kitzbühel—bestowed by Ian—is clearly a preference he shares with his wife, Tracy, which sadly wasn't the case for Ian and Ann.

As they leave on their honeymoon, Bond suggests taking the roof of their car down—which proves to be a fatal mistake—and Tracy agrees: "We can only see half the world with it up. And it's a lovely drive from here to Kitzbühel."[37] Bond fails to act on the warning sign of the red Maserati with a man and woman in the front seats: a couple representing a kind of parody of the Bonds, driving a sporty car but lacking their youth and physical appeal.

As in other novels, such as *Moonraker*, Bond's mind runs ahead to the happy future he imagines for himself and a beloved woman on a fantasized journey. There is an ominous note with Fleming's reference to bloody wars having been fought in the region. And at precisely this point, on their journey to Kitzbühel, Bond spots the red Maserati and tells Tracy, who is driving, to let it pass them because—as he poignantly states—"We've got all the time in the world." Ian's description of the Blofeld attack on them is disturbing in its imagery of disease and animality: "Bond caught a glimpse of a taut, snarling mouth under a syphilitic nose, the flash-eliminator of some automatic gun being withdrawn and then the red car was past."[38] Like the blood spilled in war, the red color of the enemy's car symbolizes death—not Bond's but Tracy's.

The intriguing question is why the idealized location of Kitzbühel, a place of such personal importance and positive memories in Fleming's life, takes on such tragic significance in his fiction. One would expect him to highlight his fond recollections of the place in which he—in various ways—discovered his talents and broke away from his family's control. Yet in these two stories—both written in 1962—Kitzbühel is the scene of the deaths of two of the people most important to Bond: his surrogate father, Hans Oberhauser, and his wife, Tracy di Vicenzo. Both of these deaths, moreover, are brutal gun murders committed by a selfish, diseased, and perhaps deranged villain (Smythe and Blofeld). Both villains also have uncanny resemblances to Ian Fleming.[39]

In this respect, it is revealing that Fleming appoints these corrupted, vengeful, and diseased versions of himself to kill people who are loved by James Bond, thereby destroying Bond's chance of happiness. The murder of Tracy on their honeymoon journey to Kitzbühel is especially tragic, for she represented Bond's hope of personal fulfillment as well as his reproductive future—his chance of being a parent and perhaps in some way offering redemption for his own orphaned state (his parents also having died in mountains, killed in a climbing accident in the French Alps at Aiguilles).

Probably for Ian, the painful experience, in later life, of losing his health and youth, including his sexual freedom, came to outweigh the happy memories of Kitzbühel. Rather than being memories of a pleasurable journey, his recollections of his time in the Tyrol were tormenting reminders of what he had lost. This attitude was shared by John Pearson, who—on meeting Ralph Arnold, confined to a wheelchair in 1965—reflected, "I got the feeling more than ever that Ian's was a doomed generation, that all his friends are dying one by one, becoming smitten with disease, loss of faculties, decay of happiness."[40]

Perhaps too there was something oppressive in the Tyrolean mountain region, despite its physical beauty, that affected Fleming's imagination even in an unconscious way. Although he looked back on his time in Kitzbühel as "that golden time when the sun always shone," was there not also something claustrophobic about the atmosphere of Am Tennerhof?[41] With its Adlerian warders keeping their young charges under their eagle eyes, observing their behavior in order to understand their inferiority complexes, and noting with disapproval the sexual escapades of Ian (as Phyllis's letter, quoted earlier, clearly indicates she judged his affairs somewhat harshly), might Am Tennerhof sometimes have felt like a prison or even an experimental clinic? In the same letter that Ann mocks Ian's longing for his days of being a "Kitzbühel Casanova," she also cites an essay by Robert Louis Stevenson that conveys this sense of entrapment that mountains can bring:

> A mountain valley has, at best, a certain prison-like effect on the imagination—the roads are indeed cleared, and at least one footpath dodging up the hill, but to these one is rigidly confined. There are no crosscuts over the fields, no following streams, no unguided rambles in the woods. The walks are cut and dry.[42]

We know, of course, that Ian and Ann often disagreed about the appeal (or lack thereof) of various environments and landscapes. Ian thought Goldeneye was Nirvana, whereas Ann wearied of it and came to dislike the tropical climate of Jamaica. Likewise, Ann grew tired of White Cliffs in Saint Margaret's Bay, Ian's coastal bolt-hole in Kent. By contrast, she adored rural Wiltshire, their grand house at Sevenhampton, and the damp countryside with its proximity to Oxford, where she had many friends. Ian, however, disliked the countryside, admitted he was "not happy about the house," and complained about the damp "encouraging mushrooms on his clothes" and having to go for dull walks in lanes and entertain dons for tea.[43]

But in the case of Kitzbühel, it is possible that what disturbed Ann consciously about the Alpine town—its claustrophobia and oppressive isolation—also left an unconscious imprint on Ian's imagination. The image of being "rigidly confined" suggests a dark side to Am Tennerhof, as a kind of reformatory to which he had been sent in his teens in order to sort out his troubled life. Ralph Arnold recalls of Phyllis Bottome, "It was a cinch for her to have all these young men with their separate problems right on her own doorstep. The Tennerhof became a sort of Adlerian menagerie on the side of the mountain."[44] Though such a view apparently conflicts with Ian's often idealized, pleasant recollections of Kitzbühel, it is possible that Piz Gloria—an Alpine clinic presided over by the highly educated villain Ernst Stavro Blofeld and his female counterpart, Irma Bunt—is the dystopian reimagining of Am Tennerhof. Blofeld's group of young female patients—whom he is "curing" of allergies while actually brainwashing them to become his "angels of death"—are the transfigured ménage of troubled young Englishmen sent to be "cured" of their psychic problems at Tennerhof. Piz Gloria is a place where Bond—though ostensibly a privileged guest—is treated more like a prisoner, his movements rigidly controlled and all his actions closely monitored. Bond is also required to adopt an alter ego—Sir Hilary Bray—entirely unlike his own personality. Bond, like Fleming, rebels against the institution's strict discipline by playing the sexual field, having covert affairs with the nubile female English patients at the clinic. Blofeld and Bunt—a sinister couple if ever there was one—preside over a facility dedicated to brainwashing the young. Finally, Bond must escape from this prison in order to save himself and in so doing utilizes his skills as an Alpine skier—skills that Fleming himself had attained at Kitz. If the Forbes Dennises looked askance at some of Ian's youthful desires and spirited behaviors, it is surely not improbable that he would have been angered by their attempts to control and train him. Ian was more ambivalent toward his surrogate parents than he acknowledged in his correspondence with them, and these mixed feelings emerge in the fiction.

Indeed, in Fleming's later correspondence with the Forbes Dennises, we can detect some ambivalence about his youthful experiences there. In the same letter in which he praises Phyllis Bottome's memoir, *The Goal* (published in 1962), Fleming criticized its portrayal of Am Tennerhof and Kitzbühel: "Have adored the book and of course the bits about Austria filled me with nostalgic memories, though I wish you had been altogether more candid about the individual horrors of the boys you and Ernan looked after!"[45] These "horrors" may refer to the bad behavior of "the boys" but may also inadvertently reveal that his experiences at Kitzbühel were not all happy ones.

There are other reasons recollections of Kitzbühel would have been a source of pain as well as pleasure for Fleming, looking back in 1962—the year in which his Kitzbühel nostalgia seems to have become most intense, judging by "Octopussy" and *On Her Majesty's Secret Service*. Recalling Phyllis's comment in a letter about Ian Fleming's "love affairs which were all catastrophic," she was doubtless thinking about some of the women Fleming met and loved around this time while he was under her supervision. Two of the women he met in the Alpine region, in particular, were parted from Fleming under traumatic or "catastrophic" circumstances. As we have seen, his relationship with Monique ended disastrously due mainly to Eve's opposition, though distance between the lovers when Ian returned to England may have been a factor. But there was a still greater trauma in store.

In August 1935, Ian was on holiday in Kitzbühel when he met an attractive young Englishwoman, Muriel Wright, with whom he began an affair. Muriel was an athletic outdoors type, an agile skier—more skilled on the piste than Fleming himself—and a talented polo player. Moreover, she was blonde, beautiful—working as a model for sportswear and lingerie—and devoted to Ian Fleming. She fell victim, however, to Ian's vow not to become emotionally involved with women after the trauma of separation from Monique. Ian kept himself aloof from becoming too involved with her and pursued affairs with other women—including Ann O'Neill, his future wife. And yet, strongly attracted to "Moo" (as she was known by friends), he kept her as his girlfriend for his own convenience. Her brother, Fitzherbert Wright, heard about how badly Ian was treating Muriel and showed up at Fleming's home with a horsewhip, prepared to thrash him. However, Ian had taken Muriel to Brighton for the weekend, and so the confrontation was avoided.

Despite his cavalier treatment of Moo, Ian was considering proposing to her. She fulfilled many of his desires in a woman, being physically beautiful and athletic, having a good sense of humor, and being willing to help Ian in any way. During the war, when Ian was working long hours in Naval Intelligence, Moo would take care of his ration book, making sure her heartthrob was properly provided for. Yet, after beginning an affair with Ann—who was married to Shane O'Neill—Ian could not commit himself to another woman. Muriel worked as a dispatch rider for the Admiralty, riding around on a motorbike. A staff member at Morlands of Grosvenor Street recalls one day in March 1944, when "a girl naval dispatch rider dashes up. Very beautiful girl in a crash helmet. Can I have two hundred cigarettes for the Commander?"[46]

In the end, it was all too late. On March 14, 1944, disaster struck. Muriel was asleep in the bedroom of her London home when a bomb hit her house. She was killed instantly by a piece of masonry that struck her on the head while she was sleeping. If Ian had been somewhat callous in his behavior to Muriel while alive, all of this diffidence vanished the moment she was dead. Ian had to go to the bombed house to identify Muriel's body, and the experience left a deep impression on him, one that stayed with him for the rest of his life. For a clearer sense of how Ian reacted to Muriel's death, we can turn

Figure 2.2. Ian Fleming with Muriel Wright, whom he met in Kitzbühel in 1935. Muriel was killed in the Blitz in 1944. *The Times/News Licensing.*

to the private diary of another of his lovers at the time, Maud Russell, who wrote:

> Wednesday, March 15, 1944
>
> This morning I heard Muriel Wright, I[an].'s girl, had been killed. Strange things happen. I heard in my room at the Admiralty that she'd been killed by debris flung up from a crater in the road coming through her roof and falling on her in bed. Most of the room was untouched. Appalled for I[an]. and found it difficult to concentrate. I know he will be overcome with remorse and blame himself for not marrying her and for a thousand other things none of which he is to blame for.[47]

If Maud was sure Ian was not "to blame" for his treatment of Muriel, Ian was less forgiving of himself. The more cynical view of Dunstan Curtis—another Old Etonian who served in Fleming's 30AU Commando Unit during the war—was that "the trouble with Ian is that you have to get yourself killed before he feels anything."[48] Even if this were true, it does not lessen the impact that Muriel's death had on Fleming. Aside from the guilt at his treatment of her, another of his Kitzbühel romances had ended tragically. Muriel was indelibly linked to the Tyrolean town where he had met her, and he would return to this tragedy with Tracy's violent death at Kitzbühel almost two decades later.

Kitzbühel and trauma were inseparably linked, then, in Fleming's imagination, as emerges clearly from the catastrophic events that take place there in his fiction. Yet, if we take account of Ian's own ambivalent feelings about marriage and family, can these events—especially the end of *On Her Majesty's Secret Service*—be interpreted straightforwardly as tragic? Ian, as is well known, identified his anxiety over his forthcoming marriage to Ann as a key motive for creating James Bond, writing his first novel as he was anticipating with some misgivings both his marriage and his first child. Hirsch offers a slightly modified version of this period, writing, "Ironically, it was because there were no guests at Goldeneye that year, while Ian waited for Anne's [*sic*] divorce to become final, that he settled down to write and produced the first draft of the thriller *Casino Royale* that was to make both his name and his fortune."[49]

Whether it was the lack of guests or his panic at the prospect of getting married, Fleming certainly got down to writing at this emotionally fraught time. Yet, at precisely the moment he was about to commit himself to marriage, Ian decides that his hero will have a narrow escape from matrimony when Vesper—to whom he is on the point of proposing—confesses she is a Soviet double agent and commits suicide. If Vesper's tragic demise touches on the premature death of Muriel Wright, it also launches Bond's career as a secret agent—vowing now to be avenged against SMERSH (the Soviet counterintelligence agency and Bond's bête noire in the novels). James Bond, in other words, has to "kill" the love he felt for Vesper in order to become 007, announcing callously that "the bitch is dead now."[50]

By the time he wrote *On Her Majesty's Secret Service*, Fleming had been married to Ann for a decade, but the marriage was by this time deteriorating due to their frequent separations and extramarital affairs. Ann was having an affair with the British Labour Party leader, Hugh Gaitskell, while Ian was involved with local Jamaican heiress Blanche Blackwell. By the 1960s, their marriage had become a source of depression and strife for both spouses.

In the light of his own marital troubles, Ian determined that Bond would have another narrow escape from matrimony in *On Her Majesty's Secret Service*, but this time *after* he had tied the knot. Bond would not resign from the Secret Service, as he planned at the beginning of the novel and had later promised Tracy he would, in order to "look after you."[51] On the contrary, he would pledge himself more passionately than ever to the death and destruction of his enemies. The new target: not SMERSH but SPECTRE (Special Executive for Counterintelligence, Terrorism, Revenge, and Extortion); not Klebb but Blofeld.

The devastating impact of Tracy's death at Kitzbühel is revealed in chapter 2 of the next novel, *You Only Live Twice*. Here the neurologist Sir James Molony explains to M what has happened to his prize agent:

> Here's this agent of yours, just as tough and brave as I expect you were at his age. He's a bachelor and a confirmed womanizer. Then he suddenly falls in love, partly, I suspect, because this woman was a bird with a wing down and needed his help. . . . So he marries her and within a few hours she's shot dead by this supergangster chap.[52]

Molony's description reveals the parallels between Bond—grieving over Tracy—and Fleming's mourning for the lover he met in Kitzbühel, Muriel Wright, snatched away from him before he could commit to her. Though Fleming did not marry Muriel—as Bond did Tracy—he did care more for her than he realized and carried memories of her for a long time afterward. Molony's description of Bond's guilt could aptly apply to Fleming: "The loss of a loved one, aggravated in his case by the fact that he blamed himself for her death."[53]

Part of Bond's code of chivalry is that he should shield defenseless creatures from harm, whether that harm be from villains or from themselves. Hence his failure to protect Tracy is especially galling, not just because Tracy is a beautiful, sexually intriguing woman but also because she appeals to Bond's protective instincts. Molony's comment that the "tough men"—such as a 00 agent with a license to kill and much blood on his hands—are "soft" is an interesting qualifier to the hypermasculinity for which Bond is renowned. Bond is known for killing villains—sometimes with his bare hands—for bedding women, and for suffering physical hardship and torture. He is less known as a caring and sensitive defender of the weak and protector of fragile environments. But this is part of Bond's identity as much as his role as an assassin.[54]

The villains that Bond eliminates are themselves destroyers, desecrators, and enemies of the precious environments that Ian himself treasured, such as the Tyrolean Alps. Major Smythe's careless damage to the fragile ice system when he kicks an overhang of snow on top of Oberhauser's body above Kitzbühel is evidence of his callous nature. Blofeld is far worse in his destruction of the fragile Apine structure of snow and ice, using flares to expose

Bond on the snowy mountains, causing an avalanche that Fleming describes as "the roaring monster at his heels."[55] The true monster is actually Blofeld, who will cause irreparable environmental damage rather than allow his prisoner to escape. A man who would start an avalanche to stop one man will hardly balk at shooting that man and his wife in cold blood. The damaging disrespect of fragile environments is not just evil in itself, for Fleming, but is a presage of further harm to human beings.

Kitzbühel was remembered by Fleming as a place of self-discovery and pleasure but also of peril and trauma. It was where he discovered new talents—such as creative writing and climbing—and found surrogate parent figures in the Forbes Dennises. It was during this period that Fleming developed his language skills, moving from Kitzbühel to Geneva and Munich to study French and German. Around the same period as *On Her Majesty's Secret Service*, Fleming wrote about his experience of the Tyrol in *Thrilling Cities*:

> I learned German in the Tyrol from Mr Ernan Forbes Dennis, husband of the famous novelist Phyllis Bottome, and then honorary Vice-Consul for the Tyrol, based in Kitzbühel. They were both ardent students of the great psychologist Alfred Adler—Phyllis Bottome wrote Adler's life—and I learned far more about life from Ernan than from all my schooling put together. But living in the Tyrol for so long made me such a devoted lover of the Tyrolese that I took against the brittle and, it seemed to me, artificial gaiety of the Viennese.[56]

Fleming dwells on the contrast between the Tyrol and Vienna but does not hint at the traumatic, oppressive associations of Kitzbühel itself. It was celebrated as a place of love and passion, associated with Monique and Muriel, and Fleming declared the Tyrolese "my favourite people in the world."[57] But it was also a place of death—as Phyllis Bottome recorded so powerfully in her 1937 Tyrolean novel *The Mortal Storm*, where the young Communist peasant Hans—Freya Roth's lover and the father of her unborn child—is hunted and shot to death by the Nazis on the Austrian-Swiss border. Was Fleming thinking of this tragic scene of Bottome's in envisaging the death of Bond's wife in the same Alpine region?

The sudden death of Muriel Wright meant that Kitzbühel would always be associated, in Ian's memory, with the violent killing of a beautiful young woman. Small wonder, then, that the same place is the setting for arguably the most tragic scene in any of the James Bond novels—the murder of Tracy. Though he may have "learned far more about life" in Kitzbühel, this location also taught Ian Fleming a harsh lesson: that for every pleasure enjoyed, there was a price of pain to be paid, and for every success achieved, there was a failure to be endured.

Chapter Three

From Moscow to Ebury Street

Fleming in the 1930s

With his failure to pass the Foreign Office (FO) exams, Ian saw his dream of a diplomatic career also go up in smoke. The setback seemed to blight his struggle for independence. And it was all the more galling because of the contrast to his brother Peter's academic and professional successes. It must have been humiliating for Ian to again depend on his mother's influence to gain him a new professional opportunity. Eve used her connection with the head of the news agency Reuters, Sir Roderick Jones, to secure her son a position as subeditor and journalist.

There could hardly have been a more exciting, if challenging, time to enter the field of journalism than the 1930s. It was a period of economic turmoil, political instability, and international anxiety as the world moved inexorably toward another world war. The Great Depression of the early 1930s, following the Wall Street crash of 1929, meant that Britain's world trade was cut in half, while other leading industrial nations—most notably the United States and Germany—also saw their economies collapse. The consequent rise of Fascism in Germany, Italy, and Spain led to the world being divided along economic and political lines. Mussolini came to power in 1922, Hitler in 1933, and General Franco after the Nationalist victory in the Spanish Civil War in 1939. The powerful Communist system of Stalin's Soviet Union, with its own vast economy and military force, was increasingly at odds not only with the United States but also with the newly empowered Fascist dictators of Europe.

Britain also flirted with Fascism in the 1930s when the British Union of Fascists, under Oswald Mosley, posed a significant challenge to the minority government of Ramsay MacDonald. In fact, Mosley had been a government minister under MacDonald and recommended—following the devastating economic fallout of the Wall Street crash—that Britain's government should take control of banking and exports. His proposals were rejected, and Mosley then left to form the New Party and later, in 1932, the British Union of Fascists (BUF). One of the union's leading supporters was Lord Rothermere, the press baron who founded and owned the *Daily Mail*. Lord Rothermere was the father of Esmond Harmsworth, who would become the second husband of Ann Charteris—the future wife of Ian Fleming. By another interesting coincidence, Ian Fleming's home during the 1930s—22b Ebury Street in Belgravia—was previously owned by Oswald Mosley, from whom Ian acquired the lease.

When Adolf Hitler came to power in Germany, he vowed to repeal the Versailles Treaty and expand Germany's empire, its nationalist goal of *Lebensraum* ("living space") being used to justify the territorial expansion into Central and Eastern Europe. The rise of Hitler's Third Reich was accompanied by an increasingly aggressive German expansionist policy that included the annexation of Austria and of Sudetenland in Czechoslovakia. The latter annexation had been authorized by the Munich agreement signed by Germany, France, and Italy as well as British prime minister Neville Chamberlain in September 1938. While many in Britain felt that the Munich agreement was necessary to prevent another war with Germany, there was also a strong and vocal opposition to appeasement with Hitler. For example, Duff Cooper—a friend of Ian Fleming's and member of Chamberlain's cabinet—was a bitter opponent of appeasement and resigned from the government the day after the Munich agreement was signed.[1]

Hitler's regime also pushed forward with the persecution of Jews and other non-Aryan peoples, providing further evidence that the Führer's agenda was anything but peaceful. Those with Jewish relatives in Germany and other Nazi-controlled countries of Europe sought desperately to help their loved ones escape before it was too late. For example, Fleming's friend and lover Maud Russell made several trips to Germany in the effort to get her German Jewish cousin and aunt (Tante Fritze) and other Jewish relations to safety. On a visit to Bonn in December 1939, Russell recorded her sense of obligation to her Jewish relations in her diary:

> In the past during any of these many periods of crisis in Jewish history there must generally have been a relation, more fortunately placed than the others, who came forward and helped. I don't feel any more Jewish than I did—and I never do much—but I feel a duty, an obligation laid on me, to help and to leave no stone unturned.[2]

Another of Fleming's literary friends, his mentor Phyllis Bottome, used her fiction to raise the British consciousness about the plight of Jews in Nazi-occupied Europe. Bottome, who moved back to England in 1936, having spent most of her life in Europe, was disappointed to find how oblivious the British were to the malignant intentions of Hitler. As Pam Hirsch writes, "She slowly realized that the British public had been lulled into a false sense of security by the damaging complacency of most of the press and the BBC."[3] In novels such as her acclaimed *The Mortal Storm*, Bottome portrayed in harrowing terms how Nazism was tearing apart German and other European societies and even destroying previously loving families such as the Roths, the family of her heroine Freya.

In 1936, the Spanish Civil War drew many anti-Fascists, including Fleming's fellow Etonian Eric Arthur Blair (aka George Orwell) to fight on the side of the Republicans against the Nationalists, the latter led by General Francisco Franco, who "crossed from North Africa to lead a military coup against the Republic." The defeat of the Republicans and installation of Franco as dictator in 1939 consolidated the Fascist position in Europe. Bottome, finding an insularity and complacency in Britain, was "astonished that the British seemed to think that what happened in mainland Europe would have no bearing on them."[4] In fact, the rise of Franco was ominous for Britain and its allies. Although Franco's Spain remained officially neutral during World War II, the strategically crucial region of the Iberian Peninsula and the Strait of Gibraltar caused great anxiety for the Allies that Franco would join the Axis powers.

The perilous combination of economic crisis, political upheavals, and moral uncertainty is reflected in many of the novels of the period, including the spy fiction of Eric Ambler and Graham Greene, both of whom became friends with Ian. For example, Ambler's *Cause for Alarm* (published in 1938) features protagonist Nicky Marlow, who is out of work during the aftermath of the Great Depression in 1937 and so travels to Milan to work for the Spartacus Machine Tool Company. But as an "innocent abroad" in Fascist Italy, Marlow is out of his depth and soon becomes embroiled in espionage and intrigue, being courted by agents of rival powers. Yet, Marlow's predicament stems directly from economic necessity due to the dreadful unemployment in 1930s Britain. As the novel opens, Marlow—under pressure with his impending marriage—loses his job and urgently needs employment:

> One thing is certain. I would not even have considered the job if I had not been desperate. Early in January, the Barnton Heath Engineering Company decided to close down the greater part of its works. It was the day after I had asked Claire to marry me that the first blow fell.[5]

Greene's *The Confidential Agent* (published in 1939) also deals with the economic factors of espionage, featuring the agent of an unnamed European power, a man named D, who travels to England to arrange the purchase of vitally needed coal for his own country. From D's perspective—his own country wracked by civil war—prewar Britain seems surprisingly calm: "The city, to D, looked extraordinarily exposed and curiously undamaged; nobody stood in a queue; there was no sign of a war except himself. He carried his infection past the closed shops, a tobacconist's, a twopenny library."[6] Greene, like Bottome, wants to alert the British reader during the economically fragile 1930s that many countries on the continent were worse off than themselves. But he also cautions that the "infection" of economic malaise and political extremism might easily be transmitted from the continent to Britain. Like Fleming, Greene's experiences in journalism (he worked for *The Times* in the early 1930s) and his extensive travels gave him firsthand exposure to the turbulent times they lived in. And these experiences of travel provided vital material for his writing.

Whether or not he envisaged a career as a novelist at this stage, Ian seems to have accepted his new career path in journalism with equanimity if not exactly enthusiasm. Compared to the prestigious and, at least in his imagination, glamorous career of a British diplomat, with its strong flavor of intrigue and espionage, the working life of a journalist may have appeared as something of an anticlimax. But if his recent failures had dented his confidence, Fleming seems to have recovered quickly enough to impress his employers at Reuters. It was there that he learned to write taut, descriptive, professional prose, a skill that would serve him well. As Robert Harling wrote, his work as a journalist meant that "Fleming had developed a talent for spare and simple prose which made memo-drafting . . . no great chore."[7] Fleming's craft was certainly honed during his years as a journalist, and these skills—required of any news reporter working to deadlines—would prove useful not only during his years in Naval Intelligence but also when he turned to writing fiction. Moreover, Fleming's experience with Reuters would stand him in good stead after the war, when he was looking for a civilian job. He stepped easily into the role of foreign manager at Kemsley Newspapers, being already familiar with the operations of a major news organization. Aside from his daily duties at Kemsley House, Fleming would produce some of his most compelling nonfiction writing—including *The Diamond Smugglers* and *Thrilling Cities*—as original articles for *The Sunday Times*. Though he is most famous for creating James Bond, one could make the case that Fleming's first calling was as a journalist and that he would not have succeeded as a novelist without this experience. Ian's novels and short stories frequently used journalistic skills of description, concise summary, and ability to convey a sense of place that he acquired while working for Reuters.

The most important assignment Fleming received while at Reuters was undoubtedly the Metro-Vickers trials in Moscow in 1933. Stalin's government had decided to make an example of Western "imperialists" accused of spying, and six British subjects working for the Metropolitan-Vickers engineering firm in Moscow were arrested under charges of "economic wrecking" and "espionage." Beginning with the arrest of the Russian secretary of Allan Monkhouse, Metro-Vickers's Moscow chief, and use of her to accuse several engineers of espionage, the case became an international cause célèbre.

Evidently, Fleming had quickly gained the confidence of his employers, for his boss, Bernard Rickatson-Hatt, sent a message to his staff in Moscow that he was sending "Ian Fleming one of our ablest young men to help coverage of trial."[8] Rickatson-Hatt remembered Ian later as a "simply first-class fellow. One could tell at once that this was the sort of chap we wanted in Reuters."[9] Though these Moscow trials are often described as Stalinist "show trials," implying that the accused were being prosecuted on trumped-up charges, there is more to this than meets the eye. It was common practice for the cash-strapped Secret Intelligence Service (SIS)—the existence of which was not officially acknowledged by the government and which had to function on a threadbare secret budget—to make use of employees of British companies overseas for intelligence-gathering purposes. As Michael Smith writes, the use of commercial agents by SIS was a matter of economic necessity:

> Treasury cuts had reduced the number of passport control offices to just nineteen across Europe at the beginning of 1931, and while these still included the important bureau covering Germany and the Soviet Union, they left whole swathes of the world to be covered by other means. SIS bolstered its overseas operations by persuading the employees of a number of companies working abroad to use this "natural cover" to mount espionage operations. It developed good relationships with a number of British firms, such as Vickers, Shell, British American Tobacco, the Hudson's Bay Company and APOC, under which the companies' employees would be encouraged to collect intelligence.[10]

Employees of companies that had offices in potential enemy territory—such as the Soviet Union—were especially sought after as sources of vital intelligence. And Smith writes, "The Service relied more heavily on Vickers for assistance than on any other company, with its representatives around the world offering an extension to the coverage provided by the SIS bureaux." It is more than likely, therefore, that the Metro-Vickers engineers tried in 1933 were indeed gathering intelligence about Soviet industrial strength, military preparations, and social organization while helping to construct the country's infrastructure. As Smith acknowledges, "The Metropolitan-Vickers Electrical Company, which provided equipment and maintenance for a number of Soviet power stations and was part owned by Vickers, was an obvious vehicle for such 'natural cover' operations."[11]

Nonetheless, the Western powers looked on such Stalinist show trials with skepticism. Clearly, the Western journalists—whether for Reuters, Associated Press, or other organs—had a vested interest in portraying the trials as a spectacle staged to aggrandize Stalin and humiliate the corrupt puppets of a capitalist system. There were no death sentences handed out to the accused. Eventually, economic and diplomatic pressures on the Soviet Union resulted in two of the six British engineers accused of espionage receiving short suspended sentences, while the rest were acquitted.

Fleming, sent on his first big assignment for Reuters, was eager to make an impression and hoped to achieve a scoop by getting to the telephone immediately after the verdict was delivered. Bryce has suggested that Ian had an accomplice outside the courtroom to whom he slipped messages about the progress of the trial. In any case, another journalist happened to be already on the telephone to his London office when the news broke, and so Ian lost out—but still emerged with credit in the eyes of his employers. Rickatson-

Hatt confirms, “Moscow was a considerable coup for Reuters, and for Ian too.”[12]

Fleming even had the gumption, while in Moscow, to write to Joseph Stalin, requesting a personal interview with the Soviet leader. While Stalin declined a meeting on grounds that he was too busy, Ian received a signed letter of apology, which he cherished and kept for many years. He also won the respect of the seasoned, thick-skinned reporters whose company he kept while in Moscow, men who had looked askance at this novice on his arrival at the trials. That the Foreign Office, on his return to London, requested a report from him about the current Soviet situation was also encouragement. Though the novelist was yet to come into being, the spy had already been born.

The success of his coverage of the Metro-Vickers trials in Moscow had paved the way, potentially, for future successes in journalism. It was typical of Fleming’s switchback course in life, however, that just as he was on the cusp of success in one career, he decided to change tack and pursue a wholly different profession. Having gained kudos for his coverage of the Metro-Vickers show trials, Fleming was offered the plum assignment of Reuters correspondent in Shanghai by Sir Roderick Jones. Fleming decided to think this offer over while he was on assignment in Berlin, covering the plebiscite that resulted in the election of Adolf Hitler as chancellor in March 1933.

Given Ian’s desire for travel—especially to exotic locations such as the Far East—and his ambition to develop his writing, this offer would have seemed an unmissable opportunity. Also, like Berlin and Istanbul, Shanghai was known to be a hub of espionage and intrigue in the 1930s. If posted there, he could have been immersed in one of the most vibrant Chinese cities, experienced a new culture and lifestyle, and collected material for potential works of literature. The posting evoked the exoticism and mystery that resonated in the fiction of Joseph Conrad and William Somerset Maugham.

Fleming was also—following the abrupt termination of his engagement to Monique—emotionally unattached and fancy-free. Who knew what enticing romantic and sexual experiences (if not entanglements) might be on offer in the Far East for a charming, handsome English bachelor in the heyday of 1930s Shanghai? Now he had the opportunity to work in one of the most exciting cities in the Asian world, and yet he turned it down. The main reason for this decision appears to have been financial ambition. Many of Ian’s friends have commented on the fact that he had always desired wealth. Fleming learned that his annual salary in Shanghai would be only £800, which he quipped was "barely enough to cover my opium consumption."[13] The problem with journalism, for Fleming, was that it was by no means a lucrative career. As the scion of a wealthy family whose fortune had been made in banking by his grandfather Robert Fleming, Ian had great expectations of a substantial inheritance someday. Pearson suggests that Ian struggled throughout his life with the "feeling that he had been cheated out of his inheritance in some obscure way after the taste of great wealth from his boyhood."[14]

Undoubtedly, he wanted to live an affluent, if not extravagant, lifestyle to match that of his wealthy friends and cronies. Because his father's fortune had passed in trust to his mother, Ian had inherited nothing and now had to make his own way and provide for himself. He continued to receive an allowance from his mother but was eager to establish some economic independence. His salary at Reuters could not allow him to maintain the affluent lifestyle he expected and desired. He therefore offered his resignation to Sir Roderick Jones.

Fleming was also under pressure from his mother—who of course had been disappointed by Ian's Foreign Office setback—to find a more remunerative career path. Fleming therefore decided to follow in his grandfather's footsteps and enter the world of finance in the City of London (the City).

In 1933, he joined the merchant bank Cull and Company before switching to the stockbroking firm Rowe & Pitman—both established and successful firms in the City. Ian's family name and connections gave him an advantage in the financial world—after all, he was the grandson of one of the most successful British Victorian bankers, Robert Fleming, a self-made millionaire. Ian had other useful connections that helped smooth his way into the City. He was close friends with Maud Russell, the daughter of German immigrants, who inherited a fortune and married Gilbert Russell, a successful banker. Together the couple bought Mottisfont Hall in Hampshire, a spectacular property that soon became one of the great magnets for the artistic, literary, and political elites of the 1930s and after. Ian Fleming was a regular visitor to Mottisfont and became Maud's lover sometime during the 1930s. According to Maud's granddaughter Emily Russell, a little-known wartime photograph of Ian in naval uniform "takes up almost an entire page of Maud's photo album."[15]

Maud's husband, Gilbert, had formed Cull and Company merchant bank with three other partners, including Anders Cull, and Maud used her influence to get Ian a job at the bank. In joining Cull and Company, Ian had the prospect of a partnership, a fact he mentioned in explaining his resignation to Sir Roderick at Reuters.[16] However, while grateful for the opportunity, he was largely ignored by the partners and soon became bored with the job. This despite the fact that he was dealing with the portfolios of such international financial magnates as Calouste Gulbenkian, who had arranged the merger of Royal Dutch Petroleum Company with Shell and became a major shareholder in the newly formed company Royal Dutch Shell. A canny businessman, Gulbenkian followed the practice of retaining 5 percent of the shares of oil companies he developed, leading to the nickname of "Mr. Five Per Cent." Despite the vast financial power of this client, Gulbenkian's biographer writes that "Fleming had found the business of handling Gulbenkian's share trades dull. History does not record whether he took any notice of his former client at the Aviz—now a balding, publicity shy man of mystery and fabulous wealth, with a fondness for White Angora Cats."[17] Referring to Fleming's visit to Lisbon while working in the Naval Intelligence Division during the war, Jonathan Conlin's description intriguingly suggests that Gulbenkian—who lived in a luxurious suite in Lisbon's Aviz Hotel from 1942 until his death in 1955—was an inspiration for Bond villains, especially Ernst Stavro Blofeld.

Unmoved by the "fabulous wealth" of clients such as Gulbenkian, Ian switched jobs, moving in 1935 to the distinguished stockbroking firm of Rowe & Pitman, where he believed there would be greater opportunity to take initiatives in order to pursue financial gain. Certainly, the signs were auspicious. Rowe & Pitman was one of the most prominent stockbroking firms in the City, having been formed in 1895 by the original partners, George Rowe and Fred Pitman. The leading light of the firm in the early twentieth century was Lancelot Hugh Smith ("Lancy"), who combined impeccable business instincts with a remarkably wide and affluent social circle. Lancy had strong ties with the United States, having built up connections with the American banking giant J. P. Morgan during his frequent trips to North America. One of Lancy's brokers at Rowe & Pitman, Arthur Wagg, wrote of him, "I have never known anyone who had so many friends or so many enemies. One could not be indifferent to him. The number of his enemies is perhaps not surprising, for he took no trouble whatever to win the good opinion of anybody in whom he was not interested."[18]

Fortunately for Ian Fleming, Lancy evidently did take an interest in him, primarily because of Ian's connection to the great banking firm of Robert Fleming. According to Hilary Bray, an Old Etonian friend of Ian's who also worked at Rowe, "Ian wouldn't have a chance now of getting away with life at Rowe & Pitman as he did in the days when he was there. He was accepted on the old boy basis because of his connections with Robert Fleming." After Fleming's recruitment in 1935, Lancy boasted that "I always felt that if they keep their heads up and their overheads down, a firm containing three members of great City families [Smith, Fleming, and Baring] must succeed."[19] Another intriguing connection at Rowe & Pitman was with the world of secret intelligence. During the First World War, Lancy's brother, Aubrey Hugh Smith, became the deputy director of Naval Intelligence under Admiral Sir "Blinker" Hall, a position similar to that later occupied by Ian Fleming under Admiral John Godfrey.[20] In fact, Aubrey was present at the luncheon at the Carlton Hotel Grill in May 1939 when Ian got the job as Godfrey's assistant.

The ties between high finance and secret intelligence were strengthened by the transition of Claud Serocold, a crucial member of "Blinker" Hall's Room 40 during World War I, into stockbroking with Cazenove and Akroyd. This company became the leading competitor with Rowe & Pitman after the war. Indeed, Serocold, distantly related to Lancy, had previously been one of the "half commission men" at Rowe & Pitman but had been obliged to leave the firm after an unsuccessful speculation. Lancy himself was involved in covert operations, being sent as head of a British mission to Sweden in 1915 to pressure the Swedes, despite their pro-German sympathies, to remain neutral during World War I and allow the free passage of goods to Russia. According to Lycett, Lancy "would spend three more years in quasi-secret activity on the fringes of intelligence and economic warfare."[21]

Most notoriously, Rowe & Pitman hired Sydney Russell Cooke in 1925 on the basis of his authorship (with Nicholas Davenport) of the book *The Oil Trust and Anglo-American Relations*. Cooke worked for MI5 during and after the war and is described by Andrew Lycett as a "prototype James Bond."[22] Like Ian Fleming, Cooke took a keen interest in the development of the young Soviet Union after the Bolshevik revolution. But where Fleming went to Russia to cover the Metro-Vickers trials for Reuters—while also preparing a report on the Soviet system for the Foreign Office—Cooke was instructed by MI5 to forge connections with leading Bolsheviks for intelligence purposes.

Cooke was the MI5 control for Clare Sheridan, the artist cousin of Winston Churchill who had sculpted the bust of Trotsky's brother-in-law Leo Kamenev and was encouraged by Cooke to do likewise with other leading

Bolsheviks in order to obtain secret intelligence. In a plot twist that could have come straight from the pages of a James Bond novel, Cooke was found shot dead in 1930, at age thirty-seven, his body found next to a double-barreled shotgun. While the inquest recorded an accidental death, Hugo Pitman—later to become senior partner at Rowe & Pitman—told a colleague of his conviction that Cooke had been shot by Russians.[23]

This atmosphere of intrigue, secret intelligence work, and danger no doubt appealed to Ian Fleming, for whom a large part of the attraction of the FO—his initial career choice—had been its ties to espionage and SIS. In fact, Ian was still in Rowe & Pitman's employ when he made his special trip to Russia, at the FO's request, and wrote his report "Russia's Strength" in the spring of 1939. Fleming would also find the connections he made in the financial world while at Rowe & Pitman, such as the Morgan banking family, helpful when he returned to the United States as Godfrey's assistant at the Naval Intelligence Division.

Unfortunately, despite his predilection for espionage and intrigue, Ian had little aptitude for stockbroking; indeed, one of the partners at Rowe & Pitman described him as "the world's worst stockbroker."[24] Ian had the right family connections and educational background (most of the Rowe & Pitman partners were products of Eton), but he had little experience of the inner workings of the stock market or understanding of the intricacies of international finance. Ian liked the idea of making money quickly, which was certainly possible in the 1930s, despite the severe economic downturn. But he did not have the persistence or, frankly, the work ethic required to create and maintain a network of prosperous clients. One of Fleming's stockbroking friends, Hilary Bray—whose name Ian would use for James Bond's cover identity as a researcher at the College of Arms in *On Her Majesty's Secret Service*—was quite blunt about Ian's shortcomings: "Ian . . . would talk very knowledgeably [*sic*] about the strategy of investments. . . . Take clients out to a good lunch and afterwards turn them over to the client investment section."[25]

Of course, "talking knowledgably" was Ian's great strength, and he refused throughout his life to be confined by the expectations or scripts provided by others. He had chosen his own path by leaving Sandhurst and spending time in Kitzbühel, Vienna, and Munich. He again showed his penchant for surprising twists by requesting an interview with Joseph Stalin while in Moscow. He would write his own script with remarkable success while in naval intelligence, coming up with some of the most imaginative deception operations of World War II. He would then, of course, reinvent himself as a spy novelist spending winters writing in Jamaica. But in the City, Ian's "considerable personal charm" and bravado could only take him so far. His literary efforts at Rowe & Pitman also met with mixed success, as his draft of a corporate history of the firm was rejected by Lancy as too biased toward the Pitmans. It is clear that he was not inclined to undertake the research, attention to detail, and—above all—dedication to the hard work of moneymaking required to make a killing in the stock exchange. His extensive (and expensive) luncheons with potential clients at Scott's or Simpson's did not yield the necessary results or profits, and Ian "is remembered for having only one regular client."[26]

Yet, one should not underestimate the value of these connections in the City to Ian's future. When Admiral Godfrey was looking for a suitable man as his assistant, he consulted Sir Montagu Norman, governor of the Bank of England, who knew of Fleming through his Rowe & Pitman connections. Even after his appointment as Godfrey's assistant, Fleming was technically still on the staff of Rowe & Pitman and would occasionally visit the offices at 43 Bishopsgate to have lunch with Hugo Pitman, who had become a close friend. Remarkably, Ian continued to draw his share of the profits from the firm even after joining Naval Intelligence.[27]

It was not only Fleming's wartime career in Naval Intelligence that played a major role in his success as a spy novelist. His experience of the financial markets, valuta, and trading in precious commodities also paid dividends when it came to devising plots for his James Bond adventures. Financial ventures, investments, money laundering, and the movement (often illegal) of lucrative commodities play a crucial part in many of the plots of Fleming's novels. While the specific sources of Bond's private income are withheld—other than the fact that he "earned £1500 a year . . . and he had a thousand a year free of tax of his own"—the villains are notable for their financial wheeler-dealings.[28] From the illicit investment by Le Chiffre of SMERSH funds in a chain of brothels, to Mr. Big's chain of shady nightclubs and smuggling of a rare supply of gold coins, to Goldfinger's smuggling of gold to India and other lucrative markets, Fleming establishes a pattern in which the Bond villains are up to their necks in dubious financial dealings. Of course, in *Moonraker* Sir Hugo Drax's personal fortune made in metals (especially the rare ore Columbite) is (apparently) legitimate, but Bond learns from Colonel Smithers at the Bank of England, in *Goldfinger*, that "gold and currencies backed by gold are the foundation of our international credit" and that Goldfinger's smuggling—a "leakage of gold out of England"—is therefore destabilizing the British economy.[29] Fleming's excursion into the world of finance furnished him with ample material for these economic-based plots.

This was all in the future, however. Meanwhile, Ian's time in the City had to be racked up as another demoralizing failure. Indeed, it fairly soon became clear to Ian and his family that he was not cut out for a career in the financial world—and he must have regretted burning his bridges at Reuters. He would eventually be saved from further embarrassing himself in the financial world by the call of duty to his country in the person of Admiral John Godfrey. As before, Ian had the backing of powerful sponsors, Rear Admiral Aubrey Hugh Smith in this case, using his connections in the City to smooth the path of Ian's transition from Rowe & Pitman to Naval Intelligence.

Fleming had other matters on his mind, however, which could not be so easily resolved by his important social connections or powerful charm. In August 1935, in Le Touquet, France, Ian met the twenty-two-year-old Lady O'Neill (née Ann Charteris), who was the wife of one of the Irish peers, Lord Shane O'Neill, with whom she already had a son, Raymond. Ann, whose mother died when she was twelve—giving her an important common bond with Ian, who lost his father when he was only nine—had married O'Neill when she was just nineteen. Ann was immediately attracted to Ian, especially his immense charm and strong personality. Ann described the meeting with Ian at Le Touquet—when he was visiting with his friends in Le Cercle—and, as Mark Amory recounts, "saw him by the swimming pool, 'a handsome, moody creature.'" Ann was not alone in being impressed by Ian's good looks. Her friend the duchess of Westminster, Loelia Ponsonby (whose name Ian would later borrow for Bond's beautiful secretary at SIS), saw him at Warwick House that autumn and considered him "the most attractive man I've ever seen." Ian—though more aloof after his disappointment over Monique—was likewise drawn to Lady O'Neill. But as another woman who knew Ian at the time remarked, "he was quite ruthless about girls . . . or perhaps absent-minded is a better word."[30]

But Ian had rivals who were equally, if not more, good looking—and who had considerably more success in life to boast of. First and foremost was his brother Peter, who Mark Amory compares with Ian in ways hardly flattering to the younger brother: "Ian was not as classically handsome as his elder brother Peter; nor was he as clever, popular, rich, serious or virtuous." Then there was Esmond Harmsworth, who had become Lord Rothermere—with some misgivings at inheriting the title, it seems—upon the deaths of his two elder brothers in World War I. At only thirty-eight, Esmond was already chairman of Associated Newspapers and proprietor of the *Daily Mail*, Britain's leading newspaper. As Amory notes, "He was also devastatingly good-looking, athletic and a sophisticated lover."[31]

Though attracted to Ann, Ian would have been struck by the contrast between Ann's opulent lifestyle—as the wife of a wealthy lord, owner of an estate in Ireland—and the rather unpromising future he could offer her as the wife of an impecunious newspaper man or unsuccessful stockbroker. According to Mark Amory, Ian—whose confidence was damaged by numerous failures and living in the shadow of "just about the most promising young man in the country" (his older brother, Peter)—"was becoming bitter, obstinate, and solitary." Interestingly, Shane O'Neill had attended Eton at the same time as the Fleming brothers and—like Ian—did not attend university. But upon the death of his father—killed in action, like Valentine Fleming, in World War I—Shane inherited his grandfather's title and the family estate in Ireland. But for Ian, the most important difference was that O'Neill had inherited the family fortune, whereas Fleming's "respectable Scottish banking family left the Fleming money to his mother."[32] Hence, the experience of witnessing Ann's lifestyle firsthand was a chastening reminder of his own rather dim prospects and lack of a secure establishment.

It didn't help matters that, as a grown man working in the City, Ian was still living in his mother's house on Cheyne Walk in Chelsea. He had no real independence, and the lack of his own home was hampering any chance of romantic success. And so Ian decided to finally move out of his mother's home, purchasing the lease to 22b Ebury Street from Oswald Mosley, leader of the British Union of Fascists. The apartment was unusual for several reasons, aside from its distinctive provenance. It had been constructed in the 1830s as a Baptist chapel, and it boasted a large portico with several Doric columns, creating a sense of grandeur that stood out from the neighboring buildings. The building stood at the other end of Ebury Street from where Mozart had lived during his visit to London in 1764. As Giblin describes, "Located on the southeastern fringe of Belgravia, the former Pimlico Literary Institute was designed by architect J. P. Gandy-Deering." Inside, the apartment was notable for its darkness. It lacked any windows, the only natural light coming through a skylight in the vaulted ceiling. The absence of natural light was compensated for by atmospheric electric lighting installed by Ian. Other distinctive features included the installation of a toilet in the alcove that once housed the church's altar.[33] Although the skylight illuminated the bedroom, the main living area was depressingly gloomy. Moreover, the skylight could not be blacked out effectively during wartime, meaning that Ian had to vacate the flat in 1940, during the German air raids, moving to the Carlton Hotel (where, fittingly, he had received the offer of a job from Admiral Godfrey over lunch in the hotel's grill room). When the Carlton sustained bomb damage, Ian moved quarters again, this time to the Lansdowne Club in Berkeley Square.

But despite its odd features, the Ebury Street apartment had two distinct advantages: it was in central London, close to the City, and it was Ian's exclusive abode, with no maternal oversight. It was to this rather foreboding dwelling that Ian invited a series of young women and offered them rather basic food such as sausages and scrambled eggs accompanied by gin or wine. In winter months, a fire would be blazing in the hearth, adding a cozy domestic ambience. A number of Fleming's girlfriends found the place off-putting, being so obviously a masculine bachelor pad with few feminine touches. According to one of his girlfriends, Lisl Popper, "His Ebury Street house was done up by a German woman in a style I used to call Renaissance Jewish. Just like something very ugly from Berlin before the war."[34]

The walls were painted gray, and, although Ian's plans to decorate the walls with an autobiographical frieze did not materialize, the décor soon became enlivened by his collection of rare first editions and other evidence of his literary inclinations. According to Lady Mark Pakenham, debutante and biographer, Ian's popularity with women was far from universal: "The average girl simply did not like him." But, of course, Ian was not in pursuit of the "average girl."[35] The women he took a strong interest in were all distinguished in some way, by remarkable beauty and/or unusual intelligence.

It was also while in Ebury Street in the 1930s that Ian launched his famed social circle of male friends, which he christened Le Cercle Gastronomique et des Jeux de Hasard. Interestingly, the first Bond film, *Dr. No*, would appropriate the abbreviation of this name—Le Cercle—for the club in which Sean Connery's James Bond makes his first appearance.[36] Le Cercle, for Fleming, was an ideal mix of male camaraderie, hedonism, outdoor pursuits, and gambling. Its members were either Old Etonian cronies such as Gerald Coke or eccentric professional types such as Duff Dunbar, a barrister and enthusiastic collector of Wedgwood china. These men had in common a passion for fine food and vintage wine and an equal enthusiasm for golf and cards. Their weeknight meetings were restricted to London, where they would meet to enjoy a gourmet meal at Ebury Street or at the club or apartment of one of the other members. Dr. Jack Beal, a member of Le Cercle who later became Ian's physician, recalled, "The basis of the group was that we were all bachelors who met once a week . . . to drink and play bridge at Ian's converted chapel in Ebury Street."[37]

The evening's entertainment would consist of a gourmet meal, lively conversation, and games of contract bridge or baccarat. Le Cercle's weekend excursions were more adventurous. They would pack up their golf clubs and head for favorite renowned courses such as Royal St George's at Sandwich or even Le Touquet on the French coast. The latter venue—where Ian first met Ann while visiting there with Le Cercle—had the advantage of offering extensive casinos, and it was a frequent watering hole or residence of various British luminaries, including P. G. Wodehouse, who moved his residence there in 1934. Le Touquet would later play an important role as the basis for the fictional location of Royale-les-Eaux in Ian's first novel, *Casino Royale*. Another member of Le Cercle, John Fox-Strangways, would have his name appropriated by Ian for the head of SIS Station J (Jamaica) in his second novel, *Live and Let Die*, and again in *Dr. No*.

Ian's emotional life became more complicated in August 1935, when he was holidaying in Kitzbühel—scene of his earlier dalliances with Tyrolean women while staying at Am Tennerhof—and met Muriel Wright, a young and beautiful Englishwoman. She appealed to Ian on a number of levels: her model good looks, with frizzy blonde hair and sweet expression, attracted him, but so did her vivacious personality and eagerness to please. Though Muriel—or "Moo," as she was called by friends—has been dismissed by some as intellectually lightweight, clearly her conversation and interests appealed to Fleming. The two became lovers, and their relationship blossomed back in England. Moo was one of the regular visitors to Fleming's apartment at 22b, and she was viewed with envy by some of the other women Ian kept in tow.

After he met Ann O'Neill the same year, however, Ian's feelings for Moo cooled somewhat. His heart was more strongly drawn to the married, mercurial aristocrat whose unattainability and high social position made her even more desirable. Even if, as Amory claims, "Ian remained what he had long been, a formidable womanizer determined to stay a bachelor," the die had been cast for his infatuation with Lady O'Neill.[38] Her very aristocratic aloofness and mystery—a woman who did not immediately fall under his spell—were the keys to her attractiveness for Ian.

All this lay ahead in the 1940s and beyond. In the late 1930s, Ian's own literary ambitions—such as they were—had either been forgotten or were carefully kept to himself. Peter Fleming had given up a promising career as literary editor of *The Spectator* in order to join an apparently hopeless expedition to find the missing English explorer Colonel P. H. Fawcett in the Amazon jungle. But whereas Ian's jettisoning of his journalistic life had resulted in failure, Peter's led to spectacular success with *Brazilian Adventure*. Despite the expedition's failure to accomplish their mission of discovering Fawcett, Peter's narrative captured the feckless hopes and misadventures of the journey with a sardonic vein of self-deprecating humor while also conveying the exotic surroundings of the Brazilian tropics and exciting episodes of travel. Peter is quite frank about the futility of the expedition: "I repeat: everything points to the whole [Fawcett] expedition having perished in the summer of 1925, probably at the hands of Indians." The sense of anticlimax, in fact, pervades the entire narrative. In the same chapter, Fleming writes, "Our abortive march towards the Kuluene accomplished nothing at all."[39]

Yet the book became a best seller and was followed by further travel books, such as *News from Tartary* (1934). Peter had realized his youthful promise, noted by TP at Durnford School, and firmly established himself as the successful author of the Fleming family. This left little room for Ian to contribute to literature, which is not to say that he had abandoned his ideas of publishing a novel someday. Philip Kindersley, who knew both brothers at Eton, recalled, "No one would have expected [literary success] of Ian. Peter of course was marked out for great things from the start but not Ian."[40]

Nor was Peter's literary success the only field in which he eclipsed Ian. While Ian was playing Don Juan, seducing various women, married and unmarried, in Britain and Europe, Peter had found the love of his life in the actress Celia Johnson, who would become famous for her role in *Brief Encounter* (1945), directed by David Lean, for which she would receive an Academy Award nomination for Best Actress.[41] Ironically, Peter's marriage to Celia did not meet with his family's approval: Eve in particular was unhappy about her son marrying one of the "fast set" of show business and cinema, but as so often Peter was able to win over his mother's opposition by his charm and persuasiveness. The stark contrast with Eve's firm prohibition of Ian's engagement to Monique was not lost on the younger brother.

Peter was now happily settled with one of the leading actresses of her generation, who gave birth to their first child, a son, in 1939. Meanwhile, Ian was still unable or unwilling to commit himself to a single woman. Once again, Peter seemed to be assuming the role of paterfamilias of the Fleming clan, in contrast to Ian, who was inevitably becoming the family's black sheep. Sandwiched between his two best-selling travelogues, Peter's marriage and establishment at the family estate at Nettlebed, Oxfordshire, placed a further gap between the two brothers. Their life courses would overlap during wartime, however, as both Fleming brothers would serve with distinction in intelligence in World War II, emphasizing their shared desire to live up to the example of their father, Valentine.

Another regular visitor to Fleming's Ebury Street apartment was Maud Russell, the wealthy heiress and patron of the arts, who became Ian's lover during this period. Her diary entry for Sunday, May 28, 1939, reflects Ian's various passions of drinking, female company, and rare book collecting: "Had a drink with I.[an] at Ebury St in his big room on Tuesday. He has just bought the first 20 or 30 copies of *Iskra*, Lenin's organ. He is making an interesting collection of the first book, broadsheet, pamphlet or paper on a particular subject."[42] Maud's description helps re-create the bookish, decadent atmosphere of Fleming's Ebury Street apartment and the origins of his remarkable rare book collection, acquired with the assistance of Percy Muir.[43]

Maud's meetings with Ian were not always so harmonious. She records in her diary for Friday, July 28, 1939, "Dined with I.[an] on Wednesday after picking him up at Ebury St where we had a rabid political talk before going to dine at Quaglino's." Though Maud does not specify the topic of this conversation, the adjective "rabid" suggests a heated debate or argument. Given the timing, the most likely topic is the looming war with Germany and the possibility of appeasement. Maud Russell was passionately anti-Nazi and saw war with Hitler's Germany as inevitable: for example, when one of her foreign friends told her "it alarmed him that England was becoming so bellicose," Maud comments, "I am glad if that is the impression foreigners now get."[44] Yet, Ian was less convinced appeasement was no longer possible, and this was very possibly the source of their disagreement.

Because of his father's death in the previous war, Ian was far from convinced that another war with Germany was desirable or even necessary. Given his later involvement with the war effort against Nazi Germany, working in Naval Intelligence, it might seem strange that he was by no means an advocate of going to war in the late 1930s. Like many of his class and background, Ian felt that Britain should make every effort to reach an agree-

Figure 3.1. Maud Russell, circa 1920s. ***Reproduced by permission of Maud Russell's estate.***

ment with Hitler and avoid plunging the nation into armed conflict that would further damage Britain's already fragile economy. In this vein, Ian wrote a remarkable letter to *The Times* on September 1938, arguing that Britain should agree to the demands of Hitler as originally outlined in the

National Socialist agenda of 1920. Fleming argued that all the other points in the agenda had been carried out and identified three that remained—including uniting the German-speaking nations in one country and expanding German colonies to feed and provide for the Germanic people.

Fleming's letter was written while Britain was awaiting the outcome of the meeting of Prime Minister Neville Chamberlain with Adolf Hitler in Munich, culminating in Chamberlain's famous "peace for our time" speech about the "deal" with Hitler. These meetings resulted in the Munich agreement, which divided up Czechoslovakia to appease the Germans, and Chamberlain's notorious declaration in which he claimed Britain and Germany had agreed never to go to war with each other again. However, within a year Britain and France would declare war on Germany following the German invasion of Poland. Neville's "piece of paper" was worthless.

Of course, Ian was not to know this when, in September 1938, Chamberlain was still negotiating with Hitler in Munich. Probably his views were shared by many, that appeasing Hitler was the best solution to avoid war. Fleming did make an important stipulation in his *Times* letter—namely, that Britain and France should only agree to these demands of Hitler's if the German chancellor first signed a rigid nonarmament pact to demonstrate that he had no aggressive intentions toward other European nations and did not plan to go to war to conquer neighboring countries. It is quite probable that Ian knew—or strongly suspected—that Hitler would never agree to such conditions and that therefore "appeasement" was dead in the water. But by offering Hitler such a deal, Britain would force the Führer's hand and make clear his aggressive intentions. The phrasing of Ian's sentences is suggestive of his skepticism:

> If and when Herr Hitler refuses a settlement on these lines—if, that is to say, it is made clear that Germany already aims once again at world domination by aggression— then it will be time to organize this country on a wartime basis and announce to Germany that we shall fight at the final act of aggression against our fundamental treaty of obligations.[45]

But, on the other hand, Fleming's letter portrays the alternatives to appeasement in scathing terms—either the "dangerous counsels of the slaughterhouse brigade" or the "vapourings" of those who thought neutrality the most desirable course and wanted Britain to be "another Holland." This letter also raises the intriguing question, whom did Ian include in the "slaughterhouse brigade," his damning phrase for warmongers? Could he have meant

Winston Churchill, who was waiting in the wings and would soon replace Chamberlain as Britain's prime minister, leading the country to hard-fought victory in World War II? This seems unlikely, given that Churchill was a close friend of his father's and wrote Valentine's obituary in *The Times* (the same paper in which Ian's letter appeared).[46]

Clearly, Ian was prepared for Britain to go to war against Germany, but only as a last resort and if it was in the country's interests. In retrospect, his letter is remarkable not so much for its position, which was shared by many, but for the fact that Ian would soon become a leader in the fight against Nazism and Hitler's Germany following his appointment as assistant to Admiral John Godfrey. Did he simply change his mind about the Nazis following their invasion of Poland and Britain's declaration of war—a volte-face that involved spending the next six years of his life doing everything in his power to defeat the German enemy? Or did Ian believe all along that Hitler had malevolent intentions and that war was inevitable?[47]

The chief question is, can his letter be construed as sympathetic to Hitler and Fascism? Ian seems to brandish his own interest in Fascist ideology—for example, by disclosing that his quotations from the 1920 National Socialist manifesto are a direct translation of a "copy in my own possession."[48] We know that Ian also acquired a first edition of *Mein Kampf*, Hitler's autobiography, for his book collection of rare editions of "landmark" publications, influential in human, scientific, and political history. But an interest in the theories of National Socialism does not equate to adherence to its principles. In Eric Ambler's *A Coffin for Dimitrios* (UK title, *The Mask of Dimitrios*)—published in 1939, the year after Fleming's letter—the protagonist Charles Latimer writes a book on Alfred Rosenberg, one of the chief ideologues of the Nazi party and the author of *Der Mythus des zwanzigsten Jahrhunderts* (*The Myth of the Twentieth Century*), originally published in 1930. Latimer's study focuses on "the economic implications" of Rosenberg's study, and it was afterward, "in the hope of dispelling the black depression which was the aftermath of his temporary association with the philosophy of National Socialism and its prophet, Dr Rosenberg, that he wrote his first detective story."[49] In other words, Ambler makes clear that Latimer's academic interest in National Socialism is far from being a personal belief and actually deepens his repugnance toward the Nazis.

Yet Fascist views were not uncommon in Fleming's circle. Interestingly, Viscount Rothermere—the father of the second husband of Ann O'Neill, the future Mrs. Ian Fleming—wrote a piece in the *Daily Mirror* in support of

Mosley's British Union of Fascists, though the *Mirror* later became anti-Nazi in its position. Rothermere owned a rival paper, the *Daily Mail*, which his third son, Esmond, would inherit following the deaths of his two older brothers in World War I. Fleming also fraternized with known Nazi sympathizers, such as Bobbie Gordon-Canning, who would be interned during the war under Defence Regulation 18B—the same regulation under which Oswald Mosley was arrested and interned.

What is clear is that Ian's rather aimless, desultory course in life was transformed by the outbreak of World War II. Had war not broken out, he might have continued working as a mediocre stockbroker, still dreaming of earning a fortune in the stock market, while pursuing half-hearted affairs with various willing women and married socialites. He would have continued to spend his leisure hours playing golf and cards with the members of Le Cercle, spending his weekends at the links of Royal St George's.

Even before war broke out, however, Ian had another chance to prove his mettle as an undercover agent. Having already reported on the Soviet situation in 1933, Fleming was asked to visit Russia again in the spring of 1939 to report on its preparations for war. Ian's official cover was that he was accompanying and reporting on a trade mission to Moscow for *The Times*. However, his actual purpose—in the role of the covert intelligence agent about which he had fantasized—was to study Russian military preparations, industrial strength, and political attitudes toward the likely allies and enemies in the approaching war.

Sefton Delmer, who worked for the *Daily Express* and later played a key role in wartime propaganda as a leading figure in the Political Warfare Executive, recalled meeting Ian for the first time on the train to Moscow in 1939 when they were both with the trade delegation. Delmer recalls, "For of course he was there doing a job for the Secret Service. No question about it. . . . This, of course, was why Ian went into Reuters. Pure cover."[50] Ian's role as a spy seems to have been an open secret.

Ian's report "Russia's Strength" is a small masterpiece of succinct reporting, condensed research, and spirited personal opinions about the probable behavior of the great nation. It is fair to say that Ian admired Russia but was antipathetic to the Soviet system, which he rejected as oppressive, monolithic, and treacherous. Long before the Soviet Union became Ian's bête noire in his Cold War spy fiction, he had warned that Russia would be an unreliable and possibly treacherous ally in time of war. On the one hand, Russia was not overtly preparing for aggressive action in war, being more concerned with its self-preservation:

> It is well known that the USSR possesses sufficient forces not only for protecting its own frontiers, but for adding quite useful weight to any international action for curbing the aggressor. It is equally well known that the Soviet Union is interested in preserving peace throughout the world and in rebuffing the aggressor. . . . It cannot be too often repeated that the Soviet Russia is, in all respects, stronger for defensive than for offensive action. Already sated with territory and natural resources, requiring leisure for political consolidation and for the progress of her "Industrial Revolution" her main ambitions now are self-protective. Broadly speaking, her chief value in any international action to curb the aggressor—supposing the aggressor to mean the Anti-Comintern powers, and postulating the continued refusal by Poland and Roumania [*sic*] to allow the passage through their territories of Russian forces—might be to guard the hinterland of her Western front, supply arms and raw materials to democratic allies on that front, and create diversions in the Far East with alarms and in the Baltic and Black Sea with her naval forces.[51]

Yet, Ian's report concluded that Britain's government should be wary of entering an alliance with Russia, which (he claimed) had little sentimental attachment to Britain and was more inclined to allegiance with Germany. Specifically, he alleged, "Russia would be an exceedingly treacherous ally. She would not hesitate to stab us in the back the moment it suited her. But not too much weight should be attached to the possibility of a Russo-German alliance at the moment."[52]

The report was circulated among the Soviet sections of the Foreign Office, offering valuable intelligence on a very sensitive and urgent political topic. A preface to the report stated, "(N.B. The writer returned from Soviet Russia last week. He has no political prejudices whatsoever.)"[53] This may be reflective of Fleming's wish to appear "neutral" on the controversial topic of Russia and Germany, but the tone of his report is undoubtedly hostile toward Russia's self-interest. Maud Russell wrote in her diary for April 26, 1939, "Lunched with I.[an] at Boulestin's on Friday. He'd just come back from doing *The Times* Special Correspondent in Russia and was wholly and completely anti-Bolshevik."[54] Though Maud does not mention (and possibly did not realize) that the report was actually written at the behest of the FO, the report's tone corresponds with what she observes about Ian's hostile attitude to the Soviet system.

The report "Russia's Strength" helped enhance Fleming's reputation in the Foreign Office and Intelligence Services and is doubtless one of the reasons Ian came to the attention of Godfrey in 1939 when he was seeking an assistant in his new role as director of Naval Intelligence. It is ironic that the very government department that had crushed Ian's hopes of a career in diplomacy and intelligence at the beginning of the decade—when he failed to gain entrance to the Foreign Office in 1931—was influential in gaining him a high position as an intelligence officer at the decade's end. Delmer's insistence that "of course" Ian was working for the Secret Service during his trip to Russia is an indication of the close connections between the FO and SIS. Ian's entrance into the world of Naval Intelligence would be the turning point of his career and one of the decisive experiences that led to the creation of James Bond after the war.

Apparently, Ian was already thinking about joining the clandestine services before Godfrey stepped in with his extraordinary job offer. Lycett argues that

> with introductions and subtle encouragement not just from Maud [Russell] but also from Forbes Dennis, who had returned to Vienna to work with refugees, and from Lancy [Smith] and his partners at Rowe and Pitman, Ian was becoming increasingly aware of the world of clandestine services. As war with Germany loomed, he seems to have identified intelligence as an area where he would like to work.[55]

Another sponsor of Ian's quest to join the world of secret intelligence was likely Gilbert Russell, the husband of Maud since 1917. Throughout their relationship, Maud—who was Ian's senior by ten years—saw her role as helping to realize Fleming's dreams, as she wrote in her diary for Sunday, May 28, 1939, Ian's thirty-first birthday,

> I think he [Ian] would like to do secret service work, or journalism, or both. He wrote a report about Russia and another about Germany after he'd been there this spring to show to his friends. G.[ilbert] read one of them and had the idea of introducing him to M.I. which he did.

Referring to Military Intelligence by its usual abbreviation (as in MI5, MI6), Maud also suggests the tantalizing idea that, as Emily Russell notes, "Gilbert may have played a part in getting Ian his job in the Naval Intelligence Division which came about at around this time."[56] In fact, only four days earlier, Ian had joined Godfrey, Aubrey Hugh Smith, and Angus Mac-

Donnell at the Carlton Hotel Grill and had been offered the position as Godfrey's assistant. His life as a spy was now underway.

Chapter Four

My Man Godfrey

Ian Fleming in Naval Intelligence

The 1930s had been, on balance, a decade of frustrated hopes, false starts, and bitter disappointments for Ian. His failure to enter the Foreign Office (FO) was a damaging blow to his self-esteem, following on the heels of the breakup of his engagement to Monique. However, Ian's promising debut as a journalist for Reuters news agency seemed to offer an exciting future as a reporter. The high point of Fleming's early journalistic career—his assignment to cover the Moscow Metro-Vickers trials in 1933—demonstrated the favorable opinion that Reuters chief Bernard Rickatson-Hatt had of their new hire, for it was one of the most high-profile news stories of the time. The venture into the City proved something of a blind alley, and Ian was more than grateful to leave this milieu so as to take up the request from the FO to visit Moscow and write his report "Russia's Strength."

When Admiral John Godfrey was appointed director of Naval Intelligence (DNI) in 1938—though he did not take up his post until February 7, 1939—war with Germany looked increasingly inevitable. With his responsibilities growing, Godfrey was looking for a suitably ambitious and capable man to assume the role of his assistant. Ian Fleming came highly recommended by Sir Montagu Norman—director of the Bank of England—and Godfrey, as we have seen, met Fleming for lunch at the Carlton Hotel Grill.

Ian passed his interview with flying colors, and the meeting resulted in his appointment as assistant to DNI despite having no previous naval background. They agreed that Ian would come into the Admiralty part time to get to know the various sections, starting in June 1939.[1] Fleming and Godfrey were very different personalities, and to some extent they complemented each other. Ian used a charm offensive to get what he wanted, spoke well and confidently, and was known for being able to win over difficult personalities. Godfrey was more taciturn and could be brusque toward people in power. Therefore, Godfrey would rely on Ian to liaise with other intelligence agencies and even government departments, including those of Britain's wartime allies. Where Godfrey's bluntness might give offence, Ian's charm was more likely to smooth ruffled feathers.

Perhaps John Godfrey lacked imagination—Macintyre describes him as "a most literal man" and cites Godfrey's own comment that "the business of deception . . . needed the sort of corkscrew mind which I did not possess."[2] If Godfrey lacked this quality, however, then Fleming possessed it in abundance. His creative mind was frequently devising outlandish plots and schemes with which to deceive and bewilder the enemy, while Godfrey could serve as the necessary restraint on his assistant's tendency to excess. Godfrey's practicality was a useful counterweight to Ian's tendency to fantasize.

Yet for all their important temperamental differences, both men, in their unique ways, were shy, and this resemblance perhaps allowed them to form a bond. Ian may have sensed something else—that in this senior naval officer and intelligence chief, twenty years his senior and somewhat gruff to boot, he had found a surrogate father, another man of distinguished military pedigree to replace the father he had lost in the previous war, when Ian was only nine years old.[3]

John Godfrey was born in 1888, only six years after Ian's father, and he served with distinction during World War I on the HMS *Euryalus* in the Dardanelles campaign. After the war, Godfrey had risen through the ranks of the Royal Navy to achieve the position of rear admiral in 1939. In addition to his high naval rank, he was now, in 1939, the head of the Naval Intelligence Division (NID), which would arguably become the most important intelligence division in wartime. With its island status and celebrated maritime history, Britain had always needed to protect its waters and coasts from enemy invasion. At the same time, the sea had launched British seafarers on their quest to explore, discover, and conquer many parts of the globe. To "rule the waves" was the heart of Britain's imperial identity. In World War II, the role of Naval Intelligence in defending Britain from the planned Nazi invasion—codenamed Operation Sea Lion—was essential in preventing the Germans from gaining air and naval supremacy in the English Channel. At the same time, the Admiralty sometimes came into conflict with the Air Ministry over who took precedence in Britain's defense of the realm.

Ian—whose instinct was to bristle and rebel against draconian authority—had already failed at one military institution, Royal Sandhurst. There was certainly a risk that he would balk at the hierarchy and discipline of the Admiralty as well. But when authority and power were embodied in a person he admired—and who reciprocated with praise of his talents and support of his ideas—then Ian was prone to reverence if not worship. Godfrey was the ideal mentor and supervisor for Ian during his years in Naval Intelligence. The admiral could be stern, stubborn, and severe—he would have serious conflicts with Winston Churchill about the role of Naval Intelligence during the war and the type of missions it should be involved in. In particular, Godfrey was opposed to Churchill's Operation Catherine, the Baltic offensive that Churchill planned as first lord of the Admiralty, shortly before becoming prime minister in May 1940. The purpose of Catherine was to stop the flow of Swedish iron ore to Germany by disrupting German naval traffic in the Baltic. In his naval memoir, Godfrey writes, "Both Charles Daniel, Director of Plans, and I disliked Churchill's operation 'Catherine' intensely. It was the naval assault into the Baltic right under the German fighter umbrella and well outside ours. Daniel made his views quite clear, but Pound said 'don't worry, it will never take place.'"[4] Though Pound was correct, and Operation Catherine was never carried out, it led to the deterioration of Godfrey's relationship with Churchill, resulting in the director's eventual removal from his post in 1942.

But, for all his irascible tendencies, Godfrey was far from being a martinet toward those serving under him, and he was willing to grant Ian considerable independence in running Room 39, the hub of the Naval Intelligence headquarters, under his command. Despite having no prior naval experience, Fleming was initially assigned the rank of lieutenant in the Special Branch of the Royal Naval Volunteer Reserve (RNVR) and was later promoted to commander. This was, of course, the rank Fleming would also bestow on his fictional hero, James Bond, whose relationship with M reflects that between Fleming and Godfrey. The mixture of respect, admiration, and at times irritation that Bond feels toward M's leadership style replay the understanding Ian had with his wartime boss. Fleming sometimes refers in the novels to the expressions of M's "sailor's eyes," emphasizing his naval background, and M, like Godfrey, has the rank of admiral.[5]

Robert Harling notes that "above all, he [Fleming] was fortunate in working for and with someone he respected and liked: the then Rear Admiral John Godfrey, a formidable man indeed . . . with steely eyes and the manner of a relentless advocate rather than that of a sea captain."[6] Godfrey would later pay Fleming the great compliment of saying that, had their respective ages been reversed, Fleming would have been director of NID and he, Godfrey, his assistant. William Stephenson, who directed the British Security Coordination (BSC) in New York and knew both men, has strongly emphasized Fleming's leadership role in his assessment: "Really, it was Ian who was the DNI through most of the war. He had far more grasp than Godfrey. And did far more work."[7]

Room 39 was the vital intelligence hub where shipping reports, U-boat sightings, opportunities to capture the German Enigma machine and cipher books, and other information relating to the war at sea were all brought together, collated, synthesized, and distributed to the most important recipients of this intelligence. As its manager, Fleming oversaw a crucial dimension of the war effort. In his memoirs, Godfrey describes Fleming's responsibilities in some detail:

> Ian was appointed to my staff in the rank of Lieutenant R.N.V.R. and given a desk in Room 39 next to my office. The appointment was a great success from my point of view. Not only did Ian carry out the multifarious duties of personal assistant (P.A.), a job which has no defined frontiers, with outstanding success, but he represented me on various inter-department committees. . . . He had command of three languages and wide outside interests and contacts. As a result, bright suggestions by many brilliant civilians working with an officer of junior rank often received more encouragement than if they had gone through normal sectional heads whose duties were concerned rather more with countries than with functions. In fact, I found a P.A. of use in most matters not directly connected with the Naval Service. It was evident by the spring of 1940 that Ian had at least a two-man job, and this led to the appointment of Ted Merret as private secretary (P.S.).[8]

In addition to his involvement in ambitious intelligence operations such as Mincemeat, Ruthless, and Goldeneye (the latter designed to keep Spain neutral and out of the war and to protect the British territory of Gibraltar in the event of German invasion), Ian was also eventually authorized to form his own commando unit, 30AU, from 1942. This unit gave the future author more opportunity to run agents in the field, seizing crucial intelligence mate-

Figure 4.1. Ian Fleming in naval uniform from the photograph album of Maud Russell, circa 1940. ***Courtesy of Ian Fleming Images/Maud Russell Estate Collection.***

rial behind enemy lines in occupied Europe. As Robert Harling describes it in "Where Bond Began,"

> Because this German unit had proved so frighteningly successful, DNI decided that the time had come to form a British naval unit along similar lines. Fleming was given the job of getting the unit into shape. No 30 Assault Unit, or 30 AU, was the title of the outfit, and it began to operate tentatively in the Middle East, working with the Eighth Army.[9]

Ian's role as controller of 30AU really developed after Godfrey had been posted to India and replaced as DNI. Despite the fact that Ian and Admiral Edmund Rushbrooke did not get along well, Ian's role in Naval Intelligence continued to bring new responsibilities: "A few months later, following Admiral Godfrey's posting to India, his successor, Rear Admiral Rushbrooke, had undoubtedly found 30AU and its manifold and frequently inexplicable activities a further oddment on his plate. Hence Fleming's current plateful."[10]

Because Godfrey has often been identified as the model for M—the head of the British Secret Intelligence Service (SIS) and Bond's chief in the novels—there is a tendency to place Ian in the role of James Bond, Godfrey's subordinate, as Bond is M's subordinate. But in many respects, Ian's role during the war was more like M's than Bond's. He was not actively involved in espionage operations—though at times he doubtless wished to be. Rather, he managed operations from the Admiralty in the heart of London, which had an impact all over the globe. Ian built intelligence networks, managed his commando unit, collaborated and coordinated with Britain's allies, and launched daring missions to seize enemy intelligence. And, at times, he sent men under his command to their deaths. Harling writes about the complexity of this control in "Where Bond Began":

> A major headache for Fleming was the remote control of this highly mobile, individual unit which he had fondly thought would be so near to hand once back in Europe. . . . He had a dozen roving splinter groups to guide and drive him mad, for all our movements were controlled in a high degree by Fleming from the Admiralty. He gave precise orders for what Intelligence suggested we should look for and where we might seek and find, from homing torpedoes to the results of German jet experiments.[11]

Fortunately, Ian had the intellectual ability, administrative capacity, and man-management skills necessary for the position. His journalistic background was also useful to Godfrey, one of whose goals during the war was to improve the relationship between the DNI and the press. Indeed, Donald McLachlan—who also worked in Room 39—likened this hub of industry "to the newsroom of a great newspaper."[12] In his naval memoirs, Godfrey explained his plan in cultivating contacts with the media:

> Firstly, to get to know all editors and some of the proprietors personally, secondly to gain the confidence of their staffs by informal weekly press conferences conducted with considerable frankness. In fact, to take the press into my confidence in the conviction that, if this was done, they would play the game.

Fleming's connections with newspaper barons such as Lord Rothermere and Lord Beaverbrook became especially useful in this regard, as Godfrey described: "It was now that I began to appreciate the qualities of my personal assistant, Lieutenant Ian Fleming, RNVR, who was within easy call the other side of the door leading to Room 39. He was well acquainted with Fleet Street, having been with Reuters before taking to the City."[13]

Ian also had an extensive social network and gift for making important connections that Godfrey lacked. Having gained valuable experience in producing intelligence reports for the FO, and having studied under a former SIS head-of-station, Ernan Forbes Dennis, Ian was already immersed in the intelligence world before he joined NID. As Robert Harling, Ian's friend and NID colleague, remarks in his memoir, "Fleming . . . had acquired, in peacetime, an unusually wide range of contacts well outside the conventional naval round—from the City and Reuters to motor-racing and skiing."[14]

Godfrey's faith in Fleming's abilities boosted his confidence in himself, and the new responsibilities stimulated a remarkable energy and determination in the assistant to the DNI. As Harling wrote after Ian's death, "To the surprise of many, and to the utter perplexity of his friends, Fleming took these demands in his stride, meeting them ably and equably, no matter if, as he said, he suffered from corns on his backside."[15] Most important, Ian's experience running intelligence operations, traveling the world, and controlling spies would provide him with material, ideas for characters and plots, and a knowledge of the secret world that would eventually form the basis for James Bond and his adventures.

In particular, Assault Unit 30—known as "Ian Fleming's Commandoes" or Fleming's "Red Indians"—specialized in the kind of derring-do, unconventional and at times reckless covert operations that would characterize

Bond's postwar adventures. Fleming himself was not actually part of the 30AU "on the ground"—but he directed it from NID headquarters at the Admiralty in London, assigning it the task of going into occupied territory behind enemy lines and vital intelligence grabbing. Several of the members of 30AU, including Dunstan Curtis, Robert Harling, and John Anthony Crawford Hugill, could be considered influences on the character of James Bond. As both Harling's memoir and Hugill's book *The Hazard Mesh* and diary (the latter in the Churchill Archive Center) reveal, Dunstan and Ian disliked each other, and the tension between them occasionally erupted.

For example, on one occasion Dunstan tried to fend off a visit to 30AU from Ian by saying that their French base was unsafe, thereby implying that Ian wanted to leave London to escape danger. Harling records bluntly that "neither had a pennyworth of understanding or tolerance for the other" and later referred to "Fleming and Curtis, those two polarities." When 30AU fell out of Ian's control, passing to Supreme Headquarters Allied Expeditionary Force, Ian dismissively suggested Dunstan's continuing role would be "nominal and operational head of the unit in the field," which Harling interpreted as a "splintered head of a splintered toy."[16] And yet, Ian's respect for Dunstan's courage as a soldier and leader of men left an imprint on Bond. Curtis later recalled that "Ian was very much in control from London at this stage. . . . From the start he gave us a very detailed shopping list—the best catch was for ciphers, anything marked *Geheim* [secret]."[17]

Ian's idea for 30AU came from the example of a German intelligence-grabbing outfit organized by Otto Skorzeny. This unit had not taken part in the main battles but set out "to grab as much British secret material as he and his men could lay their hands on."[18] Ian decided that NID should form its own "intelligence commandoes"—30AU—that worked closely with the Special Operations Executive (SOE), formed by Churchill to "set Europe ablaze," using sabotage and subversion to damage the Nazis' progress through occupied Europe. In some ways, James Bond was a composite of the members of 30AU, embodying their courage, sense of adventure, and lust for life, together with Fleming's hedonism (during one of his field visits to 30AU in France, Fleming complained that the brandy they gave him was "undrinkable"—a Bond-like comment). Robert Harling later reflected,

> Naturally, in its lifetime 30 AU had recruited some unusual citizens and some of their oddities brushed off on Bond and the rest of the Fleming oeuvre. There was the only man wholly without nerves I have ever known whose idea of an

> evening's enjoyment was to spend the night in a jeep, with two unwilling Commando comrades, in the middle of No-Man's Land.[19]

In the history of 30AU held in the UK's National Archives, the importance of its operations to intelligence gathering is made clear in a statement about its greatest achievement: the capture of the German Naval Archives:

> After a 3 days search this department was found intact at Tambach. This capture included the entire operational archives of the German navy and, from the historical point of view, is undoubtedly 30 AU's greatest achievement this war. Team 55 also discovered 2 secret establishments at Immenstadt and Obendorf together with an Air Force establishment at Rottenbach before returning to HQ on the 8th May.[20]

As Christopher Moran describes,

> Most impressively, in May 1945, they [30AU] ransacked Tambach Castle, a Nazi outpost deep in the forests of Württemberg, capturing 100 tons of operational logs, war diaries and administrative records of the German Navy, dating back to the Franco-Prussian War. According to 30AU member Robert Harling, the haul was so large that half-a-dozen 3-tonne lorries were needed to transport it to the port in Hamburg, where a fishing boat was then chartered to deliver it London.[21]

In his memoirs, Robert Harling makes clear that it was Ian's decision that the capture of the Tambach archives be made a top priority for 30AU: "Fleming decided that losing valuable archives of any war could prove a grievous loss to future marine scholarship. Such a possible loss would prompt interest for any book collector of ambition and scope." Fleming was also excited about the prospect of a personal visit to Tambach, getting him away from his London desk. In his account, Harling asked Ian afterward if "the venture helped to persuade you to feel more compassionate toward the 30AU underlings you've been chiding for the past couple of years?" Ian's response, typically, was "not noticeably."[22]

Such extraordinary hauls of intelligence "pinches" were, of course, exactly what Fleming hoped to achieve by establishing 30AU and garnering support from Godfrey and the NID. But Ian himself was not in the front line, not in the heat of the action—never a full participant in the daring adventures of 30AU but its "spymaster" figure, running operations from London. For all his involvement with the war effort, Ian was always one step removed from the line of fire. Unlike his father, Valentine, and his brother Michael, Ian's life of military action was a matter of fantasy rather than reality.

While in Naval Intelligence, Ian planned, and was involved in, other missions (apart from those of 30AU) that anticipated and provided inspiration for the Bond novels. One key example is Operation Ruthless, which was devised by Fleming in the fall of 1940 as a means to capture the naval Enigma codebooks from the Germans. The progress of the codebreakers at Bletchley Park in decrypting Enigma traffic from the Luftwaffe and Abwehr was impressive, but the naval encrypted traffic presented greater problems to great minds such as Alan Turing's. Fleming's idea was to obtain a captured German warplane/bomber from the Ministry of Defence and for himself and several others to disguise themselves as German aircrew. They would crash the plane into the English Channel and send an SOS signal, leading to their "rescue" by a German naval vessel. When the enemy rescue cruiser arrived, the British in disguise would shoot the German crew, dump them overboard, and steal their Enigma codebook.

This plan, far-fetched as it may sound, had the support of the head of the Operational Intelligence Center, Rear Admiral Jock Clayton, and Admiral Godfrey himself helped obtain the German Heinkel bomber, "which had been shot down in a raid over the Firth of Forth." After the bomber's Perspex nose was reinforced, the operation seemed set to go, but no suitable German ships appeared in the Channel on the day of the proposed operation, so it was postponed. Lycett points out that Fleming "anticipated aspects of his future fictional hero James Bond when he stipulated that the bomber's pilot should be a 'tough bachelor, able to swim.'"[23] He may well have had himself in mind.

The note from Fleming to Godfrey proposing Operation Ruthless, included by Charles Morgan in his "History of Naval Intelligence 1939–42," states,

> During the last days of August and early September a plot began to be hatched for the capture of a German enigma-cypher machine. There were earlier projects vaguely and verbally discussed but the first concrete proposal was made in an informative note by Fleming to DNI:
>
> DNI
>
> I suggest we obtain the loot by the following means:
>
> 1. Obtain from Air Ministry an air-worthy German bomber

2. Pick a tough crew of five, including a pilot, W/T operator and word-perfect German speaker. Dress them in German Air Force uniform, add blood and bandages to suit
3. Crash plane in the Channel after making S.O.S. to rescue service in P/L
4. Once aboard rescue boat, shoot German crew, dump overboard, bring rescue boat back to English port.

In order to increase the chances of capturing an R. or M. with its richer booty, the crash might be staged in mid-Channel. The Germans would presumably employ one of this type for the longer and more hazardous journey.

F[leming]. 12.9.40[24]

Fleming seems to relish the theatricality of the disguise of German uniform and the fake blood and bandages. The most likely role for Fleming himself would be the "word-perfect German speaker," as his fluency in German would be vital for communicating with the rescue boat. Fleming's role goes from being the implied leader of the group of "he and a few others" to being the "German speaker" to offering to "accompany the crew" to simply directing it from the shore. In the end, even this role failed to materialize. Ian's wish to participate in the mission was thwarted by Godfrey, who refused his permission because Ian knew too much about the secrets of Naval Intelligence and Bletchley Park to risk his capture by the enemy.

Fleming's disappointment at being excluded from the heat of the action was undoubtedly a factor leading him to create the fictional alter ego of James Bond. Whether through his own fear of danger or Godfrey's caution, Fleming was limited to a supervisory "directing" role in these operations—and so could never become the war hero that his father, Valentine, had been or that men such as Dunstan Curtis could claim (probably one source of Fleming's animosity to Dunstan was envy: the envy of the "desk man" for the man of action, the soldier in the field).

Ian sometimes romanticized or exaggerated his wartime experiences when writing about them, in the interests of telling a thrilling story. As one of the writers he most admired, William Somerset Maugham, wrote in the preface to his 1926 classic of spy fiction, *Ashenden*:

> This book is founded on my experiences in the Intelligence Department during the war, but rearranged for the purposes of fiction. Fact is a poor story-teller. It starts a story at haphazard, generally long before the beginning, rambles on inconsequently and tails off, leaving loose ends hanging about, without a conclusion.[25]

Maugham also asserts that the content needs some spicing up: "The work of an agent in the Intelligence Department is on the whole extremely monotonous. A lot of it is uncommonly useless. The material it offers for stories is scrappy and pointless; the author has himself to make it coherent, dramatic and probable."[26] Ian learned this lesson well from the master. Like his friend Willie Maugham, he would dress up the raw facts of his Naval Intelligence work to enhance the drama and create coherence. Yet, at bottom, Ian's Bond novels are nonetheless—as Maugham's stories were—based on the author's actual experiences in intelligence.

Of all the Bond novels, it is the first, *Casino Royale*, that draws most deeply on Ian's wartime experience for the chief reason that it was the novel he was dreaming about and was planning to write throughout the war. For example, it has been pointed out that Fleming had a wartime experience involving gambling at a casino in Estoril, Portugal, where he broke his plane journey to the United States with Admiral Godfrey. There are various different versions of this episode. The most dramatic was that Fleming observed a couple of Nazi officers at the casino table, decided to strike a blow for Britain against the German war effort, and so beat them at baccarat. The more likely version is that Fleming saw two Portuguese businessmen gambling and went up against them, losing his money. He then commented to Godfrey, "What if those men had been German secret service agents, and suppose we had cleaned them out of their money; now that would have been exciting."[27]

This scenario would provide the seed for the scene in *Casino* in which an enemy of Britain (an agent of SMERSH rather than the Nazis) organizes a high-stakes game of baccarat in an exclusive European casino, a game that he needs desperately to win, and Bond is pitted against him by the Secret Service. Bond—like Britain during the war—is also backed by the Americans, in the person of Felix Leiter from the Central Intelligence Agency (CIA). He is subsequently captured and tortured by the ruthless enemy in an attempt to extract information (as many British soldiers were by the Nazis). Though the novel is set during the Cold War, with the Soviets as chief adversary, it draws heavily on wartime experiences.

Other wartime experiences found their way into the pages of *Casino Royale*. While visiting William Stephenson at the British Security Co-ordination, run by Stephenson from the Rockefeller Center in New York, Fleming witnessed Stephenson travel down to a lower floor of the Rockefeller Center to steal the Japanese naval codebooks from a cipher clerk who was operating from the Japanese consulate. Fleming was clearly impressed by this feat of real-life espionage by the director, no less, of BSC. In *Casino*, Ian enhanced and sensationalized the event to describe how Bond got his first "kill"—two kills being necessary for 00 status: in the novel, Bond assassinates the cipher clerk from the facing building, with assistance from another shooter, who takes out the window before Bond makes the kill shot from his floor. As Bond tells Vesper, "I've got the corpses of a Japanese cipher expert in New York and a Norwegian double agent in Stockholm to thank for being a Double O." He explains the operation to Mathis in more detail, describing it as "a pretty sound job. Nice and clean too."[28]

Ian would write a foreword to the US edition of H. Montgomery Hyde's biography of Stephenson, in which he claimed that James Bond represented the fictional version of the spy, where Stephenson was the real thing, one of the greatest secret agents. The original typescript of the jacket copy of *The Quiet Canadian* stated, "It is no exaggeration to describe Sir William Stephenson as a real-life version of Ian Fleming's famous character of fiction, James Bond."[29] This episode gives an example of how Fleming added drama and violence to actual wartime events for fictional purposes. It also demonstrates that Stephenson, "Little Bill" (contrasted with "Big Bill" William Donovan), was one of the signal influences on the creation of Bond.

The wartime collaboration between Britain and the United States is again at the forefront in Ian's second novel, *Live and Let Die*. This novel begins in the United States, which Fleming visited several times with Admiral Godfrey and on his own, to coordinate with BSC and the Office of Strategic Services (OSS), forerunner of the CIA, headed by William Donovan. Stephenson's organization had some notable recruits, including Roald Dahl, the spy and later novelist who would also write the screenplay for the EON film of *You Only Live Twice*. Meanwhile, Ian's old school friend Ivar Bryce worked for both the BSC and the OSS running spy networks in Latin America. Bryce states, "By 1942 . . . I was a fully-fledged member of Donovan's organization, as well as Stephenson's. The OSS or Office of Strategic Services had taken shape with the presidential mandate of complete co-operation with Stephenson's far-flung secret force, the British Security Co-ordination."[30]

The ultimate purpose of BSC was to generate propaganda designed to influence American support of Britain and eventually to persuade the United States to join in the war. Despite the isolationist stance of many members of Congress, the "America Firsters," BSC was effective in securing American military support, warships, tanks, and so on, in exchange for ninety-nine-year leases on British bases in Canada and the Caribbean (the "lend-lease program"). One of the projects on which Bryce worked (he was an authority on South America and ran networks of agents there) was to create phony maps showing Nazi Germany's plans for South America if it won the war, which would significantly affect the United States as South American countries would become German colonies, as would Mexico.

Bryce planted one such map in a house in Cuba that was a contact point for U-boats in the area so that it would be discovered by the Federal Bureau of Investigation under J. Edgar Hoover, "a monster prize, something of transcendental importance that the Nazi agents would have no time to destroy." The plot required a convincing replica of the map, and "in forty-eight hours they produced a map, slightly travel-stained with use, but one which the Reich's chief map makers for the German High Command would be prepared to swear was made by them."[31] President Franklin D. Roosevelt then announced the discovery of the map, demonstrating the urgency of Americans entering the war.

Ian was involved in these propaganda efforts and helped with the setting-up of an American Secret Intelligence Service modeled on the British SIS. This began life as the Office of the Coordinator of Information, established by Roosevelt in 1941, replaced by the Office of Strategic Services, formed in 1942 under William Donovan. Following World War II, OSS was dissolved, and two years later, in 1947, the CIA was established. Donovan had visited Britain and reported favorably on the British resolve to win, in contrast to the negative appraisals of British resoluteness and probability of success delivered to Washington by United States ambassador Joseph Kennedy (father of John F. Kennedy and Robert F. Kennedy). After the war, the need for a peacetime intelligence agency was apparent, and the CIA was brought into existence.

Ian Fleming has long been credited with having written the blueprint of the OSS as early as 1940. As his first biographer, John Pearson, states, "Ian is exactly the man who could have written such a document[,] . . . one of the few people in Washington at this moment who could have written this."[32] According to Bryce, Ian was flown to Washington during the war and was locked in a room, where he wrote the blueprint for the American CIA: "The expert, immediately flown to Washington from Whitehall, was the personal aide of Admiral Sir John Godfrey, the Director of British Naval Intelligence. He was a comparatively young but exceptionally able officer, Lieutenant-Commander Ian Lancaster Fleming RNVR."[33] On his arrival in DC, according to Bryce, Fleming

> had been whisked off to a room in the new annexe of the Embassy, locked in it with a pen and paper and the necessities of life, and had written, under armed guard around the clock, a document of some seventy pages covering every aspect of a giant secret intelligence and secret operational organization. This was accompanied by a précis of the same. It was a detailed blue-print of the British service, using a century's experience of its aims, its methods, and its security. It was a *tour de force* of organizing and administrative ability, and demonstrated what I believe was Ian's greatest strength.[34]

Moreover, this blueprint, drawing on Ian's extensive experience of running agents in Europe during the war, "included a mass of practical detail on how much use could be made of diplomatic sources of intelligence, how agents could be run in the field."[35] As a reward for his help with drawing up the blueprint for the CIA, Donovan presented Fleming with a .38 Special Police Positive Colt revolver with an inscription: "For Special Services." Fleming would give a gun of this model to James Bond and refer to it again in *Thrilling Cities* when he describes how a woman in the Monte Carlo casino asks, "I suppose you've broken the bank. . . . Why don't you shoot out the lights with your .38 Police Positive?"[36] Clearly Donovan's gift of this gun made a deep impression in Fleming's memory.

Fleming's involvement with North American intelligence continued during his wartime visit to the famous Special Training Camp 103 (Camp X), a Special Operations Executive training facility set up by William Stephenson at the BSC. Located on the shores of Lake Ontario at Oshawa, Camp X has been described by Pearson as "the foremost training ground for sabotage and subversion in the New World." As well as providing preliminary training for SOE recruits, this facility aimed to produce highly skilled commandoes, saboteurs, and agents for the newly formed US Secret Service. Fleming was excited at the potential of this new training camp, having already dreamed up his 30AU commando unit. Pearson claims, "Fleming suggested that he spend a few days there as a trainee. It was to prove a formidable experience."[37] Officially, he was an observer of the training program, but according to Pearson he took part enthusiastically in some of the exercises and distinguished himself in the underwater mission, involving a long underwater swim to place limpet mines on the hull of an abandoned tanker on the lake. Such adventures would leave their mark on future Bond novels, such as *Live and Let Die*, where James Bond successfully places a limpet mine on the hull of Mr. Big's yacht, the *Secatur*.

These episodes at Camp X have become part of the Fleming wartime legend, establishing closer links of courageous action between Ian and Bond, his famous creation, by demonstrating that "once again [Ian] was living fiction."[38] Intriguingly, while in Toronto, Fleming stayed at a private home that was located opposite the Saint James-Bond United Church.[39] However, Pearson's claims have been met with skepticism by some historians. David Stafford, for example, believes "there are enough oddities and inconsistencies about the story to suggest that it is no more real than the cover invented by the average SOE agent working behind enemy lines." Stafford's chief "evidence" against Fleming's training at Camp X having taken place is that neither of the living commandants of the camp (who he interviewed) "has any recollection at all of Fleming having been there."[40] However, as Stafford himself points out, Fleming was not a famous author of spy novels at this time—the visit would have occurred in 1942 or 1943—but merely a visiting intelligence officer, of whom there were many at Camp X. Even if Fleming's outstanding achievements in the Camp X training exercises were exaggerated by Pearson, that does not prove that the visit never took place. Stafford also cites the official archivist for the SOE archive, who has been unable to locate any evidence to support the claim of Fleming's visit. However, it is entirely possible that Fleming's visit to Camp X was "off the record" and that there would be no official documentation of it. Indeed, Stafford admits, "I received considerable help from the current keeper of the SOE archive. But he, too, is bound by official policy and the SOE archive still remains a closed society."[41]

Perhaps the strongest evidence that Ian Fleming's visit to Camp X did take place is the testimony of William Stephenson, the man responsible for setting up Special Training School 103 (the official name for Camp X). Interviewed by John Pearson, Stephenson stated, "I sent Ian to our sabotage school in Canada in 1942. It was at Oshawa in Ontario, run by a man called Booker. . . . He was deeply affected by the whole thing and came through very well indeed." Stephenson also makes clear that Ian's experience at Camp X had an important impact on his later work: "Ian took extensive notes at the time and used a lot of what he learned there when he was setting up his own 30AU."[42]

Fleming was also successful, according to Pearson, in the small-arms training and distinguished himself in the agent initiative exercise, involving planting an imaginary bomb at several key locations in Toronto. Fleming, however, drew the line at shooting an "enemy agent" (actually one of the training staff at the camp) when this was assigned to test the potential recruit's ruthless killer instinct. Ian told Stephenson, somewhat shamefacedly, "You know . . . I just couldn't open that door. I couldn't kill a man that way."[43] For Ian, the violence and ability to kill in cold blood that characterized the successful secret agent would always remain a vicarious fantasy. In Stephenson's words, "You see, Ian had Bond always doing the kind of thing he would have loved to have done, but never quite could. You know, he hadn't the temperament."[44]

Such covert activities in North America demonstrate not only the close collaboration between British and American intelligence organizations during World War II but also Fleming's vital role in the formation of an American counterpart to SIS. Ian would no doubt have been treated like royalty—as Bond is when he arrives at Idlewild Airport at the beginning of *Live and Let Die*. Pearson notes that "when the British DNI and his personal assistant arrived in New York [Stephenson] was at their disposal with hospitality, advice and an office, complete with secretary, next door to his own."[45] This "hospitality" included putting Fleming up at the exclusive St. Regis Hotel, the "best hotel in New York," where Stephenson maintained his own suite while working at BSC. Bond also stays at the St. Regis, and, like Ian, was treated by his hosts as a trusted and valued ally.

Bond's chief CIA contact, Felix Leiter, is a compound of the various North American allies Fleming worked with, including Stephenson himself, and perhaps Donovan. "Leiter" was the name of the husband of a woman who had been a girlfriend of Ian's during World War II, Marion Oates (later Oates Leiter). But Felix was Ivar Bryce's middle name, and the friendship between Bond and Leiter mirrors that between Fleming and his old Eton school friend. Though British born, Bryce was Americanized in various ways, and in 1950 he married a wealthy American heiress, Josephine ("Jo") Hartford, the A&P heiress and one of the leading racehorse owners in the United States. Jo owned Black Hole Hollow Farm in Vermont, where the couple spent the summers and where Ian was a frequent visitor. With these various American influences, Bryce could plausibly "double" as an American CIA agent in Fleming's imagination, and it explains the close bond between Bond and Leiter that always seems to run deep.

Published the year after *Casino*, *Live and Let Die* also draws extensively on Ian's wartime experiences in the United States. The plot involves the smuggled gold doubloons from Captain Morgan's treasure, which Mr. Big is using to finance SMERSH operations in the United States via his network of

Black workers whom he controls with "voodoo"—details of which Ian gleaned from his friend Patrick Leigh Fermor's *The Travelers Tree*, a source from which he quotes extensively in the novel. But the idea of illicit gold hoards also connects to the Nazi gold (*Raubgold*), gold looted from the annexed or occupied countries (such as Austria and Czechoslovakia) as well as from victims of the Third Reich (including Jews and others in concentration camps). This stolen gold was then sent to overseas depositories and used to finance the war against the Allies. The reliance of Bond villains such as Mr. Big and Goldfinger on stolen gold to fund SMERSH operations revisits how the Nazis used *Raubgold* to bolster their gold reserves and supply their military forces.

During his wartime visits to the United States, Fleming enjoyed a standard of luxury not available in ration-afflicted Britain. This is also the case for Bond during his Cold War missions, financed in part by American assets. While Felix Leiter is not personally wealthy, he has the vast resources of the CIA at his disposal, illustrated by the thirty-two million francs of "Marshall Aid" that Bond uses to defeat Le Chiffre at baccarat.[46] In *Live and Let Die*, the CIA provides the "royal treatment" of specially expedited customs and immigration processing, a room at the St. Regis Hotel, and a thousand dollars of spending money. Fleming's opening to the novel captures the sense of indulgence and privilege he himself enjoyed in New York:

> There are moments of great luxury in the life of a secret agent. There are assignments on which he is required to act the part of a very rich man; occasions when he takes refuge in good living to efface the memory of danger and the shadow of death; and times when, as was now the case, he is a guest in the territory of an allied Secret Service.[47]

Important as the Anglo-American alliance was during and after World War II, it is in the pages of Ian's most "European" Bond novels—*Casino* and *From Russia, with Love*—that we find the deepest imprint of his wartime experience in Naval Intelligence. The NID's obsession with obtaining a German Enigma cipher machine and its codebooks found expression in the plot of *From Russia, with Love*, in which the Nazi Enigma machine is transposed into the Soviet Spektor machine. So desperate is the British SIS to obtain this machine that M is willing to risk sending Bond into a SMERSH trap. Just as the Enigma machine and its codebook, when captured, enabled the codebreakers at Bletchley to decrypt secret Nazi messages identifying positions of U-boats and plans to intercept and destroy British naval and mercantile traffic in the English Channel and Atlantic, so the theft of the Spektor machine would allow the British to decrypt Soviet top-secret messages. Fleming's language reveals the obsession M has with this machine and his wish to believe that the defection of Tatiana Romanova is genuine: "If she could come over to us she would bring her cipher machine with her. It's the brand new Spektor machine. The thing we'd give our eyes to have." Bond, no less than M, recognizes the vital importance of this machine in the Cold War struggle: "The Spektor! The machine that would allow them to decipher the Top Secret traffic of all. To have that . . . would be a priceless victory. . . . In the Russian secret service, loss of the Spektor would be counted a major disaster."[48]

Though M calls this machine "brand new," it actually isn't—rather, it's a recycled version of the World War II Enigma machine sought after by Fleming and NID. An added incentive for the SIS to get hold of this machine is that it would give the British an advantage over the Americans—hence the "priceless victory" it offers is not only over SMERSH but also over the CIA. Since World War II, Britain had been playing second fiddle to the Americans in the Cold War conflict and had depended on the United States for much of its vital intelligence. Despite the fact that the OSS and CIA had been based on British precursors, US Intelligence had gradually gained ascendancy in the West. George Blake, the notorious Soviet double agent, aptly expressed the role reversal between the allied intelligence services:

> It is true that SIS, with its historic reputation and long experience, had been called in to act as midwife at the birth of the CIA in the years immediately after the war when the USA had felt the need for a permanent intelligence service. . . . But soon the young stripling had outgrown its mentor and, with rather greater resources in money and manpower, had become the senior partner.[49]

Of course, Fleming sometimes undermines the "myth" of British superiority in intelligence matters—the very myth that he had helped create with deception operations during the war. The purpose of such deceptions was not only to fool the enemy about the Allied plans of invasion or attack but also to convince them that the Allies (especially British) were better prepared, more fully equipped, and more effective than was actually the case.

SMERSH assassin Donovan Grant in *From Russia, with Love* is a half German, half Irish soldier in the British army, who switches sides to the Soviet Union because they provide a better outlet for his murderous instincts.

This merger of interests between Germany and the Soviet Union—a reflection of the pact between Hitler and Stalin—is a theme in several of the Bond novels. It also features in the third novel, *Moonraker*, where the villain, Graf Hugo von der Drache (aka Sir Hugo Drax) is a former Nazi who now serves as an agent of SMERSH. While von der Drache's vengeance against Britain is motivated by hatred for Germany's victorious enemy in the war, his planned act of destruction—sending an atomic rocket into the heart of London—is sponsored and financed by the "new enemy," the Soviet Union. Ian had the imaginative foresight to fuse together the anti-German phobias from the war with the continuing menace of Communist Russia.

Was Fleming motivated to write Bond's adventures in part because his own intelligence experience had largely lacked the action, excitement, and adventure that he fantasized? In the notes of his interview with Admiral John Godfrey, John Pearson speculates, "Is it possible that Bond is the supreme man of action because F. was nothing of the sort?"[50] While Fleming was too preoccupied with the demands of running Room 39 to have experienced much boredom, there may be some validity to the idea that Bond was "compensation" for Fleming's removal from the battlefield, his protection from the action of war. With this in mind, we should not expect to find exact correlations between Fleming's wartime experiences and the episodes of the Bond novels. Rather, his time in naval intelligence planted the seeds that grew in Fleming's mind until they bore fruit in Bond's memorable adventures.

How are we to assess most productively the importance of Fleming's work in Naval Intelligence as a source and inspiration for his James Bond novels? In his naval memoirs, Godfrey makes an interesting distinction between "truth," "reality," and "publicity" in intelligence matters: "'Truth' therefore means what NID thought was the truth. 'Reality' is what actually happened, undiscoverable in its entirety until we had access to German records after the war. 'Publicity' is what the world, the country, the Navy and Admiralty departments were told at the time."[51] This distinction helps us understand the influence of Fleming's naval intelligence work on his Bond novels. In his books, Fleming writes the "truth" of intelligence work as he sees it, with certain elaborations and exaggerations, but the "reality" of what actually happened may never have been known, even to Fleming himself. Equally, Fleming's novels served as a crucial form of "publicity" in presenting to the world certain myths about the excellence of British intelligence organizations, both during and after the war. Self-evidently, there is an element of propaganda in this publicity function due to the distortions and elaborations Fleming deploys in writing Bond's adventures. Operational failures in real life become successes in fiction; the mundane operation is transformed, in Fleming's imagination, into the thrilling mission.

Ian's postwar nostalgia for his role in NID should also not be overlooked as an influence on his fiction. His war years in Naval Intelligence were clearly an intensely absorbing experience, giving Fleming a sense of purpose and excitement. Ian's friend and lover Maud Russell frequently observes in her wartime diary how engrossed Ian is in his intelligence work: at one meeting in October 1939, Russell recounts that Ian is "so absorbed in and fascinated by his work [in NID] that he can barely detach his mind from it." In November 1940, she notes, "I[an] has been on some dangerous job again. He cannot ever tell me what they are."[52] The secrecy and potential danger of intelligence work were addictive to a temperament such as Ian's. Even the Bond villains evoke a certain nostalgia for the clarity of wartime hostilities, when the whole country, indeed the entire Allied forces, knew who the enemy was. Fleming still exploits the anxiety and fear about Nazi Germany from World War II—for example, Le Chiffre having been found in the Dachau concentration camp in Germany. Though his precise ethnic origins are unknown, he is a living symptom of wartime trauma.

Fleming's nostalgia for the war is most apparent in his naming of his Jamaican winter home after one of his most important wartime operations. Fleming was able to realize his dream of living in Jamaica thanks to the generosity of Maud Russell, who gave Ian the £2,000 needed to buy the land and the £3,000 required to construct the house.[53] He had considered naming the house Shame Lady after an indigenous plant that grew in the garden but eventually settled on Goldeneye. Because all the James Bond novels were written at Goldeneye, Bond is indelibly linked to Fleming's wartime espionage and sabotage work.

Goldeneye—the most ambitious and far-reaching operation that Ian planned while working in Naval Intelligence—was a complex project involving cooperation between the various branches of armed services and between international forces including Britain, Spain, and the United States. Goldeneye was primarily devised as a precaution against the German invasion of Spain and the strong possibility that the Axis powers would gain control of the Iberian Peninsula. Although Franco's Spain was officially neutral in the war, its sympathies apparently lay with Germany, and Spain was under increasing pressure to join the Axis powers. This would, of course, have threatened the British territory of Gibraltar, and Fleming's plan for Goldeneye was designed to protect Gibraltar from Nazi control. Fleming was particularly concerned about Axis radar installations being placed in the Strait of Gibraltar, the narrow passage between Spain and North Africa, thus threatening Allied naval strategy and shipping interests in the Mediterranean.

Orchestrated by the British naval attaché in Madrid, Alan Hillgarth, Goldeneye also involved plans for sabotage of Spanish ports and naval installations should a German invasion take place. While visiting Gibraltar in February 1941, primarily to establish a secure cipher connection between Gibraltar and London—specifically with the Operation Goldeneye liaison office—Fleming also met with William Donovan of the Office of Coordinator of Information (the precursor of the Office of Strategic Services) to discuss coordination on Goldeneye with American intelligence. Fleming subsequently suggested that an Anglo-American intelligence committee be set up to coordinate intelligence gathering from the Iberian Peninsula.

Goldeneye was on high alert during the buildup to Operation Torch, the planned Allied invasion of North Africa. However, the original ambitious plans for Goldeneye had to be modified due to lack of resources, as revealed in "Progress Report on Goldeneye" from April 30, 1941, which stated that "two Sub-Lieuts. RNVR have arrived from UK and four more are to follow. No further [naval] personnel can be sent from U.K." This shortfall of manpower meant that several important Spanish ports, including Barcelona and Valencia, had to be removed from the list of sabotage targets in the event of German invasion. However, the report also noted that "a conference was held at Government House on 8 April with the object of giving the Foreign Secretary and CIGS the latest information regarding the situation in Spain and Spanish Morocco and Goldeneye."[54] The presence of the foreign secretary—at the time Anthony Eden, the future prime minister—at the meeting demonstrates that the knowledge and management of Goldeneye went to the highest levels of British government.[55]

The high international importance of Goldeneye suggests why Fleming chose the name of this operation for his postwar Jamaica home. In the event, the German invasion of the Soviet Union in June 1941 (Operation Barbarossa) led to a change of priorities by the Axis powers. With so many forces taken up by the Soviet invasion—especially with the Germans' failure to capture Moscow in the fall of 1941—Operation Felix, the Axis plan to invade and capture Gibraltar, was abandoned. Moreover, Admiral Canaris—the head of the Abwehr—had been conspiring to convince General Franco not to enter the war on the Axis side. Consequently, the German invasion of Spain did not take place, and Operation Goldeneye was shelved in 1943. Like other ambitious operations Ian conceived while in NID—such as Ruthless—Goldeneye was an elaborate plan that was never actually put into action. Yet, it planted more seeds of ideas for plots that would come to fruition with the adventures of James Bond ten years later.

The case of Operation Goldeneye is an excellent example of how the general outlines and objectives of Naval Intelligence operations, rather than the specific details and locations, informed Fleming's fiction. None of the Bond novels is set on Gibraltar, and the Iberian Peninsula is generally a neglected locale in Fleming's fiction despite its vital strategic importance during World War II.[56] Yet, some of Fleming's best fiction incorporates aspects of Goldeneye, notably "Tracer"—the plan to install a stay-behind surveillance and espionage unit inside the Rock of Gibraltar in the event of a German invasion. The preparations included building a "hide," a secret compartment within the Rock of Gibraltar, with observation slits on the east and west sides allowing surveillance of both the Straits of Gibraltar and the Mediterranean. A group of men were trained as stay-behind agents, a water tank was installed to allow them to survive "underground" for up to a year, and other preparations were made for an extended stay.[57]

In the story "From a View to a Kill," James Bond discovers a Soviet "stay-behind" spy unit in the Bois de Boulogne after they ambush and kill several SHAPE (Supreme Headquarters Allied Powers Europe) motorcycle couriers and steal their classified documents. The elaborate preparations made for this concealed espionage unit resemble Tracer: the agents are hidden underground, in a clearing in the woods, concealed by a rose bush that opens mechanically to let the spies and their motorbike in and out.

Goldeneye leaves its mark in other ways on Fleming's fiction. One of the most innovative aspects of the Bond novels is their demonstration of the interdepartmental collaboration between SIS and other intelligence, security, and government organizations. Not only does M report directly to the prime minister, but also Bond collaborates with "sister" organizations such as MI5 and Scotland Yard (notably in *Moonraker* and *Diamonds Are Forever*). He also cooperates with the College of Arms in *On Her Majesty's Secret Service*—although this is not a government agency, its chief, Sable Basilisk, is eager to assist with secret operations and assures Bond, "I did my national service with Intelligence in BAOR [British Army of the Rhine], so please don't worry about security." As Sable Basilisk goes on to advise Bond, "we have in this building probably as many secrets as a government department—and nastier ones at that."[58] In other words, the College of Arms is the civilian equivalent of a secret intelligence agency, which is why Bond can count on their discretion and is able to adopt the persona of Sir Hilary Bray so easily.

Bond also works closely with the intelligence organizations of other countries, including France (René Mathis of the Deuxième Bureau), the United States (Felix Leiter of the CIA), and Japan (Tiger Tanaka of the Japanese Secret Service). The importance of international collaboration for Bond's success reflects the coordination of intelligence gathering between allied nations during Goldeneye and indeed throughout the war. This interdependence of intelligence agencies certainly counters the myth that James Bond is a lone wolf, a solo agent who is always reluctant to share missions or intelligence. The image of a solitary agent, emotionally detached or withdrawn, who is unable or unwilling to cooperate with others, is part of the Bond mythology in need of debunking. For despite Bond's imaginative origins in 30AU—a group force if ever there was one—he is often portrayed as an asocial solo killer. Even Dame Stella Rimington, former head of MI5, declared that Bond "is no more than a licensed killer with no mission but to destroy."[59]

In fact, the missions where Bond is required to work alone are the ones he is most unhappy about, precisely because it casts him in the unwanted role of assassin. These occur in short stories such as "For Your Eyes Only" and "The Living Daylights," in which Bond is sent by M on a solo mission to kill an enemy. As Bond reflects in "For Your Eyes Only," he is sent to carry out "the revenge of the community," and Bond refers to such missions based on revenge or necessity as "rough justice" or, more cynically, in "Octopussy," as "dirty work."[60]

In most cases, Ian goes to great lengths in his fiction to show the interdependency of the various intelligence organizations as well as the heavy reliance of SIS headquarters on the station chiefs around the world. These include essential agents such as John Strangways—head of Station J in Jamaica, who appears in *Live and Let Die* and *Dr. No*—and "Darko" Kerim Bey, head of Station T in Istanbul, who orchestrates the delivery of the Spektor machine by Tatiana Romanova. Without the contributions of such vital agents based overseas—M refers to Kerim as "one of the best men we've got anywhere"—Bond's missions would never get off the ground.[61]

Much of the effort Ian devoted to Goldeneye and other operations during the war was spent on building relationships and coordinating with foreign intelligence organizations, especially with William Stephenson's BSC in New York and William Donovan's OSS in Washington, DC. In fact, it was for just such skills at liaising and network building that Godfrey chose Ian as his assistant. Despite his headstrong personality, Ian was recognized as a master of collaboration and compromise. Therefore, from the very first novel, Bond is shown to be plugged in to a network of intelligence agents, even though he is *primus inter pares*. In *Casino Royale*, Bond's access to essential information about Le Chiffre relies on "material made available by Deuxième Bureau and C.I.A. Washington."[62]

Moreover, Gibraltar—the protection of which was the objective of Goldeneye—represents the kind of threatened, embattled British enclave or possession (during a period of imperial decline) that Fleming frequently uses as settings in his novels. In fact, there is evidence that Fleming envisioned Bond's role as launching a rearguard action to shore up Britain's shrinking empire. In *Thrilling Cities*—the travelogue based on travels that Fleming made in 1959–1960 for *The Sunday Times* and published in 1963—Fleming lamented that "it was a source of constant depression to observe how little of our own influence was left in that great half of the world where we did so much of the pioneering." Fleming notes that "American culture, communications and trade have almost a monopoly" in Japan, and, in *You Only Live Twice*, published the year after *Thrilling Cities*, Bond is sent to Japan to convince a reluctant Tiger Tanaka, head of Japan's secret service, to share a vital intelligence stream about Soviet nuclear preparations, known as "MAGIC 44."[63] This devastating intelligence also shows the fragility of the Anglo-American alliance that Fleming had worked so hard to develop during World War II: "It would probably destroy the Anglo-American alliance since it can be assumed that America will not risk a nuclear war involving her territory for the sake of rescuing a now more or less valueless ally."[64] The intelligence sharing and cooperation that characterized the Western Allies against the Axis powers (including Japan) during the war has collapsed and been replaced by competition, distrust, and rivalry.

Bond therefore forges new alliances with Britain's and America's former World War II enemy, Japan, to counter this shortfall of intelligence from the United States. However, Japan—represented by Tiger—will demand a heavy price for British access to MAGIC 44. And Bond's new friend and ally Tiger tells him some painful home truths about British postwar decline, reproaching Bond—and Britain—with his unflinching assessment: "You have not only lost a great Empire, you have seemed almost anxious to throw it away with both hands. . . . When you apparently sought to arrest this slide into impotence at Suez, you succeeded only in stage-managing one of the most pitiful bungles in the history of the world."[65]

If Tiger's views of modern Britain are reactionary, Bond's defense of his nation is nostalgic for the nation's victories in World War II. He blames Britain's current malaise on the fact that the country has "been bled pretty thin by a couple of World Wars" but reminds him, "We still climb Everest and beat plenty of the world at plenty of sports and win Nobel prizes."[66] Yet, as Bond well knows, this is empty rhetoric because all the trump cards are in Tiger's hand. Eventually Bond's defense of his country's pride and reputation must take the form of personal risk and direct action. The price Bond will have to pay for sustained access to the vital intelligence source is to assassinate a foreign resident, known as Dr. Guntrum Shatterhand, who has created a "garden of death" at his Japanese castle.

By naming his Jamaica home—and the birthplace of James Bond—after a major wartime operation, Fleming created a symbolic monument to the wartime alliances and intelligence agencies of Britain and the United States. Fleming was certainly aware of the symbolism of Gibraltar as one of the few pieces of the British Empire remaining, and naming his home Goldeneye made a statement about the British possession of Jamaica.[67] Goldeneye represents a paradoxical combination of vulnerability—Gibraltar as a potentially isolated target of Axis hostility—and fortitude, part of British resilience in the face of a powerful and potentially deadly enemy. Although the planned efforts to rescue Gibraltar from the Nazis were never executed, the idea behind this mission was planted in Fleming's imagination, and Bond's role as the representative of these qualities of courage and determination is key to the success of the novels.

M's memorable "obituary" of Bond in *You Only Live Twice*, which pays homage to Bond's "outstanding services to his country," casts doubt on the reliability of Ian's novels as a credible account of actual wartime espionage. M laments that "a series of popular books came to be written around him by a personal friend and former colleague of James Bond. If the quality of these books, or their degree of veracity, had been any higher, the author would certainly have been prosecuted under the Official Secrets Act." Yet, on the other hand, what better smokescreen for Fleming than to dismiss his own novels in this way as "romanticized caricatures of episodes in the career of an outstanding public servant."[68] Due to Fleming's deliberately making Bond's adventures seem farfetched and romanticized, few readers would suspect that what they were reading was based on actual intelligence operations from World War II. Fleming's friends, as Christopher Moran and Trevor McCrisken note, "mockingly . . . accused him of sitting behind a desk all day, concocting fanciful ploys to stick it to Hitler that were immediately dismissed by his exasperated superiors . . . a pen-pusher."[69] This was far from being the truth.

Yet, Ian did at times grow frustrated by the bureaucratic burden of his job in Naval Intelligence. He sometimes felt that the thick of the action was taking place somewhere else. Maud Russell writes in her diary for November 27, 1941:

> He is beginning to want a more active life than he gets at DNI though he is lucky enough to move about quite a lot. He wanted to know what I thought about him resigning and going to King Alfred's Training Ship and getting a MTB [Motor Torpedo Boat used by the Royal Navy during the Second World War]. I said I didn't think he would get much excitement there. . . . I daresay he is more useful where he is.[70]

This was the irritating refrain Ian had grown used to—he was more *useful*, his talents better adapted, as an administrator than he would be in more active service. Godfrey's prohibition against Ian joining the crew disguised as German airmen in Ruthless may serve as an example of the limitations placed on him. Yet, he longed to experience more action and excitement during wartime. Even William Stephenson recalled, "Of course, it troubled him that he saw no action in the war, but I doubt if he'd have been very good in action."[71] His creation of James Bond was in part a response to these frustrations of wartime bureaucratic responsibility.

Another important wartime operation in which Fleming was involved, Operation Mincemeat, marks the pinnacle of what Nicholas Rankin has termed the British "genius for deception." The actual operation was launched by a piece of writing called the "Trout memo," which was issued by the NID and distributed to the chiefs of wartime intelligence on September 29, 1939, at the beginning of the war. Though it officially came from Godfrey, the Trout memo was likely written by Fleming: as Ben Macintyre remarks, "it bore all the hallmarks of his personal assistant, Lieutenant Commander Ian Fleming. . . . The ideas were extraordinarily imaginative and, like most of Fleming's writing, barely credible."[72]

One of the proposals in this memo was based on an idea from a detective novel by Basil Thomson, called *The Milliner's Hat Mystery* (published in 1937). The novel's detective, Inspector Richardson, discovers that every document in the pockets of a dead man found in a barn has been forged using a special ink. This seed of creating a "new" and false identity for a dead man planted itself in Fleming's imagination, and the eventual harvest was Operation Mincemeat. While the details of this operation have been related numerous times, the extent of its impact on Fleming's work as a novelist has not been adequately discussed.[73]

The objective of Mincemeat was to disguise the 1943 Allied invasion of Sicily by convincing the Germans that Britain and its allies planned to invade Greece and Sardinia rather than the actual target. In order to deceive the enemy about the planned invasion target, the body of a deceased vagrant—Glyndwr Michael—was obtained and dressed in the uniform of a Royal Marines captain. A false identity was created for this corpse—namely, Captain William Martin of the Royal Marines—with documents and identification papers placed on him that "proved" this identity. For all intents and purposes, the orchestrators of the operation—Ewen Montagu and Charles Cholmondeley —had created an elaborate fictional character for the purpose of wartime deception:

> Hour after hour they discussed and refined this imaginary person, his likes and dislikes, his habits and hobbies, his talents and weaknesses. In the evening, they repaired to the Gargoyle Club, a glamorous Soho dive of which Montagu was a member, to continue the odd process of creating a man from scratch.[74]

Previous experience had demonstrated to Naval Intelligence and Fleming that secret papers obtained by the Spanish would duly be passed on to the Germans, despite Spain's official neutrality. As Charles Morgan wrote,

> Shortly before the launching of Torch, a Catalina had crashed off Spain. A body had been washed ashore and we knew that the papers on the body had reached the Germans. This suggested that the Spanish could be relied on to pass on what they found, and that this unneutral habit might be turned to account.[75]

The body of "Captain William Martin" was released from a submarine (rather than being dropped from a plane as originally planned) near the Spanish coast and picked up by Spanish fishermen at Huelva, on the southern coast. The body of "Martin" had a briefcase attached to it containing documents—correspondence between British generals suggesting that the Allies planned to invade Greece and Sardinia—designed to deceive the Germans. The plot relied, of course, on the corpse—more specifically, the contents of the briefcase—washing up on the Spanish coast (rather than drifting out to sea) and being passed on to the Germans. These hoped-for outcomes duly occurred. The identity of Martin was solidified by "pocket litter" such as a letter from Martin's fiancée and a photograph of the invented fiancée, Pam (actually an SIS clerk, Jean Leslie). Charles Morgan concluded that Mincemeat "is a small classic of Deception, brilliantly elaborate in detail, completely successful in operation."[76]

In effect, the creation of Captain William Martin was not just an elaborate subterfuge but a brilliant piece of imaginative fiction, perhaps only surpassed in wartime by the "Garbo Network"—the plethora of imaginary Abwehr agents invented by Spaniard Juan Pujol García and his MI5 case officer Tomás Harris to deceive the Nazis about the target of the D-Day landings. Not only was Fleming behind the stroke of creative genius that led to Mincemeat, but the lessons learned from it also left a deep imprint in his imagination. The obsessiveness with which Montagu and Cholmondeley invested "Martin" with various habits, tastes, and attributes is very similar to how a novelist constructs a character out of such materials.

The same techniques also shaped the creation of James Bond, who—like Captain Martin—was a fictional character constructed from diverse materials and might also be described as a "man who never was." There have been various ingenious attempts to identify James Bond with one particular original—whether Dusko Popov, the Serbian double agent who played a vital role in the "Double Cross" system of World War II; or Sidney Reilly, the "Ace of Spies" from World War I; or BSC chief William Stephenson; or indeed Gustav (Gus) March-Phillips, the Dorset-based SOE agent. But, ultimately, Bond cannot be traced back to a single person because Bond was (and is) a fictional composite (like Martin) pieced together from various sources, real and imagined, in the workshop of Fleming's inventive brain.

Fleming's fantasy life was always highly active. As Mark Simmons writes, "Vice Admiral Norman Dening, who worked with Fleming at the time, felt a lot of his ideas 'were just plain crazy' yet '. . . a lot of his far-fetched ideas had just the glimmer of possibility in them.'"[77] As a novelist, Ian tried repeatedly to alert his reader to this fantasy basis of Bond, reminding us that our "hero" is merely a figment of Fleming's—and our own—imagination. For example, Donovan Grant (the SMERSH assassin) taunts

Bond with his fabricated identity on board the *Orient Express*: "You see, old man, you're not so good as you think. You're just a stuffed dummy and I've been given the job of letting the sawdust out of you."[78] Interestingly, Grant's view echoes Fleming's own opinions about James Bond around the time of *From Russia, with Love*. He wrote to his reader at Jonathan Cape, William Plomer, who had worked in NID during the war as editor of the *Weekly Intelligence Report*, "My greatest fear is staleness. It is so difficult to communicate zest if it isn't there, and though I still enjoy writing about Bond, I constantly find myself piling on adjectives . . . to fill the vacuum created by my waning enthusiasm for this cardboard booby."[79]

If Bond can be considered Fleming's version of "the man who never was," it should not surprise us to find so many strands of wartime deception, disguise, and intrigue woven throughout the novels. Notably, in *Moonraker*, Bond assumes the role of a security expert from the Ministry of Supply to replace the murdered Major Tallon at the rocket base run by the Nazi Hugo Drax. Bond fits the necessary requirements of the job description, several of which echo the prescription for participants in Operation Ruthless: "must be bilingual in German, a sabotage expert, and have had plenty of experience of our Russian friends."[80] Whereas, in Operation Mincemeat, the fictional identity of Captain William Martin was superimposed on a dead body (Glyndwr Michael), in Ian's novel Bond is sent to take the place of a dead man. The evidence is that Bond's identity is fluid, malleable, and interchangeable with a range of different characters.

Bond's most elaborate disguise is that of Sir Hilary Bray, an employee of the College of Arms, in *On Her Majesty's Secret Service*. Fleming filched Bray's name from his Old Etonian friend, who also worked for Rowe & Pitman after the war and spent time with the Flemings at Goldeneye in Jamaica.[81] In the novel, Bray's wartime background also overlaps with Bond's in significant ways, as "this man's got a good war record and sounds a reliable sort of chap. He lives in some remote glen in the Highlands, watching birds and climbing the hills." Bray's war record, interest in birds, and Scottish background all parallel Bond's. Bond explains the plan simply to M: "The idea is that I should be him. Rather fancy cover, but I think it makes sense." Where the William Martin fake identity was designed to deceive the Germans about the intended target of the Allied invasion of Europe, Bond's disguise as Bray is planned to mislead Blofeld about Bond's true mission: "If Blofeld takes the bait, I go out to Switzerland" in order to "get him over the frontier to somewhere where we can do a kidnap job on him," in a kind of reverse version of the Venlo incident of November 1939 in which two British SIS agents were lured over the Dutch border and captured by the Abwehr.[82]

Unsurprisingly, while disguised as Bray, Bond continues his 007 habits of smoking, drinking, and seducing young female patients at Blofeld's clinic. However, Bond's reckless sexual exploits do jeopardize his cover identity, and it is only a matter of time before Blofeld smells a rat, asking Bond point-blank: "I suppose you would not be connected in any way with the British Secret Service, Sir Hilary?" In self-defense, Bond plays up the theatrical disguises conventionally associated with intelligence work: "Can't quite see myself running about behind a false moustache. Not my line of country at all."[83] Blofeld's suspicions lead Bond to believe his cover has been blown and to engineer his escape from Piz Gloria.

Bond is also troubled by his betrayal of a fellow agent, Shaun Campbell, who, having been captured by Blofeld, recognizes Bond at Piz Gloria and asks for his help while in Blofeld's presence. Like an inmate of a prisoner-of-war camp in World War II, Bond saves his own skin at the expense of his colleague: "There had been no alternative except to throw him to the wolves." Indeed, there are resemblances between Piz Gloria and a high-security Axis prisoner-of-war camp such as Colditz Castle, especially the difficulty of escaping from the "prison." Ruby asks Bray/Bond, "How *are* you going to get away? You know we're practically prisoners up here." Beneath the benign appearance of the "clinic," Piz Gloria is a guardhouse where unwitting "patients" are confined along with foreign agents such as Bond. Bond is constantly under surveillance by Blofeld and Irma Bunt and meanwhile even makes secret notes in his passport about the true identities of the female patients at Blofeld's clinic.[84]

Fleming plants an intriguing clue about the influence of Operation Mincemeat on Operation Bedlam and the plot of *On Her Majesty's Secret Service*. During Bond's escape from Piz Gloria, he is pursued by Blofeld's men on skis, and they approach a snow fan clearing newly fallen snow. This curiously pure image of snow is soon destroyed by the gruesome fate of one of Bond's pursuers: "God! The man had tried to follow him, had been too late or had missed his jump, and had been caught by the murderous blades of the snow-fan! Mincemeat!"[85] The word *mincemeat* is unnecessary for the meaning of the scene—Fleming has made clear the horrible fate of Blofeld's henchman—but it functions as a code for the influence of the wartime operation on the novel.

Some of the most compelling evidence of the influence of Mincemeat on the Bond novels appears in *You Only Live Twice*. Chapter 20 ends with Bond, having killed Blofeld and escaped his castle in a hot-air balloon, in freefall, "plummet[ing] down toward peace, toward the rippling feathers of some childhood dream of softness and escape from pain."[86] *The Times* "obituary" by M that begins chapter 21 seems to confirm that Bond has been killed in the fall. Yet, having been fooled by Fleming before—most notably with Bond's apparent demise at the end of *From Russia, with Love*—the skeptical reader might consider it is quite possible that M's obituary is itself a piece of deception designed to convince Bond's enemies that he is dead in order to protect him and make him more effective as an agent. There is no indication—outside of the text of the obituary itself—whether M truly believes Bond is dead or alive or how he feels about it.

In fact, as we learn in the following chapter, Bond is still alive, having been saved from drowning by Kissy Suzuki. The loss of his memory resulting from the fall from the sky means that in one sense he has "died"—at least as Commander James Bond. He has become—perhaps permanently—"Taro Todoroki," a Japanese fisherman and Kissy's lover. She is advised by the doctor that "it may be months even years before he regains his memory."[87] This is trauma-induced amnesia, not a deliberate cover, but it serves its purpose just as well.

M's deception plot, like Operation Mincemeat, is designed to blur the lines between fact and fiction, between life and death. Yet, it has the opposite goal to Mincemeat: its purpose being to convince the enemy not that a dead man is someone else but that a living man—a naval commander and British spy—is actually dead and no longer of any importance. It allows Bond the opportunity to live in the obscurity and oblivion he has sought since the death of his wife, Tracy. Yet, the construction of an elaborate deception to mislead the enemy is common to both operations.

Lewis Gilbert's EON Productions' 1967 film of *You Only Live Twice* is more direct about the faking of Bond's death as a smokescreen for further operations. The film opens with Bond's apparent assassination by enemy agents in Hong Kong, and we then witness his corpse, wrapped in a canvas shroud, being buried at sea. The newspaper headline, shown next to an observer of the scene, confirms "British Naval Commander Murdered," and the naval funeral adds authenticity to this printed "fact." But then we see two Royal Navy frogmen "rescue" Bond's corpse from the seabed and carry him to a British submarine, where the canvas wrappings are removed and Bond returns to life. Bond's meeting with M on the submarine confirms that the purpose of arranging Bond's "death" was a deception: "Now some people will pay less attention to you," M advises.[88] What was implicit in the novel is made explicit in the film.

These examples illustrate the pervasive importance of deception, the creation of false identities, and faking death to various of Bond's adventures. Though these deception plots were based on Fleming's wartime operations, there is no evidence that Fleming himself used disguises or false identities while in NID. However, Godfrey's memoirs indicate that he and his assistant certainly liked to travel incognito, under a shroud of secrecy. When, on occasion, their cover was blown, the two men were highly discomfited. For example, on a trip to the United States in 1941, Fleming and Godfrey were on the same flight as Elsa Schiaparelli, the Italian fashion designer. Godfrey recounts:

> Our mission was supposed to be highly secret as the United States was still technically neutral. . . . Anyhow, Ian and I were in plain clothes travelling as Mr Godfrey and Mr Fleming and being careful to avoid all contact with the press. Walking down the gangway on arrival at La Guardia airport, New York, we became conscious of a battery of cameras aimed in our direction and realized that the target was Mme. Schiaparelli. . . . It was too late to do anything about it and whether we liked it or not the cameras and press depicted us in close attendance on this distinguished lady.[89]

This amusing anecdote is a reminder of the high stakes involved in Godfrey and Fleming's travels to the United States as well as the importance of being undercover on their missions. If it seems more akin to the satirical tone of Graham Greene's *Our Man in Havana* than *On Her Majesty's Secret Service*, it does show many of Fleming's trips abroad during World War II were sub rosa.[90] The parallels reveal that the kinds of elaborate deception, disguise, and identity theft proposed in the Trout memo and executed in Mincemeat were the very materials Fleming drew on for his novels.

Fleming's friend Robert Harling wrote that, even during the war, "Fleming was at that time, I sometimes think, his own brand-image for the later Bond."[91] Ian, like his fictional creation, was also a master of deception in NID, as Harling recalls his various roles as liaison with other departments: "Fleming was the admirals' link with an appalling range of activities inseparable from modern war: from the cracking of codes to the practice of deception."[92] Godfrey warns, in his memoirs, that deception is a double-edged sword that ends up damaging its perpetrators: "Deception plans and propaganda have sometimes deceived their initiators and have a way of coming back at one, through agents, prisoners of war, refugees, neutral capitals and foreign attachés, in a form that gives them the appearance of truth." The ultimate example of this "reversal" of deception was the double-cross system in which German undercover agents in Britain were turned by MI5 against the Nazis and used to feed them misinformation. Godfrey also suggested that it is sometimes necessary to deceive even those on one's "own side"—especially those in positions of power—noting that Fleming "learnt, perhaps sooner than I, that intelligence may be a sticky commodity which sometimes needs sugar coating and that the purveyor of bad tidings is unwelcome."[93]

Some of Ian's novels illustrate this crucial point that the instigators of "deception plans" may themselves fall into the trap of mistaking "the appearance of truth" for "reality." Deception plans are, by their very nature, opportunistic and improvisational. Operation Mincemeat was brought to life by the discovery that the Spanish authorities had previously passed the dead bodies from a crashed British Catalina seaplane, discovered off the coast of Cadiz, to the Nazis. The Allies' main fear was that the Germans would discover a letter in one of the victims' pockets, containing evidence of the Allies' invasion plans of North Africa, Operation Torch. Although the letter had not been discovered, the fact of the evidence being passed to the Germans provided inspiration the British needed for Mincemeat.[94]

As many studies of World War II deception have revealed, for every successful deception operation there is an aborted or disastrous one often hidden in the background. In his preface to Godfrey's memoirs, Steven Roskill remarks, "Unhappily the very nature of Intelligence work demands that its successes shall never be made public, and so it too often happens that the accomplishments of those who achieved the successes receive little understanding and scant acknowledgment."[95] However, this very secrecy also means that intelligence failures, too, are often concealed from the public. Fleming may have created good "publicity" for British secret intelligence—even propaganda—with his thrilling portraits of a British spy hero outwitting his country's enemies, but he also raised the curtain on some embarrassing if not disastrous intelligence failures. For example, Bond's failure to obtain the genuine Spektor machine in *From Russia, with Love* reflects the collapse of Fleming's plot to capture the Enigma codes in Ruthless.

The most successful and creative double agent of the war, Juan Pujol García—Agent "Garbo"—volunteered to work for the British but was initially rejected. Having been recruited to the Abwehr and based in Lisbon, Pujol García invented entire networks of fictional spies reporting back to Germany. Because he had never visited Britain at this point, Pujol García used guidebooks to Britain, train timetables, and information gleaned from British newsreels to fabricate convincing spy reports. Later, when Pujol García was recruited by the British and given the code name "Garbo" (due to his extraordinary skills as an actor), he was given a base in Hendon and assigned an MI5 handler, Tomás Harris, who spoke Spanish fluently. Together, Pujol García and Harris developed extensive networks of fictional subagents, including a Venezuelan businessman based in Glasgow and an officer at a British airbase, who could deliver the disinformation desired by MI5 to the Abwehr. So highly prized was Garbo by the Germans (whose code name for him was "Arabel") that he received lavish funding from the Nazis and high praise from the German leaders.

Garbo's fictional spy networks—which were probably the inspiration for another landmark postwar spy novel, Graham Greene's *Our Man in Havana* (1958)—enabled the Twenty (XX) Committee under J. C. Masterman to feed the Germans misinformation about the Allies' military forces, battle preparations, and invasion targets. Garbo's networks were instrumental in convincing the Abwehr that the Allies planned to invade France at the Pas-de-Calais, in June 1944, with a small force arriving at Normandy merely as a distraction from the main target. The Germans were convinced by this deception, moving most of their forces to protect the Pas-de-Calais. This allowed the Normandy landings to succeed, despite heavy casualties, and accelerate the end of the war.

The influence of Agent "Garbo" is reflected in *From Russia, with Love*, in which the Soviet agent Tatiana Romanova is repeatedly likened to the Swedish actress Greta Garbo. Even Darko Kerim, who has good professional instincts, suggests that for the photograph of Romanova to be placed in Bond's passport, "an early picture of Garbo would serve. There is a certain resemblance."[96] While the creation of a passport using false identities—that of David and Caroline Somerset—and fake photographs is an echo of Mincemeat, the "Garbo" reference (which occurs seven times in the novel) is a clue to the influence of Pujol García's inventions on Bond. Romanova is—like Pujol García —a great actor playing a part, that of the lovestruck woman smitten with the handsome British secret agent, designed to lure Bond and M into a trap. Indeed, this Garbo-esque deception plot is successful, and it is only due to luck that Bond survives.

Yet, the villains—whether agents of SMERSH or SPECTRE—are more successful than the Western intelligence organizations and governments at deception. They are also successful in setting traps for the British and their allies, leading them to place their own agents—including Bond—in great peril. The prize for master of deception among Bond villains must go to Sir Hugo Drax. Recalling that the original plan for Operation Mincemeat presented to the Twenty Committee by Charles Cholmondeley in 1942 had the code name Trojan Horse, there is no more effective Trojan horse operation in the Bond novels than that of Graf Hugo von der Drache.[97] Von der Drache's brilliance is to create an alias that is highly prominent, a celebrity in fact, using the cover identity of Hugo Drax, a "national hero," to penetrate the highest echelons of British society. Even Bond is forced to feel admiration for Drax's providing Britain with the independent nuclear deterrent the country so desperately wanted.

Britain's desire to strengthen its position in world affairs—especially vis-à-vis the Americans—is a common theme in both *From Russia, with Love* and *Moonraker*. In the former novel, M is desperate to obtain the Spektor cipher machine from SMERSH because it will raise Britain's status. Peter Hennessy has written of the heated debates among Clement Attlee's postwar Labour government about the desirability of obtaining an independent nuclear weapon. Ernest Bevin, the foreign secretary, argued that, despite the exorbitant cost, Britain had to obtain such a weapon. Sir Dennis Rickett's notes of one meeting summarize Bevin's position: "Our prestige in the world, as well as our chances of securing American co-operation would both suffer if we did not exploit to the full a discovery in which we had played a leading part at the outset."[98]

As Ian and Godfrey recognized—along with Masterman and the XX Committee—the most effective deception operations do not simply present false information to the enemy; they exploit the wishes, weaknesses, and fears of the opposition, offering them the prospect of something that they desperately wish to be real even if it seems too good to be true. There was no greater master at this ability to exploit the enemy's desires and fears for deception than Winston Churchill. As Nicholas Rankin writes, in World War I,

> as First Lord of the Admiralty in 1914, one of [Churchill's] earliest "Most Secret" memos of wartime gave instructions to build a dummy fleet of ten large merchant vessels mocked up in wood and canvas to look like far bigger battleships in silhouette. . . . Three of these "battleships" were sent to the

> Dardenelles in February 1915 to lure the German fleet out into the North Sea.[99]

The prospect of having British battleships at their mercy like sitting ducks proved irresistible to the Germans, who fell into the trap.

Does Fleming imply, with the brilliant deceptions practiced by the sinister duplicitous villains of his novels, that there is something ethically dubious about deceiving the enemy, even though it may prove a winning stratagem? Deception is a form of lying, which Judeo-Christian morality condemns as a sin, indeed the work of the devil. The Gospel of John states, "You are of your father the devil, and the desires of your father you want to do. . . . He is a liar and the father of it."[100] Like spying—which was portrayed as a form of covert, often mercenary, activity unworthy of a gentleman, even in classic spy novels like *Riddle of the Sands*—lying and deception traditionally violate the code of honor for "English gentlemen."

Of course, in time of war, many taboos and prohibitions are lifted, most obviously that of killing. To kill in peacetime is generally considered murder, but in wartime the same act may be condoned as a legitimate act of war. Therefore, deception was considered justified because it became necessary to win the war. As Nicholas Rankin writes,

> War is an extraordinary state that changes the normal rules: a crime like killing may become a duty. Deception or deceitfulness in ordinary life is wrong, because it corrodes trust, the basic glue of human relationships, but deceiving your enemy in wartime is common sense. If the war is just, then deception is also justified.[101]

These justifications of deception may hold water during wartime, but after the war they can be viewed in a different and harsher light. Fleming, writing the Bond novels after the war, looked back on the Allies' deception operations, as well the sacrifice of lives that resulted, with some misgivings. The moral obloquy of deception is conveyed in the phrase "black propaganda," of which Fleming—like his friend Sefton Delmer—became a master. However, in the novels he attributes the blackest arts of deception to the villains, whom Bond must expose and destroy. It is Ian's way of displacing the guilt for a necessary wartime evil onto the enemies of Britain.

As Ian complained to Michael Howard, creating original and memorable villains was the most demanding part of writing spy fiction: "One simply can't go on inventing good villains. They are far more difficult to come by than heroes or heroines."[102] To counter this difficulty, Ian would draw on wartime deception operations as the source for his villains, just as he did for Bond himself.

Of course, the Second World War provided the ultimate villain in the person of the Nazi leader, Adolf Hitler. William Stephenson's characterization of Hitler during 1940 is worth quoting, for it sheds some light on Fleming's creation of the Bond villains:

> The Führer is not just a lunatic. . . . He's an evil genius. The weapons in his armory are like nothing in history. His propaganda is sophisticated. His control of the people is technologically clever. He has torn up the military textbooks and written his own. His strategy is to spread terror, fear, and mutual suspicion.[103]

In this description of Hitler, we can recognize the prototype of the archvillain and Bond's nemesis, Ernst Stavro Blofeld, as well as elements of other Bond villains—especially those that psychologically manipulate and control their underlings with terror, like Mr. Big and Dr. No. The Führer's combination of technological sophistication and dark propaganda foreshadows Fleming's evildoers, and the purpose of SPECTRE is very similar. But with time the idea that Hitler was the origin of all evil in the war began to be modified.

Godfrey's memoirs give us an idea of the kind of Allied wartime activities that Ian was troubled by in retrospect during the postwar period. He writes, for example, about the formation of a special section of NID (17Z),

> whose function was, by means of insidious propaganda, to undermine and destroy the morale of officers and men in the German (and for a time, the Italian) Navy. This was achieved by the use of overt and covert wireless broadcasts, by the distribution of leaflets from the air, by the spreading of rumours and by other subversive means.

Godfrey continues in a vein that reveals how closely involved Ian was with these "insidious" propaganda practices:

> Donald McLachlan was genuinely pleased when I asked him after dinner at 36 Curzon Street if he would like the post. He accepted and I then asked him and Ian Fleming to put the machinery in motion for creating a Naval Section (17Z) in collaboration with the PWE [Political Warfare Executive]. I was greatly relieved and confident that there would be no lack of sting with him, Ian Fleming and Sefton Delmer in charge. As section 17Z developed I formed the personal view that *an element of perfidy, verging on the unscrupulous, was*

> *one of the ingredients essential to its success, and that this was being adequately looked after.*[104]

While post-traumatic stress disorder is usually ascribed to those who have directly experienced armed combat in war—partly due to its earlier denomination as "shell shock" or "combat neurosis"—it can also affect those involved in the planning and execution of missions. Just because the Allies' nefarious actions and "perfidy" have been overshadowed by the horrors of the Nazis' "Final Solution" and Holocaust, that does not mean they did not cause psychological harm to their perpetrators as well as targets. Writing the Bond novels was more than just a way for Ian to amuse himself while on holiday in Jamaica. It was also a form of therapy, a way of exorcising some of the dark and "perfidious" activities that might be viewed as breaches of the laws of combat, or "war crimes." While interviewing Ernest Cuneo, John Pearson reflected, "It is not until you meet these ex-Intelligence people that you understand how Secret Service work really does put a mark on a man for life."[105] This reference to a "mark" is not necessarily a compliment.

William Plomer—who would become one of Fleming's key editors at Cape—notes the traumatic material that Fleming had in mind for his thrillers: in his piece "Ian Fleming Remembered," Plomer recalls,

> Once during the War, when some of its worst phases were past, we . . . found time to speak of what we intended to do when it was over. With a diffidence that came surprisingly from so buoyant a man, he said he had a wish to write a thriller. He may not have used exactly that word, but made it quite plain that he had in mind some exciting story of espionage and sudden death.[106]

In referencing that Ian's plan to write fiction was forged after the "worst phases" of the war—that is, during a post-traumatic stage—Plomer seems surprised by Fleming's "diffidence." Rather than the enthusiasm and excitement that Plomer might expect from Ian at the prospect of writing a thriller, Ian's reaction is that of one who needs to write in order to explore traumatic material. He needed to expiate some guilt, or to achieve catharsis by writing about the terror of "sudden death" that haunted him, as it had so many times during the conflict. This is in addition to the personal psychic wounds of losses such as Muriel Wright, his wartime lover killed in an air raid, or his brother Michael, also killed during the war.

According to Lee Richards, Ian played a central role in the "black propaganda" work of NID:

> [Sefton] Delmer's friend and personal assistant to the Director of Naval Intelligence, Commander Ian Fleming, became the Royal Navy's general supervisor of psychological warfare. In September 1941, under Fleming's watchful eye, the unit NID 17Z was formed to liaise with PWE on propaganda matters. NID 17Z was formed by the former *Times* journalist Lieutenant Commander Donald MacLachlan. Like Delmer, MacLachlan "knew a great deal about how to get under the German's skin."[107]

The new "black propaganda" department made the utmost of the communications media and technology available at the time, and "the collaboration between McLachlan and Delmer led to the creation of the largest and most successful of the clandestine radio stations, when *Kurzwellesender Atlantik* went on the air on 22 March 1943. This shortwave transmitter was principally designed to attack the morale of U-boat crews." As Richards argues, "Fleming played a leading part in intelligence, deception, and psychological warfare operations."[108] Indeed, an important part of Fleming's wartime work was involved in "black propaganda," sometimes broadcasting fabricated news bulletins on the "black propaganda" radio stations such as those operated by his friend Delmer.

Ian's friend and lover Maud Russell—who would herself work for NID 17Z, as a result of Ian's advocacy of her application—recorded in her diary for April 9, 1940: "I listened to Ian broadcasting to the Germans in German. He wasn't bad. His voice is higher than I thought. I had never noticed the pitch of Ian's voice before. He says the stuff given him to broadcast is dreadful, dull stuff and he tries to improve it."[109] This ability to "improve" the "dull stuff" of reality, using his creative imagination to make it more exciting, would become a vital element of his ability to appeal to readers as a spy novelist.

Of course, Fleming was hardly unique in exploiting and "improving" his wartime intelligence background for spy fiction. As Ben Macinytre observes, "The greatest writers of spy fiction have, in almost every case, worked in intelligence before turning to writing. W. Somerset Maugham, John Buchan, Ian Fleming, Graham Greene, John le Carré: all had experienced the world of espionage firsthand."[110] Indeed, the powers of observation, the need for solitude (even isolation), a vivid imagination, attention to detail, and a gift for effective and *persuasive* communication—to convince people that something fabricated is true—are skill sets shared by the two professions of spy and writer. Where Harling believed that Fleming was already the "brand-image" of James Bond while in NID, it would be more accurate to say that he was already the spy novelist in embryonic form.

In one of the "appreciations" of Ian Fleming included as appendices to Godfrey's naval memoirs, Anthony Curtis claimed, "Fleming's famous accuracy of detail was a brilliant journalistic illusion. The loving care for minutiae with which he describes a game of golf or a meal of soft-shell crabs enabled him to get away with murder in climactic scenes of wild penny-dreadful improbability."[111] It is hard, perhaps impossible, to separate truth from fiction in Fleming's work when so many of the wartime escapades in which Fleming was involved seem so improbable and extraordinary.

Yet, some have suggested that Ian's "authority" and "expertise" were themselves a form of deception. In writing about John Hayward, the authentic bibliographical expert behind the *Book Collector* magazine that Fleming bought from Lord Kemsley and managed for years, John Pearson states, "Typically [Ian] left the work to others—chiefly to Percy Muir and to its unpaid editor, John Hayward. . . . Fleming never wrote for it or really directed its policy. All the same, the magazine was 'his.' He was very proud of it."[112] If this seems a bit unkind—displaying Pearson's perhaps unconscious wish to penetrate Fleming's "façade" and expose him as a fraud—it does point to one of Fleming's skills as a writer, his ability to *convince* the reader of his authority on a range of subjects about which he knew relatively little.

Ian's tone of "expertise" and authority would become part of his contract with the reader, his guarantee that the reader is in expert hands and can trust Fleming's information, knowledge, and judgments. Ian had become an expert at deception and propaganda during the war, and he transfers this particular type of expertise to James Bond in the novels. Yet, what are the spy and the spy novelist—perhaps the novelist more generally—if not deception artists, whose practice and profession it is to deceive? The *New American Oxford Dictionary* defines the confidence man as "a man who cheats or tricks someone by gaining their trust and persuading them to believe something that is not true."[113] Perhaps Ian's ultimate confidence trick may have been the reverse: to convince the world that his novels were "high flown and romanticized caricatures" based on fantasy rather than founded on the truth of espionage operations, as they most certainly were.[114]

Aside from the specific operations and propaganda of Naval Intelligence that influenced the character and adventures of Bond, one of the most concrete inspirations for the Bond novels that Fleming obtained while in NID was Admiral John Godfrey as the inspiration for M. It is notable, given the wide variety of conflicting theories about the "real-life" origin or inspiration for James Bond, that there has been relatively little controversy about the authentic basis for M. A recent book about Maxwell Knight, the top agent-runner in MI5, has suggested that he might have been a source of M's character, partly given the initial "M" by which Knight was known in MI5. Another figure sometimes alluded to is Mansfield Cumming, the first head of SIS (MI6) who was known as "C," which has since become the identifying initial for all directors of SIS.

However, most accounts of Fleming's life and work accept Admiral Godfrey as the basis for M, and the official Ian Fleming Publications website makes this link in its biographical page.[115] Of course, Godfrey was director of Naval Intelligence, whereas in the Bond novels M is head of SIS. However, M is referred to as "Admiral"; and in *The Man with the Golden Gun*, his full identity is revealed as Admiral Sir Miles Messervy. Bond, of course, has the rank of commander, and his military background is also naval—so there is a clear transposition of the naval intelligence framework during World War II to the postwar SIS context.

In 1939, Godfrey chose Fleming as his "man" and never regretted it: he explained, "With literally the manpower of Great Britain to choose from, I had to pick the sort of man who could give me the service I needed. I chose Ian Fleming and was never to be disappointed."[116] As Moran and McCrisken note, "As Godfrey' s right hand man, [Ian] was given a remarkable licence to coordinate with a host of secret government departments. At NID, he was not just *a* desk officer; he was *the* desk officer, who knew everything and everyone."[117] The selection of Ian as Godfrey's personal assistant was, by all accounts, mutually beneficial.

Yet, such descriptions of Fleming's outstanding performance as "assistant" to Godfrey raises the question, who was really in the "service" of whom? Godfrey wrote in his memoirs that "I once said that Ian should have been D.N.I. and I his naval advisor. If he had been ten years older and I ten years younger this might have had the elements of a workable proposition."[118] William Stephenson reinforced this perception, noting, "When I first saw Ian during the war he was with Godfrey, but it was evident that he was more the DNI than DNI himself. A very serious, war-winning type."[119]

This was no doubt flattering to Ian, but it also reminds us of the fact that his role in NID was largely administrative, bureaucratic, management—rather than active, in-the-field, "heroic." In reality, Fleming's role was less like that of Bond and more like a junior M: he initiated missions, organized intelligence gathering, sent his "men" (such as his "Red Indians" or commandos) out on dangerous missions, supervised them, and would sometimes chastise them when they failed to deliver the necessary intel. Room 39 collated, condensed, and coordinated the vital naval intelligence material through spy networks, signals, and other sources and decided which agencies or government departments would most benefit from this intelligence.

Godfrey's familiar name, among NID staff, of "Uncle John" suggests the avuncular role rather than stern disciplinarian that is M. Fleming makes M considerably older than Bond, gives him a more puritanical and disciplinarian type of personality, and, of course, the roles are much more distinct: M does not travel with Bond into the field (though, in the Bond films, he sometimes appears out in the location of the mission). M is not a "handler" in the sense of being Bond's case officer but is his superior officer in an intelligence, military, and administrative context. When it came to his novels, in any case, Godfrey was recruited as Fleming's "man" and rendered sterling service as the embodiment of British intelligence leadership and authority. If Godfrey had made Fleming's career by choosing the young journalist as his "man," Fleming returned the favor by making "My Man Godfrey" more famous as the spymaster for Bond than he was as the head of NID.

Ian's nostalgia for the hard work, freedom, adventure, and improvisation of the Naval Intelligence Division during World War II is at the very heart of the James Bond novels. Ian especially hankered after the collective wartime conviction that Britain was leading the free world against a tyrannical, sophisticated, and technologically advanced enemy—endowing its people, armed forces, and intelligence services with heroic status. These nostalgic longings for fantasies of power and influence—as well as some haunting guilt over wartime deceptions and personal losses—could all be embodied, in various ways, in the heroic persona of Bond, James Bond.

Chapter Five

After the War Was Over

Goldeneye and Kemsley House

After the war, Ian faced an anticlimactic return to a civilian world in which he had never really found his niche. Robert Harling summed up Ian's career thus far: "He was terribly lazy all his life except for the one time during the war at the Admiralty. This was the one time he found himself really extended. His capacity for work was phenomenal and he was terribly good."[1] Journalism and stockbroking had both proved unsatisfactory, and the latter had hardly "extended" Ian. It was to the former career, though, that he returned after the war, accepting the job as foreign manager at Kemsley Newspapers. Yet, Fleming's strongest ambitions were to write the "spy story to end all spy stories" (as he told Harling) and to live in Jamaica (as he confided to Bryce). Neither of these were traditional professional goals—especially in the eyes of his mother—but his plans show that Ian wanted a change of direction and hoped that the war could be a watershed in his life. He had lost a brother (Michael) and a lover (Muriel Wright) to the war, but, on the other hand, he had gained a renewed sense of purpose and ambition.

There is no doubt that Ian missed the action, intensity, common purpose, and unique role he played in the Naval Intelligence Division (NID) during the war. John Pearson referred to "a sort of doldrums from which he was rescued from by the war. . . . This saved him a terrible fate."[2] Ian was in danger of returning to these "doldrums" after the war was over. Though challenging in its way, his role as Kemsley's foreign manager for *The Sunday Times* was hardly a substitute for the heady experience of power to decide on top-secret missions and could not replace Ian's immersion in wartime conflict and espionage. Eventually, Ian found the antidote to "accidie"—his greatest fear, boredom and inertia—in his fantasy world by creating a character with whom he could vicariously continue the potent mix of adventure, danger, romance, and conflict with deadly enemies that the war had delivered. In *From Russia, with Love*, Fleming described Bond as "a man of war," adding that "peace was killing him."[3] This could equally apply to Ian, and there were seven years of "peace" to endure before Ian began to write his first spy novel.

The war had been long, brutal, and punishing for Britain, even though the nation emerged victorious from these trials. Those who served in its intelligence services, including NID, worked insanely long hours, spent many weary days traveling, and in many cases suffered the same shortages, rationing, and hardships (such as intensive German bombings) that civilians endured in Britain. If they were spared some of the physical horrors of the battlefield, they still suffered the psychological traumas of war.

Despite having no naval background, and although he had left Royal Sandhurst under a cloud, Ian had thrived in the challenging environment of wartime NID. His connections, of course, had helped him get the position as Godfrey's assistant: his friend Ivar Bryce noted, "No doubt his name was mentioned in quiet conversations in hallowed clubs, and jotted down in little notebooks by small gold pencils belonging to people who count."[4] But even so, Ian still had to prove himself worthy of the position.

One of the most astute observers of how much Ian's wartime intelligence work meant to him is Maud Russell, his friend and lover, who worked in the NID propaganda department, 17Z, from 1942. Russell (who used the shorthand "I." for Ian) writes in her diary for September 20, 1939—less than three weeks into the so-called Phoney war—"Dined with I. at the Berkeley this evening. He loves his NID better than anything he has ever done, I think, except skiing." The following week, Russell wrote enthusiastically, "I. is fascinated by his work."[5] If this was the case at the beginning of his appointment, his absorption and interest, as we have seen, only intensified as the war progressed. At the end of the war, this left a vacuum that Ian needed to fill.

The war in Europe ended with triumph for the Allies in May 1945, and on VE Day, Ian could be justifiably proud of the role he had played in the victory. Naval Intelligence was arguably the most important clandestine service during the war, and its contribution to the cracking of the Enigma cipher machine—which most historians agree shortened the war by months or even years—was inestimable. And other departments had also contributed to cracking the codes, as Christopher Andrew—noting that "Dilly" Knox succeeded in breaking the Abwehr Enigma machine in December 1941—points out that the intelligence derived from the decrypts confirmed by spring 1942 that "the Security Service controlled all German agents operating in Britain."[6]

Besides providing Ian with the engrossing experience of wartime service, his six years in NID had also offered a solution—at least temporarily—to the burning question, what was he to do with his life? This problem returned with a vengeance in 1945. What was the best course for a former journalist, now in his late thirties, without a substantial private income and with no established career path? He was still nominally a partner in Rowe & Pitman, the stockbrokers, but his prewar experiences there did not encourage him to return full time to stockbroking.

One answer to his dilemma had been found, at least in Ian's fantasy, during a visit to Jamaica with Ivar Bryce in November 1944. The purpose of the trip was to attend an Anglo-American naval intelligence conference in Kingston, to plot strategy for dealing with the threat of U-boats in the Atlantic and Caribbean. As Bryce notes in his memoirs, "The sinkings in the Caribbean had reached a most alarming total. . . . Two hundred vessels had succumbed to enemy torpedoes in one month. . . . The combined efforts of our two great navies seemed unable to destroy the U-boats or even to deprive them of their weapons and their fuel."[7] Therefore, emergency measures were necessary.

Rather than staying at a hotel in Kingston, Ian and Ivar retired to Bryce's home, Bellevue, in the Blue Mountains—a plantation with an eighteenth-century "great house." However, Bryce recalled, "the road to Bellevue was very bad indeed," and the torrential rain and lack of supplies in the house—no gin, so they were forced to drink grenadine, and only a "stringy tasteless chicken" for dinner—convinced Ivar that Ian must have had a miserable time. Bryce recalled in his memoir "rain that streamed from the roof like a continuous waterfall" and noted of their grueling schedule, away before dawn and back after dark, "it was very depressing for me."[8]

However, Ian surprised his closest friend on the flight back to New York with his next remark:

> You know, Ivar, I have made a great decision. . . . When we have won this blasted war, I am going to live in Jamaica. Just live in Jamaica and lap it up,

> and swim in the sea and write books. That is what I want to do, and I want your help.[9]

There was only one problem: How was an impecunious journalist who had been, according to his brother Richard, "the very worst stockbroker in the world" and who had received no inheritance, despite his grandfather's wealth, to afford this dream of a private tropical eyrie?[10] Maud Russell knew about Ian's dream of living in Jamaica after the war and feared that he would be lured back into intelligence work instead. She wrote a gloomy prognosis in her diary about Ian's future when he was considering a job in intelligence, on July 13, 1945:

> He is likely to be offered a new job he thinks he won't be able to refuse. It would carry with it the rank of Commander if he cared to remain in uniform. Goodbye then to Jamaica and a lazy life, negroes and palms and the dreams that have sustained him during the hard work of these last years. I felt a pang for him. He will go on, straight on, without rest or pause, he will never get free. He will wear himself out and lose his youth. His muscles will melt away, his back will get bent, he will sweat away at this job for ever till his dreams fade and none are left to take their place.[11]

This horrible image of decay and disillusionment is reminiscent of Lord Henry Wotton warning the youthful Dorian Gray about the ghastly fate that awaits him as he ages and his beauty fades. Maud's comments reveal not only how much she cared about Ian's future but also how long he had been dreaming about a life of tropical ease after the war. His ideal destination had not always been Jamaica, for previously Tahiti and even Hawaii had been mentioned by Ian as possible retreats. Her diary entry suggests Maud was willing to make almost any sacrifice to bring Ian's dreams to fruition.

While Ian was in Ceylon (now Sri Lanka) on NID business in early 1945, he had a strange experience when a Sinhalese came to tell his fortune. When Ian asked the fortune-teller whether there were important women in his life who had greatly influenced him, the reply came that there were two. One was his mother, the other a widow who had "given him money for what purpose the soothsayer didn't understand."[12] Maud, of course, had been widowed since her husband Gilbert's death in 1944. This prediction of her benevolent role in his life was more accurate than even Ian understood at the time.

Ultimately, Ian turned down the intelligence job in order to accept Kemsley's offer, a decision that Maud approved of: "He feels he must break away. So Jamaica is on again. I am sure he is right not to let himself grow old, unhealthy and apoplectic sitting for ever in London on mysterious committees and having no leisure, no freedom, no unbuttoning." Ian's decision reopened the possibility of a Caribbean bolt-hole, and Maud believed the journalist's life "will be best for him provided he can have four months to himself in Jamaica . . . every winter." Ian even suggested that Maud too should take a house on Jamaica. She declined, but this did not reflect any lack of support for his plans. In order to allow Ian to buy the land and build his Jamaican home, Maud made him an extraordinarily generous gift of £5,000, £2,000 of which was used to buy the land, while the remaining £3,000 went on constructing the house.[13]

By the time Ian came to negotiate the terms of his job with Lord Kemsley, the four-month annual sabbatical had been trimmed to two months. Even so, Kemsley was taken aback by Ian's request (really a demand) for two months paid leave, not being used to such stipulations from those he offered work to. As Bryce notes, "Lord Kemsley was not accustomed to conditional acceptance when he made an offer, and appeared startled when Fleming said he was interested in the job but would only accept it IF it was understood that for two months of every year he would be absent in Jamaica."[14]

With the job in place, all Ian needed was a suitable piece of land to purchase. As he had promised, Bryce did indeed help his friend secure the desired property, a former donkey track on the clifftops near Oracabessa. With the help of a Jamaican land agent, Reggie Acquart, Ivar found the prime real estate with its own "secret beach" and visited it in person before approving the purchase on Ian's behalf. Bryce's first impression was of delight at the property: "It was rough grass land scattered with a sprinkling of big trees, banyan and silk cotton, with a fringe of bush toward the harbor side. The view was enchanting—a bay of clear aquamarine protected by a broad and tangled reef across the mouth of it."[15] Fleming now had his Jamaican retreat, and on hearing the details of the property, he cabled Bryce with characteristic zeal, "Pray pause not Ian."[16] Now all Ian needed was to build the house and find the inspiration to "write books" there. Ian's literary ambitions—suppressed for some time first by the great success of Peter's books and then by the demands of wartime intelligence work—had been rekindled by the release from the absorbing challenges of working in Naval Intelligence. The imaginative boldness and skills at deception and communication that could devise wartime operations such as Ruthless and Mincemeat could now be adapted to creating fascinating fictional spy plots.

As foreign manager of a major newspaper group, Ian would run networks of foreign correspondents, a task he was, as Bryce noted, well prepared for by his experience of running agents for NID during the war. Ian apparently

> defined his working life as "an old-age pensioner's version of Room 39." This absence of novelty well suited him, he contended. He had been appointed to a top job—foreign news manager—in the Kemsley Group. I suspected that he had secretly hoped that he would also have been offered a directorship.[17]

Ian's communications skills—enhanced by the demands of wartime memo writing and propaganda—and ability to work under pressure of tight deadlines also suited him for the position. He told Harling that he chose his job title for himself, "as more befitting the job he intended for himself: directing the group's foreign correspondents around the globe from hot spots to hotter spots."[18] The new job as foreign manager would require travel overseas, a prospect that Ian relished. The title of Kemsley's news service was Mercury, named appropriately after the herald and messenger to the gods in Roman mythology as well as the god of travelers. As Bryce wrote about his friend's new appointment, "Ian was delighted and it was thus that the pattern of his life thenceforward was established."[19]

This "pattern" would eventually come to include the annual production of a James Bond novel each winter, starting in 1952. But before this there were several years spent building and settling into Goldeneye—the name Fleming chose for his Spartan bungalow built on the clifftop—and enjoying the pleasures of swimming, snorkeling, and socializing in the tropical paradise of Jamaica. Bryce had suggested naming the house Shame Lady after an indigenous Jamaican plant, but Ian settled on Goldeneye after his wartime operation. At Goldeneye, the friendships of neighbors such as Noël Coward and Blanche Blackwell made Fleming's Jamaican recesses a time of great happiness, and Bryce concluded that "Jamaica gave him more pleasure than all his triumphs wrapped up together. His happiest days were to be spent there."[20]

Without the extraordinary generosity of Maud Russell and the willingness of Lord Kemsley to grant Ian's annual two-month winter holiday, the conditions necessary for James Bond's creation would never have been possible. Maud, as far as we know, took no credit for providing Ian with the means to achieve his writer's haven in the Caribbean. However, Kemsley himself came to realize the important role he had played in the creation of the world's most famous secret agent. Harling recalls meeting Kemsley, after the sale of his newspaper group to Roy Thomson, observing that "his lordship was deriving a curious latter-day pride from recalling the eccentric contract he had granted Fleming with those curious holiday arrangements. That those spells in Jamaica ultimately contributed substantially to the emergence of Bond was undoubtedly true."[21]

With the dreamed-of Jamaican home secured, there remains the puzzling question, why did it take Ian seven years after the war to write his first novel, given that he had nurtured ambitions to write books before the war ended if not long before? Doubtless there were lingering feelings of inferiority to Peter, who had become a famous author in the 1930s and was still known as the "literary Fleming" after the war, receiving the Order of the British Empire in the 1945 King's Birthday Honors list. Peter had also served with distinction in intelligence during the war, thus equaling Ian's accomplishments. In his 1962 article "How to Write a Thriller," Ian explained this delay simply:

> For the first six years I had plenty to do during these months exploring Jamaica, coping with staff and getting to know the locals, and minutely examining the underwater terrain within my reef. But by the sixth year I had exhausted all these possibilities, and I was about to get married—a prospect which filled me with terror and mental fidget.[22]

But Ian had to adapt to the postwar world in other ways than his own career and living arrangements (Fleming had kept his flat in Atheneaum Court but was looking for a larger accommodation). For the world was rapidly changing, as the common enemy and shared hardships of war gave way to resurgent individual ambitions, class conflicts, and political tensions. In political terms, a dramatic change occurred in 1945 with the election of a Labour government, the first since 1931. Despite having led Britain to victory in World War II, Winston Churchill was ousted by Clement Attlee's Labour Party in a landslide victory, marking the first time the Conservatives had lost the popular vote in forty years. Maud Russell recorded attending an election party at the Rothermeres' on July 26, 1945, where clearly the guests' expectation was that the Conservatives under Churchill would win another term. Though the election had been held on July 5, less than two months after VE Day, some of the UK polls were delayed and the results had to be counted, the final outcome not being announced until July 26. This also allowed time for the transportation of votes from those in the military and diplomatic corps serving overseas. The result reflected the largest ever national swing from one party to another in British general election history.

Among the partygoers at the Rothermeres' was Sir John Anderson, who had been dubbed "the home front prime minister," having served in several capacities in the cabinet during the war, including as home secretary. Anderson was being tipped as a future prime minster, and Russell wrote, "Anderson remained completely unmoved as the results poured in. Either he'd foreseen them, or he has the finest self-control, or else he is a block of wood." Russell also predicted, "The Socialists will be in for five or 10 years and where now is Sir John's premiership? I couldn't resist laughing a good deal at the results and some of the long, foolish faces."[23] Maud's reaction suggests that her private sympathies may well have been with the Labour Party, despite the overwhelmingly Conservative company she was in. However, Ian—for whom Churchill was a personal hero—was also at the party, choosing to drown his electoral sorrows in vodka and wandering forlornly around the house. Maud noted "he kept on coming back to me" as though returning to his emotional center of gravity. The new political regime of Attlee and the birth of the welfare state was almost certainly a factor in Ian's refusal of the offered job in intelligence; as Maud reported, "He feels he must break away."[24]

Ian was not by and large a political animal. Indeed, he gave as his reason for refusing the job title of "foreign editor" at *The Sunday Times*—that "he would be expected to pen a weekly think piece on the state of the world. . . . He had neither the political conviction nor the pontifical prose suited to such a task."[25] Instead, he preferred the title of "foreign manager." His instincts and background were generally Conservative (his father having been Conservative member of parliament for Henley), and his writings contain expressions of socially conservative or even reactionary views. Yet, in other ways, Ian's views of sexual liberation, personal freedom, and reproductive rights were quite progressive for the time period. While Bond may show disdain for Tilly Masterton's sexual "confusion" in *Goldfinger*, Fleming by no means condemns Viv Michel for asserting her own reproductive choice by having an abortion in *The Spy Who Loved Me*. Viv describes the experience "as mentally distressing but as physically painless as I had expected."[26] Rather, the fault lies with her callous lover, Kurt, who ends their relationship when he learns of her pregnancy, wishing to marry "into the Teutonic strain."[27] Likewise, Ian does not moralize about Viv's first sexual experience in a cinema, while portraying her lover Derek in a negative light for his exploitation of her. Ian sometimes wrote critically about the welfare state and trade unions, but his views did not align neatly with any political party.

Despite his foibles, Kemsley was known as a hard taskmaster. Ian's new job involved setting up the Mercury networks of foreign correspondents for *The Sunday Times* and other newspapers in the Kemsley Group. Importantly, these networks of correspondents also had "informal connections to British intelligence," keeping alive Ian's relationship with the world of espionage.[28] It was, in fact, this very professional opportunity that came between Ian and the fulfillment of his literary ambitions. Harling notes that "Fleming's social life in peacetime London seemed little different from his wartime round: a workaday business life with an unusual concentration on evening commitments."[29] While in London, Ian's days were occupied at the Grays Inn Road office at Kemsley House, where he operated the Mercury News Service—the global network of over eighty correspondents whose names and territories were marked in dotted lines on a large yellow map on the wall of his office.[30] William Stephenson had encouraged Ian to accept the offer to set up Mercury, being convinced Ian "was fascinated by the whole thing of Intelligence and . . . couldn't bear to let it go."[31]

The image of this large map suggests interesting parallels between the role of foreign manager and that of spymaster. It has been widely speculated that this network of foreign correspondents was also a network of spies, for some of his recruits were undoubtedly in the pay of the Secret Intelligence Service (SIS). The profession of journalism—like the diplomats in the Foreign Office—could be an excellent cover for espionage, providing a pretext for extensive travel, observation, and note-taking about foreign industrial and military preparations as well as civilian affairs. Ben Macintyre notes of Fleming's remarkable control over the Mercury News that "these correspondents (some of whom were spies) were hired, fired, paid and commissioned by Fleming."[32]

Mark Edmonds raises the tantalizing possibility that Fleming was already playing out his own "Bond fantasies" in the years before penning his first novel: "The job almost certainly blurred into the opaque half-light of the intelligence world. What was Fleming up to? . . . Perhaps in his work at the paper he saw himself not as Bond, but M, the head of MI6."[33] Just as journalism had provided cover for espionage when he traveled to Moscow for Reuters in the 1930s, so the role of Kemsley's foreign manager was the ideal pretext for continued postwar intelligence gathering.

But Ian's day job was far from being his raison d'être. For most of the year, evenings were spent socializing with friends, playing bridge, or dining with eligible women: or as Fleming described Bond's love life in *Moonraker*, "making love, with rather cold passion, to one of three similarly disposed married women."[34] Ann's husband, Shane O'Neill, had been killed in action in World War II. As an attractive and highly eligible widow, Ann had several suitors, including Ian and Lord Rothermere. In fact, Ann's marriage to O'Neill had been troubled for some years, and she had fallen in love with Esmond Rothermere even before the war. She wrote,

> In August 1936 I went to Austria and met Esmond Harmsworth. I had by then given up all hope of falling in love, but we fell in love with each other . . . and remained in love till early war years, though from 1939 onwards I grew more and more attracted to Ian and very curious about him.

This love tangle became even more complex when Ann convinced Rothermere that they must get married or separate. The couple went through the "rigamarole of giving evidence at Bournemouth (Esmond went back on this two months later)."[35] The "evidence" referred to was that of contrived adultery, which was necessary to secure a divorce from O'Neill.

However, Ann returned to Shane O'Neill at Ian's insistence. When the news came of Shane's death in Italy, in October 1944, it is clear that Ann's affections had by this time transferred to Ian: "The night before I married Esmond [June 28, 1945] I dined with Ian, and we walked and walked in the park. He said several times, 'I want to leave some kind of mark on you'; if he had suggested marriage I would have accepted."[36] However, Ian was too protective of his emotional detachment and bachelor lifestyle to propose marriage at this point.

Nonetheless, he continued to dine regularly with Ann, even after her marriage in 1945 to Lord Rothermere. After the war, Ian lived in Hays Mews, Mayfair, from autumn 1947, returning to the exclusive area of London where he was born. He also remained close to Maud Russell, with whom he could reminisce about working in Naval Intelligence during the war. He would also join old friends such as Duff Cooper and Ivar Bryce—when the latter was in London on one of his numerous transatlantic crossings—for gambling and dining excursions in the City.

Weekends were spent playing golf and socializing with a close circle of friends. Ian joined the Royal St George's golf club at Sandwich in November 1948—having been proposed for membership by his stockbroker friend Hilary Bray—and this soon became his favorite course, and refuge, in England. His regular attendance at the golf course was made easier when Noël Coward arranged for him to take over the lease of Eric Ambler's seaside home at

Saint Margaret's Bay in the summer of 1949. As Peter Lewis writes, Ambler had drifted into screenwriting after the war, but

> in 1948 his friend Noël Coward advised him to "forget all this film nonsense" and "write more books." During the next two years, living in a house owned by Coward that was subsequently let to Ian Fleming when he was about to create James Bond, Ambler wrote much of *Judgment on Deltchev.*[37]

Coward also had ulterior motives in persuading his friends to lease the properties near White Cliffs, which he had purchased in 1945 and restored with the help of a stage designer friend, Gladys Caltroph. He wanted to keep the hoi polloi at a distance:

> On the long beach of St. Margaret's Bay there were then only four houses and *White Cliffs* was the closest to the sea. Coward wanted to purchase them all in order to secure his privacy, but in the post-war days of 1945 there was a housing shortage in South East England and thus Coward was forbidden to purchase more than his one house. To ensure Coward's privacy, two of the other houses were bought by Coward's friends, novelist Eric Ambler and Cole Lesley, and the third by Coward's mother and Auntie Vida. Despite investigation by Fleet Street and a suspicious Ministry of Works, no breach of the law was discovered.[38]

In late 1951, Fleming would make a further commitment to living on the Kent coast, buying the lease of Coward's own home, White Cliffs, at Saint Margaret's Bay. This had the advantage of giving Ian direct access to the sea, and he spent many happy hours gazing through his telescope at the shipping in the English Channel. The house at White Cliffs also provided easy access to Royal St George's golf course. There was some good-humored banter with Noël Coward about the state in which Coward had left the house: Fleming demanded £100 for repairs to the property, but Coward offered only £50, prompting Ian to complain about his friend's "insolent niggardliness."[39] When he felt like a change from Royal St George's, another favorite location for Ian to play golf was Huntercombe at Henley-on-Thames, near the Flemings' old haunt of Nettlebed in Oxfordshire. But his preference was for the Sandwich course he described in *Goldfinger* (using the fictionalized name "Royal St Marks") as "the greatest seaside course in the world."[40]

Ian was also absorbed by the exciting project of building Goldeneye and overseeing the construction of its garden. Ian made a trip with Ivar Bryce in January 1946 to secure the property, returning home to England aboard the

Queen Mary.[41] Once built, Goldeneye provided an oasis of tropical pleasures that included swimming and snorkeling off the private beach; exploring the reef; enjoying the delights of tropical fruits and cuisine; and, of course, socializing with neighbors, friends, and visitors. Chief among these neighbors and friends was his friend from Kent, Noël Coward, who built a house nearby in 1948, naming it Blue Harbour. Another was Ivar Bryce, who was living in Jamaica year-round at this time, and Fleming was a frequent visitor to the Bryce home, Bellevue, where his Jamaican adventure had started in 1944. There were also frequent excursions to Montego Bay, sometimes renting a cottage there and attending social functions such as the opening of the Sunset Lodge Club. In the immediate postwar years, Jamaica was fast becoming an international hotspot for celebrities and the wealthy jet set.

Ian's two precious months at Goldeneye each winter slipped by very easily in a stream of social engagements, gardening, and tropical rest and relaxation. He had frequent visitors, including Ann Rothermere, Loelia Ponsonby (the duchess of Westminster), Ann's brother Hugh Charteris, Duff and Diana Cooper—his old friends from the Russells' home of Mottisfont—and the travel writer Patrick Leigh Fermor, who visited Goldeneye to research his anthropological work *The Traveller's Tree* in the winter of 1947–1948. This work would be used by Ian as a source on voodoo and quoted extensively in his second Bond novel, *Live and Let Die*. Fermor, unlike Coward—who mockingly referred to the single-story house as "Goldeneye, Nose, and Throat"—approved of the Spartan conditions at Goldeneye, for example, the lack of glass in the windows, arguing that the design of the house

> "might serve as a model for new houses in the tropics . . . great windows capture every breeze, to cool, even on the hottest day, the large white rooms." Even better, the "enormous quadrilaterals" framed a "prospect of sea and cloud and sky, and tamed the elements, as it were."[42]

Despite his mockery, Coward was converted by his visit to Goldeneye in 1948 and decided he had to build his own home on the coast. He remained a frequent visitor. Despite their being neighbors in Kent, Matthew Parker notes that the "unlikely close friendship" between the two men "was, at its heart, a friendship made in Jamaica. . . . Through all Fleming's adventures at Goldeneye over the next fifteen years, Coward would be a continual presence."[43]

Sometimes Ian's social arrangements at Goldeneye went awry, as when he invited Rosamond Lehmann, expecting that he would be on his own in the house. However, Lehmann, who "had her sights set on Fleming," arrived to find Ann installed in the home, and as a result "all hell broke loose, and eventually Fleming had to bribe Coward with his Leica camera to take Lehmann off his hands."[44] Ann reports that Rosamond Lehmann said of Ian that he "got off with women because he could not get on with them." Despite the fact that fellow novelist Elizabeth Bowen, to whom Ann repeated the comment, pointed out that she had used it in *Death of a Heart*, Ann believed "it was certainly true of Ian."[45]

Despite such occasional mishaps, Ian had a full life in Jamaica, enjoyed the glorious winter climate, the intense social life, and the pleasures available to an attractive bachelor. Yet, he still doubted his abilities as a writer. The fact that Ian had not started his "spy story to end all spy stories" did not mean he was detached from the literary world. Part of his job involved finding suitable books for serialization or review in *The Sunday Times*, and his circle of literary friends (including Ann's social circle) made him ideally placed for such a role.

For example, on February 17, 1950, Ian wrote Jonathan Cape with

> warmest thanks for sending me a copy of Popski's book. I am sure it will get a fine showing throughout our papers. I shall be sending you your file copy of "All Night at Mr Stanyhurst's" next week. Please forgive the delay. It is a remarkable story and I am sure you ought to reprint. Any news of Ernest Hemingway's book?[46]

The book by Popski referred to by Fleming was *Private Army*, the life of Lt. Col. Vladimir Peniakoff (Distinguished Service Order, Military Cross), published in 1950. Fleming had attended a Jonathan Cape dinner at the Savoy to celebrate Popski's life on May 3, 1949, and was seated next to the guest of honor.

Fleming also wrote to Cape about possible serialization in *The Sunday Times* of Fitzroy Maclean's *Eastern Approaches*, an account of the Scottish adventurer's exploits behind enemy lines in North Africa, as part of the newly formed Special Air Service in World War II, and in Russia and Yugoslavia after the war. Ian wrote to Cape on May 3, 1949, about Maclean's book (published in 1950),

> Alas, I am afraid it will be no use to us for serialisation. It would require too much cutting about and there are not enough single incidents of the right length to fit into our papers. It occurs to me that the book might suit the *Daily Telegraph* much better since they could run the series daily.[47]

Given that Fitzroy Maclean has been identified by some as a possible model for James Bond, Fleming's interest in this volume is of particular note. In fact, the volume may have given Ian some ideas for his own spy novel; Ben Macintyre, stating that Fleming "rejected [*Eastern Approaches*] rather pointedly, insisting that the author had claimed too much credit for himself," believes this is "something Fleming would surely not have done had Maclean been the inspiration for Bond."[48] But the opposite could be true—that Fleming was already thinking about a spy character of his own and did not want to publicly associate himself with, or seem to endorse, a real-life action hero such as Maclean. Fleming passed responsibility for the book to his brother Peter, informing Cape that "I have persuaded Peter to review it for *The Sunday Times*, which I hope will please both you and Fitzroy."[49]

That Ian felt himself to be in some sense competing with Maclean is evident from a later letter he wrote to Jonathan Cape on May 15, 1953, complaining about his modest royalties for *Casino Royale*. Cape had offered Ian a three-book deal, but Ian suggested he might do better with another publisher. Fleming griped that "only yesterday, I was talking to a Cape author rather younger than myself, who had been granted a flat 20% on his *first* book with you. This was a severe blow to my 'amour propre.'"[50] But regardless of whether Maclean was a source for Bond, the success of Maclean's book apparently inspired Ian to write about his own fictional spy hero.

Through his work for *The Sunday Times*, Fleming was involved in the literary world of postwar England and already on good terms with the publisher who would eventually bring James Bond into the public realm. Ian did not create James Bond out of a vacuum but drew on his extensive readings of spy fiction as well as his experience in intelligence operations. Likewise, his first book did not come out of the blue but grew from Ian's immersion in postwar literary culture. It was one of Ian's wartime colleagues in Naval Intelligence, William Plomer, who proved most influential in this respect. However, Ian had mixed feelings about the literary set cultivated by Ann before and during their marriage. Having found a London house in Victoria Square in early 1952, around the time that he began *Casino*, Ian was dismayed at how the house became a center for the literati and "came to see Victoria Square as permanently festooned with effeminate intellectuals." The highbrow writers patronized by Ann looked down on Ian's "pornography," and "some of them mocked Fleming's novels and . . . as his success grew, so did the mockery."[51]

But Ian had other, more worrying concerns than such social unease at this time. As early as December 1946, Fleming had complained of tightness in his chest while staying with Ivar Bryce in New York. This was the first occurrence of what he would later call "the Iron Crab," a metaphor for the heart disease that would eventually kill him.[52] In 1946, while in New York, Ian visited a "Dr. F.G.," whose report stated, "The patient admits to smoking seventy cigarettes a day and drinking at least a quarter of a bottle of gin."[53] In April 1948, Ian visited Sir John Parkinson, a Harley Street specialist, again complaining of chest pains. While James Bond shows minimal ill effects from smoking sixty cigarettes and drinking numerous cocktails a day (we are told in *Thunderball* that Bond's "average daily consumption of alcohol is in the region of half a bottle of spirits of between sixty and seventy proof"), Ian's health was another matter.[54]

Fleming repeatedly ignored his doctors' warnings to cut back on his drinking and smoking and continued to consume large amounts of tobacco and alcohol for the rest of his life. We must recall that Fleming lived and worked in an era and society when smoking was the norm, and it was a regular occurrence for businessmen to enjoy a two-martini lunch. At social gatherings with Coward, Bryce, the Rothermeres, the Coopers, and the Russells, the cocktails usually flowed: Ann relates in a letter to Diana Cooper of February 10, 1951, about one such occasion when Ivar Bryce's yacht ran aground in a storm off the Jamaican coast, while Ann, Ian, and Noël Coward were "swigging martinis." She also notes that, when the group returned to recover their possessions from the grounded yacht the next day, "Ian salvaged the gin," revealing of his own priorities.[55] On top of these indulgent habits, Ian had also endured six years of extremely stressful, high-intensity intelligence work during the war, working very long days under immense pressure, and this also took its toll. Fleming did not suffer his first heart attack until April 1961, but the warning signs were already present long before this. Fleming's lifestyle was not sustainable, but as he implied via Darko Kerim's sentiments in *From Russia, with Love*, he would not change it in order to extend his life.

An additional impetus to Fleming's creative purpose came in the summer of 1947, when his mentors from Kitzbühel, Phyllis Bottome and Ernan Forbes Dennis, arrived to stay at Goldeneye. Fleming usually confined his Jamaica visits to the winter, but he was on hand to welcome his former teachers, whom he would later describe as surrogate parents. The Forbes Dennises loved staying at Goldeneye, especially "go[ing] down to the small private beach with its lint-white sand accompanied only by Ian's fox terrier, Charles, and float in the warm clear water threading through the forests of coral." The previous year, Phyllis had published her first spy novel, *The Life Line*, with Faber in Britain and Little, Brown in the United States. As her first novel to appear since the war, *The Life Line* set the tone for her future work in combining the thriller form with social critique, and the results were encouraging. Bottome's biographer, Pam Hirsch, writes, "*The Life Line* sold well. Phyllis was by this stage adept in combing what might seem like distinct elements of psychology, social criticism, and political critique, all within a dramatic narrative that kept her readers eagerly turning the pages."[56]

What made this work distinctive compared to her previous books was that it was unabashedly a spy novel, its hero Mark Chalmers being, as Hirsch notes, "recruited as a spy by his chum Reggie in the Foreign Office" and then "parachuted into Austria after the Anschluss." As a "study of the anti-Nazi underground forces in Europe," Bottome's novel also imitated the gentleman amateur school of spy fiction developed by John Buchan and more recently used by the Scottish-born novelist Helen MacInnes. MacInnes's best-selling debut *Above Suspicion* (1941) featured an Oxford couple, Richard and Frances Myles, who are recruited by a Foreign Office friend and sent to communicate with an endangered British spy in Nazi-controlled Austria. MacInnes had pioneered the use of the Austrian Tyrol as an exciting venue for spy fiction, and Bottome would follow suit in *The Life Line*. Bottome's novel also has a feminist slant, reflecting "her distaste for any regime that kept women as second-class citizens," but her priority was to create a page-turning story of espionage in wartime.[57]

While the alleged specific parallels between *The Life Line* and Fleming's fiction have already been noted, it is important to recognize here that the timing of Bottome's novel was significant for Ian. She presented Ian with a copy of her novel on their visit to Goldeneye, and Fleming read it avidly, admiring Bottome's style and plot construction. He realized that, in the new era of geopolitics—only recently dubbed the "Cold War" by Bernard Baruch in a speech of April 16, 1947—many novelists would be looking to exploit the global confrontation between the Soviet Union and the United States (and Britain) for fictional purposes.[58] If he planned to make his contribution, he would need to get to work before other writers cornered the market.

It was not until another writer, one even closer to him personally, published a spy novel that Fleming's inertia was finally overcome and *Casino Royale* begun. His older brother, Peter—who had established his success with travel books in the 1930s and whose intelligence career during the war mirrored Ian's own—decided to enter the field of spy fiction. In 1951, he published *The Sixth Column*, a spy novel that contained elements of dry humor, even spoof, but whose protagonist was, as Ben Macintyre notes, "a thriller writer who creates a protagonist with marked similarities to Bond."[59] Fittingly, Peter dedicated this novel to "my brother Ian," as though attempting to spark his younger sibling into literary action. However, by making his protagonist a thriller writer rather than an actual spy, Peter Fleming brings in a metafictional element, an implicit satire of the farfetched conventions of the spy genre. In this respect, he echoes Eric Ambler's first novel, *The Dark Frontier*, with its "doubling" of Henry Barstow and his superhero alter ego Conway Carruthers, or even *A Coffin for Dimitrios* in which Latimer, the protagonist, is a detective novelist who reflects throughout on the conventions of his genre.

Peter acknowledged the tongue-in-cheek tone of the novel in his introduction: "It is true that not all the strange occurrences with which the narrative deals are treated with that high seriousness which transfigures the work of more respectable authors." However, the novel deals with a conspiracy to undermine the British character, which, Peter suggests, reflects a genuine concern about the morale and culture of postwar Britain. The head of Section D. 2 (d)—a division of Military Intelligence (MI5) dedicated to countering "suspected attempts to upset the balance of nature in the United Kingdom"—is presented with a discovered document known as "Plan D." This document had been found on an airplane by the sister of one of Section D. 2 (d)'s secretaries, and its contents address "the most promising methods of accelerating the current deterioration of the British national character with a view to undermining and eventually eliminating British influence in the affairs of the world."[60]

There are some intriguing parallels between Peter's novel and Ian's work: for example, in *Thrilling Cities*, Ian lamented "the fantastically rapid contraction of our [i.e., British] influence, commercial and cultural, across the globe," suggesting that both Fleming brothers were genuinely worried about Britain's waning power and influence in the postwar era.[61] Even though the preoccupation of Section D. 2 (d) with attempts to upset "the balance of nature" might initially seem ludicrous, it anticipates the consistent focus on environmental threats and ecological damage posed by the villains in Ian's novels. For example, Peter's make-believe section of MI5 suspects that the "grey squirrel had been deliberately introduced into these islands by German agents before the First World War" and imagines "how easy it would be for the King's enemies to infiltrate into Great Britain birds, beasts, insects, or indeed fish, which might have unbalancing and perhaps even disastrous effects on our precarious agricultural economy!"[62]

Peter's work anticipates the unnatural plots of Ernst Stavro Blofeld in *On Her Majesty's Secret Service*, where Bond's nemesis indeed attempts to destroy Britain's "precarious agricultural economy" by using female "angels of death" to introduce bacteriological agents, thereby infecting the UK's crops and livestock with sterility. In *You Only Live Twice*, moreover, Blofeld—under the pseudonym Shatterhand—introduces alien and poisonous species of plants, flowers, and fish into Japan, creating a "garden of death" designed to lure suicides to its fatal snares. In both novels, Blofeld's conspiracies can be traced back to the presumed threat to Britain's "balance of nature" presented in *The Sixth Column*. Even Plan D—a conspiracy to create enemy "agents of influence" among Britain's literary, political, and cultural elites—is coopted for action by Section D. 2 (d) on the grounds (in Captain Volpard's words) that "monkeying about with our national character! If that's not upsetting the balance of nature I'm damned if I know what is!"[63]

Given Ian's passionate interest in the environment and the balance of nature, it is not surprising he latched on to this aspect of his brother's spy novel. His experience at Goldeneye had introduced him to the pleasures of snorkeling, which became something of an obsession, and he became fascinated with the undersea world. One of Ian's heroes was Jacques Cousteau, the famous French marine explorer and conservationist, and he sought to imitate his idol on a small scale at Goldeneye. As Ross Kenneth Urken writes,

> In 1949, Ian Fleming bought a blank naturalist's notebook which he grandly labeled "Sea Fauna or the Finny Tribe of Goldeneye." Bound in leather and its title embossed in gold, he took it with him when he departed London for his beloved Jamaica, where he would immerse himself in the island's natural beauty and dive among its plentiful barracudas. He called two of the larger specimens Bicester and Beaufort, similar to creatures seen in "Thunderball," one of a dozen novels he would later write about a certain British spy.[64]

These underwater adventures became a valued part of Ian's life at Goldeneye and would also go on to have a profound influence on the Bond novels.

James Bond's vital role, as a defender of fragile ecosystems and protector of endangered life forms, in novels such as *Live and Let Die*, *Moonraker*, and

Dr. No, displays Ian's more extended development of the "balance of nature" mandate of Peter's imaginary MI5 section in *The Sixth Column*. Even Captain Volpard's quip about "all those questionnaires about cormorants which you said nobody would trouble to answer" would find an echo in *Dr. No*, where the eponymous villain has made his fortune from guano, or the droppings of the green cormorant, which provides an innocuous front for his plot of interference with American rockets.[65] Bond's attention is drawn to the evil doctor by his hostility to another bird, the roseate spoonbill—thus upsetting the balance of nature on Crab Key, a British possession.

Given the ongoing rivalry between the Fleming brothers, the timing of their publications is significant. Ian began work on his first novel, *Casino Royale*, in February 1952, less than six months after the publication of *The Sixth Column*. As we know, Ian kept his ear close to the ground about developments and news in the publishing world, and there could have been no more interesting story than his brother publishing a spy novel. Had Peter yet again beaten him to the prize of literary acclaim? In view of its satirical tone and style, Peter's novel would perhaps have greater influence on spy spoofs such as Graham Greene's *Our Man in Havana*. But Peter certainly also contributed to the creation of James Bond by laying down this marker of his own spy fiction.

There were other nonliterary factors at work, pushing Ian closer toward launching his career as a spy novelist. Ian's fears that the brilliant World War II successes of Naval Intelligence, the Secret Intelligence Service, and the Special Operations Executive would be wiped out by postwar ineptitude and betrayal seemed confirmed in May 1951, with the disappearance of Guy Burgess and Donald Maclean. The "missing diplomats," as Ian's friend Cyril Connolly described them in his book, had both been posted in Washington, DC, and had access to classified material concerning the US nuclear program. The worst fears of the British and American governments would be confirmed when the two men showed up in Moscow. The finger of suspicion pointed to Kim Philby, a high-ranking officer of SIS, as the "third man" who had tipped off Burgess and Maclean, threatening an even greater spy scandal. Meanwhile, unbeknownst to Ian or to British intelligence, another important SIS agent, George Blake, was still actively handing secrets to the Soviet Union, including the details of Operation Gold—the secret tunnel dug by the British and Americans under the Soviet sector of Berlin in the early 1950s in order to tap classified Soviet communications between East Germany and Moscow. As Steve Vogel writes,

> It was not just documents that George Blake was turning over to the KGB. It was names as well—the identities of agents working for SIS. Most of them were East Germans, though they included Soviets and other nationalities. As with documents, Blake could not put a number on how many agents he betrayed. "I can't say, but it must have been maybe five hundred, six hundred," he later said.[66]

Though Blake would not be exposed as a Soviet double agent and confess until 1961, the culture of betrayal was rife in SIS long before that. As would later emerge, Guy Burgess had been instructed by Kim Philby to tip off Maclean about his impending arrest, resulting from the investigation of him by British and US intelligence agencies. They were looking for a British embassy mole (codenamed Homer) in Washington, DC, who was leaking information to the Soviets. Philby was at this time a senior officer in SIS who was posted in Washington, DC. Burgess, however, apparently panicked and decided to flee with Maclean, taking the SS *Falaise* from Southampton to the French port of Saint Malo, on May 25, 1951.

Philby's close friendship with Burgess—with whom he had shared his house in the US capital—made him a prime suspect and led to the accusations of his being the "third man." He was investigated by both SIS and MI5, but the lack of conclusive proof meant that Philby was not prosecuted but allowed to retire discreetly from SIS.[67] SIS was inclined to defend one of its senior agents from scandal and, as MacIntyre notes, "did not take kindly to having one of its officers accused of treachery without hard evidence, let alone the suggestion that the Foreign Office was staffed with drunken, mentally unstable sexual deviants."[68]

Burgess was clearly the loose cannon in this group of Soviet double agents, who became notorious as the "Cambridge Spies," although Maclean could also be indiscreet. Michael Smith writes, "Burgess began as an ideological traitor, but was soon much more concerned with being needed by the Soviets. . . . Ultimately, Burgess needed someone, the KGB in this case, to need him, and to make him believe that he was someone who mattered." The selfishness of Burgess's flight is reinforced by the fact that by disappearing so abruptly he implicated not only Philby but also the "fifth man," John Cairncross, as MI5 found a classified document in Burgess's flat with "an accompanying note written by Cairncross which referred to the discussions between Stalin and Beneš over the 1939 invasion of Czechoslovakia." Under interrogation, Cairncross insisted "his relationship with Burgess was entirely innocent and he had no connection with espionage." Though the prosecution of Cairncross wasn't pursued, he was now on the SIS's radar as a likely traitor. Late in life, Cairncross retained a "strong ideological conviction that spying for the Soviets had been the right thing to do."[69]

Ian, like many others with backgrounds in British intelligence, was appalled by the scandal surrounding Burgess and Maclean's disappearance and probable defection. Having worked so hard during World War II to strengthen ties between British and American intelligence, Ian knew only too well the damage the Burgess and Maclean scandal would cause not only to the prestige of British intelligence and diplomacy but also to Britain's "special relationship" with the United States.[70] If highly placed, trusted British diplomats such as Burgess and Maclean could betray their countries and allies, why should the United States allow Britain access to its most highly classified material?

Ian's shocked reaction to the defections of Burgess and Maclean, and dismay at the suspicions that fell on Philby, was personal as well as political. Alaric Jacobs claimed that Ian knew Philby "quite well" and indicated that Philby had used his work for *The Times* as cover for his SIS involvements.[71] These men, traitors all, came from a similar class and educational background as Ian. As an Old Etonian, he was further chastened by the fact that Burgess had also gone to Eton, bringing disgrace to the school as well as the country. Burgess had then attended the Royal Naval Academy at Dartmouth (whereas Fleming had been at Sandhurst) before going on to Trinity College Cambridge, the same college as Kim Philby (Maclean was at Trinity Hall). Notably, Ian himself—unlike Peter—had not been to university in England, and in creating his spy hero he made sure that Bond would share this lack of an Oxbridge education and dedicate his career to bringing down the Soviet system that had seduced and recruited the Cambridge spies.

The timing of the defections was impactful on the creation of James Bond in that they occurred just as Ian was gathering his energies to finally start writing his spy novel. Fleming had already decided to make his hero a professional spy, one who had honed his intelligence and combat skills during World War II—seeing much more direct action than his creator—and had then continued in the secret world after the war. Whereas Fleming had turned down the offer of a job in intelligence after the war, Bond accepted a job, or rather (in euphemistic SIS-speak) made a "post-war application to continue working for the Ministry in which . . . he had risen to the rank of Principal Officer in the Civil Service."[72]

Born under the shadow of betrayal, scandal, austerity, and failure that haunted SIS in the early 1950s, James Bond had to be something more than a tough spy hero. He had to restore the confidence and morale of British intelligence but also provide a boost for Britain as a nation. Still enduring the hardships of postwar rationing and shortages, experiencing the birth pangs of the welfare state under Attlee's Labour government (which stayed in office until Attlee called a snap election in October 1951, losing narrowly to the Conservatives under Churchill), the British people were still reeling from the aftermath of World War II.[73] The cost of the Korean War, beginning in 1950, had added further burdens to the British taxpayer, resulting in another austerity budget from Chancellor Hugh Gaitskell. This war—coming so soon after the end of World War II—also engaged tens of thousands of British troops in combat in a remote overseas conflict. For many, the advantages of supporting the United States in the fight against Communism were outweighed by the economic and emotional cost of another war.

Ian, enjoying his annual tropical vacations in Jamaica while others endured the winter freeze in the United Kingdom, felt it his patriotic duty to create a hero who did more than reflect his own aspirational lifestyle fantasies and need to escape from dull routine. Of course, Bond would live well, dress with style, be handsome and charismatic, be equipped with the latest technology, travel to exotic locations, and be irresistible to women. Beyond this, though, Bond would have to provide a shot in the arm for his ailing nation, a reminder of Britain's wartime spirit under Churchill and unassailable courage in fighting the Nazis. Bond's Britishness would be an indelible and enduring part of his identity as a spy hero.

Ian was assisted in this patriotic purpose by the events of history. On February 6, 1952, King George VI died, and his daughter Elizabeth became Queen Elizabeth II of the United Kingdom and the Commonwealth. George's death occurred while Fleming was in Jamaica, writing the novel published the following year as *Casino Royale*. Hence James Bond would, from his first appearance, always be on Her Majesty's Secret Service, and this transition to a new generation in the monarchy offered a fresh start to Fleming's spy story as well. Elizabeth represented a break with the wartime past, with Britain's imperial history, and the beginning of a new, more modern era of the Commonwealth.

In fact, Ian hoped that the timing of *Casino*'s publication would coincide with the coronation of Queen Elizabeth in 1953, though in the event the novel's publication predated the coronation by several weeks. However, the inclusion of "Royale" in the title reflected Ian's eagerness to tie the novel and its hero with the British monarchy. In a letter to Jonathan Cape, Ian—always with an eye on the literary market—suggested the publication date of April 15 for *Casino*, as "The 'Royale' in the title may help to pick up some extra sales over the coronation period."[74] This association between Bond and the monarchy has continued up to the twenty-first century, notably with the queen's arrival, via "parachute," at the Olympic Stadium during the Danny Boyle–directed Opening Ceremony of the 2012 London Olympic Games chaperoned by none other than 007 (Daniel Craig).

The new queen seemed to promise Britain renewed hope, and even the coronation reflected a new age of mass media, for it was the first crowning of a British monarch to be televised. This was at Elizabeth's own insistence, despite the misgivings of the prime minister, Winston Churchill. Clearly the new queen wished to connect with her people in a new, more media-savvy way. As the first female monarch since Queen Victoria, the accession of Queen Elizabeth to the throne ushered in a period of frenzied patriotism, with three million spectators thronging the streets to witness the event. It was a gilded occasion in more ways than one: the queen and the duke of Edinburgh were driven in the Gold State Coach from Buckingham Palace to Westminster Abbey. As though in reciprocity, Ian ordered his own "golden typewriter," writing Ivar Bryce in May with the request that his old friend smuggle the machine into the country from the United States.

With the public euphoria surrounding the coronation of the new queen, the scandals of the Cambridge spies could be forgotten—at least temporarily. Yet, there were other cracks appearing in the veneer of British self-assurance and global authority. In 1947, India—the largest possession in the British Empire—had gained its independence, leaving Britain bereft of the "jewel in the Crown" of its overseas territories. Other nations in Asia and Africa would decolonize in the 1950s and 1960s—including Ghana and Nigeria—marking the end of Britain's imperial reign. Fleming, like many of his friends (such as Noël Coward), believed in the value of the British Empire and was despondent about its rapid collapse after World War II. Unlike most, however, Ian had the opportunity to respond to the actual decline of Britain's power by creating a fantasy of its resilience in James Bond. Seizing the new spirit of patriotic enthusiasm, Ian could dedicate himself to creating a spy hero who would triumph over the enemies of queen and country and keep Britain at the "top table" of international affairs.

Bond is an agent of the British Empire despite the fact that this empire was rapidly shrinking when he was created. As James Chapman argues, "Fleming's Bond is undoubtedly one of 'the Breed,' that group of instinctively competitive, patriotic, honest and square-jawed defenders of the realm."[75] But while Fleming had long been an avid reader (and, at Durnford, listener) of the imperialist spy thrillers of John Buchan, "Sapper," and Oppenheimer, he saw his own first novel as an opportunity to update and upgrade that tradition. While Bond might preserve some traces of the Edwardian "clubland heroes," his identity emerged from the culture of the second half of the twentieth century, belonging to the jet age and the Cold War. Britain seemed to have a promising edge in this technology, as the British de Havilland Comet airline was the first commercial jet airliner to be in service, starting in 1951.

In 1952, Jamaica was still a British colony, allowing Ian the illusion of being part of a colonial class of British expatriates (at least in winter months). The tranquil and private location overlooking the Caribbean Sea allowed Ian the leisure to become immersed in his fantasy realm without distraction from ringing telephones, flickering television screens, heavy traffic, or (with a few exceptions) unwanted visitors. The tropical climate allowed him to relax and enjoy the hedonism that (along with its corollary, a Scottish-bred puritanism) was a powerful strand in his character. Jamaica provided Ian with the mental and emotional freedom he needed to create original fiction.

While in Britain Attlee's government was installing a welfare state that sought to strip away privilege from the dominant class and redistribute its wealth for the good of society (at least in theory), Jamaica could still be a bubble of luxury for the elite. In Jamaica, Ian could escape to a world where he was still "Commander."[76] At Goldeneye, he could indulge and elaborate on the beguiling myth that Britain's empire was still in its heyday and that his spy hero James Bond was always going to protect its interests and vanquish its enemies. He and his friends would meet for cocktails at Goldeneye or Blue Harbour or one of the new hotels in Montego Bay and congratulate each other on their delightful and enviable lifestyles, blocking out the bleak winter climate and deteriorating prestige of the mother country. Goldeneye was the perfect oasis in which Ian could conceive and create his postwar fantasy of British importance and power.

But was Bond really a spy fantasy? It is tempting to see Ian's job at Kemsley Newspapers as a continuation, in a different form, of his wartime espionage in Naval Intelligence. During the war, the wall behind Fleming's desk in the Admiralty's Room 39 was papered with maps showing the locations of his agents, including 30AU personnel. The wall behind his desk at Kemsley House also had a large map with the locations of his various "correspondents" or agents. Ian's salary at Kemsley of £4,500 plus £500 expenses seems unusually generous for a journalist but reasonable if Fleming was also running spy networks through Mercury. An archive at *The Sunday Times* also reveals that Fleming had a copy of *Bentley's Complete Phrase Code* in his office, which seems unusual even in the competitive world of journalism but standard practice for intelligence work.[77]

If Ian was indeed running agents from London, with some of his "correspondents" also on the payroll of the security service, then the long delay in writing his spy story is less surprising. The fact that Ian "refused" a new postwar job in intelligence in order to work for Kemsley—Maud Russell noted that "the newspapers are offering him handsome jobs"—did not mean Ian had forsworn further connections with espionage.[78] Rather, the job with Kemsley provided an ideal cover for Ian to continue running agents—the intelligence-gathering expertise of foreign correspondents being second only to professional diplomats and spies—under a respectable, civilian cover.

Perhaps Fleming didn't need to create a fictional spy immediately following the war because he was still recruiting and running real ones. Only later when the Mercury Network was well established, and he "had become increasingly bored with executive life at the paper," did Fleming commit himself to inventing a fictional spy who could fulfill his fantasies of action and adventure.[79] The combination of an impending marriage and loss of his bachelorhood, a damaging spy scandal, and the publication of his brother's spy novel were the sparks that led Ian to give life to the spy hero who had been gestating in his imagination for years if not decades.

Chapter Six

The Spy Story to End All Spy Stories

Casino Royale

When Ian's friend Robert Harling—who was a member of Fleming's 30 Assault Unit (30AU) during World War II—asked him what he planned to do after the war, Ian hardly missed a beat: "In due course, I am proposing to write the spy story to end all spy stories."[1] As things turned out, however, his debut novel was not "the spy story to end all spy stories" but the launch of the most famous fictional spy of all time: a character that remains alive and iconic, in both literature and film, in the twenty-first century.

Beginning with *Casino Royale* in 1952 (published the following year), Ian produced a new Bond novel each winter in Goldeneye, Jamaica, up to and including the year of his death in 1964.[2] For many readers, *Casino* remains the best Fleming novel in the canon—this, indeed, was Raymond Chandler's opinion about the superiority of the first in the series. In any case, *Casino* was a remarkably accomplished, mature debut and one that almost single-handedly dragged the spy genre from the Edwardian gentlemen's club into the Cold War era and modern jet age. What made this remarkable novel so different from its predecessors, and how did it come to be so influential on the course of spy fiction and popular culture?

First, Ian made the conscious decision that his protagonist would be a *professional* spy. Today, in an era when so many spy novels and films feature characters from the Secret Intelligence Service (SIS), Central Intelligence Agency (CIA), Mossad, or KGB, this might seem an obvious choice. But at the time, most of the significant precursors in the spy novel featured amateur agents or "accidental spies"—gentlemen (and sometimes women) who happened to stumble upon a plot of international intrigue, often threatening the national security of Britain. Even Ashenden, Maugham's spy protagonist, uses his job as a professional writer as cover for his work in intelligence. Maugham's analysis of the workings of the government agency is quite minimal, the emphasis being on Ashenden's sophisticated "man of the world" persona while engaged on his missions abroad. The typical protagonists of Eric Ambler—another important influence on Fleming—are "everymen," engineers or journalists or writers, who happen to be drawn into a conspiracy, often backed by an international bank or major corporation for whom war is a matter of profit, not ideology or nationality.

Dennis Wheatley's serial spy hero Gregory Sallust is a professional, of sorts, and Jeremy Duns has recently made a persuasive case for the influence of Wheatley's spy fiction on Fleming. Referring to Wheatley's 1936 novel *Contraband*, Duns notes,

> The line about Sallust's scar giving him an almost satanic look appears, with minor variations, in several novels in the series: it tends to show "a livid white" against his dark features when he is angry. Like *Contraband*, *Casino Royale* opens with a handsome, world-weary British secret agent gambling late at night in a casino in northern France (the fictional resort of Royale-les-Eaux, which Fleming modelled loosely on Deauville and Le Touquet).[3]

However, there is comparatively little detail in the Sallust novels about his professional life or the spy organization he serves. Another of the popular spy novelists of the period, Helen MacInnes, launched her career with *Above Suspicion* (1941), featuring Richard and Frances Myles, a married couple from Oxford sent on a mission to Europe, for whom espionage is clearly an amateur pursuit.

Ian's decision to professionalize the fictional spy reflected important changes in the attitude and structure of British intelligence after the war. As one wartime SIS recruit, George Blake—who later achieved notoriety as a Soviet double agent—writes,

> The pre-war Secret Service had been very much a kind of club of enthusiastic amateurs, autocratically ruled by the Chief, who could take them on, sack them and pay them as he deemed fit, not bound by any Civil Service rules and regulations. The new SIS, which emerged after the big post-war reorganization was a properly established Government Department with a personnel department, gradings, regular promotions, pension schemes and annual increments.

> There were many old hands who shook their heads at all this new-fangled bureaucratic paraphernalia.[4]

Ian being no lover of bureaucracy—despite his wartime role in the Naval Intelligence Division (NID)—it is quite possible that he too lamented the passing of the age of inspired amateurism and improvisation in which he had thrived while in NID. However, as a new author anxious to carve out a niche in the marketplace for spy fiction, Ian knew he had to reflect the changing realities of professional intelligence. Bond, as we are told in *Moonraker*, worked in a large organization, and his "typical routine day" involved "the duties of an easy-going senior civil servant." Even his salary reflects his rank: "He earned £1500 a year, the salary of a Principal Officer in the Civil Service."[5] Bond—except for the occasions when he's on a mission—is a bureaucrat tied to an office as Ian was in Naval Intelligence.

Fleming's breakthrough was to establish these professional credentials and surroundings of Bond but set them against an exciting background for his various assignments. The opening of *Casino* is defined by the emphasis on Bond's professional status. He has a "controller" based in Jamaica, his chief is in London, and his access to intelligence about the villain Le Chiffre comes through a classified dossier held by SIS. Bond is a highly trained expert who has learned the tricks of the trade, which he demonstrates by leaving minute "burglar-alarms" in his room in the Hotel Splendide, designed to reveal if his possessions have been searched.[6] Bond has a remarkable instinct of self-preservation, allowing him to survive even a bombing attack that occurs early in the novel. As a member of the 00 section of SIS, he also collaborates with highly trained agents of foreign intelligence services—most notably (in this novel) René Mathis of the Deuxième Bureau and Felix Leiter of the CIA. Bond is part of a professional culture of intelligence work, and his mission is authorized at the highest levels of government.

Perhaps most important, we learn that James Bond, as a member of the 00 section, possesses a "license to kill." He has earned this license by carrying out two kills in the line of duty, both of which are described in some detail early in Fleming's first novel. One of the killings—the assassination of an enemy Japanese cipher clerk working in the Rockefeller Center in New York—was based on an incident Fleming actually witnessed while in New York during World War II. The invention of an imaginary "00 section" is a masterstroke by Fleming, for it places Bond in an elite unit within the SIS, giving him special powers and privileged status and identifying him as a top professional agent.

The opening words of *Casino Royale* have become among the most famous in spy fiction history. However, the most surprising feature of this opening is how off-putting the setting is from a sensory perspective: "The scent and smoke and sweat of a casino are nauseating at three in the morning. Then the soul-erosion produced by high gambling—a compost of greed and fear and nervous tension—becomes unbearable and the senses awake and revolt from it."[7] Despite Ian's love of *jeux de hasard* and casinos, there is no romance or glamor to this scene of nocturnal gambling. It is hard to imagine Childers's Davies and Carruthers, or Buchan's Hannay, making their first appearance in a casino, let alone in the seedy atmosphere depicted by Ian. Not merely its gritty, unpleasant setting but also the mood of cynicism and exhaustion marked *Casino Royale* as something entirely new in spy fiction. The atmosphere is closer to one of the hardboiled detective novels of Dashiell Hammett or Raymond Chandler, which Ian enjoyed reading, than to earlier spy fiction.

The tone of seedy and corrupt pleasures mixed with danger is perhaps based on Ian's own enjoyment of such louche surroundings. According to Ivar Bryce, "He liked gambling. Liked it for the sensations of risk, excitement it gave him."[8] Fleming introduces his spy hero with uncanny insight into his thoughts and feelings because he is based on Ian himself: "James Bond suddenly knew that he was tired. He always knew when his body or his mind had had enough and he always acted on the knowledge. This helped him to avoid staleness and the sensual bluntness that breeds mistakes."[9]

The novel's opening raises several questions in the reader's mind, such as, what kind of profession requires someone to be in a casino at three in the morning, and why would it involve a fear of making "mistakes"? The author then tantalizingly suggests that Bond may be a criminal planning a robbery of the casino. Even though we soon learn Bond was not "personally concerned [with robbing the caisse], but only interested," there is something jarring and inappropriate about a British spy hero contemplating such criminal action.[10]

The source of the idea for an epic battle between East and West—SMERSH versus SIS—over the baccarat table has been widely discussed. Ian's wartime stopover in Estoril, on Portugal's Riviera, while accompanying Admiral John Godfrey on a visit to the British Security Co-ordination in New York, led to his trying his luck in the casino. Ian took on a couple of Portuguese businessmen in suits at baccarat and soon lost all his money, which did not impress Godfrey. As well as a popular tourist resort, Estoril was known during the war as a center of espionage and diplomatic intrigue, drawing spies from both Allied and Axis nations. As they were leaving the casino, Fleming shared a fantasy with his Naval Intelligence boss—that those Portuguese businessmen had been Nazi officers and that Fleming had been able to strike a blow for the Allied war effort by defeating them at cards.

Yet, it is a long way from this fleeting experience in Estoril to the casino at Royale-les-Eaux. By the time Ian came to write this scenario, the war had been over for several years, and the nature of the enemy would have to be updated to reflect the changed world of the Cold War. Ian's boldest move was to make the game of baccarat the centerpiece of the entire novel rather than merely the prelude to it. But the fundamental concept of *Casino Royale*—that of a British hero taking on a sinister, ruthless foreign enemy agent in a high-stakes card game with international implications and deadly consequences—had been brewing in Ian's mind for years.

In Le Chiffre, Ian created not only one of his most sinister villains but also a product of the trauma and conflict of World War II. In the chapter titled "Dossier for M," we read not only about Le Chiffre's present activities as an agent of the Soviet Union who is now facing a "financial crisis" but also of his past as a displaced person and inmate of Dachau concentration camp. Suffering from amnesia caused by the war (though the dossier suggests this was feigned), this man chose his name—which literally means "the number"—because "I am only a number on a passport."[11] As is often the case with his villains, Fleming inserts a mixed-race element, raising the possibility that Le Chiffre was imprisoned in Dachau due to his partly Jewish ethnicity, though Fleming also identifies Polish, Prussian, and Mediterranean blood in his background. Le Chiffre is a product of a broken postwar Europe, his loss of memory and speech being symptoms of the destruction of the past, indeed the loss of identity, of Europe as a result of World War II. Though Dachau began as a camp for the internment of political prisoners, it later was used for the imprisonment of Jews and criminals. The camp featured brutal punishments and executions, causing its inmates to live in terror. Hence Le Chiffre's dumbness, when discovered, can also be read as a paralyzing response to the trauma of the war that killed millions of soldiers on either side and came horrifyingly close to destroying the Jewish population of Europe.

On the other hand, *Casino* has one foot firmly in Europe's prewar past, when Ian and his cronies in Le Cercle went on pleasure excursions for golf and gambling to the French coastal resort of Le Touquet, the inspiration for the novel's location of Royale-les-Eaux. Ian's first novel reflects nostalgia for a time of elegance and luxury before the destruction and devastations of war, and it used this to account for the rebuilding of the resort. While this French location is vital to the novel, it is significant that Bond is controlled from Jamaica—the island where the novel was written and where, in effect, Bond was born.

Ian's wartime experience working closely with the United States—assisting William Stephenson with British Security Co-ordination, working with Bryce and the Office of Strategic Services, and helping to draw up the blueprint for the CIA, the new American intelligence service, for William Donovan—is also influential in *Casino Royale*. While in the casino, Bond makes friendly contact with an American who turns out to be the CIA agent, Felix Leiter. Their first exchange symbolically takes place over ordering a drink, when Bond requests his famous version of a martini—later christened a "Vesper"—eliciting an admiring response from Leiter. Felix was the middle name of Ian's old Eton friend Ivar Bryce, with whom he shared many adventures and indulgences in Britain, Europe, the United States, and Jamaica. Their shared delight in risky exploits is shown in Bond's close friendship with Leiter, which is based on yet transcends their professional relationship.

At the same time, Fleming makes it clear that Bond is in charge—despite the reality of America's superiority both economically and politically in the postwar era. Leiter admits, "Washington's pretty sick we're not running the show"—that is, the operation to destroy Le Chiffre—and concedes that he is there to provide backup and follow Bond's orders.[12] Of course, later in the novel, the economic muscle of the United States is demonstrated forcefully after Bond loses the first round of baccarat to Le Chiffre.

While the Cambridge spy scandal of Burgess and Maclean is not explicitly mentioned in *Casino*—as it is in *From Russia, with Love*, for example—its impact is clear in the theme of a Soviet double agent betraying secrets under the very noses of the British SIS. Bond will reproach himself for having missed the various clues that "now stood out like signposts" about Vesper's treason—reflecting the self-recrimination of British intelligence and the Foreign Office at having been betrayed by "their own" men, trusted agents Burgess, Maclean, and—as it later transpired—Kim Philby and George Blake. With a sense of disgust, Bond realizes "the real enemy" had been working alongside him all the time—a hidden foe in contrast to the clear demarcation between ally and enemy in World War II.[13]

Ian boldly gave the postwar spy scandal a significant twist by reimagining the double agent as a beautiful female employee of SIS, allowing her to exploit one of Bond's major blind spots—his "weakness for women."[14] It is Bond's inability, first, to take women seriously as colleagues and, subsequently, to view Vesper as more than a sexual "distraction" or potential romantic partner—that leads to his painful undoing.

One of the most off-putting elements of *Casino Royale* for the modern reader is the flagrant, even virulent, nature of Bond's misogyny. On being told by Mathis that his female assistant has arrived from SIS, Bond responds with anger, "What the hell do they want to send me a woman for? . . . Do they think this is a bloody picnic?" Mathis—who presumes Bond's chauvinistic interest in Vesper's physique—also vouches for her professional qualifications, which include speaking fluent French, and assures Bond of her seriousness. Yet these various accomplishments do not assuage Bond's objections to this "pest of a girl."[15]

The question asked by many readers is, does Bond speak for Fleming in his initial dismissal of Vesper's worth as an agent? While Ian may have shared some of Bond's attitudes to women—assessing them first as potential sexual partners, for example—we should be wary of assuming Bond is simply a fictionalized mouthpiece for Fleming. For as the novel will make clear, Bond's failure to take Vesper seriously makes him dangerously vulnerable and becomes a serious flaw in his professional self-defense. Rather than endorsing Bond's blunt misogyny, then, Fleming displays its dire consequences.

The complex blend of hedonism and puritanism in Bond's character, however, undoubtedly reflects that of his creator. Likewise, the compartmentalizing that leads Bond to wish to separate his work from his leisure reflects Ian's preference for quite rigid boundaries between different areas of his life and groups of friends. John Pearson portrayed *Casino Royale* as launching a double life for Ian Fleming:

> During the six years following *Casino Royale*, when he wrote his most memorable books, Ian was at his happiest, as he lived two separate lives—the daily round of an unhappy marriage and the exciting Walter Mitty world he escaped to in the person of James Bond. And during these six brief years Bond was Ian's slave and faithful friend.

Pearson continues these insights into Ian's dual personality, arguing that "nearly everyone who knew him well comments on the way he seemed to enjoy compartmentalizing his life, keeping his various sets of friends rigorously apart, so that those to whom he was very close in one role would not be aware of those equally close to him in another."[16] The drawback to Pearson's emphasis on Bond as Fleming's escapist fantasy is that it ignores the extent to which the novel reflects the actual political and ideological conflicts of the period—especially the profound duality of the Cold War. Not only were East and West separated by an "Iron Curtain," but double agents were living similarly stratified and duplicitous lives, posing as loyal British spies and diplomats while secretly undermining the capitalist system of Western democracies from within.

Ian famously claimed that he began writing *Casino Royale* to distract himself from anxiety about his impending marriage to Ann Rothermere (née Charteris). A confirmed bachelor at the age of forty-four, despite his numerous affairs and long romantic and sexual involvement with Ann, Ian entered the married state with trepidation and reluctance—out of a sense of duty rather than desire, it seems, when Ann became pregnant with his child.

It may or may not be a coincidence that a number of Fleming's lovers in real life had names beginning with "M" (Maud Russell, Monique de Bottomes, Muriel Wright, Millicent Rogers)—the initial he also frequently used to address his mother, Eve. It is surely not happenstance, however, that so many of his fictional heroines have names that—like Eve—possess religious or even biblical significance. "Vesper"—the first female character he created—means an evening prayer, though it is also a literary name for Venus (the goddess of love) in her incarnation as the evening star. The woman Bond would eventually marry is named Teresa—the name of the Spanish Saint Teresa of Avila whose "Autobiography" (1567) is among the great works of Renaissance mystic/spiritual literature. Teresa di Vicenza prefers to be called "Tracy," telling Bond, "Teresa was a saint. I am not a saint."[17] But the spiritual association of the name remains. In the later novels—beginning with *On Her Majesty's Secret Service*—Bond's new personal secretary is Mary Goodnight, another religious association with the Virgin Mary and the night.

As her name suggests, Vesper is indeed a creature of the night—she belongs, with Bond, at the nocturnal casino sessions where the battle with Le Chiffre takes place. She is also, like Venus, a beautiful woman capable of stirring great desire and passion in men. Vesper is at home in the darkness in another sense—her clandestine work as a double agent for the Soviet Union is secretive and best conducted under the shadows. The traumatic late scene at Le Chiffre's villa near Royale—when Bond is tortured while Vesper, apparently, is being brutalized by the villain's men—takes place at night, when the eyes of the civilized world are closed in sleep. Like the atrocities perpetrated at concentration camps during World War II, Le Chiffre's tortures are shrouded in darkness. And, of course, it is at night that Vesper takes her own life in the French hotel, writing her confession to Bond before taking a fatal overdose of sleeping pills. One of the ironies of the iconic status of Bond is that Vesper is remembered for having given her name to a potent cocktail rather than for these more mystical associations.[18]

Despite Bond's harsh dismissal of her at the novel's end—"The bitch is dead now"—it is clear to the reader that Vesper betrayed SIS and her country out of love for her Polish fiancé rather than malice toward Britain and its intelligence service.[19] It was in order to protect him—to save his life—that she betrayed SIS secrets to the MWD. Though Bond has lost Vesper to Le Chiffre, he is mistaken about her motives. As would be the case with other Fleming novels, there is far more complexity to the "Bond heroine" than either Bond or the reader realize at first.

The card game between Bond and Le Chiffre can be read as an extended metaphor for the Cold War hostilities between East and West (similar to the chess match in *From Russia, with Love*). It is typical of Ian's technique as a writer that he grounds the global ideological conflict, something of an abstraction, in the concrete and thrilling situation of a competitive game. The battle of wits and nerve over baccarat, with its swings and reversals of fortune, is the "field" in which Bond and Le Chiffre test their mettle, struggle for dominance and power, and ultimately seek to destroy their opponent. *Casino* is, in fact, the most extreme case of this "game" motif—for the card game is not merely a prelude to the later conflict, as in *Moonraker* and *Goldfinger*, but the very heart of the plot.

Bond and Le Chiffre are the two best card players in the game, and each represents a hostile intelligence organization—SIS and SMERSH, respectively. Each "side" in the Cold War has put forward its most skillful card player for the contest. There is one important difference in their positions, however. Bond is the "official" candidate of Britain's SIS, sent by M to defeat Le Chiffre and destroy his networks of financing for the SMERSH "fifth column" in France. By contrast, Le Chiffre has organized the game at the Casino Royale because he has embezzled funds from his organization and has to recoup these losses before they are detected. Le Chiffre, then, has "gone rogue" on SMERSH and is in a more vulnerable position. This precarious situation makes him, if anything, even more dangerous and ruthless. Quite simply, Le Chiffre cannot afford to lose.

Fleming suggests that his novel, like the card game, follows a set of rules, moves through different phases, and will eventually produce a definite "winner." Fleming maximizes the suspense of the story by having Bond first lose all his funds to Le Chiffre (at the end of chapter 11), apparently suffering an ignominious defeat. Then, in the first of many such reversals in the canon, Bond will return to life with a new financial backer in the person of Felix Leiter of the CIA (perhaps an ironic comment on Bryce's personal wealth, which Fleming enjoyed the fruits of during trips to Jamaica, New York, and Vermont).

The risk, of course, is that the lengthy description of the card game—even for readers who know the rules of baccarat—could become tedious and repetitive. Ian circumvents this by creating dramatic scenes showing Le Chiffre's willingness to take any measures, fair or foul, to stop Bond winning. A key example is the incident of the "deadly tube" rifle disguised as a crutch and pointed at Bond's spine to force Bond to withdraw his bet. Fleming here creates a dramatic sequence from the potentially static card game, as Bond acrobatically flips head-over-heels and takes out his would-be assassin. Essentially, Ian shows that Bond cannot just rely on his card-playing skills to win this game but must be adaptable, active, and able to respond with violence to the villain's "moves" whether they fall within the rules of the card game or not.[20]

Even before the baccarat game begins, an attempt is made on Bond's life by the Bulgarian assassins. One might ask why Le Chiffre—who desperately needs to win everyone's money to make himself whole—would eliminate one of the key players with a large purse. The answer must be that he already fears Bond as his chief rival and will sacrifice the opportunity of winning Bond's money for the security of removing him from the game. Ian draws on one of his wartime memories, the Russian attempt to kill Von Papen in Ankara, for a compelling scene in his novel.

As the game unfolds, Le Chiffre will always be holding the trump card, unknown to Bond or the reader. The name of this card is Vesper Lynd. While Bond has important allies in Mathis and Leiter, Le Chiffre has the best agent of all—a double agent, secretly working for him while trusted by the other side. All of Bond's secrets—from the cards he holds to the origin of the mission with M and the SIS intelligence background on Le Chiffre—are open for scrutiny by his adversary, without Bond's knowledge.

Near the end of the novel, after Le Chiffre has been killed by SMERSH, Bond ruminates on whether his role in killing the evil man has actually done any good. Mathis advises Bond not to reflect too deeply or become too human, or we would lose a "wonderful machine."[21] For Mathis, Bond is a mechanical contrivance, an assembly of parts designed for a specific purpose: the destruction of Britain's (and by extension, the West/NATO's) enemies. The same could be said about Fleming's novel—it is a "wonderful machine" that could be reproduced, with significant variations, each time Ian returned to Goldeneye for his winter break. And its purpose is to develop the myth of British supremacy during the Cold War by displaying the superiority of the SIS over SMERSH, of Western capitalism over Soviet Communism.

From the outset, the James Bond novels showcased and celebrated a certain lifestyle based on freedoms, commodities, and experiences available only in the West (even if to a limited selection of the populace). In terms of their "lifestyle ethos," there is a certain irony—even a contradiction—in the idea that Fleming's Bond novels represent a significant leap forward from the "clubland heroes" of the early spy novels. The heroes of novels by "Sapper," Dornford Yates, John Buchan, Erskine Childers, even William Le Queux are defined by their membership of and appearance in gentlemen's clubs (usually in London), a membership that defines their social and even their professional identities.

The main action of *Casino Royale* also takes place at a kind of club. Though the casino is open to the public, the crucial action takes place in a *salle privée*, or private room.[22] Bond first describes Le Chiffre gambling in this private room, and his epic battle at baccarat takes place in the same (or a similar) private space. Membership is restricted only to the players in the game and their friends and accomplices. In fact, membership of this club is restricted to upper-middle-class white men and women, defined by their professional status or work as intelligence agents. The social privilege of membership seems to transcend any ideological differences.

Not only did Fleming himself belong to several gentlemen's clubs in London, including Whites, the Portland Club, and Boodles, but he also formed his own exclusive social, dining, gambling, and golfing club called Le Cercle Gastronomique et des Jeux de Hasard, which consisted mainly of Old Etonian friends such as Duff Cooper, "Boofy" Gore (later Earl of Arran), Gerald Coke, John Fox-Strangways, and others in London. The one defining feature of this club is that it consisted only of upper-middle-class men; no women were admitted.

The "Royale" of the novel's title also connotes, despite its French location, a particularly British exclusivity and privilege. As his correspondence with his publisher, Jonathan Cape, reveals, Fleming wished to time the publication of his novel to coincide with the coronation of Queen Elizabeth II in 1953 and was disappointed when this could not happen. Fleming desired the "royal connection" with Queen Elizabeth, both for the publicity it would generate and because the "Royale" of his title suggested prestige, exclusivity, and "class" that would appeal to readers—or at least to the sort of readers Fleming wished to appeal to.

In the course of the novel, Bond, Mathis, and Leiter—an elite "club" of Western intelligence agents—join forces to organize an operation against their common enemy, Le Chiffre. He is a criminal, a sexual pervert (or "flagellant"), as well as the agent of an enemy power, the Soviet Union. And yet this "club" of Western allies treats Le Chiffre as an equal because of his membership of the same club. They play the same game, even if they don't always play by the same rules, and enjoy the same privileged lifestyle.

Following the unwritten rules of honor and loyalty to other "members," Leiter provides Bond with thirty-two million francs to allow him to continue in the game against Le Chiffre. Leiter calls this money "Marshall Aid," linking it to the US government plan, under Presidents Roosevelt and Truman, to provide vast financial support for the reconstruction of war-ravaged Western Europe after World War II.[23] Seen as an important measure to combat the spread of Soviet-backed Communism through Europe at a time of great economic instability, the Marshall Plan showcased the United States' superior economic power and political influence as compared to European countries, even those that had been on the victorious side of the war. Bond accepts this gift of money, though he pays it back after collecting seventy million francs in winnings.

When Bond defeats Le Chiffre at baccarat with the nine of hearts—"a whisper of love, a whisper of hate"—the villain does not accept his losses like a gentleman.[24] Instead, he lures Bond into a trap, kidnaps him, and brutally tortures him in order to make Bond give up his winnings. The method of this torture—beating Bond's genitals with a carpet beater to the point of emasculation—further demonstrates Le Chiffre's ineligibility for the "club" of honorable men. It is an atrocity, designed to inflict the maximum of pain and result in Bond being "no longer . . . a man."[25] Ironically, Le Chiffre's own employer—SMERSH—inflicts the punishment for dishonor, sending an assassin to put a bullet between his eyes for having embezzled money from them. Because SMERSH does its own dirty work, by killing those who betray it, Bond is spared the trouble of eliminating the ungentlemanly villain.

Vesper is another matter. Despite the fact that she is a member of the intelligence "club" in *Casino Royale*—accepted by Bond, Mathis, and Leiter—she ultimately proves unworthy of membership. While working alongside her male allies, Vesper is secretly a Soviet double agent, feeding secrets about Bond's mission and other classified information to the enemy. Her only honorable action, by the code of this club, is the suicide she commits immediately after writing her confession.

Ian's revisions to the original typescript of *Casino Royale* reveal his changing views of the novel's main themes. For example, he revises a passage about luck to emphasize that

> luck was a servant and not a master. Luck had to be accepted with a shrug or taken advantage of up to the hilt. But it had to be understood and recognized for what it was and not confused with a faulty appreciation of the odds, for at gambling, the deadly sin is to mistake bad play for bad luck.

Of course, Fleming ensures that Bond will ultimately have the good luck he needs to defeat Le Chiffre—in the form of the winning card that he changed to the nine of hearts from the original choice, the "curse of Scotland" (nine of diamonds), because its name suggests it is an unlucky card rather than a lucky one. But nonetheless Bond will, as he anticipates in a clear foreshadowing, eventually be "brought to his knees by love or by luck . . . he too would be branded with the deadly question mark."[26]

There were other literary influences at work on Ian as he wrote his first novel, especially given its focus on an exclusive "club" of intelligence agents. In 1937, Geoffrey Household had published his first novel, *The Third Hour*, which, Andrew Lycett notes, "Ian thought tackled contemporary issues in an exciting and realistic manner."[27] Despite its quite sophisticated approach to contemporary politics and international relations, Household's novel still promotes the idea of an exclusive circle. The group of friends at the novel's center, led by the liberal English businessman/adventurer Toby Manning, establishes a fellowship based on shared values and a disdain for the crassness of mainstream commercial culture. This "fellowship" will be organized as something between a monastic order and an exclusive, members-only social club.

Household provides an appendix to the novel with the rules and principles of this fellowship—dubbed The Order of the Third Hour—which dictate that the catering in the order will be of a standard to match the best club. This anticipates Fleming's description of M's gambling club, Blades, in *Moonraker*: "The food and wine are the best in London and no bills are presented, the cost of all meals being deducted at the end of each week *pro rata* from the profits of the winners."[28] And, in *Casino*, the relationship of Bond and Vesper is forged over an expensive, luxurious dinner in the sumptuous restaurant of the Hotel Splendide during which Bond tells his companion, "I take a ridiculous pleasure in what I eat and drink."[29] For Fleming, distinction in matters of food and drink are essential for membership.

In *The Third Hour*, each member must relinquish his or her property in order to enjoy the benefits of the "club," and new members can only be approved by a unanimous vote of the Grand Committee (i.e., all current/existing members), as "the abilities and tastes of each individual were so clearly defined that he or she fell inevitably into their natural office."[30] That the club is politically tolerant enough to allow a Nazi (even a former one) like Irma von Karlskreuz to join shows how the alignments of interwar politics are less important than this idea of "nobility" and honor. Women are also admitted to this club, although only in exceptional cases.

One of the secrets of Ian's success as a spy novelist was that he invoked an atmosphere of sophistication, luxury, and exclusiveness at a time when many of his compatriots—shivering through the bitter winter of London while Fleming was writing in tropical breezes at Goldeneye—were still suffering from scarcity, rationing, austerity, and postwar decline. Some foods—such as sugar and meat—were still rationed when Ian wrote his first novel. International travel was only for the rich, or for those in the armed forces, while even the television set was an unattainable luxury for many British households in the 1950s. Bond, then, moves in a world of glamor, material affluence, and freedom that was not accessible to many of his readers.[31]

Ian—a surprisingly good reader of popular moods and changing trends—realized that the coronation of the new queen brought a wave, if not a frenzy, of patriotic feeling to a still war-ravaged country. He felt that his own novel—boasting its own patriotic British hero—would chime in with and benefit from this surge of national feeling, as the British people celebrated a royal family that lived in a luxurious condition regular Brits paid for yet could never afford. This contradiction—that the British people, struggling with shortages and hardships, would celebrate an aristocratic, noble class with which they had almost nothing in common—was related to the contradiction of Bond himself. Bond's name and lifestyle evoke wealth and privilege—

from the treasury "bonds" of the financial markets and the exclusive area of Bond Street to Bond's own swanky Chelsea flat and vintage Bentley automobile and luxurious restaurants.

As the torture scene in Le Chiffre's villa demonstrates, though, the luxury Bond enjoys on his missions is paid for with the suffering of his vulnerable body. The idea that the pleasures and pains of the agent's life are mutually dependent is a point made clear at the opening of *Live and Let Die*, identifying the "moments of great luxury in the life of a secret agent" as "occasions when he takes refuge in good living to efface the memory of danger and the shadow of death."[32] On closer inspection, the passage reveals the dark side of a secret agent's life—that he is always facing mortality—in an echo of Psalm 23: "Even though I walk through the valley of the shadow of death, I will fear no evil for you are with me; your rod and your staff, they comfort me."[33] Like King David, James Bond is bound by the duty of leadership to walk in this "shadow of death."

But this "shadow of death" proves hard to efface given the extremity of Bond's suffering. The scene in which Le Chiffre tortures Bond with a carpet beater is remarkable and groundbreaking in a number of ways. It breaks the taboo on graphic depiction of violence in spy fiction, in which physical pain may be alluded to in general terms but not described in explicit detail. The scene also violates the code of the hero's omnipotence by emphasizing Bond's vulnerability: "He was utterly a prisoner, naked and defenceless."[34] Fleming's readers at Cape found the scene powerful but disturbing because of the sexualized nature of the assault on Bond. Michael Howard "thought its cynical brutality, unrelieved by humour, revealed a sadistic fantasy that was deeply shocking."[35]

For Le Chiffre, the choice of Bond's genitals as a target is a pragmatic matter, simply the most effective method of extracting the information he desires—namely, the location of Bond's check for forty million francs. Le Chiffre's attitude is brutally direct: "One can cause a man as much pain as is possible or necessary. . . . It is not only the immediate agony, but also the thought that your manhood is being gradually destroyed and that at the end, if you will not yield, you will no longer be a man."[36]

But the attack on Bond's sexuality is also symbolic because it is in precisely the area of sex that Bond differs so much from the "clubland heroes"—his predecessors in spy fiction. In the essay "The Moments of Bond," Tony Bennett and Janet Woollacott point out that "Bond and the 'Bond girl' embodied a modernization of sexuality. . . . Bond thus embodied male sexuality that was freed from the constraints and hypocrisy of gentlemanly chivalry, a point of departure from the restraint, a-sexuality or repressed sexuality of the traditional English aristocratic hero."[37]

Le Chiffre's abuse of Bond includes infantilizing him, calling him "my dear boy," reducing his ordeal to the level of childhood games. If, as discussed, Bond's and Fleming's wartime prowess at spy games are the source of their heroic status, Le Chiffre destroys this fantasy: "'My dear boy,' Le Chiffre spoke like a father, 'the game of Red Indians is over, quite over. You have stumbled by mischance into a game for grown-ups and you have already found it a painful experience.'"[38] This is surely one of the most meaningful utterances in the novel. It touches not only on the plot but also the biographical sources of the fiction, as the reference to "the game of Red Indians" alludes to Fleming's commando unit in World War II, 30AU, which was known as "Ian Fleming's Red Indians." Using Le Chiffre as a mouthpiece, Ian is pointing out that the "games" of World War II—amateurish, improvised, yet exciting—have been replaced by a far more deadly battle between professional spies of East and West, in which the stakes are higher and the requirements more strenuous.

Fleming notes that Le Chiffre "spoke like a father"—a punishing father, the reality of which Fleming, whose father was killed in World War I when Ian was only nine, was scarcely aware. Rather, the scenario is the memory of a sadistic schoolmaster beating his pupils. Fleming had experienced the harshness of bullying and corporal punishment at Durnford and Eton. But if Le Chiffre is to be compared to a parent, why not to a mother? It was Eve, of course, who (in Fleming's view) brutally curtailed his nascent romantic desires by terminating his relationship with Monique.

The comment quoted earlier that this ended Ian's chance of a "normal life" suggests the emasculating impact of Eve's interference. Andrew Lycett describes Fleming's consequent feeling as "a complex construction built not just from his experiences with Monique but also from his feelings of disgust and inadequacy at the consequences of catching gonorrhoea at Sandhurst, and from his powerful love-hate relationship with his mother."[39] Ian's ambivalence toward Eve, a punishing mother, is reflected in the torture scene, in which two men combine to make a sadomasochistic couple: "There came a wonderful period of warmth and languor leading into a sort of sexual twilight where pain turned to pleasure and where hatred and fear of the torturers turned to a masochistic infatuation."[40] The torture scene is so disturbing partly because of this suggestion that Bond, at a certain point, enjoys being tortured and feels a perverse desire for his torturer. No doubt scenes such as this planted the seeds for subsequent attacks on the "snobbery, sadism, and violence" of the Bond novels in the late 1950s, which were a delayed reaction to Fleming's careerlong assault on conventional proprieties. It is clearly a homoerotic scenario of far more intensity than any heterosexual scene in the novel. Vesper's role in the scenario, for Bond, is limited to his imagination of her as an innocent victim being tortured and perhaps violated by Le Chiffre's henchmen.

The full irony of this assumption of Bond's can only be appreciated, of course, after the revelation that Vesper is, in fact, a Soviet double agent. Far from being a "poor wretch" or "poor little beast" haplessly caught up in the violence, Vesper is the author of Bond's agony. It is her betrayal—including the revelation to Le Chiffre that Bond had hidden the check somewhere in his room—that leads Bond into the deadly trap. In this, his first novel, Fleming thus boldly pulls the rug from underneath the reader's feet, shattering our generic expectations about the "heroine" being a desirable yet helpless victim whom the hero Bond must rescue from the villain.[41]

Bond's survival features a radical reversal of fortune in which Le Chiffre—the sadistic schoolmaster abruptly stripped of his cane and power—receives his comeuppance from a stronger man. Bond watches with amazement a transformation in his tormentor's body: "Suddenly Le Chiffre had grown another eye, a third eye on a level with the other two . . . without eyelashes or eyebrows."[42] This neat bullet wound—a professional assassination by SMERSH—puts Bond out of his misery but also creates a vacuum in the novel. It is the only Bond novel in which the presumed "villain" is killed before the final act of the story, and it prepares the way for the most astounding revelation anywhere in Fleming's fiction: that the beautiful, intelligent, compassionate Vesper Lynd—and not the grotesque, perverted Le Chiffre—is the novel's true malefactor.

Before this revelation, Bond—and the reader—have been reassured by the doctor about the possibility of "repairing your body without bothering too much about your mind." The notion that the traumas inflicted by Le Chiffre and Vesper—both sexual and psychic—might be irreparable does not occur to the good doctor. Bond seems to accept the verdict that he is a "machine"—to be repaired, like his damaged Bentley, by expert mechanics—and that Vesper will play a key role in his sexual recovery: "He had intended to sleep with her as soon as he could, because . . . he wanted *coldly to put the repairs to his body to the final test*."[43] If Bond's body "works"—if he can perform sexually with Vesper—the implication is he has recovered. Only later Bond novels would return to the idea that Bond's physical and psychic scars have not healed, that he has become if not physically emasculated then emotionally traumatized.

As Bond was built to be a machine, Ian decided his future installments would be composed on a very special kind of instrument. He ordered a "golden typewriter," in August writing to Ann, "This is only a tiny letter to try out my new typewriter and to see if it will write golden words since it is made of gold."[44] Nor was this the only type of machine that emerged from the success of *Casino Royale*. The typescript of Ian's novel benefited from the close and critical scrutiny of various professional readers, including William Plomer and Daniel George at Cape. Together with Kenneth Williams; the founding partners, Jonathan Cape and G. Wren Howard; Cape's director, Michael Howard; and Fleming's older brother, Peter (who signed his corrections "Dr Knittpick"), these readers formed Fleming's team of editors and critics for future books. As Jon Gilbert writes, "This was a production scenario typical for each successive James Bond book, and the publisher's offices at Bedford Square (and its staff) were later nicknamed 'The Factory' by Ian Fleming."[45] If Fleming's hero—and his novels—were "machines," then it was at this "Factory," refining the products of Ian's brilliant imagination, that they were produced.

Casino Royale was published on April 13, 1953, and received enthusiastic responses from revered fellow authors William Somerset Maugham and Raymond Chandler. John Betjeman, the future poet laureate, wrote in *The Daily Telegraph*, "Ian Fleming has discovered the secret of narrative art. . . . The reader *has* to go on reading," while Chandler praised Fleming as "the best thriller writer since Eric Ambler."[46] Although the initial sales did not live up to Ian's optimistic expectations (he had lobbied Cape in vain for an initial print run of ten thousand), it was clear that he had established an important new spy hero and that future adventures would follow. In the wake of the defections of Burgess and Maclean, Ian's novel showed that a British SIS agent could still be trusted, could still be effective against the Soviet Union. Bond also demonstrated, no less crucially, that a British spy hero could work productively alongside the American CIA against their common enemy: the Soviet Union.

That same month—April 1953—a real-life British SIS agent launched his postwar career in London. George Blake, returning from a harrowing three years of captivity and physical suffering in North Korea during the Korean

War, was invited to resume his work for SIS and was interviewed by "C," Major General Sir John Sinclair. Blake would later note that "to James Bond fans . . . he is well known as M," and Blake's return would be greeted in M's curt style of welcome: "'Pleased to see you back with us, Blake' he said to me as he got up from behind his desk to shake hands with me."[47] Cursory as this greeting was, unknown to Sinclair—or indeed to anyone else in SIS—Blake was not another James Bond but a real-life Vesper Lynd. While Ian typed away, working toward fame and success with his thrilling adventures of a British spy hero battling SMERSH, Blake would be busily burrowing inside the bowels of SIS and leaking its most prized secrets to the Soviets for years to come.

Chapter Seven

The Edge of Danger

Thrilling Environments of Ian Fleming

Is James Bond for the birds?

The origin of James Bond's name is just as important as its transformation into a cinematic and popular culture icon. As many familiar with Fleming's writings know, Ian took the name of his famous spy from the author of a well-known book of ornithology, *The Field Guide to the Birds of the West Indies*. First published in 1936, as *Birds of the West Indies*, the 1947 edition of James Bond's study had pride of place on Fleming's bookshelf at Goldeneye. As Ian told the story in interviews, this choice of a name was a matter of coincidence. While writing his first novel, Fleming recounted, he was fishing around for a suitable name for his spy hero when his gaze happened to fall on Bond's book in his bookshelves at Goldeneye. Deciding this was just the sort of "flat, quiet name" without any "romantic overtones" he wanted, Ian simply "stole it and used it" for his hero.[1] With this casual act of identity theft, the career of the most famous fictional spy in history—and one of the best-known characters in twentieth-century literature—was born.

There is some evidence, however, that this act of naming was not simply random. It was more than a chance selection of a name at once memorable and simple with additional associations of wealth and even royalty. James was the name of the Scottish Stuart kings, as the Scottish Fleming would know, while Bond—as Sable Basilisk points out in *On Her Majesty's Secret Service*—is "the name of one of the most famous streets in the world—I refer of course to Bond Street."[2] One clue to the name's significance is that Fleming described the *Field Guide* of James Bond as "one of my bibles out here" in Jamaica.[3] To name his character after the author of one of Fleming's "bibles" is to inscribe this character with a sacred value. Saint James is an apostle, in church history—though it is another saint, Saint Francis of Assisi, who has become associated with patronage of birds, animals, and natural environments. And it is with Saint George, the patron saint of England, that Bond compares himself (in *Goldfinger*). Yet, James Bond's affection for and protection of birds and other nonhuman lifeforms is an important theme in many of his novels and stories. This leads the observant reader to the conclusion that Fleming's naming of his character had more purpose and design than usually believed.

Bond's close and sympathetic connection to birdlife, nonhuman lifeforms, and natural environments may seem at odds with his popular image as a harbinger of death and destruction, equipped with the latest technology. However, Kingsley Amis—the author of the first Bond continuation novel, *Colonel Sun* (1968), as well as the first book-length study of Fleming's work, *The James Bond Dossier* (1965)—noted in 1991 that Bond is "tough, yes, resourceful, all that but fully capable of indignation, compunction, remorse, tenderness and a protective instinct toward defenceless creatures" and cited "The Hildebrand Rarity" and *Thunderball* as key examples.[4] Bond's violence is generally directed toward the villains, whose plots he attempts to stymie, and these malefactors are often guilty of committing destructive violence against nature. Not only do they inflict damage to birds, animals, natural landscapes, or oceanic life, but also the Bond villains often weaponize natural lifeforms in order to threaten not only 007, but humanity.

In the first novel, *Casino Royale*, it is trees—rather than birds—that furnish the evidence of James Bond's close interdependence with the natural world. The plane trees along the boulevard outside the Hotel Splendide play a key role in Bond's survival. As natural protectors of Bond, they first shield him merely from the heat of the sun, as they "gave a cool shade." But these trees provide a more important form of protection when the Bulgarian assassins—"two men in Straw hats"—try to blow Bond up with a bomb. After the devastating explosion, Bond realizes that the trees have been sacrificed in his place, being "leafless and charred" and "two of them had snapped off near the base and lay drunkenly across the road." With no sentimentality, Fleming reveals that the trees have died so that Bond may live. If this seems like a fanciful, romantic interpretation, Fleming makes it explicit when Mathis arrives on the scene: "By that time Bond was standing with his arm round the tree which had saved his life."[5] While this saving of Bond's life may seem coincidental, it also suggests a benevolent intention. Bond, in return, has become a tree hugger.

Trees had a special place in Fleming's heart. Despite his later negative comments about rural life in Sevenhampton, Wiltshire, Ivar Bryce records that arboreal life was Ian's special preference for the landscaping of Goldeneye:

> He hated pot plants and flower arrangements and bunches of blooms, just as he hated flower-beds—he called them kittens' graves—and artfully planted pathways and herbaceous borders. He loved big trees, however, and night-scented shrubs and flowers with nectar that attracted humming-birds. He grew proud of a few special species which grew naturally and boasted impressive names, which he could memorize.[6]

Ten years after he wrote *Casino*, Fleming returned imaginatively to the fictional resort of Royale-les-Eaux for Bond's tenth adventure, *On Her Majesty's Secret Service*. Not only does this novel return us to Bond's childhood, and memories of happy seaside holidays, but it also revitalizes Bond's important role as a defender of the natural environment. The ecological focus of this novel is grounded in the critical value of Britain's agricultural economy to its national survival.

As Fleming well knew, during World War II, Britain's agricultural fertility was of great importance to the country's survival. Given the threat of an enemy blockade against the British Isles, the heightened demand on scarce natural resources during wartime, and the inevitable food shortages caused by blockades and disrupted imports, Britain's self-sufficiency in agriculture became an issue of national security. Added to this urgency was the shortage of manpower caused by war, with many agricultural workers volunteering or being conscripted for the armed forces. In order to address this labor shortage, the Women's Land Army was formed under the Ministry of Agriculture and Fisheries in 1939 and staffed by female volunteers (later conscripts) who worked on the land to ensure Britain's agricultural production was sustained.

The so-called Land Girls became a regular feature of the rural landscapes of Britain, and they were joined by conscientious objectors and other male citizens deemed unfit for active military duty. The purpose of the Women's Land Army, along with newly introduced technologies and fertilizer methods, was not simply to maintain Britain's prewar agricultural production but to increase it to bring the nation as close to self-sufficiency as possible. One wartime farmer, John Warren, interviewed by the BBC, reminisced about the arrival of "Allis-Chalmers tractors, and they were bright orange, and they were brilliant. And they came on rubber tyres and they came on iron tyres." As Warren also recalled, "The other thing that was introduced in the war was a thing called nitro-chalk. It was the first time that we'd actually had artificial fertilisers available. I don't know where—it was obviously imported from abroad."[7]

Britain proved remarkably successful in increasing its production, staving off the worst effects of Hitler's U-boat torpedoing of commercial fleets in the Atlantic and English Channel. This ability to meet increased demands on domestically produced foodstuffs also yielded dividends to the agricultural business. As Warren also recollects, "The war produced much better financial returns for all the farmers. Prices improved tremendously."[8] As Hitler realized, the most effective way to defeat Britain—apart from widespread bombing or military invasion (the latter of which had been abandoned after the Nazis' defeat in the Battle of Britain)—was to starve its citizens into surrender. Thus, agricultural production became a national security issue, and Britain's farming industry might be considered a legitimate wartime target.

Toward the climax of *On Her Majesty's Secret Service*, Fleming introduces the "Man from Ag and Fish" (named Franklin) who points out that Britain "happens to be the most highly agriculturalized country in the world. We had to make ourselves so during the war to keep ourselves from starvation. So in theory we would be an ideal target for an attack of this kind."[9] In his Alpine clinic atop Piz Gloria, Blofeld has devised a biological agent of war more deadly than anything produced under the Nazis. He also recruits his own apocalyptic version of the Land Girls—a group of British women, all taken from rural and agricultural communities, chosen because of their allergies to the foodstuffs produced by their families' farms or holdings.

Blofeld's threat is so potentially catastrophic that Bond is sent out to Piz Gloria in disguise as Sir Hilary Bray (the name of an Old Etonian friend of Ian's), where he will uncover the deadly plot against Britain's agricultural production. On his return, Bond confers with representatives of the Ministry of Agriculture and Fisheries to better understand Blofeld's toxic agents and develop countermeasures. The ministry is reduced to the defensive measure of trying to protect Britain's agriculture from decimation. Franklin is initially fooled by Blofeld's benevolent cover story, believing "that a man on top of an alp is making efforts to improve our agriculture and livestock." However, he recalls a news story about Christmas turkeys being afflicted with pest outbreaks, a warning that alerts both him and M to Blofeld's malign intention to devastate Britain's crops and livestock. Their discussion leads to the essential and disturbing question, "How much do you gentlemen know about Biological Warfare?"[10]

Number 501 from the Secret Service, the head of the Scientific Research Section—a man called Leathers—reports that both sides had developed biological warfare agents in the war but that neither the Allies nor the Axis powers had ended up using it. In fact, Fleming shows that weaponizing nature to attack Britain's agriculture is still a threat at the height of the Cold War. The biological warfare planned by Blofeld is an especially potent economic weapon, for without its crops and livestock, Britain "would be a bankrupt country within a matter of months." Fleming provides details of the varieties of biological warfare (BW) groups and also the specific harmful agents that might be used by Blofeld, including anthrax, potato blight, cereal stem disease, crown rust of oats, and harmful insects "such as the Colorado beetle."[11] This list of pests and BW agents adds verisimilitude to Fleming's plot, being an example of what Kingsley Amis called the "Fleming Effect"—"the imaginative use of information, whereby the pervading fantastic nature of Bond's world, as well as the temporary, local, fantastic elements in the story, are bolted down to some sort of reality."[12]

The brilliance of Blofeld's plot is that it exploits a method of warfare that no one in Britain, during this atomic age, had been thinking about or taking defensive measures against: "We talk about the new poison gases, the nerve gases the Germans invented in the war. We march and counter-march about radiation and the atom bomb."[13] Blofeld's fiendish scheme to weaponize natural biological agents and British women against the natural reproductive cycle of land and livestock represents a more primal threat of extinction. The deadly nature of BW agents is that they cannot be detected by the human senses and are therefore especially hard to intercept. Only Bond's observations about the suspicious activities and high-tech laboratories at Piz Gloria, with their rows of test tubes and dim red lighting, provide the evidence of Blofeld's BW plot against Britain.

The most compelling evidence of Blofeld's unnatural attack is that it fits the archvillain's character profile and preferred methods of assault. In *Thunderball*, Blofeld's surrogate Emile Largo used barracuda and sharks as a "natural" shield to protect the underwater cave near the Bahamas in which he conceals nuclear weapons stolen from NATO. Largo is confident that any human intruders would "bring shark or barracuda" to the area, forming a natural defense against discovery. We also learn that Blofeld is outside the natural reproductive cycle and is in this respect an "unnatural" being: "For the rest, he didn't smoke or drink and he had never been known to sleep with a member of either sex."[14] The trait of being sexually neuter is something Blofeld has in common with other Fleming villains, such as Donovan Grant, Rosa Klebb, and perhaps Goldfinger, but is linked especially closely to Blofeld's attack on human and organic reproductive cycles.

Bond's mission in the mountainous environment of Piz Gloria in *On Her Majesty's Secret Service* is especially daunting for him. Even though Bond later proposes to M that he and Marc-Ange Draco return to Piz Gloria to destroy Blofeld's laboratory, Bond reflects, "That damned mountain! He never wanted to see the bloody thing again!"[15] Why such hostility toward a mountain? We know that Bond's parents were killed in a climbing accident in the Aiguilles Rouge when Bond was only eleven, and this trauma has influenced his feelings about mountainous regions. Moreover, some of Ian's mixed feelings toward the Kitzbühel Alps and the Tyrol, influenced by his own traumas, influence Bond's negative response to Piz Gloria.

Bond's description of the region as "damned" also foreshadows the most devastating trauma in the whole Bond canon: the death of his wife, Tracy di Vicenzo, at the hands of Blofeld and Irma Bunt. Blofeld avenges his failure to inflict sterility on Britain's agriculture by causing another kind of sterility: by killing Bond's wife, the SPECTRE chief destroys Bond's reproductive future, any hope he had of creating a new life—and new lives—with Tracy.

Bond is still suffering from the catastrophe of Tracy's death in the next novel, *You Only Live Twice*. In fact, he has become so paralyzed by depression that M is at the point of firing Bond from the Secret Service—completing the rupture that had begun in *On Her Majesty's Secret Service*, when Bond had actually written a letter of resignation. Bond's struggles reflect, in many ways, Ian's growing difficulties with creating new plots and resentments toward his publishers' demands that he produce a new novel each year: as Ian wrote to William Plomer, "The only trouble with killing off one's villains is that one has to invent new ones."[16] The advantage of Blofeld as a serial villain—the nemesis for Ian's serial hero—was therefore self-evident.

To find out more about Bond's condition, M consults a neurological expert, Sir James Molony. For Molony, "the problems he was required to solve intrigued him greatly because they were both human and vital to the state." Molony confirms that Bond's reaction to Tracy's death is a natural response to trauma: "It's a form of psycho-neurosis, and it can grow slowly or suddenly. In your man's case, it was brought on out of the blue by an intolerable life-situation . . . the loss of a loved one."[17] The state of Bond's mental health reminds us that Blofeld has, in fact, struck a severe blow not only against Bond but against Britain's national security by disabling its top secret agent.

Bond's cure treatment involves a new mission: he is sent by M to Japan to liaise with Tiger Tanaka, the head of the Japanese Secret Service. His objective is to gain access to a vital intelligence stream known by the code name of MAGIC 44. Fleming wrote in *Thrilling Cities*, in the chapter on Tokyo, "I was full of reservations about Japan. Before and during the war they had been bad enemies and many of my friends had suffered at their hands."[18] But in *You Only Live Twice*, Tiger is now an ally of Britain and of Bond and wants his help gaining access to this vital intelligence source, which intercepts encrypted Soviet communications relating to a planned nuclear attack on Britain.

As in *On Her Majesty's Secret Service*, Bond is faced with an existential threat against "all life" in Britain, although the enemy appears to have reverted to the Cold War adversary of the Soviet Union. The text also contains the chilling information that Britain can no longer depend on the protection of its closest wartime ally, the United States of America: "THIS WILL . . . PROBABLY DESTROY THE ANGLO HYPHEN AMERICAN ALLIANCE SINCE IT CAN BE ASSUMED THAT AMERICA WILL NOT RISK A NUCLEAR WAR INVOLVING HER TERRITORY FOR THE SAKE OF RESCUING A NOW MORE OR LESS VALUELESS ALLY."[19] In requesting Tiger's help to secure more detailed information about this deadly threat to England, Bond is faced with further accusations that Britain is in irreversible decline, a now-obsolete former world power.

The only way Bond can convince Tiger that Britain is still worthy of receiving such high-grade intelligence is to demonstrate his personal heroic qualities. In preparation, Tiger briefs Bond about a new arrival in Japan, a man known as Dr. Guntram Shatterhand, whose expertise is in horticulture and botany and who has imported a variety of subtropical species to populate the garden of his newly acquired castle on Kyushu, on the South Island of Japan. The visitor's proposal sounds benevolent, or at least innocuous: "Doctor Shatterhand was prepared to spend no less than one million pounds on establishing an exotic garden or park in this country which he would stock with a priceless collection of rare plants and shrubs from all over the world."

This summary omits, however, one sinister quality these plants have in common—they are all poisonous and deadly. Tiger describes Shatterhand as a man who "collects death," and his presence has become a national security concern for Japan due to the high incidence of suicide in Japanese society. Tiger outlines the cultural obsession with "honor" that requires self-immolation in order to cleanse the stain of dishonor or failure. This means that Shatterhand's deadly ecology, or "garden of death," has become the chosen venue for those many Japanese citizens wishing to kill themselves.[20]

In an echo of Blofeld's previous plot to launch biological warfare against Britain, Tiger provides Bond with a comprehensive list of the deadly plants installed by Shatterhand "together with comments by our Ministry of Agriculture." Like the list of deadly BW agents provided by Ag and Fish in *On Her Majesty's Secret Service*, Tiger's list adds verisimilitude to the plot of *You Only Live Twice* by grounding it in botanical actuality. The list divides the poisons into "six main categories" of deliriant, inebriant, convulsivant, depressant, asthenic, and irritant. He then lists various specimens of these imported poisonous plants, the scientific basis of which demonstrates Shatterhand's expertise as a horticultural collector. In addition to the poisonous plants, Shatterhand has populated the lakes, ponds, and streams of his castle with the deadly piranha fish, which "can strip a whole horse to the bones in less than an hour."[21]

In creating the character of Tiger Tanaka, Ian was influenced by people he had met in Tokyo on his trip for *The Sunday Times* to write *Thrilling Cities*, such as "Tiger" Saito, the editor in chief of *This Is Japan*, "the massive and beautifully produced annual which the privileged receive through the Japanese Embassy around Christmas time." Describing Saito as "a chunky reserved man with considerable stores of quiet humour and intelligence" who "looked like a fighter," Fleming relies on him (as well as the Australian journalist Dick Hughes) as a guide to the Japanese capital and its culture.[22] Likewise, Bond depends on Tanaka in *You Only Live Twice* to inform him about social attitudes and conditions in postwar Japan in which suicide, Tiger reports, has reached epidemic proportions. While Shatterhand feigns dismay at the fact his garden has become the destination for suicides, Tiger believes that the "castle of death" is a deliberate attack on Japanese society, using Japan's own weakness for this malign purpose: "If anyone is to blame, it is the Japanese people."[23]

Because Shatterhand's garden of death has become an urgent Japanese national security issue, Tiger proposes an exchange of MAGIC 44 for Bond's assistance in eliminating their unwanted invader. In order to protect Britain's national security, Bond must risk his life, entering the "garden of death" in order to eliminate Japan's enemy within—a malignant guest they originally welcomed with open arms (much as the British welcomed its enemy Sir Hugo Drax as a benefactor in *Moonraker*). Tiger proposes this mission as a quasi-mythical quest and test of Bond's heroic qualities: "You are to enter this Castle of Death and slay the Dragon within."[24]

Bond agrees to assassinate Shatterhand in exchange for MAGIC 44, but his motivation for this killing soon changes as, in a powerful scene of recognition, Bond is shown a photograph of Shatterhand by the Japanese police superintendent. His reaction is visceral: "There was no doubt, no doubt at all! He had grown a drooping black moustache. He had had the syphilitic nose repaired. There was a gold-capped tooth among the upper frontals, but there could be no doubt."[25] Bond's knowledge that this is Blofeld is confirmed by a picture of "Shatterhand's" wife, whom he recognizes as Irma Bunt. Blofeld's metamorphosis—he has a drastically different appearance in each novel—is another sign of his "nonhuman" status, a chameleon-like ability to transform his appearance in order to adapt to different environments.

The modus operandi of Blofeld's villainous projects is to use natural lifeforms for unnatural purposes: the BW agents appear in nature, but Blofeld's cultivation and malevolent dissemination of them are highly unnatural. Likewise, in *You Only Live Twice*, the subtropical plants and fish that he stocks his garden with are natural species, but they—like Blofeld himself—are not native to Japan. Moreover, their being imported and collected in one place is also unnatural, while their use as lures for Japanese suicides is depraved.

Blofeld's choice of Japan as a target is pragmatic rather than ideological, suggesting he is a deadly virus who finds the weakness in the "immune system" of any host nation in order to destroy it. In Britain's case, the national Achilles' heel was its economic dependence on agriculture and livestock, a result of wartime circumstances but still in effect long after the war. In Japan, the vulnerable point is the nation's honor code, resulting in suicide as a constant temptation to avoid or expunge the stain of dishonor. As Tanaka explains, "Honour is a very serious word in Japan, Commander."[26] Of course, Japan is also now an ally of Blofeld's primary foe, Britain. Blofeld targets these national weaknesses with deadly purpose, and like the most dangerous viruses, he changes form according to the defense system.

But if Blofeld is the virus, then Bond is the vaccine. Blofeld embodies sterility, sickness, depravity, and death. But Bond—the antidote—also contains elements of these toxins. Bond is like a remedy of homeopathic medicine, being a smaller dose of the same virus that threatens to disable the healthy body. Because Britain, Switzerland, and now Japan are infected with Blofeld's virus, the only cure is to deploy Bond with his "license to kill" to eliminate it. Tiger makes clear the moral necessity of his employment to do the world's dirty work: Shatterhand's assassination "could not be carried out by a Japanese. Bond's appearance on the scene was therefore very timely." But in order to defeat Blofeld, Bond also must become a chameleon, transforming his appearance "into something more closely resembling a Japanese."[27]

Bond's moral conscience is eased by the pragmatic necessity of destroying the Blofeld virus, although the assassination is also justified by his private vendetta. After recognizing Blofeld, Bond reflects, "This was now a private matter. It had nothing to do with Tiger or Japan. It had nothing to do with MAGIC 44. It was ancient feud."[28] Though Bond does not disclose his knowledge of Shatterhand's true identity to Tiger or M, for fear of losing his "prey," there is no doubt in the reader's mind that Blofeld—the doctor of deadly science—is Bond's personal target. Bond's "license to kill" is necessary in order to protect the lives of innocent civilians and to destroy a greater evil.

Once inside the "garden of death," Bond uses his extensive knowledge of deadly lifeforms, plants, and fish, asking himself which of the snakes are likely to attack him. Fleming's fascination with the deadly toxins of nature was apparent with the scorpion in *Diamonds Are Forever* and the poisonous centipede in *Dr. No*, but Blofeld's garden intensifies this theme at the heart of the novel. As a chilling demonstration of the fatal consequence of lack of knowledge of poisons, Bond witnesses an intruder with a grotesquely swollen head, poisoned by Blofeld's garden, whose only refuge is to throw himself into a lake populated by piranhas.[29]

The references to the piranha had special significance for Ian, whose brother Peter had ridiculed the deadliness of this South American freshwater fish in his first book, *Brazilian Adventure*. Traveling through the Amazon jungle in search of lost English explorer Colonel Fawcett, Peter and his companions are wading through a river infested with what they believe are piranhas. Peter gives a colorful account of the fearful reputation of this fish:

> We remembered all that we had read, all that we had been told, about the rapacity, the vindictiveness of these fish: how a shoal of them, if you ventured into waters which they infested, would tear the flesh from your bones before you could scramble ashore again: how because of them a man could not safely immerse so much as a finger in the rivers of Central Brazil: how those cruel and undeniably imposing teeth could cut you to ribbons in a trice.

Having created this image of deadly predators, Peter—far from playing up the actual dangers—brings an absurdist note to the proceedings, demystifying the threat of this infamous species with withering irony: "We could not but admire the rigid self-control with which they ruled their blood-lust." Concluding "these tigerish creatures might have been poultry for all the harm we took from walking among them," Peter clearly relishes "the belief that we were exposing a fallacy; we were debunking the piranha."[30]

Ian, however, has no such intention of debunking the myth of the piranhas' ferocity. On the contrary, he plays up the horrible voracity of the fish, describing the scene melodramatically as the poisoned victim enters the lake: "The man raised his head and let out a single, terrible scream. . . . James Bond wiped the cold sweat off his face. Piranha! The South American freshwater killer whose massive jaws and flat, razor-sharp teeth can strip a horse down to the bones in under an hour." Like Dr. No's dystopian island of Crab Key, Blofeld's "garden of death" is infested with the "smell of Sulphur [that] hung in the air," an odor Bond traces to its sinister source of "bursting mudboils."[31] Fleming intensifies the unnatural setting, infernal atmosphere, and oppressive effects by concentrating all the deadly species of plants, fish, and reptiles into a single confined space, one paradoxically associated with cultivation and civilization: the garden.

This "garden," though, is a diabolical perversion of the biblical Garden of Eden, the perfect world created by God for Adam and Eve. Its landscape is designed for torments rather than delights. Bond watches as a Japanese gentleman, dressed in a top hat and black suit, calmly walks into one of the sulfur pools and is boiled alive, as "the pervading stink of Sulphur reached Bond's nostrils."[32] Blofeld, a maleficent power, has replaced life with death, a pastoral idyll with the scenes of hell. Yet even in the original garden, the presence of the poisonous serpent was a reminder of the temptations of evil. Blofeld's garden is itself the fatal temptation for those who wish to end their own lives. In entering this garden, Bond faces his own extinction.

Even though the military forces of Japan could easily destroy Blofeld's castle with an air attack, Bond is faced with the reality that he alone can do this job and that he needs only his bare hands. In this way, Fleming reduces Bond himself to a state of nature, forced to rely on his own natural weapons and instincts for survival, using the most primitive of methods to tackle a sophisticated and technologically advanced enemy. Fleming again draws on the work of one of his favorite contemporary novelists, Geoffrey Household, whose classic spy novel *Rogue Male*, published in 1939, dramatized the survival of the lone hero relying on his own natural instincts, using cunning and a primitive skill set to defeat a powerful enemy.[33] More recently, Household had developed the theme of a hero struggling to survive in a state of nature in *A Rough Shoot* (1951) and *Time to Kill* (1952). His hero, Roger Taine, is similar to Bond in being able to adapt to and exploit the natural environment for his self-defense.

Blofeld's garden is perhaps the ultimate test of Bond's survival skills, for he is deprived of the technical support and manpower of the Secret Intelligence Service. Having effectively "gone rogue" in his quest for revenge, Bond's skill, courage, and powers of observation remind us that his heroic qualities are primal and instinctual, not dependent on advanced technology. Officially, the high incidence of suicide in Japan is not Bond's problem, but he is morally appalled by a practice he views as unnatural. Bond's self-appointed role is to stem this tide of self-murder and cleanse the world of a deadly plague.

In the novel's bizarre climax, Bond defeats Blofeld in a medieval-style duel—his opponent dressed in full body armor as protection against the poisons of his own garden. Rather than kill his nemesis with a sword—Blofeld's weapon of choice—Bond strangles him to death, using the "bare hands" that he has, commando-like, always relied on in a state of nature. Bond reverts to savagery in this killing, being "in the terrible grip of blood lust," but this is justified by the horrible injury Blofeld inflicted on him by killing Tracy.[34] Bond then escapes from the castle using Blofeld's own hot air balloon but falls from the sky like a modern Icarus, plunging into the ocean and losing his memory. Having destroyed the "virus" of Blofeld, Bond pays the price with the loss of his own identity, having no recollection of his previous existence as 007. It is as though Bond cannot survive—or is no longer necessary—without the stimulus of the evil force he was sent to eliminate. Bond's moralizing conclusion about Le Chiffre—"By his evil existence, which foolishly I have helped to destroy, he was creating a norm of badness by which . . . an opposite norm of goodness could exist"—still applies in the last novel Fleming published in his lifetime.[35]

Blofeld even claims that his destructive purposes are actually in the true interests of humanity. By stealing atomic weapons from NATO in *Thunderball*, he asserts, SPECTRE prevented the weapons falling into "the hands of a Castro," which "could lead to the wanton extinction of mankind." Blofeld then justifies his BW attack on England by presenting himself as the surgeon for "a sick nation," which "might . . . have been forced out of her lethargy into the kind of community effort we witnessed during the war." Blofeld presents himself not as an agent of Britain's destruction but as the catalyst needed to jolt a declining nation out of its sickness. Blofeld's diagnosis of his own malaise, "a certain lassitude of mind which I am determined to combat," also resembles the "accidie" Bond sometimes suffers from, as in *From Russia, with Love*. His motives are obviously selfish, his arguments probably specious, yet he claims the "garden" fulfills a civic service to Japan by preventing the Japanese government from having to deal with the messy, often bloody, public means by which its citizens kill themselves.[36] In his perhaps insane view of his conspiracies, Blofeld insists he will ultimately heal and save rather than destroy the targets of his biological or botanical attacks.

Blofeld's deadly attacks on the environment use natural bio-forms to assault nature itself, making him a kind of anti-ecology figure. Whereas other Bond villains exploit, weaponize, or damage natural environments in their quests for power, Blofeld exploits the flaws and vulnerabilities in natural systems to destroy the system itself. Blofeld, in his shapeshifting incarnations, is carefully crafted by Fleming to represent the environmental antithesis of Bond. Where 007 values and protects the natural world, Blofeld devastates it.

Intriguingly, Fleming gave his own birthday to Blofeld—May 28, 1908—inviting readers to make the connection between the author and his archvillain. Both author and villain shared an interest in scientific knowledge and advancement. Fleming's book collection, focusing on rare editions that advanced scientific knowledge and inquiry, included Marie Curie's paper on penicillin, Charles Darwin's *Origin of Species*, and Einstein's theory of relativity. This demonstrates his fascination with the power of scientific inquiry. While the fact he assembled this collection does not of itself mean Ian was a scientific expert, it does demonstrate his enduring interest in science and ecology. Moreover, Fleming increasingly came to share Blofeld's urgent desire to eliminate Bond, to rid himself of the burden of writing a new 007 adventure each year.

But in most respects, Fleming's interest in natural environments and non-human life is closer to Bond's than Blofeld's. Fleming was also a keen birdwatcher, especially while in Jamaica, always keeping a pair of binoculars by the window at Goldeneye. According to Hilary Bray, one of the physical limitations that hit Ian hardest after his heart attack in 1961 was that when staying at Goldeneye, "[he] could no longer look for birds or flowers. No longer live in and out of the water."[37] Natural history was one of the subjects Fleming was most passionate about, and Gilbert White's classic *History of Selbourne* was another of the prized books in his collection. From one angle, Fleming's interest in nature and the environment always had an ulterior motive—either collecting commodities like books or shells, or playing golf in a "natural" setting at Royal St George's, or snorkeling at Oracabessa Bay, studying what he called the "Finny Tribe of Goldeneye."[38] It would be inaccurate to categorize Fleming as a "rambler" or a man who enjoyed extended solitary time in the countryside, for example. When he and Ann moved to Sevenhampton in Wiltshire, in the 1960s, he complained about the prospect of living "in the middle of a lot of plough with deadly little walks down lanes."[39] And yet, throughout his life he was attracted to locations of outstanding and fragile natural beauty, including the White Cliffs and Isle of Thanet on the Kent coast, the Green Mountains of Vermont, and the Jamaica coastline near Oracabessa.

Ian had a deep fascination with the flora, fauna, and bird life of each place he lived in. His novels and stories also contain extensive passages of vivid descriptive prose about natural landscapes, creatures, and dynamics. One could cite the memorable description of the scorpion preying on a beetle before being crushed by a man at the opening of *Diamonds Are Forever*, or the thrilling underwater scenes featuring predatory fish in *Thunderball*, or the lyrical description of James Bond and Gala Brand's walk across the White Cliffs in *Moonraker*. Bond's interest in the natural world and his protection of "defenseless creatures," in other words, derives from the enthusiasm and passion of his creator, which emerged during his early years at Durnford School.

It is reasonable to wonder, though, why Fleming would assign these conservationist qualities to his tough, masculine, apparently ruthless secret agent. Recalling that Ian was influenced by the gentlemanly adventure heroes of John Buchan and "Sapper," as well as the hardboiled detectives of Raymond Chandler and Dashiell Hammett—who are very much urban-based, cynical, and thick-skinned investigators—it might seem surprising that he would assign such sensitivities to nature to his professional spy. Even Bond's boss, M, has little time for his agent's environmental concerns, dismissing the Audubon Society—which seeks to protect a colony of endangered roseate spoonbills in *Dr. No*— as an irritating distraction from the important business of gathering intelligence about threats to the security of a British colony.

Bond's ability to blend in with a natural environment is often on display, notably in "From a View to a Kill," where he is camouflaged and merges with a tree branch to avoid detection: "He was dressed from head to foot in parachutists' camouflage—green brown and black. Even his hands were covered with the stuff, and there was a hood over his head with slits cut for the eyes and mouth."[40] Bond is on the trail of a nest of enemy spies who have assassinated a British dispatch rider carrying classified information while riding in the Bois de Boulogne. Bond's suspicions are alerted by a report of gypsies having encamped in a clearing nearby, and he holes up in the clearing.

Bond is almost deceived by the silence and innocuous-seeming tranquility of the glade. His sensitivity to natural beauty lulls him to ignore the danger signals, observing the movements of two wood pigeons, a pair of hedge sparrows, and a "fat thrush [that] finally located its worm." Bond is warned of impending danger by his sensitivity to the behavior of birdlife: "It was the pigeons that gave the first alarm. With a loud clatter they took off and dashed into the trees. All the birds followed, and the squirrel. . . . What had sounded the alarm?" Thus alerted, Bond observes an even more unusual disturbance in the natural world, as "slowly, inch by inch, a single thorny stem, an unnaturally straight and rather thick one, was rising through the upper branches." Bond watches as the "rose" extends on its stem and rotates around the glade, and he then looks on with amazement as the rose bush opens up and several previously hidden men emerge into the clearing.[41] The rose bush is the perfect concealment for the enemy spies to wait in their lair until unsuspecting dispatch riders go past on the road. Without his patience and camouflage, Bond would have missed the dangerous signs of the enemy. Like the hidden cell designed for a stay-behind unit on the Rock of Gibraltar in Operation Tracer, these men are concealed within a natural environment. Bond's attention to the specific flora and landscape reflects Ian's own interest in the varieties of natural life. Yet, Ian's writing simultaneously creates a sinister impression of natural beauty and serenity as covers for menacing warlike activity.

This short story provides a vivid example of how the "natural" environment can conceal deadly dangers that only a highly trained observer such as Bond can detect. Fleming has a post-Darwinian attitude toward the natural world as a constant battlefield in which the appearance of tranquility is a disguise for the "struggle for existence." Fleming's rosebush concealing a nest of enemy spies is his fictional equivalent to Darwin's famous "tangled bank" that concludes *On the Origin of Species*:

> It is interesting to contemplate an entangled bank, clothed with many plants of many kinds, with birds singing on the bushes, with various insects flitting about, and with worms crawling through the damp earth, and to reflect that these elaborately constructed forms, so different from each other, and dependent upon each other in so complex a manner, have all been produced by laws acting around us. . . . Thus, *from the war of nature, from famine and death, the most exalted object* which we are capable of conceiving, namely, the production of the higher animals, directly follows.[42]

Like Darwin's, Fleming's writing probes beneath the surface of an apparently tranquil natural scene to discover the violent "laws" working beneath it—laws of "war, famine, and death," a constant battle for survival. These laws can be detected in all Fleming's works, whether in the form of underwater battles, fights to the death on land, or wider human conflicts.

We know that Ian particularly enjoyed two types of landscape—coastal regions and mountains. Ian enjoyed living by the sea—in Jamaica and Kent—and these coastal landscapes also provided many of the memorable settings for the Bond novels, as will be discussed in the next chapter. Fleming's early experience of mountains came at Kitzbühel, Austria, where he went to live and study with the Forbes Dennises at Am Tennerhof (see chapter 2). Here the teenaged Ian learned to ski and also enjoyed active mountain climbing in the Tyrol region of the Alps. After the war, Ian also enjoyed the surroundings of the Green Mountains of Vermont while staying with his friend Ivar Bryce at Black Hole Hollow Farm.

Unfortunately, Ann did not share Ian's passion for mountain scenery, as is apparent in her complaints about the Tyrol. More significantly, by the early 1960s, she could no longer enjoy the winter sojourns at Goldeneye as is apparent in her letters from the period. As Ann set her heart on the expansive (and expensive) rural retreat of Warneford Place (later known as Sevenhampton Place) at Sevenhampton, Wiltshire, she hoped that Ian would sell Goldeneye. But she soon realized that the Jamaican home was essential to Ian's sense of identity. She wrote him in March 1962, "I cannot ask you to give up Jamaica because of your great love for it, and because we are leaving Sandwich [in Kent], but I can and do ask you understand that a two months holiday for you should be made bearable for me if we are not to break asunder." To her friend Clarissa Avon, Ann wrote even more emphatically in February 1964, "I *loathe* the tropics, can only think of this glorious early English spring and burgeoning bulbs at Sevenhampton." Their different taste in environments is a strong sign of their deteriorating marriage, and Ann's dismay at witnessing "Ian struggle to give birth to Bond" with "but half the typewriter banging of last year" is another reason for her dislike of Goldeneye.[43]

Ian also enjoyed rural and mountainous surroundings in the United States, especially at the Vermont home of his lifelong friend, Ivar Bryce. Bryce had married the American heiress Jo Hartford in 1953, and one of her properties was the beautiful Black Hole Hollow Farm in upstate Vermont, where Ian was a frequent visitor, despite the fact he did not get along with Jo.[44] He made particular use of the location in *Diamonds Are Forever*, which is set in part in Saratoga, not far from Bryce's farm. According to Christie's Real Estate, "Fleming often stayed in guest quarters known as the Yellow Room. From there he would take long treks into the woods surrounding the estate and return at eventide. In an old guest register, Fleming once wrote, 'Lived here like a king—an uninvited one—in fragrant and luxurious solitude.'"[45] The opportunity for solitude was one of the chief attractions of the mountain setting, and it was Bryce who noted that, throughout his life, Ian needed to spend at least three-quarters of an hour per day on his own.

However, there were also more convivial experiences at Black Hole Hollow Farm. While staying at Bryce's property in August 1954, Fleming visited the Saratoga races with his friend the lawyer Ernie Cuneo, and the two also made a visit to a sulfur baths in the area. However, rather than reaching the upmarket facility they had planned on visiting, Fleming and Cuneo ended up in a seedy, rundown establishment, which provided the inspiration for the "Acme Mud and Sulphur Baths" in *Diamonds Are Forever*. Many of Fleming's trips to the United States after the war took place in the winter, when he was either on the way to or returning from Jamaica. However, his visits to Black Hole Hollow Farm usually took place in summer or autumn, when the weather was conducive to long walks, and the spectacular fall colors would attract the eye. The Bryces' farm was an ideal bolt-hole for Fleming to plan his next Bond novel or to revise typescripts of his most recent one. It also provided the opportunity for strenuous exercise of the kind witnessed by Cuneo, who accompanied Ian on a climb up the 880-foot Goose Egg Mountain.[46] As another testimony to Ian's great love of the outdoors, Bryce also recalls physical pursuits for Ian: "In Vermont he would always wander about the mountains, play golf, often barefoot, sit by the dam gazing at nothing for hours on end, and then come back and tell us he'd seen a pair of horned owls, or some other bird."[47]

Ian used this remote upstate Vermont/New York location in several works of fiction besides *Diamonds.* In "For Your Eyes Only," the hideaway for the Nazi villain Von Hammerstein—a farm at Echo Lake—is based on Black Hole Hollow Farm. Its privacy and seclusion are beautifully conveyed in the story, and yet the house's use as the base for a villain—who has murdered the parents of the heroine, Judy Havelock—endows it with a menacing atmosphere. Fleming describes the mansion based on the model of Bryce's Vermont farm: "Echo Lake looked what it was—the luxurious retreat, in deep country, well away from atom bomb targets, of a millionaire who liked privacy and could probably offset a lot of his running expenses against the stud farm."[48] The reference to Echo Lake's "stud farm" reflects the Bryces' interest in horse breeding, while its distance from "atom bomb targets" is a reminder of the remoteness from New York City, which Bond had once described as "the fattest atomic bomb target on the whole face of the globe."[49] But Echo Lake is not safe from the primitive weapon of the crossbow, with which Judy will gain her revenge on Gonzales and Von Hammerstein, her parents' killers.

Bond's professional skills are similar to those of a naturalist, able to blend in with the natural environment, hiding in the forests on his approach to Echo Lake. He becomes aware of Judy's presence by his acute senses: "Animals and birds do not break twigs. Dead wood must carry a special danger signal for them." Bond's reflections on Judy mark her as his female equal, another natural predator: "The girl looked like a beautiful unkempt dryad in ragged shirt and trousers. . . . The beauty of her face was wild and rather animal."[50] Judy demands that she take the kill shot, and Bond is impressed by Judy's ability to blend in with the natural surroundings of the woods, claiming her place as one of the later "Amazon" heroines featuring in his fiction.

As a bird lover, Bond is further incensed by Von Hammerstein's cruelty toward avian life: he hears a burst of gunfire followed by hand-clapping and watches in horror as "the kingfisher, a handful of tattered blue and grey feathers, thudded to the lawn and lay fluttering." This act of brutality to a defenseless and beautiful bird seals Von Hammerstein's fate and strengthens Bond's purpose. Bond exists in a Hobbesian state of nature in which he is designated the hunter to punish crimes against nature. Together, Bond and Judy exact vengeance on the Nazi and his Cuban henchman, and Fleming describes how—after killing Gonzales—"the echoes of much death, rolled to and fro across the valley."[51] The natural world, Fleming reminds us, also harbors the forces of fatality.

Fleming's most extensive use of the upstate New York/Vermont location occurs in *The Spy Who Loved Me*, a narrative experiment of writing in the first-person voice from a female perspective. The Adirondacks setting of the Dreamy Pines Motel, where the action takes place, is vividly realized. Whereas the Spangled Mob are drawn to Saratoga Springs by the horseracing and gambling, the gangsters in *The Spy Who Loved Me* are attracted by the prospect of easy money from an insurance scam. The prospect of violating Viv Michelle, Ian's nubile heroine, is an unexpected bonus for their vile intentions.

Dreamy Pines is, of course, a tourist resort of sorts, reflecting Ian's ambivalence toward the tourist industry more generally. His description of the motor court is a mixture of charm and artifice in the landscape: "The whole construction and design was the latest thing—glazed pitch-pine frontages and pretty timber roofs all over knobbles, air-conditioning, . . . all the gimmicks."[52] By using the New York and Vermont backwoods as a haven for gangsters, Fleming suggests, in his post-Darwinian vision, that the peace, tranquility, and remoteness of these locations are deceptive fronts for a deadly menace, killers worse than any predator from the jungle. The location and its hostile invaders also create surprise for the reader, as we scarcely expect to encounter such malevolent figures in this picturesque, rustic setting.

Fleming's insight that remote and apparently tranquil woodland environments could harbor forces of evil and danger also features in the Berlin chapter of *Thrilling Cities*. Fleming uses a rural location for a recurring nightmare in which an apparently lonely, isolated environment conceals a deadly threat to Britain. Describing the scene "in the Harz Mountains, or in the depths of the Black Forest," Fleming relates a "recurrent waking nightmare" in which "a green and smiling field slides silently back to reveal the dark mouth of a great subterranean redoubt." Fleming describes how "the tip of a gigantic rocket emerges above the surrounding young green trees. England has rejected the ultimatum."[53] Like a much larger version of the "unnatural" rose stem in "From a View," or like the rocket emerging from Drax's launchpad carved into the White Cliffs, the missile is concealed but threatens deadly violence to Britain.

Fleming reveals personal reasons for his fear and dislike of Berlin—telling the reader, "From this grim capital went forth the orders that in 1917 killed my father and in 1940 my youngest brother."[54] But it is not from the "grim capital" itself that the rocket will be launched. The remote forests are a more effective hiding place than the city for such a secret weapon. Perhaps unsurprisingly, given Fleming's personal antipathy, Berlin is not used as a setting for any of the Bond novels. However, it is used in an important short story, "The Living Daylights," which has the distinction of being the work of fiction published in the inaugural issue of *The Sunday Times Magazine*—then known as *The Sunday Times Colour Section*—on February 4, 1962.[55]

The story's original title was "Trigger Finger," and it was published in the United States under the title "Berlin Escape," conveying the impression that Berlin is a city both Fleming and Bond wished to "escape" from.[56] Admittedly, it is a stretch to consider Berlin as a "natural environment." The city—at least the section where Bond is to take cover for his mission—is "a waste of empty bombed space . . . of waist-high weeds and half-tidied rubble walls." It is neither town nor country, unpopulated by humans or animals. On this mission, Bond himself loses his humanity, being reduced to a weapon "fired off by M like a projectile at some distant target where a problem waited for his coming." His task is simply to assassinate the Soviet sniper known as "Trigger" before the enemy shooter can kill an escaping British spy. Ravaged by war and political division, Berlin is a vacant territory where nature has begun to reclaim the landscape, with its "broken, thickly weeded bombed ground."[57] This site was chosen as the British agent 272's crossing point from East to West Berlin precisely because its rubble and heavy weeds provide excellent cover. It is this reversion to a natural state that places Berlin in the company of other deceptively harmless environments.

Like Ian, Bond dislikes Berlin as "a glum, inimical city," and his reaction reflects the dirty work he is sent to perform there. Yet, even in this bleak urban setting, Bond's behavior and preparation are similar to those of an avid birdwatcher looking out for a rare species. The first task is to camouflage himself, thus his gun is painted black, and he also wears "a black velvet hood stitched to a waist-length shirt of the same material." If Bond is dressed like an executioner, his purpose is to locate the hiding place of Trigger and kill the assassin without being seen. His apartment and its covered window are like a birdwatcher's hide, and of course Agent 272 is the endangered species he must look out for and protect against a shooter. Bond possesses the most important quality of a birdwatcher: immense patience. This is Bond's strong suit, as he waits in darkness, night after uneventful night, for Agent 272 to make his appearance on the stage later to become famous as "Checkpoint Charlie" compared to "a well-remembered photograph."[58]

While awaiting his target, Bond forgoes a visit to a local brothel in favor of "a strenuous walk in the Grunewald," the vast forest on the outskirts of the city. Though Bond's reflection that "virtue triumphed" may be self-mocking, it is telling that "virtue" is linked to pleasure in natural scenery: "The pretty young trees round the long lake had already been touched by the breath of autumn and there was occasional gold amongst the green."[59] It reminds us of Bond's role as protector of defenseless creatures, including birds, animals, and plants.

In the case of "The Living Daylights," Bond's chivalry leads him to spare the life of "Trigger" when he discovers that she is the blonde cello player whose natural vitality and beauty he has already admired: "She was vivid with movement and life and, it seemed, with gaiety and happiness." When she disappears, Bond suffers a "sharp pang of longing, this thrill of animal magnetism" a reminder of the importance of his "animal instincts" to 007.[60] Fleming uses bird imagery to make her taboo as a target: "And then, in the Sniperscope, Bond saw the head of 'Trigger'—the purity of the profile, the golden bell of hair—all laid out along the stock of the Kalashnikov! She was dead, a sitting duck!" Bond cannot bring himself to kill a "sitting duck" and contents himself with scaring "the living daylights out of her."[61]

Fleming was also fascinated by the destructive powers of nature, drawn to living things that prey on others. In his memorable descriptions of the underwater world, Fleming wrote of sharks, squids, barracudas, and other species that survive by killing and can become—for humans—deadly adversaries. Fleming writes a powerful description in *Thunderball* of a barracuda attacking a man, in which blood, described as "black smoke," spreads through the water, and the barracuda—"seven or eight feet of silver and blue torpedo"—goes in for the kill.[62] Fleming leaves the reader under no illusion that even the beautiful Caribbean sea can conceal deadly predators that pose a threat to man.

If Fleming sees the natural world as a site of continuous struggle—often a deadly one—for survival and dominance, this does not diminish the beauty of this world. Fleming is as gifted as any writer of his generation at conveying the aesthetic vitality and sensual beauty of natural objects and locations.

His strong sense of place was cultivated by his journalistic training as well as wide travel experience that included years of patient observation of birds, plants, seascapes, and landscapes. Fleming's writing can evoke geography, topography, flora, and fauna with a passion and exuberance that recalls the adventure fiction of Robert Louis Stevenson and John Buchan. Yet, for Fleming, natural beauty can also be a fatal trap designed to lull the observer into admiration and lower his or her self-protective radar and defenses. Absolute silence is itself, of course, unnatural and can be a warning signal.[63] But even when natural sounds are audible and a pastoral harmony seems visible, this can be the prelude to a major disturbance of sudden violence or aggression. The calm waters of the Caribbean may be suddenly thrown into chaos by the thrashing attack of a barracuda on its prey. The quiet, peaceful thornbush may project its "rose" that is actually a periscope and then open to release a cell of enemy spies. And the rapid, playful flight of seagulls around a clifftop may be suddenly interrupted by an explosion planned with a view to a kill.

Fleming is rarely didactic about the urgency of preserving fragile ecosystems or indeed on any other environmental matter. But the evidence of his writings, throughout his career, points to his deep and abiding passion for the natural world; his close attention to the appearance and behavior of birds, animals, and sea creatures; and his fascination with environmental change. This compulsive literary interest in describing, and cherishing, the natural environment is in itself an ethical standpoint—it assumes that the nonhuman world is just as important as the human. Nature is worthy of this kind of admiration and contains enough interest and drama to reward the writer's—and the reader's—attention.

Fleming also takes an ethical position by attributing the most ecologically destructive, irresponsible behaviors to villains who emerge—even if they are not immediately identified—as existential threats to human survival and security. Milton Krest's use of deadly poison to capture a rare fish, the Hildebrand Rarity, causes havoc and destruction among the fish "community," which Bond thinks of as "friendly people." In fact, Bond compares his role in the destruction to "the bomb-aimer at Nagasaki," although the real villain is "a big, a fully grown predator, a man called Krest. . . . He was just going to kill—almost for fun."[64] Krest, who also brutally abuses his beautiful wife, Liz, is eventually hoist by his own petard when Liz kills him by stuffing the Hildebrand Rarity down his throat while he sleeps.

Fleming's fiction repeatedly shows violence toward the natural world and nonhuman life as warnings of dangerous and deeply antisocial traits such as psychosis, megalomania, sexual abuse, fantasies of omnipotence, extreme narcissism, and obsessive avarice. He proposes, through his descriptive techniques and novelistic imagination, a moral equity between human and nonhuman lifeforms, whether on land, in the sea, or in the air. It is this equality that makes the "Death of a Pelican" deserving of as much empathy as the brutal wounding of a CIA agent; that causes Bond to feel gratitude for the trees that sacrifice themselves to protect him; and that leads him to cover up the murder of Krest, recognizing it as a form of natural justice.

Bond's environmental concerns are not mere window dressing to his character. Like his real-life namesake, who made numerous trips to the Bahamas and Caribbean from 1927 to 1935 while researching *Birds of the West Indies*, Bond is aware that environmental vulnerability, ecological damage, and the threat to natural resources are also vital national security issues.[65] Bond's sensitivity to threats of environmental destruction, in fact, is an essential part of his equipment as a spy and defender of Britain's security.

The greatest anxiety during the Cold War was, of course, the threat of nuclear war between the United States and the Soviet Union, as the superpowers came to the brink of annihilation during the Cuban missile crisis in 1962. Although the threat of nuclear Armageddon—and the extinction of the human race—is always in the background to Fleming's novels, it is on a scale unimaginable and therefore too abstract to serve his plots. Instead, Fleming portrays menace and devastation on a smaller, more concrete scale. A man shooting a harmless bird, destroying an iconic natural landmark, or damaging a fragile ecosystem are ominous signs of turpitude rather than the apocalypse of mutually assured destruction. Bond's recognition of these sinister signs often starts him on the trail toward greater plots of destruction, making him an early warning system for damaging toxins and existential threats to humanity.

Chapter Eight

"Such Stubborn Retreats"

The Bondian Worlds of Jamaica and Kent

There are many fascinating and unique locations and natural environments that feature in the James Bond novels and stories. Ian's nonfiction also explores some of the most intriguing and exotic places in the world. Yet, two locations stand out as especially important and frequent in Ian's writings: the Caribbean island of Jamaica and Ian's favorite English county of Kent. Ian owned homes in both locations, by the coast, and both properties—Goldeneye and White Cliffs—allowed him to indulge his love of the sea. Ian's fascination with the history, topography, landscape, flora, and fauna of these places is evident in some of the most memorable Bond novels, including *Live and Let Die*, *Moonraker*, *Dr. No*, and *Goldfinger*.

What was it about the environments of Jamaica and Kent that possessed such enduring fascination for Ian, not only as places to live but also as settings for some of his best writing? Ian cherished the sense of remoteness and privacy of his homes at Goldeneye and White Cliffs and, of course, their access to dramatic seascapes. But what other features of the landscapes and environments fueled his imagination? In order to answer this question, we must delve into some of the hidden features of the Jamaican and Kentish coasts that drew Ian to them.

By the time Ian left Naval Intelligence at the end of World War II, his head was already full of ideas for spy adventures inspired by his wartime operations. Fleming's experience in intelligence work and the insights he gleaned into espionage during this period had provided the furniture and décor for a structure that already existed in his imagination. But the missing ingredient was a place in which he could find the time, peace of mind, and freedom from distraction necessary to write and express his creative energies. He found this place in Goldeneye.

After the war, Fleming's friend Ivar Bryce helped him find the piece of prime land on the north coast of Jamaica near Oracabessa—the site of a former donkey track—with the help of a local land agent, Reggie Aquart. The land cost £2,000—a lot of money in 1946 but still a bargain considering that Jamaica was attracting more and more of the rich and famous to its shores in the postwar period. Ian then spent another £3,000 building his somewhat Spartan bungalow, which Bryce described as "a cubist arrangement of concrete surfaces" with its glass-free jalousie "windows" and uncomfortable furniture.[1] Naming the house Goldeneye, after Ian's important wartime Naval Intelligence Division operation to defend Gibraltar, marked its significance as a retreat where Ian would continue to inhabit the heady world of espionage but in imaginative form.

It is hardly surprising, given the creative freedom Ian enjoyed at Goldeneye, that the tropical landscapes and coastal environment of Jamaica play a central role in the plots and locations of the James Bond novels. In the second novel, *Live and Let Die*, Bond is entertained in luxury by the Central Intelligence Agency (CIA) in New York and visits, among other places, the strip joints of Harlem before heading off to Jamaica in pursuit of Mr. Big, the Haitian-born SMERSH agent. Mr. Big owns his own private island (the "Isle of Surprise") off the coast of Jamaica, where he has discovered Captain Morgan's lost treasure and proceeds to smuggle the antique contraband coins into the United States. Because the funds are being used by Mr. Big to finance SMERSH spy networks, the Secret Intelligence Service (SIS) and James Bond set out to eliminate him. Mr. Big also poses a threat to the British colony of Jamaica, and as Captain Dexter of the Federal Bureau of Investigation reminds Bond, Jamaica is "your territory."[2]

A key figure in introducing Bond to the hidden places and natural treasures of Jamaica is Quarrel, the loyal and supportive Cayman Islander with whom Bond finds companionship. Quarrel befriends Bond and trains him with great survival skills, educating him about the unique natural features of the island. Clearly, there is a hierarchy between them—Fleming compares their relationship to that between a Scottish laird and his retainer—but there is also respect and affection. As Vivian Halloran has argued, Quarrel can also

Figure 8.1. Ian Fleming looks up from his typewriter in Goldeneye, Jamaica. ***Mara Vivat/Contributor/Getty Images.***

be seen as "Bond's double. Bond's recognition of Quarrel's blood suggests that he views him as a kinsman."[3]

The Jamaican landscape of *Live and Let Die*, still fresh and vivid in Fleming's imagination, is one of the most memorable aspects of the novel. Jamaica is shown as an island of outstanding natural beauty, cultural vitality, and tropical delight. Ian was still fairly confident of his—and Britain's—colonial position in the Caribbean in the early 1950s, and there is no doubt in the CIA agent Felix Leiter's mind that Jamaica is in Bond's (and Britain's) jurisdiction. This may be self-delusion on Bond's part, but Leiter of the CIA will play second fiddle and "move right on to Jamaica with you, Mr Bond."[4]

At this early stage of the Cold War, the US-UK alliance remains intact and amicable.

The situation had changed significantly by the time Fleming wrote his second Jamaica-based novel, *Dr. No*, published in 1958. By this time, American influence in the Caribbean had expanded, Fidel Castro was on the brink of installing a Communist government in nearby Cuba, and Britain's days as a colonial power were waning. In describing the Queen's Club—the haven for the island's colonial class—Fleming anticipates the demise of both this institution and the colonial society it represents as though he were a prophetic tour guide:

> This mansion is the social Mecca of Kingston. It is Queen's Club, which, for fifty years, has boasted the power and frequency of its blackballs. Such stubborn retreats will not long survive in modern Jamaica. One day Queen's Club will have its windows smashed and perhaps be burned to the ground.[5]

Fleming's description also tells us something important about the way he views imperiled natural environments and other unique locations throughout the Bond novels. In Fleming's imagination, there is a fragility and vulnerability to such environments: their beauty and appeal is connected to this fragility and the danger of their destruction. Many of the most memorable and cherished locations in Fleming's novels can be characterized as "stubborn retreats"—they are set away from the beaten track, tourist traps, or urban centers; they provide a welcome escape from the stresses of modern life; and they manage to survive despite the attempts of some, usually the villains, to destroy them.

In addition to protecting these endangered places and species from harm, Bond also receives crucial assistance from nonhuman sources concerning the dangers he faces. In a notable pattern, birds and other animals become Bond's "agents in the field," warning him of hostile intentions and impending threats from enemy actors. Without wanting to make Bond sound like Hugh Lofting's Dr. Doolittle, he does communicate in various ways with nonhuman lifeforms in order to protect them or save himself and other humans from disaster.

Fleming's choices of location in the novels are based on more than simply their appeal as an attractive "background" or exotic setting for Bond's adventures. In the Bond films, the viewer often gets the impression that exotic locations have been chosen simply to provide a visual spectacle and stimulating display of "local color." In Fleming's novels, by contrast, the locations are densely researched; rendered in careful, atmospheric detail; and play an integral part in the story lines. When Ian has Bond visiting another culture, he does not simply follow the tourist map but explores regional differences, samples local indigenous culinary specialties, and has meaningful encounters with locals away from the tourist traps.

Except when he is hosted overseas by others (as in *Live and Let Die*) or required to stay in exclusive hotels as part of his mission (as in *Casino Royale*), Bond does not generally choose the luxury options. Rather, he often opts for simpler, more characterful accommodations, such as the Kristal Palas in Istanbul, which Bond chooses from "a perverse liking for the sleazy romance that clings to old-fashioned Continental hotels." He is often blessed with a local guide—such as Quarrel in *Live and Let Die* and *Dr. No*, Darko Kerim in *From Russia, with Love*, or Tiger Tanaka in *You Only Live Twice*—who can bypass the obvious tourist destinations and introduce Bond to more "authentic" experiences (notably, the gypsy camp in *From Russia, with Love*, where Kerim tells him to eat exclusively "with the right hand, James").[6]

Ian's choice of locations for the novels was inspired by his own travel experiences. One steaming hot night in September 1956, for example, Ian found himself in Istanbul for the Interpol General Assembly meeting. He had traveled there with Sir Ronald Howe, commissioner of the Metropolitan Police, who managed to get him into the conference. Fleming was hoping to glean ideas from the conference for his next novel, as the agenda included drug smuggling, forgery, human trafficking, and other topics that fascinated him. But instead, on this night, he witnessed a dramatic orgy of street violence as Muslims in the city rose up against Istanbul's Greek Orthodox residents in a stunning display of ethnic hostility. The violent uprising required military intervention, including "cavalry and Sherman tanks," to suppress it.[7]

In his effort to describe the mayhem, Ian tapped in to his great gifts for conveying violent action and setting, writing in *The Sunday Times*, "a car went out of control and charged the yelling crowd and the yells changed to screams and gesticulating hands showed briefly as the bodies went down before it."[8] This was exactly the kind of "strong sensation" Ian looked for on his travels, and though the violence was unusual, it helped him settle on Istanbul as the setting for his next novel, *From Russia, with Love*. Ian returned to England on the Orient Express, also a key setting for the novel.

When not busy working and socializing in London, Ian gravitated to Kent, especially his favorite stretch of coast between Dover and Sandwich.

The Kent locations of novels such as *Moonraker* and *Goldfinger* offer detailed descriptions of places along the coast, such as Dover, the White Cliffs (where he was living in Noël Coward's former home) at Saint Margaret's Bay, Sandwich (location of the Royal St George's golf club), and Reculver on the Isle of Thanet. Bond, like Ian, is happy to stop off at a local pub to sample the beer and listen to gossip.

Ian was also immersed in the history of the region, going back to the important role of the Cinque Ports in the twelfth to fourteenth centuries, and the crucial construction at Chatham Naval Dockyard from the sixteenth century. Because of their stubborn resistance to William the Conqueror and the Normans, the Kentish people adopted the motto "Invicta" (undefeated) for the county, and this undaunted spirit continued during Kent's vital role as a base for Royal Air Force bombing raids during World War II. Its importance as a base for military activity also made Kent a primary target for German bombings, and in the 1950s—when Fleming lived there—the area still bore many of the scars of enemy bomb damage from the war.

Ian's delight in coastal scenery and proximity of the sea made the Kent coast an ideal retreat from London—only a short drive along the A10—while the location of his favorite golf course at Sandwich was a further enticement. But more than this, Kent represented a key boundary—the name deriving from the Celtic word *kantos* or "border"—and defense against the threat of foreign invasion, being the closest spot in the British isles to Continental Europe. On the one hand, the White Cliffs of Kent represented an image of Britain as a "fortress," with its "snarling milk-white teeth" presenting a warning to potential invaders.[9] On the other, Kent's proximity to Europe made it vulnerable, a potential target for enemy invasion and spies. This vulnerability was highlighted in early spy novels such as Childers's *The Riddle of the Sands* and, especially, Buchan's *The Thirty-Nine Steps*, in which the Black Stone—the German spy ring—has its hideout on the Kent coast near Broadstairs.

Kent's ambivalent status as both a defensive bulwark and a vulnerable point of the country explains the sinister presence of Bond villains such as Hugo Drax and Auric Goldfinger in the county's coastal reaches. These locations are attractive in being at once remote, private, and secure, while also providing quick escape routes from Britain to Continental Europe. Ian's interest in Kent goes beyond the military history and espionage potential of the county, though. Kent is one of Britain's most fertile agriculturally productive regions, known as the "Garden of England." Ian's minute attention to the landscape, flora, and fauna of Kent makes a familiar "domestic" location appear exotic to the reader, drawing our attention to features of the natural landscape we may have overlooked.

In Britain, the Kent coast remains detached from the great metropolitan energy and hubbub of London, even while its easy access by car makes it attractive to Londoners seeking a weekend retreat. Ian shows that the Kent coast is under threat from another kind of "invasion"—that of mass tourism, which would transform the landscapes of Margate, Ramsgate, and Southend-on-Sea (in neighboring Essex) into crowded seaside resort towns. Though such privileged, remote retreats might be endangered, they are also resilient—and James Bond's role is to cherish, protect, and guard them. The connection between Kent and Jamaica, in Ian's imagination, is that both locations are "stubborn retreats" threatened by hostile invasion.

"THAT DAMNED BUSINESS ABOUT THE BIRDS": FLEMING AND BOND IN JAMAICA

When Ian began writing the James Bond novels in 1952, Jamaica was still a prized colony of Britain. The colonial lifestyle and tropical landscape of Jamaica appealed greatly to Fleming and his cohorts, who obtained land and built homes at bargain prices while living out a fantasy of colonial prestige. They enjoyed tropical fare at home and at the colonial enclaves such as the Liguanea Club at Kingston (founded in 1910), on which Fleming based Queen's Club in *Dr. No*. Ann's letters make various references to being served by "black slaves," suggesting that such disturbing racial prejudice was not viewed as offensive in her circle. Even though Fleming was on friendly, even affectionate terms with his staff—especially his cook, Violet—there was never any doubt who was in charge. He was referred to by his staff as "The Commander," recognizing his rank in the navy (the same as Bond's rank).

However, the days of the British Empire were fast disappearing—especially after the independence of India in 1947 and Nigeria in 1960. American influence was increasingly evident in the Caribbean well before Jamaican independence in 1962. This was partly a factor of America's geographical proximity and also attributable to American fears about the spread of Communism, a potential Caribbean "domino effect." After Cuba fell to the Communist regime of Fidel Castro in 1959, American governments were increasingly anxious about the spread of Soviet influence and control in the Caribbean, located right on America's doorstep. This would reach a crisis point with the Cuban missile crisis in October 1962. Soviet influence in Jamaica was also a source of concern with the US government. Hence the explosion of American-style capitalism; building hotels and resorts, restaurants, and shops was both a symptom of profitable mass tourism and a desire to annex the island through "soft power" of American cultural influence.

Ian would convey his criticism of the United States—also evident in US-based novels such as *Diamonds Are Forever*—by the unfavorable contrast of its resorts and tourist venues to the vitality of Jamaica. In *Live and Let Die*, Bond helps Solitaire, Mr. Big's clairvoyant mistress, escape from her captor and travels with her (under the assumed names "Mr and Mrs Bryce") on the Silver Phantom down to Saint Petersburg, Florida. Here, Bond is appalled by the proliferation of "oldsters"—retired senior citizens who (in Bond and Leiter's view) are just grabbing some sunshine on their way to the grave. Bond objects, "It sounds rather like Bournemouth or Torquay. But a million times worse." He then witnesses benches "thick with oldsters sitting in rows like the starlings in Trafalgar Square."[10]

Ian had traveled to Saint Petersburg with Ann the previous year—1953—taking the Silver Meteor train (on which the Silver Phantom is based), and he was appalled by the scenes of genteel decline and physical decay that he witnessed. Fleming later wrote of Bond in *You Only Live Twice* (quoting Jack London), "I shall not waste my days in trying to prolong them. I shall use my time."[11] Fleming's epitaph engraved on his headstone in Sevenhampton is the Latin phrase "*omnia perfunctus vitae praemia, marces*," which can be translated as "having enjoyed all life's prizes, you now decay."[12]

Ian's reflections on the inevitability of decay and the determination to seize each day and live without concern for the future may have been influenced by his Saint Petersburg, Florida, experience. These somewhat negative, if not dystopian, impressions of American society are a stark contrast to Bond's return to the gorgeous tropical exuberance of Jamaica. For example, Fleming describes Bond's drive with Quarrel "towards the northern plains through some of the most beautiful scenery in the world, the tropical vegetation changing with the altitude." Yet the reference that Bond had previously been on a mission to Jamaica after the war "when the Communist headquarters in Cuba was trying to infiltrate the Jamaican unions" is a warning of the present threat: the Communist SMERSH agent, Mr. Big.[13]

Mr. Big's use of voodoo to terrorize his various gangs of Black workers has roots all over the Caribbean. For his research, Fleming drew on *The*

Traveller's Tree (1950) by Patrick Leigh Fermor, a good friend of his and Ann's, who has been described as "a cross between Indiana Jones, James Bond, and Graham Greene."[14] Fermor's book was referenced by Ian to illustrate the central role of voodoo in the fabric of Caribbean life. In particular, Fermor made a link between voodoo and political rebellion, noting that

> it was the unifying force of Voodoo, far more than the advent of New Ideas from Europe, that impelled the slaves at the time of the French Revolution to revolt. The new ideas merely provided the opportunity and implanted in their opponents the mood of doubt. The first chain-breakers—Mackandal the poisoner and Boukman . . . were both Voodoo initiates, and the Haitians were carried to victory by the inspiration of their equatorial numina.[15]

Mr. Big uses voodoo to establish a tyranny over his followers rather than to incite rebellion. In order to take on Mr. Big, Bond cannot work alone. He therefore enlists the help of Quarrel, a Cayman Islander who works with him at a remote coastal house called Beau Desert. This extended sequence represents Fleming's most overt "Crusoe fantasy"—or "Robinsonade"—in which Bond is supported and trained by a native "Man Friday" in a remote location resembling a desert island.

Like a Caribbean "rogue male," Bond returns to a state of nature, adhering to a strict regimen of exercise, abstention from smoking and drinking, and a healthy sea-based diet, which brings him to a peak of physical fitness and alertness. In Fleming's novel, Bond has to place himself in the hands of a West Indian man in order to prepare for battle with his Caribbean adversary, Mr. Big. Bond in Jamaica has to shed the trappings of Western "civilization" (many of which are bad for his health) in order to return to a more primitive and virile state. Quarrel's influence is essential, informing Bond about Jamaican native plants, "the poisons of the forest and the healing properties of tropical herbs."[16]

Following this training period, Bond is in shape both to kidnap Solitaire and endure tortures such as being dragged over a coral reef by a speedboat. Bond eventually goes diving and places limpet mines on Mr. Big's luxury yacht, displaying a blend of technological know-how and primitive skill and cunning. Ian had excelled at underwater exercises at Camp X—William Stephenson's training camp at Oshawa on Lake Ontario—where "the final test came at night with a long underwater swim rather like the one James Bond performed in *Live and Let Die* when he fixed the limpet mine to the hull of the *Secatur*."[17] The scene in *Live and Let Die* also exploits the "Crabb" fiasco in which SIS sent a veteran Royal Navy frogman—Lieutenant Commander Lionel "Buster" Crabb—to spy on Nikita Kruschev's cruiser *Ordzhonikidze* docked in Portsmouth harbor in April 1956, when the Soviet leader was in Britain for meetings with Prime Minister Anthony Eden. Unlike Crabb—whose headless corpse washed up over a year later in Chichester Harbor—Bond successfully plants limpet mines on the enemy's yacht. Ian again transforms messy reality, even operational disaster, into thrilling fiction.

Combining the technical skill and military resources of the West with the physical strength and vigor of the "natural" man, Bond is more than a match for Mr. Big. When the limpet mines detonate, Bond witnesses Mr. Big, floating in the Caribbean Sea after the explosion, being eaten by a ravenous shark. The horrific death of the villain is a fitting metaphor for Mr. Big, a human "predator," who weaponizes natural creatures to destroy his enemies but is himself consumed by those same creatures.[18]

Ian's original title for *Live and Let Die* was "The Undertaker's Wind"—a title that links the work even more closely to the Jamaican environment and climate.[19] In the published novel, this wind, though not part of the title, plays an important role in the plot, and it is Quarrel, the "native" man, who explains its significance to Bond in chapter 17:

> "On-and-off shore breeze de sailors call it," said Quarrel. "De Undertaker blow de bad air out of de Island night-times from six till six. Then every morning de 'Doctor's Wind' come and blow de sweet air in from de sea. Leastwise dat's what we calls dem in Jamaica." Quarrel looked quizzically at Bond.
>
> "Guess you and de Undertaker's Wind got much de same job, Cap'n," he said half-seriously.[20]

This comparison between Bond and the "undertaker's wind" is a fascinating suggestion that Bond has the role of a natural "cleanser" of pollution or "bad air." Quarrel, in his role as the native shaman figure and guide, gives Bond access to indigenous knowledge and people who would otherwise not be known to him. Rather than being identified as an agent of British colonialism—an alien, oppressive authority—Bond is endowed by Quarrel with a natural and decontaminating efficacy. At the same time, the associations between "undertakers" and death reminds us that Bond's role—his power of "cleansing"—is that of an assassin, authorized by his "license to kill" to rid the British colony of a foreign menace. Death is the focus of Fleming's eventual title and is alluded to by Bond, who is still in New York with Leiter and Captain Dexter of the Federal Bureau of Investigation, who advocates a policy of "live and let live": "'In my job,' he said, 'when I come up against a man like this one, I have another motto. It's "live and let die."'"[21]

Mr. Big—like other Fleming villains—tries to weaponize the natural world and the environment, dragging Bond and Solitaire across the coral reefs surrounding his island, attempting to cut them to pieces on this beautiful, fragile, yet deadly natural material. Mr. Big plans to feed his captives to the sharks, just as the Robber had used Felix in Saint Petersburg. Yet, ultimately, it is Mr. Big who becomes shark food.

Ian chose Jamaica as the setting for several James Bond novels and stories so as to exploit his own knowledge of the landscape, topography, climate, and society of the island. The remoteness of Beau Desert—which we later learn (in *Dr. No*) was owned by the family of Honey Rider—creates a sense of isolation for Bond and Quarrel. Like Ian when he returned to Jamaica each winter, Bond feels a mood of homecoming as he leaves the US mainland for the Caribbean: "Bond was glad to be on his way to the soft green flanks of Jamaica and to be leaving behind the great hard continent of Eldollarado."[22] With the contrast between "soft" natural Jamaica and "hard" commercialized America, Fleming implies that Jamaica is somehow immune to the ruthless capitalism and materialism of the United States. Yet as businessmen-villains like Mr. Big and Dr. No testify, the ruthless greed of capitalism (ironically, in the service of Communism) knows no national boundaries and is fast encroaching.

The setting of Jamaica also brings a tropical, exotic element to the Bond novels, enhancing their appeal for the British reader who had never been—and more than likely never would go—to the Caribbean. When *Dr. No* was selected as the first Bond novel to be filmed by the Salzman/Broccoli team, EON Productions, the choice could hardly have been more fortuitous for Ian. Fleming was in Jamaica during this winter of 1962, writing *On Her Majesty's Secret Service*, but still found time to interact with the film's stars, director, and crew. He assisted with scouting for shooting locations and set up a vital production assistant in Chris Blackwell (son of his close friend and lover Blanche Blackwell and today the owner of Goldeneye). Among other things, including location scouting, Chris Blackwell assumed responsibility for finding local musicians to perform on the film's soundtrack, including the distinctive numbers "Underneath the Mango Tree" and "Three Blind Mice."

When Ian wrote *Dr. No* (in 1957), Cuba was already on the brink of being taken over by the Communist revolutionary leader Fidel Castro and thus becoming effectively a Caribbean satellite of the Soviet Union. Therefore, Britain's influence on and colonial control of Jamaica was in jeopardy during the Cold War but remained crucial to protect the island from similarly being taken over by Soviet-influenced Communists. Fleming, of course, predicted that eventually Jamaica would throw off British rule and claim its independence—an inevitable fate that he foreshadows at the start of *Dr. No*. But, meanwhile, Jamaica could serve both as a reminder of Britain's former imperial role and as a symbol of her continuing strategic and political importance.

Ian's fantasy in *Dr. No* of Britain's role as protector of American national security—a reversal of the actual respective powers of the NATO allies—also draws on war memories. The eponymous villain is half German, half Chinese—combining enemies from Britain's two most recent wars—and has established his base on Crab Key, a private island just off the coast of Jamaica. Crab Key comes to the attention of SIS because of a controversy over a colony of endangered birds—roseate spoonbills—which has been disturbed by Dr. No's activities. The officials and rangers from the Audubon Society who were sent to investigate all meet with violent deaths. But the reason Bond is sent to Jamaica—on what is supposed to be a kind of rest cure after his near-death experience in *From Russia, with Love*—is the sudden disappearance of Commander Strangways, the head of Station J, along with his female assistant, Mary Trueblood.[23]

As he digs deeper—again enlisting Quarrel as an ally—Bond learns that No's activities pose a direct threat to America's national security. Dr. No's underground facility on Crab Key allows him to sabotage American missiles launched from Cape Canaveral, sending them plunging into the sea or, more fiendishly, redirecting them to hit American mainland targets such as Miami. Dr. No's background is explicitly anti-American: he used to be a member of the Chinese Tongs before he embezzled their funds, having his hands cut off as punishment. That he is on America's doorstep is a matter of grave concern for the CIA, but they are powerless to intervene because he is on British territory. Hence Fleming's novel is a reminder that Britain's long history on Jamaica gives the nation a unique role in Caribbean politics and intelligence gathering.

In addition to its renown as the basis for the first EON Bond film, *Dr. No* deserves recognition as Fleming's most sustained attempt to focus on the environment and nonhuman lifeforms critical to both ecological health and political security. The themes of environmentalism (especially the threat posed by the novel's villain, Dr. Julius No, to bird life and ecological balance) and James Bond's role as a protector of the environment are more central to *Dr. No* than in any other work by Fleming.

Bond's role as a defender of Britain's interests overseas includes his being a protector of fragile lifeforms and ecosystems around the globe. Bond, as previously mentioned, was named after an American ornithologist. There are other potential sources for the name James Bond: there is a character with this name in an Agatha Christie short story of the 1930s, and a boy named James Bond attended Fettes Grammar School in Edinburgh—the school that Fleming's fictional hero attends after being expelled from Eton College. Yet, the origin that Fleming chose to showcase in interviews was the American author of *Field Guide to the Birds of the West Indies*.

The origin of the novel is also unusual. Fleming had been asked to write a screenplay for a television series, titled *Commander Gunn*, for the American producer Henry Morgenthau.[24] The series was to feature an agent called James Gunn, who travels to Jamaica to confront a villain who is based in a fortified castle, from which he is threatening the world with nuclear attack. When the television series project foundered, Fleming adapted the ideas from the abandoned screenplay for a new novel. Hence, the novel is an adaptation from another medium—television—that would itself be adapted into film.

Dr. No begins with M consulting the famous neurologist Sir James Molony (Fleming gives the name of his own dentist to the eminent doctor) with his concerns about Bond's condition. Molony assures M that Bond, with his remarkable constitution, has survived the dose of "fugu poison" he received from Rosa Klebb (at the end of *From Russia, with Love*) but recommends a period of recuperation for the injured agent. M, therefore, decides to send Bond on a "holiday" to Jamaica, to investigate the disappearance of head of SIS Station J, John Strangways. While most at SIS, including M, believe that Strangways has eloped with his attractive blonde assistant, Mary Trueblood, Bond is less convinced. Having worked with Strangways on a previous Jamaican assignment in *Live and Let Die*, he doubts he is the type to simply disappear, even with an attractive female companion.

Bond is especially intrigued by the investigation Strangways was conducting just before his disappearance. The island of Crab Key is the property of a "Chinaman," Dr. No, who runs a fertilizer business there, collecting the dung of the guano bird with its remarkable nutrient properties for commercial sale. The endangered roseate spoonbills on Crab Key had been decimated, and the wardens sent by the Audubon Society to protect them are found dead. Then, a team of officials sent by plane to investigate is killed when their plane crashes. M and his chief of staff are contemptuous of all the fuss about the spoonbills, dismissing it as "that damned business about the birds." Whereas M ascribes the interest in protecting the spoonbills to foolish old ladies with too much time and money, Bond takes the threat to the birds and the environment altogether more seriously: "It just strikes me that four people seem to have died more or less because of these birds. Perhaps two more did—Strangways and the Trueblood girl."[25]

In fact, as the reader knows from the dramatic opening to the novel, Strangways has been assassinated by three hitmen, posing as "three blind men," outside the Queen's Club, where he was playing cards with colleagues. In Fleming's portrayal, the killers are a sinister mixed-race caste he calls "Chigroes" and soon identified as the henchmen of Dr. No.[26] Without knowing Strangways's fate, Bond realizes that the attacks on the birds may be warnings of a deeper menace that also threatens human life and society. M sees Bond's interest in the birds as a trivial distraction, telling him to "hurry up and get your holiday over. You may not have noticed it, but the rest of the world happens to be in a bit of a mess."[27] As a secret agent named after a famous naturalist, it is Bond's special gift to understand that damage to bird habitats on Crab Key is also bad news for humans.

Fleming's representation of the environment, with the stark contrast between Jamaica and Crab Key, is curiously mixed in *Dr. No*. Jamaica itself is celebrated for its stunning natural beauty, the friendliness and hospitality of its people, and the vitality of its culture. Bond's journey there is tinged with nostalgia for his previous adventure in *Live and Let Die*, and the descriptions of the Jamaican landscape are richly detailed and poignant in their appreciation of natural beauty: "The setting sun flashed gold on the bright worms of tumbling rivers and streams. 'Xaymaca' the Arawak Indians had called it—'The Land of Hills and Rivers.' Bond's heart lifted with the beauty of one of the most fertile islands in the world."[28]

By contrast, the descriptions of the imaginary Crab Key are dystopian in their evocation of filth, decay, and corruption. Despite being the home of the beautiful spoonbills, the island is dominated by their avian opposite, the guano birds. The overwhelming impression is the sickening, ammonia stench of the guano droppings that provide Dr. No with his excremental "cover" for espionage and sabotage. The landscape of Crab Key is dominated by oppressive swamps and festering rivers that Fleming describes with attention to pestiferous corruption: "Soon, as they got away from the sea, it began to smell bad with the bad egg, sulphuretted hydrogen smell of marsh gas. The mosquitoes and sandflies began to find them. They liked Bond's fresh body."[29]

The malaise of Crab Key is represented, in racial terms, by the Chinese influence on Jamaica. The portrayal of Dr. Julius No is clearly influenced by the Sax Rohmer Fu Manchu novels, and Fleming—writing soon after the Korean War—taps into the xenophobic anxiety of a "yellow peril" invading British territory that Rohmer exploited in the early twentieth century. Fleming adds to this mix his own phobias about mixed race as a sign of villainy. Interestingly, James Bond also has a mixed ethnic background—his mother, Monique, being Swiss, while his father, Andrew, is a Scotsman from Glencoe. As Vivian Halloran has remarked in an interesting article, "James Bond's mixed Scottish and Swiss heritage and his upbringing abroad mark him as as much of a hybrid figure as any of the villains he encounters in his assignments."[30] However, it all depends on the elements mixed together: the presence of German or Chinese blood is a sure sign for Fleming of villainy, as it is with Hugo Drax (*Moonraker*) and Donovan Grant (*From Russia, with Love*) as well as Dr. No.

Yet, the greatest racial stigma of the novel is assigned to the Chigroes, a mix of Chinese and Black Caribbean who emerge from the dystopian world of Crab Key to infect Jamaica with crime and corruption. Just as Crab Key is a corruption of the idealized Jamaica, so the Chigroes are portrayed as a contaminated race, not "proper" Caribbean like Quarrel but not pure Chinese either. The fact that the Chigroes offer the first violent attack on British rule in Jamaica in the novel—with Strangways's assassination—marks them, in Fleming's novel, as deadly and evil.

Fleming's arbitrary division of various species and landscapes—birds, humans, and territories—into "pure" and "impure," "good" and "evil," is both revealing and disturbing. Bond's role in the novel is to identify Dr. No as a villain through his sponsorship of the Chigroes and also by his destruction of the fragile ecosystem of Jamaica—an environmental violence that presages a greater geopolitical threat to Britain and the United States in the New World (both the Caribbean and United States). Bond's instinct to protect and respect the birds pays dividends for his mission to protect Britain's interests.

M's chief of staff makes angry reference to "this damned business of the birds" and is more prophetic than he realizes. The birds, not spoonbills but green cormorants, are indeed a commercial "business," and they are mephitic in odor and ugly in appearance—"damned" indeed. It is fair to say that owlish Dr. No does not give a hoot about the guano birds—though he does supervise the manufacturing of the profitable fertilizer from their droppings. Dr. No is clearly a canny businessman as we learn from the chief of staff's report: "Some bright chap had the idea of buying the island and starting to work it again. . . . This man imported plenty of cheap labour and soon had the place working at a profit." Both birds and humans, in fact, provide "cheap labour" from which Dr. No extracts his profit. The damage to the landscape, the mountains coated with a permanent layer of excrement, is irrelevant to him. The two official Western institutions investigating problems on Crab Key both have things out of proportion. While the Audubon Society cares about the birds but not the people who have died or disappeared, SIS cares about its agents but not the birds: "Nobody at the Colonial Office or in Jamaica's in the least interested" in the fate of the spoonbills.[31] Having reached a stalemate, the case is passed on to Bond to "solve."

The idea that apparently minor crises in Fleming's novels can be indicative of greater perils has been touched on by Christoph Lindner, who argues,

> Crises in Fleming are no longer directed toward individuals or individual communities, but rather toward entire nations, whole continents, and, often, the human race itself. *Moonraker* (1955), *Thunderball* (1961) and *Dr. No* all contain potentially genocidal atomic conspiracies. On a similar scale, *On Her Majesty's Secret Service* (1963) threatens biological warfare in an attempt to annihilate Britain's agricultural and livestock industries.[32]

The drawback to Lindner's emphasis on vast scale and global conspiracy is that it assumes the reader already knows in advance about the huge scale of the villain's operation. Lindner neglects the reader's process of discovery, in which a global conspiracy is revealed gradually, through small warning signs. Traveling through the landscape of Fleming's novel, the reader becomes as engaged with the quest to protect the spoonbills as Bond himself.

Dr. No also represents a significant advance in Ian's portrayal of women, as the influence of his Jamaican lover Blanche Blackwell on his later heroines becomes evident. Interestingly, despite suggestions that Dr. No uses slave labor in his guano factory, the only direct reference to "slavery" in the novel is made in the context of Bond's relationship with Honey Rider, the native woman who works alongside him. Although her ancestors presumably built their fortune on slavery, Fleming's context is Honeychild's offer to sleep with Bond on Crab Key; when he demurs on the grounds he has to keep watch, Honey makes him promise that he will sleep with her when they get back to Jamaica: "The voice whispered triumphantly, 'Now you owe me slave-time. You've promised.'"[33]

Through Bond's affair with Honey, Ian allows his hero to abandon his role as colonial master with a "license to kill" and also give up his position as male dominator of women: "With him she had no inhibitions. They were two loving animals. It was natural. She had no shame." The idea of the human as a "natural" animal is celebrated in this scene of passionate sexual love. Ian unlocks the conventional hierarchy of power between man and woman, as Honey demands that Bond take off his clothes, again reminding him of his obligation to her; when Bond hesitates—"But"—Honey utters the novel's final words, a woman's statement of command: "Do as you're told."[34]

To be clear: Crab Key is a fictional environment, a product of Fleming's imagination. It was based in great detail on a real island that Fleming visited in 1956, the year before he wrote *Dr. No*, to do a piece for *The Sunday Times* on the Bahamian island of Great Inagua. The landscape of this small island was dominated by stinking mangrove swamps, and Ian—accompanied by Ivar Bryce—joined an expedition that visited a flamingo colony and then drove around the swampy island in a converted Land Rover with extra-large wheels to handle the marshy terrain. They were recording the various types of guanay bird for the Audubon Society and staying with the Ericsons, a family that owned a salt mine on the island.[35] Ian was struck by the contrast between the beauty and elegance of the flamingoes and the less attractive but more profitable guanay bird (aka the green cormorant) whose migrations they were there to record.

In creating Crab Key, Fleming replaced the flamingoes of Great Inagua with roseate spoonbills—a beautiful, endangered, and economically useless species that attracts the protective support of the Audubon Society. The spoonbills represent an "aristocracy" of birds—vulnerable in the modern capitalist society, yet privileged and immune from the laws of "survival of the fittest." Huge resources are expended to protect this fragile species, which perhaps would not survive without such protections—and this use of resources is the root of M's ire, as he struggles to secure adequate funds for (in his view) his far more important work as chief of SIS.

By contrast, the guanay birds are prolific in their breeding, and economically productive, yet aesthetically unappealing. From Pleydell-Smith at the Colonial Office in Jamaica—one of Fleming's potentially boring "experts" who turns out to be more interesting than expected (the formula would be repeated with Colonel Smithers in *Goldfinger*)—Bond learns that "the guanay is a machine for converting fish into guano." Fleming's mischievous suggestion that capitalism and its colonial enterprise is a matter of turning excrement into profit can hardly be missed. The wartime memories of an attacking fleet of enemy bombers (still present in Fleming's mind from World War II) provides a fitting image for the guanays, as

> they began to back-pedal in the air and then go into shallow dives, hitting the water like shrapnel. Almost at once a fresh file appeared from the west, then another and another that merged into a long stream and then into a solid black river of birds. For minutes they darkened the skyline and then they were down on the water, covering several acres of it, screeching and fighting and plunging their heads below the surface, cropping at the solid field of anchovy like piranha fish feasting on a drowned horse.[36]

It is as though the German blood of Dr. No has transformed his guanay birds into a squadron of enemy Messerschmidt fighter planes or Heinkel bombers—yet, they are both the bombers and the bombs, landing in the sea "like shrapnel." Did Ian's memory linger on the horrifying scene of his lover Muriel Wright, lying asleep in her London home, instantly killed by a piece of masonry from the German bombs during a night raid in 1943? Again, the image of the feasting piranha fish anticipates the perils of Blofeld's "garden of death" in *You Only Live Twice*.

The grotesque portrayal of "the guanera that gave the mountain its snow-covered look" also carries echoes from Ian's past.[37] The image anticipates the "snow-covered mountain" lair of a later Bond villain, Ernst Stavro Blofeld, atop his private Swiss Alp in *On Her Majesty's Secret Service*, plotting his own assault on the balance of nature—a biological warfare against Britain's livestock and agricultural production.[38] But it also harks back to the snowy mountains of Kitzbühel, where Ian felt indebted to his protectors, and surrogate parents, the Forbes Dennises. The cormorants, however, don't need protecting—only harvesting—and the relationship between "owner" and birds is purely economic.

The death of Dr. No has poetic justice, the villain being fittingly buried by Bond under a mound of his own guano, suffocated by the bird dung that has made him his profits. Dr. No's plot has exposed the fragility of the British colonial presence/domination of Jamaica. Dr. No also raises the troubling prospect that the "mixed" or impure breed is more robust—has more vitality and potency—than the "pure" breed. Cynthia Baron argues that *Dr. No* "discloses an anxiety about the 'integrity' of the boundary between colonizer and colonized, which was being threatened by the unprecedented immigration of people from the former colonies."[39] While this point is demographically and historically correct—as a context for the novel and the film—there is no manifestation of such immigration to Britain in Fleming's novel. In fact, having dispensed with the villain, Bond escapes imaginatively to an idealized and archaic Britain that has no suggestion of non-White faces: "His mind drifted into a world of tennis courts and lily ponds and kings and queens, of London, of people being photographed with pigeons on their heads in Trafalgar Square."[40] As Halloran observes, "Despite the increasing presence of black Britons in Wales and England, they do not appear in Fleming's novels."[41] Ultimately, it is Bond's—and Fleming's—fantasy of a traditional Britain that represents the natural order of peace and environment of harmony. Nowhere is this fantasy of a "treasured," yet imperiled, England more apparent than in Fleming's portrayals of Kent.

"ENGLAND AT MY FEET": IAN FLEMING'S KENTISH NIGHTMARES

The Kent hamlet of Pett Bottom is easy to miss. Located just south of Canterbury, the hamlet consists of a few houses and the Duck Inn, a pub and restaurant that also offers accommodations. When my wife and I went in search of it, in the summer of 2016, we drove down a long lane that seemed to lead nowhere before happening on the road that led to the place we sought. The pub was busy on this sunny July afternoon, but we stopped for a drink to enjoy the atmosphere. Perhaps the Duck Inn's chief claim to fame is that Ian Fleming enjoyed drinking there after a round of golf at the Royal St George's golf club at nearby Sandwich. A plaque on the front wall of the pub proclaims that Fleming wrote *You Only Live Twice* there in 1963. This is a dubious claim, as Fleming actually wrote the novel in January and February of 1963, at Goldeneye in Jamaica. Perhaps, though, he made some revisions to the typescript in Kent. Certainly, it was in *You Only Live Twice*—the final Bond novel to be published in Ian's lifetime—that he identified Bond's own connection with the hamlet.

M's obituary of Bond in *You Only Live Twice* states that following the deaths of Bond's father, Andrew Bond of Glencoe, and his Swiss mother, Monique Delacroix, in a climbing accident, Bond was looked after by "an aunt, since deceased, Miss Charmian Bond, and went to live with her at the quaintly named hamlet of Pett Bottom near Canterbury in Kent." It is to this unlikely and remote spot that Ian sent Bond during the troubled time of mourning for the loss of his parents, where "his aunt, who must have been a most erudite and accomplished lady, completed his education for an English public school."[42] This choice of Pett Bottom for Bond's orphaned childhood home also reflects the importance of the shire of Kent for Ian's literary development and creative imagination. It is far indeed from the tropics of Goldeneye where Bond was born, yet Kent would be second only to Jamaica as a recurrent setting and source of inspiration for Fleming's novels.

Two of Ian's most memorable villains—Sir Hugo Drax and Auric Goldfinger—have their English bases on different stretches of the Kent coast, plotting attacks on Britain's economy and populace. Ian liked to give some of his own identity traits and tastes to his villains, and Drax's and Goldfinger's gravitation to Kent links them closely to their creator. Bond also enjoyed his time in the county, perhaps in nostalgia for his childhood associations of Pett Bottom. The seaside ports of Dover, Deal, and Ramsgate have established Kent as a significant gateway to Europe, and the region is associated with the continental trips Ian frequently made. For those arriving at or leaving Britain by ferry, the White Cliffs of Dover are a visible symbol of British national borders, being the most striking visible feature of the coast from the English Channel.

When it came to finding a home in Kent, Ian wished to live as close as possible to the sea. Noël Coward—his neighbor in Jamaica—decided he'd had enough of his seaside Kent house, White Cliffs at Saint Margaret's Bay, and Fleming was eager to take over the lease. Coward "complained that the Bay had become 'a beach crowded with noisy hoi polloi' and he therefore made the decision to return to the peace and quiet of *Goldenhurst*, his previous home in inland Kent. He left on 16 December 1951, having sold *White Cliffs* to Ian Fleming."[43] The increase in "hoi polloi" was probably due to the greater use of motor vehicles in the postwar period, making travel to the Kent seaside towns more accessible.

According to Fergus Fleming, Ian chose to live at White Cliffs because "it had a view of the sea, was in Fleming's favourite county, Kent, and most importantly was within easy reach of the Royal St George's, one of England's premier golf courses."[44] White Cliffs lacked the private beach and tropical waters Ian enjoyed at Goldeneye; however, it offered a unique vantage point on the English Channel, a dramatic spot from which he could gaze for hours through his telescope at the shipping in the channel, perhaps looking for that elusive German rescue boat whose absence had thwarted Operation Ruthless during the war. Kent had been a key location during World War II—both a target for German warships and U-boats and a site of gun emplacements from which to shell the enemy fleets. Present-day signage at Saint Margaret's Bay identifies the location as "Hellfire Corner" and states:

> During the Second World War this part of Kent was thrust into the forefront of the battle to control the Channel. Big guns along the French coast could fire directly at Dover and the surrounding area. To counter this, several gun batteries were built along the cliff top and around St Margaret's to shell enemy shipping in the Channel. Other, bigger guns were used to fire at the enemy batteries and strong points in France.[45]

Even today, there are gun batteries still visible on the cliffs. A house at the other end of the beach at Saint Margaret's Bay suffered a direct hit, leaving debris over the beach for several years. Churchill made Dover his wartime base for several spells, emphasizing the town's strategic importance especially as the Normandy landings were being planned. A system of tunnels had been carved into the chalk of the White Cliffs dating back to the Napoleonic Wars. After the war, "the tunnels were extended, given alphabetical names as you go down: A—Annexe, B—Bastion, C—Casemate, D—DUMPY, for Deep Underground Military Position Yellow, and E—Esplanade. Annexe was excavated in 1941 to create a military medical aid station for immediate care for wounded soldiers." According to placards at the site,

> Following the fall of France in 1940, the original tunnels of Casemate level were extended by two further levels. Above came Annexe, constructed as a secure underground hospital. Below came Dumpy, its larger spaces designed to be the heart of a new Combined Operations Headquarters for the Royal Navy, Royal Air Force and the Army, jointly charged with protecting the Straits of Dover and the coast of Kent.[46]

Some of the more prominent owners of Kent holiday homes left the area due to the wartime shelling, but Coward was not deterred from buying the property in 1945. He even tried to purchase all the properties in the area near White Cliffs to ensure his privacy but was prevented from doing so due to the shortage of housing in the postwar period. Therefore, "to ensure Coward's privacy, two of the other houses were bought by Coward's friends, novelist Eric Ambler and Cole Lesley, and the third by Coward's mother and Auntie

Vida. Despite investigation by Fleet Street and a suspicious Ministry of Works, no breach of the law was discovered."[47] During Coward's residence, White Cliffs became a lively social hub for the theatrical and arts set, with visitors such as Katharine Hepburn, Spencer Tracy, Daphne du Maurier, and, of course, Ian Fleming. The location also allowed Coward to travel easily to London or Paris.

Ian would often drive down to Saint Margaret's Bay on Friday afternoon, after his week's work at *The Sunday Times* offices in London, in time for a round of golf and a predinner cocktail in the club house. Ann recalled that on weekends "his routine was to go to the golf club at 12:00 where I think he used to drink and talk to his friends, have an early lunch, play golf, have tea in the golf club and come home about 6:00."[48] She was less enamored of White Cliffs than Ian was and somewhat resented being abandoned while Fleming went off playing golf with his cronies: she later complained to Evelyn Waugh in September 1960, even after they had sold White Cliffs, "T-B does not want to leave Sandwich, he is on the golf committee and his only happiness is pink gin, golf clubs and men."[49] The Flemings remained at White Cliffs until 1957. Hence, Ian resided there, for at least part of the year, during the period in which he wrote some of his greatest Bond novels, including *Live and Let Die*, *Moonraker*, and *From Russia, with Love*. *Moonraker*, the third Bond novel, is the only one in the series to be set entirely in Britain, and much of the action takes place in Fleming's beloved Kent.

When Ann grew tired of living in the somewhat run-down White Cliffs, where everything became impregnated with the smell of the sea, she lobbied for a move to an inland location. The result was that they moved to the Old Palace, an eighteenth-century eight-bedroom house at Bekesbourne near Canterbury. Far from solving their domestic problems, however, this move exacerbated them. The conflicts were worsened by the fact that, since Caspar's birth in August 1953, Ann had stopped going to Jamaica during the winters. Ian had made it clear that he did not want Caspar at Goldeneye while he was trying to write his novel, as the child would be too much of a distraction.[50] Ann—for whom the tropical allure and Spartan bachelor conditions of Goldeneye had in any case started to pall—decided that she would stay in England. Ian wrote sympathetic letters to Ann, who was stuck in the Old Parsonage while he was bathing in the Caribbean Sea at Goldeneye, and it is clear that she loathed the house. Ian writes in 1958, "I perfectly see your point about the house and I only beg that where we finally settle will have something that appeases my savage breast—some outlet for activity."[51]

It was while wintering in Jamaica in 1954 that Ian returned imaginatively to the Kent coast that was his favorite part of England. Rather than sending James Bond on an exotic adventure to the Caribbean tropics or French coastal resort—as he had in the previous two novels—Ian decided his hero would face a domestic mission. The novel was written with film specifically in mind, and Ian felt that the "Englishness" of the story would add to its cinematic appeal. While this may have seemed a risky strategy—given that overseas travel and exotic adventure were already established as part of the "Bond formula"—Fleming would delve into the local landscape, flora, and fauna of Kent in such detail that it would seem exotic to the reader. He would exploit the dramatic wartime history of the Kent coast between Dover and Deal, making it the setting of a new crisis in the Cold War.

In fact, the World War II tunnels in the White Cliffs of Dover continued to be used throughout the Cold War. However, the burrowing into the Kent coast carried out in Fleming's fictional world was orchestrated by a former Nazi, Hugo von der Drache, alias Sir Hugo Drax. The presence of this foreign enemy on British soil—ironically being fêted as a "national hero"—would tap into the fears of German invasion that had also inspired the pre–World War I spy classics by Erskine Childers, William Le Queux, and John Buchan.[52]

The title of his third novel gave Fleming more trouble than any of the others—and it would be published in the United States under a very different title: *Too Hot to Handle*. Fleming's eventual choice for the British version has a different regional significance, for "moonraker" is a colloquial expression for a person born in Wiltshire—the county in which Fleming would make his final home in England and in which he was laid to rest. Although the title was supposed to convey the distant flight of the rocket, it also anticipated Fleming's burial place.

Bond's journey to Kent relies heavily on coincidence. Having exposed Sir Hugo Drax (aka "The Columbite King") as a cheat at bridge at Blades club in London, Bond then learns from M that the security officer at Drax's base, Fallon, has been murdered in an apparent *crime passionnel* by one of Drax's German staff, who viewed Fallon as a rival for the affections of Drax's assistant, Gala Brand. Following this revelation, Bond is assigned to take the position of the new head of security from the Ministry of Supply.

When he learns of the trouble at the Moonraker plant, Bond is told "the cover-plan is that it's part of the big radar network along the East Coast. . . . It's on the edge of the cliffs between Dover and Deal." Located at this symbolic boundary of British territory, fifty of Drax's rocket engineers are Germans. Bond is unclear why SIS should become involved in a case on British soil but is informed by M that, because SIS had cleared the German workers, they were in some sense responsible for them. Bond's journey to the Kent coast gives Fleming the opportunity to highlight some of the county's landmarks as 007 finds himself "thrashing the big Bentley down the Dover road along the straight stretch that runs into Maidstone."[53] Bond's first pleasure in Kent is that of driving in a region free of the gridlock of London. This resembles Ian's pleasure in driving down to Kent at high speed from London after his working week at *The Sunday Times*, enjoying the feeling of freedom driving his Ford Thunderbird on open roads.

Bond's route takes him out of Canterbury along the Deal road, stopping for a drink at the World Without Want Inn. This inn—based on one of Fleming's favorite Kent watering holes, the Swingate Inn—was where the fatal shooting of Fallon took place. On Bond's arrival at the Moonraker plant, what strikes the reader about Drax's rocket base is not just its coastal location but the sense of reclusiveness and remoteness: the large house is "half-hidden behind a wall six feet thick, that rose straight up off the surface of the concrete."[54] Drax not only desires privacy but also has something to hide.

On arriving at the Moonraker base, in the distance Bond sees a "squat dome surged up about fifty feet out of the concrete."[55] This is the silo for the Moonraker rocket, and its presence in this concrete jungle created by Drax is another warning sign that this development and technology are a threat to the natural environment. Throughout these chapters, Fleming emphasizes the suppression and destruction of the fragile ecosystem that Drax's base causes.

The contrast between Drax's concrete world and the natural environment is beautifully rendered during Bond and Brand's idyllic walk along the Kent coast. Although she initially gives Bond a frosty reception at dinner, Brand seems to change when out in the open country and shows more warmth toward Bond. For Fleming, the sexual inhibitions and emotional aloofness associated with "Englishness"—and we note that Brand's initials are those of Great Britain—seem to dissolve in the outdoors and with proximity to the sea. Her "cover" as Drax's secretary requires the suppression of her emotions, and Brand admits to Bond, "I'm sick of the sight of all this concrete." Fleming suggests that they are both escaping a kind of prison of the senses in their walk in the Kent countryside. They are "soon out of sight of the firing point and the high wire fence," strengthening the impression of escaped inmates. Brand's "reserve melted quickly in the sunshine, and Bond enjoys the fact that she "laughed happily at his ignorance of the names of the wildflowers, the samphire, Viper's bugloss, and fumitory round their feet."[56]

Significantly, Brand shows a greater knowledge of wildflowers than Bond, identifying her as one familiar with the natural environment. Yet, although Bond may not know the names of the flowers, he is apparently *au fait* with the latest research on botany. When Brand thoughtlessly picks a "bee orchis," Bond responds by chastising her: "You wouldn't do that if you knew that flowers scream when they are picked." In response to her incredulity, Bond explains,

> There's an Indian called Professor Bhose, who's written a treatise on the nervous system of flowers. He measured their reaction to pain. He even recorded the scream of a rose being picked. It must be one of the heart-rending sounds in the world. I heard something like it as you picked that flower.[57]

Brand suffers from what botanist Matthew Hall diagnoses as "plant blindness," the symptoms of which include "failing to take notice of, or focus attention on the plants in one's life[,] . . . thinking that plants are simply the background for animal life[,]" and "overlooking the importance of plants to human life."[58] Brand cannot be accused of the first symptom but does exhibit the other two. The scene establishes Bond, by contrast, as one sensitive to and respectful of the moral identity and feelings of plants.

Like Brand, the reader may have difficulty taking seriously the idea that James Bond, a licensed professional killer, would have such sensitivity to the feelings of plants. In fact, Brand believes that it is inappropriate for a 00 agent to care about flowers, as he is in "the business of killing . . . not just flowers either. People." Her claim that Bond is sentimental about plants also accuses him of hypocrisy—objecting to her picking a flower while he himself has extinguished human lives. Bond's retort is highly revealing of Fleming's protective attitude toward the nonhuman world in the novels: "Flowers can't shoot back."[59]

Bond's duty is to protect not just British national security interests—the reason for his presence at the Moonraker base—but also the defenseless creatures of nature, those living things who "can't shoot back." This is not part of his official mission, and M would probably react with scorn to Bond's protection of flowers, as he did to Bond's concern for the roseate spoonbills on Crab Key. But, just as he avenged the senseless murder of a harmless pelican in *Live and Let Die*, Bond here takes exception to the thoughtless killing of a plant. This does not imply that Brand is an enemy but that she is—despite her knowledge of flora—less sensitive to environmental issues than Bond.

The specific identity of the plant Brand picks might suggest that the scene is part of a flirtatious game between her and Bond. The "bee orchis" is a type of orchid whose flowers have the appearance of bees. Therefore, their pollination occurs through pseudocopulation, in which the flowers mimic female insects, thus attracting males into pollinating the flowers. In this respect, the scene suggests, Brand is sending out deceptive sexual signals to Bond, inviting him to woo her although her sexual "availability" is actually illusory. As we—and Bond—learn at the end of the novel, she is already engaged to another man, Detective Inspector Vivian, and she never had any intention of eloping with Bond. Her engagement ring—which Bond had assumed she wore to deflect the unwanted sexual attentions of Drax—is genuine. We can conclude that Bond has deceived himself about Brand's sexual intentions. Brand alludes back to flower imagery when, at the end of the novel, she tells a disappointed Bond that "there are plenty of others waiting to be picked."[60]

However, the word *orchis* derives from the Greek word meaning "testicle," due to the appearance of its paired subterranean tuberoids. In this context, Brand's plucking up the orchis is a symbolic emasculation of Bond, and it is easy to understand why he would object to the plant being uprooted in this way. Having been severely beaten in the genitals by Le Chiffre in *Casino Royale*—a torture that he was betrayed into by Vesper Lynd—it is understandable that Bond would be sensitive about these body parts with Brand. Yet, Brand repents of her thoughtless act and tells Bond, "If you're right I shall never pick a flower again as long as I live."[61] Beyond protecting his own vulnerable body parts from further attack, Bond has taught a valuable ecological lesson to his colleague. Fleming inverts the stereotypical gender roles in which women are deemed to be more sensitive and "closer to nature" than men.

The happiness of Bond and Brand during their "Golden Day" captures some of the better times experienced by Ian and Ann Fleming in the early years of their marriage. While living at White Cliffs in the 1950s, the couple enjoyed going for walks along the cliffs and the beach at Saint Margaret's Bay, watching the birds, looking out at the sea, and swimming during the warmer months. Often their coastal treks would end up at the Granville Hotel in Saint Margaret-at-Cliffe, where they would enjoy a cocktail and a fish lunch or supper. A contemporary advertisement for the Granville described the hotel as "charmingly situated, commanding the finest position in the Bay." It elaborated further on the "comfortable accommodations, cuisine for the connoisseur, a wide range of table and vintage wines, with a well stocked cocktail bar and individual service cheerfully performed."[62] All these features of luxury, of course, appealed to Ian's taste for comfort and gourmandizing.

On Boxing Day, 1954, Ian and Ann may well have taken just such a walk along the beach toward Saint Margaret-at-Cliffe. It had been a grueling Christmas, and the presence of their London cook—brought down to ease the domestic burden over the festive period—did not make things easier. The cook had not got along with the Flemings' nanny, who looked after two-year-old Caspar among other domestic duties. Ian had hired the cottage next to White Cliffs, which had been temporarily vacated by its owner, in order to accommodate the cook and her partner. As they walked along the shingle beach, arm in arm, Ian and Ann reflected on the trials of their festive period.

"I can't believe we set fire to the cottage next door yesterday, Ian! It is such a disaster," sighs Ann mournfully.

"Well, Peter Quennell seemed to enjoy the drama. He used to be in the fire service, you know, during the war?"

Ann guffaws. "Wasn't he sacked, though? For smoking on the job?"

"Yes, poor fellow—and it was his first real fire, too! All the others had been false alarms. The silly bugger hosed down the wrong floor of the building."

"Who on earth smokes when you're trying to put out a fire?" asks Ann scathingly, indulging her habit of gossiping about all her friends when they're not present.

Ian put his arm around her shoulders. It is one of the rare occasions when they join in mockery of someone else. "Peter insists that one of his colleagues stuck the cigarette in his mouth, saying 'Have a fag, Quenn'! Believe it if you will. Anyway, he was dismissed."

"Well, I feel a lot safer knowing he's out of the brigade." Ann chuckles.

"Darling, while we're on the subject of careless smoking—are you quite sure you didn't accidentally drop your lighted cigarette in the linen cupboard? The fire brigade claim that's definitely where the fire began."

Ann rankles at this accusation and deliberately removes Ian's arm from her shoulder. "Of course not! It was almost certainly a short circuit in the electrical system that started it."

Ian sighs. He will have to pay the bill for the fire damage, and he can already see the royalties for his soon to be published novel—*Moonraker*—going up in smoke. A seagull darts between them and ducks quickly into the channel, apparently in search of a fish. "Well, you do sometimes forget you're smoking. You almost burned my eye out when you kissed me once!"

Ann rankles again. "Bloody nerve. Talk about the pot calling the kettle black—you chain smoke seventy a day, Ian, and you know how bad it is for your heart."

Ian kicks a sea-worn stone into the sea. "Why should I give up the pleasures of life? Life's too short. Anyway, what on earth did you stuff all those clothes and whatnot into the linen cupboard for? It was an accident waiting to happen!"

Ann stops walking and turns to face him, her face now a mask of anger. "Didn't you see the terrible state the owner left the cottage in? Those disgusting school ties draped everywhere, and filthy towels! Cook would have resigned on the spot if she'd walked into a pigsty like that. Why didn't you inspect the place first?"

Ian decides it's not worth the fight. The sun has come out, which has lifted his mood despite the chilly atmosphere.

"Let's go and sit down—over there, on that grassy mound underneath the cliff?" Ann suggests, relenting toward him.

"Err . . . I'd rather not sit underneath the cliff, to be honest," Ian objects mildly. He takes out his gunmetal cigarette case, extracts one of his Moreland specials, and lights it.

"Why on earth not? It's a lovely, peaceful spot." Ann is reluctant to move away from her preferred seat.

"Well, if you ever read any of my manuscripts, you'd know why not! My hero sits under the cliff with his girl in the most recent one, and it doesn't work out too well."

"Why on earth did you name it *Moonraker*? Don't you know that means someone from Wiltshire?"

"Well, don't you think it's preferable to the title my American publisher is using—*Too Hot to Handle*?"

Ann winces. "Oh, how perfectly ghastly. Don't you have any veto power over your pornography?"

Ian ignores the slighting remark about his Bond novels. "Let's go to the Granville, then, and have a drink?" he suggests.

Ann glances at her watch. It's 10:00 a.m. "A bit early to start boozing, isn't it?" she asks disapprovingly.

"Don't be a bore, darling. It's Christmas!"

An hour later, flushed in face and more cheerful in mood after a bracing walk, they enter the bar of the Granville Hotel. There is a fire blazing in the hearth, and the barman greets them warmly as semiregular customers. Ian orders a large double scotch on the rocks, and Ann asks for a gin and tonic. While he's at the bar, Ian books a table for lunch at twelve in the main dining room. They take their drinks to the corner table of the bar, next to a large window overlooking the sea. A copy of *The Times* lies there on the tabletop, and Ian glances at the front page. Ann, meanwhile, puts her coat on the chair back, sits down, and lights a cigarette.

"Oh my God!" Ian exclaims, having pulled the newspaper closer to inspect the front page.

"What's the matter?" asks Ann indifferently. Ian's most emotional reactions are usually confined to golf, cars, and his royalty statements—in only the latter of which she takes much interest.

"A BOAC Boeing Stratocruiser crashed yesterday in Prestwick in Scotland. Twenty-eight people dead!"

Ann looks appalled. This is close to home, as they are due to travel to Jamaica in a couple of weeks. "That's awful, darling. How did it happen?"

Ian has continued to read the news story. He didn't read the paper or listen to the radio on Christmas Day, and so the news has only now reached him. His face, which was ruddy from the chilly air of their walk, has turned pale.

"The pilot tried to land in driving rain at Prestwick, in the small hours of Christmas Day. Bloody fool missed the runway. It was supposed to fly on to New York."

Ann is shaking her head in dismay. "That's the same route we fly!" she points out.

"Same route, same airline, same bloody plane—Boeing 377!" Ian expostulates.

"That settles it. We're traveling to New York by sea next month!" Ann exclaims.

"Nonsense! This crash means it will be safer than ever to fly. The airlines will triple-check every mechanical detail after today."

Ann looks disgusted. "Well, suit yourself—but you're on your own if you decide to fly," she says grimly and stubs out her cigarette.

Ian looks at her, his expression one of resigned melancholy. "Don't worry. I'm used to that," he mumbles.

* * *

Living this close to the sea in Kent, as in Jamaica, was a source of creative inspiration for Ian, and he used the cliffside location of Saint Margaret's for one of the most dramatic and memorable scenes of *Moonraker*, in which Bond and Brand narrowly escape death from a rockfall. As well as displaying the natural beauty of the area around Saint Margaret's, this episode also highlights the power, danger, and beauty of the Kent coastline. In particular, the chapter evokes a sense of awe at England's ancient history: when Bond and Brand leave on their afternoon expedition along the Kent coast, they "stopped for a moment on the edge of the great chalk cliff and stood gazing over the whole corner of England where Caesar had first landed two thousand years before."[63]

Like his creator, Bond stands gazing out over the English Channel, observing the ships on their various routes. The setting for the couple's excursion seems pastoral, "a panorama full of colour and excitement and romance," as Bond becomes closer and more attracted to Brand. Yet, the ominous reference to "evil sands" out at sea is a reminder of the dangers, as well as the attractions, present in the environment.[64] Beneath the beauties of the Kent coast, Fleming suggests, danger is lurking.

Where else would Fleming choose as a backdrop to this extraordinary adventure of Bond and Brand but "the two-mile stretch of shingle that runs at low tide beneath the towering white cliffs to St Margaret's Bay"?[65] Fleming specifies the precise location of his own home, White Cliffs, as a setting for the greatest danger encountered by his hero and companion. While on the beach, Bond finds himself imagining how a team of enemy saboteurs might attack the Moonraker rocket through its exhaust tunnel. He is trained to think about all possible methods of destruction, even during his periods of relaxation. Under the pretext of looking for a deep channel in the water, where an enemy ship might approach, Bond decides he will take a swim. The icy English Channel is a far cry from the tropical waters of the Caribbean sea he had bathed in in *Live and Let Die*, yet Brand agrees to a swim too, and this leads to an Edenic experience together in the water.

But it is short-lived: no sooner have the couple left the icy water, lying on the sandy beach beneath the cliff to dry off after their swim, than they suddenly face death. Fleming again showcases his hero's close connection to the natural world. It is Bond's habit of watching the birds, observing the "soaring beauty of the herring gulls as they ranged effortlessly among the air currents," that saves their lives. Bond notices that the gulls, who had been playing near the clifftop, have suddenly dashed away "with a single shrill scream of fear."[66] Reacting to this warning, he then sees a plume of smoke and, by throwing himself over Brand, is able to protect her from the landslide of chalk that falls on them. Bond later realizes that someone had placed an explosive in the clifftop, causing the huge chunk of chalk to fall, and that it was only their proximity to the cliff that saved them from being crushed. This is a harsh reminder that Bond can never lower his guard, even when the natural environment seems peaceful and benevolent, and that the White Cliffs so beloved by Fleming could be deadly.

By planting his base at the iconic White Cliffs, Drax appears to reaffirm his standing as a patriot who plans to serve the interests of his country by delivering it its own nuclear weapon (a high priority of the postwar British government). Yet, Drax actually intends to use this coastal location to attack the heart of the country in London; he warns of this by gloating that during a recent test, the chalk had melted from the heat of the rocket, and he gloats sarcastically, "Hope we don't burn down the famous white cliffs."[67] The collapse of the White Cliffs above Bond and Brand foreshadows the impending deadly collapse of Britain's economy and society—both disasters produced by Drax's explosives.

In typical Fleming fashion, he sends the injured Bond and Brand for refuge and repast to his own favorite watering hole in Saint Margaret's, the Granville, where they have a hot bath "followed by two stiff brandies-and-sodas for Brand and three for Bond followed by delicious fried soles and Welsh rarebits and coffee."[68] Bond is never so physically damaged or anxious for revenge as to prevent him enjoying the pleasures offered by a fine hotel. One of Ian's hallmarks as a writer is the detail he lavishes on the food and drink consumed by his hero, even when one would suppose Bond is in no state of mind to enjoy it. In any case, the pleasures of the table also provide another warning to Bond, noticing that the dinner table at Drax's house had been set for only three people. Clearly, the pleasure of Bond and Brand's company was not expected.

Drax's choice of exclusive automobile is another clue to his hostile intentions: Bond admires the Type 300 S sports model Mercedes yet notes it is "typical of Drax to buy a Mercedes. There was something ruthless and majestic about the cars." The comparison between Drax's "ruthless" car and

Bond's supercharged Bentley mirrors the rivalry not just between Bond and Drax but between postwar Britain and Germany. Germany as the new power emerging from the ruins after World War II is threatening Britain, yet Bond recalls nostalgically the days when Bentleys "had whipped the blown SS-K's almost as they wished."[69]

Significantly, Bond is not present when Brand, traveling as Drax's passenger, manages to steal the notebook in which Drax keeps his figures of the gyro readings for the Moonraker. Stunned by her discovery, in the bathroom at the Thomas Wyatt Inn in Maidstone, that Drax's figures for the gyroscopic readings were totally different to hers, Brand becomes the first British agent to discover his plot against England. Caught by Krebs while trying to return the book to Drax's pocket, Brand is then knocked unconscious and held captive in a house "at the Buckingham Palace end of Ebury Street."[70] Just as Fleming locates Drax's Moonraker base near his own home in Kent, so he assigns the Nazi his London base in Ebury Street, where Ian maintained an apartment at 22b between 1934 and 1945. Ironically, Fleming's residence at Ebury Street coincided with his work for Naval Intelligence during World War II, plotting the downfall of Nazi Germany (though he had to leave the flat during the Blitz because its skylight could not be blacked out effectively).

Yet, it is Brand, not Bond, who is able to calculate that the rocket would be fired—if Drax's secret gyro settings were used—right into the heart of London. Brand envisages a horrifying doomsday scenario of human extinction, "the great bloom of flame a mile wide. And then the mushroom cloud. And nothing left."[71] While Bond remains in blissful ignorance, waiting for Brand to join him at a restaurant, Brand experiences Fleming's own "recurring nightmare" about a German rocket attack on England as he related it in *Thrilling Cities*. In *Moonraker*, however, the atomic rocket does not emerge from beneath the ground in the Harz Mountains of Germany but from the very White Cliffs of Kent where Fleming made his home.

Drax's proud subsequent confession—to a captive Bond—of his German origins and Nazi sympathies confirms that he is a sworn enemy, not a friend, of Britain. A crucial part of Drax's story of how he made his fortune, became a Knight of the Realm, and deceived his hosts draws attention to the symbolism of the location for his rocket base: "England at my feet. Every bloody fool in the country! . . . Under the very skirts of Britannia. On top of her famous cliffs." Drax's speech boasts that England has already been invaded: both Nazis and Russians have unimpeded access, the "famous cliffs" providing no effective defense. His comment, "we work like devils," adds to the sense of impending evil facing Britain.[72] Even the earlier reference to the historic significance of Kent as the site of Caesar's invasion has become ominous—a reminder that England has been invaded and colonized by a foreign power before and may be so again.

The true defender of Britain against Drax's murderous plot of environmental disaster is not the famous White Cliffs but James Bond himself: the "protector" of Britannia against her destruction by a malevolent enemy. Like Mr. Big and Dr. No, Hugo von der Drache will become a victim of his own weaponizing of a natural environment. As "Sir Hugo" prepares to leave aboard a Soviet submarine, another reason for his choice of Kent for his base appears: the ease with which he may escape before the havoc to England wipes out millions. Soon after he reveals his identity with the "Heil Hitler" salute, the Soviet submarine is "thrown out of the water upside down," destroyed by his own Moonraker rocket.[73]

Fleming would use the iconic Kent coast as a key location in a later novel, *Goldfinger* (1959). This novel famously deploys Ian's favorite golf course, the Royal St George's at Sandwich—disguised for fictional purposes as the Royal St Marks—for a significant contest between Bond and Goldfinger. But while the windswept links of Royal St George's are a highlight, the novel also dwells on the more obscure, hidden reaches of Kent on the Isle of Thanet and Reculver. Goldfinger's English base leads James Bond along his favorite route into Kent—driving down the A2 in his Aston Martin DB-III—in order to explore "those melancholy forsaken reaches of the Thames which Goldfinger had chosen for his parish."[74] The duality of this location—easily reachable from London yet with a sense of remoteness and seclusion—also appealed to Fleming.

On this mission, Bond has traded the turbocharged Bentley he drove to Kent in *Moonraker* for a SIS-modified Aston Martin DB-III, loaded with gadgets that include switches to change the color of the car's lights and a radio designed to pick a homing device. The film version of *Goldfinger* (1964), directed by Guy Hamilton, would, of course, add more sophisticated gadgets to the Aston Martin (upgraded to a DB-V), including the ejector seat, but Fleming's version already equips his hero for the challenges of "Goldfinger-land." In describing Bond's car journey, Fleming directs scorn on the growth of tourism in Kent, as "Bond left the Canterbury road and switched on to the incongruously rich highway that runs through the cheap bungaloid world of the holiday lands—Whitstable, Herne Bay, Birchington, Margate."

Bond's reflections while driving toward Goldfinger's haunts are very different to those as he approached Drax's base in *Moonraker*. Bond already knows that "Goldfinger—the jeweler, the metallurgist, the resident of Reculver and Nassau, the respected member of Blades, of the Royal St Marks at Sandwich—was one of the greatest conspirators of all time."[75] Specifically, M knows that Goldfinger is the financial wizard funding SMERSH operations in Europe while also damaging Britain's economy. Hence, Goldfinger's retreat in Kent immediately has a sinister atmosphere as the site for the enemy's conspiracy and smuggling operations from Ramsgate, where his contraband would pass unsuspected.

Perhaps the most surprising thing about the famous golf match between Bond and Goldfinger is that it took Fleming so long in his career to use his favorite golf course as a setting in his fiction. Given the prominent role of competitive games in the plots of the Bond novels, it would seem an obvious move from the casino to the fairway. When Fleming did eventually decide to use Royal St George's, in his seventh novel, it proved worth the wait. Golf is far from being a recreational pursuit in *Goldfinger*. Bond is under intense pressure from M to beat his opponent, and we are reminded of the game's critical significance as a Cold War encounter by the reference to Manston NATO airbase, largely populated by US Air Force personnel, some of whom Bond will observe drinking in the bar at the Channel Packet. His concern about their "toting a hydrogen bomb round the skies over Kent" again shows a protective instinct toward the beloved shire and perhaps an unease about the American military presence in England.[76]

On arrival, Bond recalls his own personal experiences of playing golf as a teenager at Royal St Marks when he had the potential to become a professional. However, golf had ceased to be as important in his life, and "he'd never been back—even when there had been that bloody affair of the Moonraker at Kingsdown, ten miles down the coast."[77] The allusion to *Moonraker* situates his current novel in the same region, locating the importance of Kent as a unique environment for Bond and Fleming alike.

In the golf match that follows, Fleming provides meticulous detail about each hole of the Royal St Marks based on his precise knowledge of the Royal St George's. This information is not superfluous but provides authenticity and interest, whether or not the reader has any interest in golf. The evocative detail of the chapter can be sampled by the description of "the tenth at the Royal St Marks is the most dangerous hole on the course. The second shot, to the skiddy plateau green with cavernous bunkers to right and left and a steep hill beyond, has broken many hearts."[78] The association of the course with "danger" extends beyond the risks of the bunkers, warning us that Bond faces a serious threat in his antagonist. Meanwhile, with the beautifully wild golf links as a backdrop, Bond continues his duel with the man who has provoked a visceral dislike in him.

Bond's assumed role as "the type of ruthless, hard adventurer who might be very useful to Goldfinger" is not, after all, that different from his actual character. Having outwitted the cheating Goldfinger by switching his golf ball, Bond is then invited to dinner at his adversary's home in Reculver. His reactions to Goldfinger's house show the negative side of Kent, a far cry from the beautiful White Cliffs or the stunning seaside vistas of Royal St Marks. Goldfinger's Kent home, pretentiously named The Grange, seems to be hiding from the world. In his imagination, Bond associates the "smell of trapped sunshine, rubber plants and dead flies" with the house.[79] Like some of the Fleming family homes—such as Joyce Grove and Braziers Park—The Grange is grand without being inviting or aesthetically pleasing.

Bond also notices an industrial blot on the landscape, hearing the noise of the factory lurking behind the home, whose "plumed chimney reared up like a giant cautionary finger from the high conifers" and turns it into a manufacturing center that pollutes the environment. The oppressive, deathly atmosphere of The Grange does not improve when Bond is admitted to the house by the lethal Korean chauffeur, Oddjob. Bond's summing up the house shows it as the opposite of the fertile garden reputation of Kent's countryside: "What a dump! What a bloody awful deathly place to live in. How did one, could one, live in this rich heavy morgue amongst the conifers and evergreens when a hundred yards away there was light and air and wide horizons?"[80]

Fleming uses this contrast between the claustrophobic house and the open spaces of Kent as a very effective way to suggest Goldfinger's obsessive privacy. Although the house is surrounded by trees, they are evergreens, thus divorced from the seasonal changes of rural landscapes. The house is typical of Goldfinger in the very fact that it gives away nothing about his personality. Bond, during Goldfinger's temporary absence, learns that he has been under surveillance the whole time, with three concealed cameras recording his every move. Fleming conveys not only the sinister oppressiveness of Goldfinger's ostentatious home but also his use of civilized ritual—such as the dinner with Bond—as a veneer for his threats of violence. Like Drax and

Dr. No, Goldfinger uses the meal as a pretext to show his power as he tells Bond how easy it would be for Oddjob to kill him with a single blow.

The Bond villain uses fine food and wine to display his status, and its rituals as weapons in the conflict with Bond, evidenced by the description of Goldfinger as one of the "rich men who use their riches like a club." Ironically, Goldfinger himself takes no pleasure in these luxuries, deeming drinking alcohol and smoking to be "unnatural." Oddly, the unnatural villain Goldfinger makes an appeal to nature in his diatribe against poisons: "Smoking I find the most ridiculous of all the varieties of human behavior and practically the only one that is entirely against nature."[81] Bond, a heavy smoker like Ian, distrusts Goldfinger's negative description of the habit. There is more evidence of Goldfinger's unethical behavior in his cruelty to animals, as he delivers his cat to Oddjob for his dinner.

Kent deserves attention as the location in which Bond obtains definite proof of Goldfinger's malevolent nature and launches the journey to his smelting operation in Switzerland and ultimately to his stud farm in Kentucky from which the villain plans his Operation Grandslam. Unlike Drax in *Moonraker*, Goldfinger does not use Kent as his principal base but merely one of several bolt-holes, where he can prepare for his attack on the US economy by stealing the United States' gold reserve from Fort Knox.

Reculver is by far the most oppressive and sinister Kent location used by Fleming, embodied in the portrayal of The Grange as an unnatural home that excludes the beneficial influences of the natural elements. This is not a world Bond wants to be part of, preferring the bracing air of the White Cliffs or Sandwich. Yet, it is surprisingly effective cover for Goldfinger and reveals an important function of the Kent location. The very "English" associations of Kent are symbolic, from the White Cliffs of Dover to Kent's key role in the Battle of Britain during World War II.[82] Kent's idyllic reputation as "the garden of England" is undermined by the presence of villains working to harm the country and destroy its natural environment.

While the importance of Kent locations in the Bond novels reflects Ian's attachment and affection for the region, there is something ominous about the eagerness with which Britain embraces these wealthy yet inimical patrons. The country that defended itself against Hitler's vast military campaign has become complacent and overly materialistic, greedy for a nuclear weapon that will bring an imaginary parity with the United States. Fleming's fleeting reference in *Goldfinger* to the American pilots flying the hydrogen bomb over Kent is an unpleasant reminder for the reader of the reality of Britain's

Cold War status as a satellite of the United States. Perhaps Ian, sitting at his window in White Cliffs, scrutinizing the shipping in the English Channel through his telescope, imagined himself as a kind of Cold War sentinel, guarding against the possibility of a hostile armada heading for its shores. Celebrating Kent as one of England's most beautiful natural environments and attractive coastal locations, Ian never loses sight of its wartime history—and possibly its future—as the enemy's number one target.

Chapter Nine

Fleming's Women, Bond's "Girls"

The Bond girl. Physically beautiful, with perfect body and radiant face. Yet, beneath her physical charms, she is often troubled and haunted by the past, controlled by an evil and dominating man, and in need of rescue by . . . who other than James Bond? She is grateful and passionate toward her savior, often giving him her body out of gratitude. Yet, she is strangely passive in many respects, dependent on Bond's masculine protection, support, and love. Her complexion, height, hair color, and race are variable—but she is invariably slim and beautiful, as though created for the pages of *Playboy* magazine. Sometimes intelligent, other times less so, but always—either overtly or subtly—emotionally needy. Despite her appeal, she is disposable, her fate being to be replaced by an equally radiant beauty when "James Bond returns" or—still worse—to be killed off before the end of the story. She dies, as she lives, in order to validate Bond's freedom as the eternal playboy bachelor.

Such is the pervasive stereotype of the gorgeous women who feature in the James Bond adventures, an image that has been popularized and cemented by the EON films more so than by Ian Fleming's novels. This stereotype is, of course, inherently sexist—women are treated primarily (or exclusively) as objects of visual pleasure and sexual desire, Bond presumably fulfilling the vicarious fantasies of his male viewers by seducing, bedding, and then disposing of them. The Bond girl has become a cultural icon, like the Bond villain or indeed Bond himself. She represents a widespread image of femininity in popular culture that is troubling precisely because it is determined by Bond's (and male) needs and desires rather than her own. As Lisa Funnell reminds us, "Bond has historically been defined by his relationships with women and particularly through heterosexual romantic conquest."[1]

Those who pay close attention to Fleming's novels, however, will discover a significantly more complex attitude to female characters, women's lives, and their relationships with 007. It is true that the women in the novels—other than those clearly marked as villains, such as Rosa Klebb and Irma Bunt—are typically beautiful (at least in Bond's eyes), but they are more three-dimensional than their cinematic counterparts. Many of the women Bond forms relationships with have troubled pasts, carefully hidden secrets, daunting skills of dissimulation and deception, and razor-sharp intelligence. In some cases, the women Bond amorously engages with are sharper, more perceptive and insightful, and more intriguing than Bond himself.

This is not to deny that Fleming's James Bond's responses to women can be overtly misogynistic. In the first novel, *Casino Royale*, Bond fulminates against Vesper Lynd, his newly appointed coworker from Secret Intelligence Service, before he even meets her, mentally dismissing her as "this pest of a girl." Bond rants, "Women were for recreation. On a job, they got in the way and fogged things up with sex and hurt feelings and all the emotional baggage they carried around."[2] Such unprovoked hostility prompts the question, what could be the source of such strange animosity toward an unknown woman? For many readers, the answer is easily to hand: Bond is a mouthpiece for Ian's own misogyny, which had festered through a long battle for independence with his mother, Eve, who terminated his engagement to Monique Panchaud de Bottomes. Ian's subsequent vow to be "bloody-minded about women"—using them for his pleasure and then disposing of them—produces, it is assumed, Bond's sexist behavior.

Yet, we should not forget that Bond—despite having a number of similarities to Fleming—is not the author but a literary character. Ian is not shy about exposing Bond's flaws, blind spots, mistakes, and shortcomings throughout the novels. In correspondence with his readers and editors, Ian would often point out Bond's mistakes, claiming to Wren Howard that in *From Russia, with Love*, "there is no harm in letting Bond make a fool of himself" by dismissing Tatiana Romanova's warnings about "Captain Nash."[3] Bond is also making a fool of himself by dismissing Vesper sight unseen—and Vesper, like "Nash," turns out to be a Soviet agent in disguise. Bond is blind to her treason, and by the end of the novel he will be on the point of proposing marriage to her before she takes her own life.

Even when Bond does not express such antagonism toward a female character, he can behave offensively to women in other ways. Bond focuses initially on their physical appearance, paying at times obsessive attention to their breasts, buttocks, legs, and faces (the latter judged in terms of physical beauty rather than personality). In *Moonraker*, Bond is frustrated by the unresponsive, cool reception he receives from Gala Brand—a colleague from Special Branch—being more concerned with getting a sexual reaction from her than with her professional competence. But this does not prevent him from objectifying her body, especially "the swell of her breasts, which were as splendid as Bond had guessed from the measurements on her record-sheet."[4]

Such episodes reinforce the popular image of James Bond as a fast-living, womanizing playboy, objectifying women with no interest in or respect for their hidden qualities or inner personalities. Bond is the eternal bachelor, living alone, enjoying an affluent lifestyle, and remaining essentially a solo operator. This also extends to his love relationships—which seem temporary, selfish, and pragmatic. Perhaps in the 1950s and even 1960s, Bond's non-committal playboy lifestyle was a source of envy, admiration, and emulation, at least for heterosexual male readers. Some of Fleming's stories and novels were published in Hugh Hefner's *Playboy* magazine—founded in 1953, the same year *Casino* was published—which appears to cement this association of Bond with the affluent, sexually adventurous, and consequence-free playboy lifestyle.[5] The theory was that Bond was who every man wanted to be and who every woman wanted to be with.[6] But viewed through twenty-first-century eyes, Bond's treatment of women appears exploitative, misogynistic, and retrograde. In the eyes of modern readers and viewers, he condemns himself with notorious, sexist tirades such as that against the lesbian Tilly Masterton (in *Goldfinger*), whose "hormones," Bond asserts, had "got mixed up."[7]

Most spy novelists before Fleming did not dwell on sexual relationships at great length, preferring to follow the "Boy's Own" model of male-focused adventure. We should keep in mind that introducing a robust sexual theme was Ian's strategy for bringing the spy novel into the "adult fiction" category for the modern age. Indeed, Ian's postwar spy fiction and cultural influence has sometimes been linked to the "sexual revolution" that would follow in the 1960s, when men and women would challenge and break free from stifling, conventional gender and sexual norms and strive for sexual freedom and equality. Women, inspired by second-wave feminists like Gloria Steinem and Erica Jong, would seek personal, professional, and sexual fulfilment without being tied to the conventional roles of mother, wife, and daughter. From 1960, the invention and commercial marketing of the Pill, a revolutionary new form of birth control, liberated women to express their sexuality without fear of pregnancy, effectively separating sex from reproduction. Gay men and lesbians in both Britain and the United States were liberated by the decriminalization of homosexuality in Britain (1967) and the Stonewall riots in 1969, initiating an era of gay pride. Heterosexual men, too, could enjoy new sexual freedom, after the burdens of World War II, perhaps choosing not to marry but to pursue the license and pleasures of commitment-free bachelorhood.

How much of this sexual revolution is attributable in any way to Ian Fleming is debatable, of course. But Bond's sexual adventures certainly form part of the picture of changing attitudes to sexuality in the postwar era. Ian created Bond just at the point where he felt he was giving up his own bachelor "freedom" to marry Ann Rothermere, and he became a father for the first time in the year *Casino* was published. While he apparently doted on his son, Caspar, Ian nonetheless was daunted by his new responsibilities and relished the fantasy of Bond's commitment-free promiscuity. But if Bond represents an escapist dream of freedom for the affluent, single male in 1950s Britain, one should ask, what is the cost of this fantasy to the women he becomes involved with?

Does Bond really fantasize about submissive, compliant women whose greatest pleasure is to serve him? One might reach that conclusion from the sentiments he expresses at the beginning of the short story "Quantum of Solace": he tells the governor of Nassau, Bahamas, where he has been on a mission, "I've always thought that if I ever married I would marry an air hostess" because "it would be fine to have a pretty girl always tucking you up and bringing you drinks and hot meals and asking if you had everything you wanted." But if we read on in the story, we find that these words are intended by Bond to be provocative nonsense: "Bond had no intention of marrying anyone. If he did, it would certainly not be an insipid slave. He only hoped to amuse or outrage the Governor into a discussion of some human topic."[8] And the governor, in turn, will go on to tell Bond a haunting cautionary tale about just such a marriage as Bond imagines, in which the husband chooses his wife for her looks and a (deluded) belief in her submissiveness. The governor's theory of the "quantum of solace"—the "basic factor in human relations"—translates to the minimum amount of compassion and affection that is required to make a marriage work and without which it is doomed to fail.[9] The story, written as a homage to Ian's good friend Somerset Maugham, was composed in the summer of 1958 and seems especially poignant in the light of the gradual deterioration of Ian's own marriage to Ann.[10] Sometime in late 1961 or early 1962, Ian wrote Ann using language that reflects the mood of the story: "The point lies in only one area. Do we want to go on living together or do we not? In the present twilight we are hurting each other to an extent that makes life hardly bearable. That inhuman state of affairs has got to be ended."[11]

Many of the women Bond becomes involved with have jobs or other means of economic independence, are unmarried, and have professional and personal ambitions of their own. They are free to express their sexuality and follow their own desires without fear of moral judgment. Admittedly, in Fleming's novels these women, more often than not, express their sexuality by falling for Bond, and their desires frequently lead them to Bond's bed. The exceptions—women such as Gala Brand, who rejects Bond's advances, and Tilly Masterton, who prefers Pussy Galore—prove the rule. The women who resist or reject Bond's desire are sometimes punished for it, as is the case with Masterton, who is killed by Oddjob and dismissed by Bond as a "poor little bitch" who "didn't think much of men."[12] By contrast, Pussy Galore, who is also a lesbian, surrenders to Bond's desires and thus survives.

Those women, such as Solitaire (in *Live and Let Die*) and Domino (in *Thunderball*), whom Bond rescues from the villains soon discover that they have exchanged one form of servitude for another. By depending on Bond for their escape, they attach themselves to a man who doesn't care about them except as a means to the end of gaining information and the destruction of their former "masters." Many of Bond's women disappear at the end of the novel in which they feature, becoming a brief question mark for the reader before they are replaced by another nubile beauty in need of salvation, another installment in "the spy who loved me."

Other women in Bond's life occupy subordinate if not subservient roles. For example, the secretaries Bond interacts with at Secret Intelligence Service headquarters at Regent's Park are a blend of motherly and sisterly affection, their chief function being to grease the wheels of the bureaucracy and smooth the ruffled feathers of their male bosses. They type letters and documents "for their eyes only," provide the agents with tea or (in Bond's case) coffee, and worry about agents' safety when they are in the field. Miss Moneypenny, Loelia Ponsonby, and Mary Goodnight, though different from each other in some respects, are alike in being attractive women who accept without question their subordinate role in the male-dominated spyocracy.

When it comes to domestic women, there is the nonpareil Scottish "treasure" of a housekeeper, May. Though she refuses to call Bond "sir," she serves him faithfully, providing for his every domestic need. As a Scot, May is a reminder of Bond's parentage, and she is motherly toward him in certain ways, keeping a sharp eye out for intruders (such as the suspicious "man . . . here . . . about the Televeesion" she reports on to Bond in *From Russia, with Love*).[13] May is presented as the ideal servant, preparing Bond's breakfast exactly as he likes it, keeping his flat clean without making any demands.

Yet, on further inspection, Bond's relationships with women in the novels and stories are more complex, and often more troubled, than they at first appear. To appreciate the hidden dimensions of female characters in Ian's writing, we need to delve into Fleming's own involvements with a number of highly intelligent, complex, and in some cases influential women throughout his life. For despite his reputation for philandering, Ian also became deeply emotionally involved with his lovers, and for him these relationships were not easily disposable distractions. At the very least, the parallels between the emotional difficulties, romantic conflicts, and personal traumas in Ian's life and the events of his novels and stories should allow the reader to see the Bond books as more than escapist masculine fantasy.

No doubt, Fleming helped create the myth of Bond as the permanent playboy bachelor with comments such as that explaining how he came to write his first novel, *Casino Royale*, while anxious about his impending marriage to Ann: "To give my hands something to do, and as an antibody to my qualms about the marriage state after 43 years as a bachelor, I decided one day to damned well sit down and write a book. The therapy was successful."[14] And yet, in the first six Bond novels, Bond twice seriously contemplates proposing marriage to the woman he's working with (Vesper in *Casino* and Tiffany in *Diamonds Are Forever*). He is prevented from marrying Vesper by her revelation that she is a Soviet double agent and subsequent suicide. In Tiffany's case, Bond discusses marriage with her while also introducing some levity in his requirement that any woman he marries must know how to make béarnaise sauce. In an intriguing suggestion of his homoerotic attachment to his boss, Bond also reveals that he is "almost married already. To a man. Name begins with M."[15] Early in the next novel, *From Russia, with Love*, we learn that Bond's affair with Tiffany has broken down—much to M's relief—and that she has left him to return to the United States with an American military man she plans to marry.

On two other occasions in the first six novels, Bond and the woman he's currently involved with impersonate a married couple: he and Solitaire pose as Mr. and Mrs. Bryce (using the name of Ian's close friend Ivar) in *Live and Let Die*, while Bond and Tatiana Romanova pose as David and Caroline Somerset in *From Russia, with Love*. These cover identities, designed to protect the couple from detection by enemy agents while traveling by train, also indicate Bond is comfortable in the "role" of a married man. He is also romantically involved with the women who pose as his wives. At the end of *Moonraker*, Bond imagines eloping with Gala Brand on a romantic journey through France. Though there is no direct mention of marriage, Bond asks himself "was he getting serious about this girl?" and is bitterly disappointed to learn that she is about to marry another man (one Detective Inspector Vivian from Special Branch).[16]

As these examples illustrate, marriage was very much on Ian's mind throughout the years when he wrote the Bond novels. Was marriage a "role," he wondered, that Ian could play, and who should be his leading lady? A desire to marry Ann had been on Fleming's mind for a long time before they actually wed. He wrote Ann in February 1949,

> I would love to nest with you forever and you are absolutely the only person I have ever contemplated saying this to. But apart from the money side we must be absolutely sure that we should be happy or it would be a crime for me to drag you out of a basically happy life.

Ian also reminded Ann of the negative effects their marriage would have on her current husband, Lord Rothermere; her children, Fionn and Raymond, from her first marriage to Shane O'Neill; and her potential of becoming "a great person in England."[17]

While it might appear he was trying to discourage Ann from divorcing Rothermere for selfish reasons, he was more worried about the adverse effects of their union on others: "I know all the other side. Our two lovely years, our basic love and faith in each other and in our stars. They would be enough to sail our ship if it weren't for the harm we would do." These doubts about whether to get married cannot be attributed to misogyny on Ian's part, for Ann was also doubtful whether to "get off the merry go round" and make a commitment to Ian. She writes to her brother Hugo Charteris in 1950 about her dilemma, "If E [Esmond Rothermere] would push or I [Ian] pull it would be easier, but one cannot blame Ian for only saying 'Barkis is willing.'"[18]

There was also an important difference between their respective situations in the early 1950s: Ann had to decide whether to give up a high-society marriage to a wealthy lord and newspaper baron in favor of a (relatively) impecunious journalist who could not keep her in the style she was accustomed to. She also had the well-being of her two children (from her marriage to O'Neill) to consider. By contrast, Ian, though now in his forties, had never been married and barely earned enough to maintain his Jamaican home—which had been purchased with a gift from another lover, Maud Russell—and his hopes of an inheritance had not materialized.

Ian's social life still consisted largely of a circle of male friends, such as the members of Le Cercle and his golfing gang. This pattern continued long after their marriage. Only a few months before Ian's death, in February 1964, Ann reported "Ian's profound disappointment that women are to be present" on what was supposed to be an all-male golfing trip. She noted that Hilary Bray—an Old Etonian friend of Ian's—"has not grasped the extent of Ian's desire to be his alter ego in this company."[19]

On the other hand, their letters sometimes reflect anxiety on Ian's part about other men's interest in him. While staying in Tangiers at Easter 1957 to interview "John Blaize"—Ian's pseudonym for John Collard, protagonist of his nonfiction book *The Diamond Smugglers*—Ian reported, "My life has revolved around a place called Dean's Bar, a sort of mixture between Wiltons and the porter's lodge at Whites. There's nothing but pansies and I have been fresh meat for them." A few years later, soon after arriving for the winter at Goldeneye, Ian was suffering from bronchitis and a high fever. Ann reported that Noël Coward played the role of nurse, adding, "Noël has always found T-B fearfully attractive and jumped at the opportunity to handle him. While Noël fetched ice-cubes from the Frigidaire T-B's language was something horrible, he blamed me for exposing him to homosexual approaches."[20]

James Bond, despite being a fictional character, became a constant companion to Ann and Ian throughout their troubled marriage. Bond provided the financial security they required to live comfortably, but he was also a source of tension between the couple. Ann's mocking nickname for Ian, "Thunderbird" (abbreviated as T-B) derived from his purchase of a Ford Thunderbird in 1955 to reward himself for having sold the film rights to *Casino Royale*. But it also had a close resemblance to "Thunderball," the name of the novel that plunged Fleming into a damaging legal battle with Kevin McClory, whose victory in the case led Ann to speculate gloomily that they would have to sell their property. After Ian's death, Ann would write an essay, "How James Bond Destroyed My Husband," lamenting the malign effects of her husband's imaginary alter ego.

In truth, Ann showed little interest in or respect for Ian's literary efforts, often referring to the Bond novels as "Ian's pornography" or "horror comics." She encouraged her friends to participate in the condescending mockery of Ian's work. It is clear that neither Ann nor her literary friends—such as Evelyn Waugh and Cyril Connolly—considered Ian Fleming a serious writer. Yet, as Ann knew only too well, the success of the Bond novels, baffling as it might be to her and her literary friends, provided their family with comfort and luxury.

Ian had no pretensions toward being part of the "avant-garde" and did not embrace highbrow culture but preferred golfing with his friends or playing cards and drinking gin to visiting galleries or attending operas (he once humorously suggested that roller skates should be provided to visitors of museums and galleries). And yet one could not dispute the prestige of Ian's publishing house, Jonathan Cape, one of the most respected publishers in Britain. That their own chief editor, Michael Howard, had been strongly opposed to publishing *Casino Royale* made little difference. Fleming would soon become the prize asset of Cape's list of authors, helping to keep the business afloat in difficult economic times (especially with the introduction of paperback fiction into the market).

Tempestuous, troubled, and sometimes tortured as the Flemings' marriage may have been, Ann's strong personality certainly did match Ian's will and offered important checks to his excesses and follies. These complications in Ian's actual relationships with women lead one to look for deeper levels in his portrayals of women in fiction. To grasp the complexity of Ian's relationships with women, and the extent to which the women in the Bond novels mirrored these relationships, we need to return to Ian's early years and the formative influence of his mother, Eve.

Perhaps the decisive conflict in Fleming's relationship with Eve, as previously discussed, occurred over her ending of his relationship with Monique Panchaud de Bottomes. Monique's father, however, was less willing to accept the abrupt termination of the affair and began proceedings for breach of contract. Ironically, Eve herself would later be involved in a breach of contract case involving a contest for the affections of the aged marquis of

Winchester between herself and a Parsi woman, Bapsy Pavry. During that case, in November 1957, Ian accompanied his mother to court and thus suffered some of the humiliating public exposure of the scandal. Eventually the judge decided in favor of Eve, though he "thought both of them silly."[21]

Equally, Fleming's involvement with Muriel Wright during World War II would profoundly shape his later fictional portrayals of women. Moo—as she was known by her friends—was a talented skier (far more adept than Fleming himself, whose heavy smoking was already impeding his athletic prowess). Her qualifications for a "Bond girl" seemed perfect! Moo came from a respectable Derbyshire family who occupied the spacious home of Yeldersley Hall. Lycett reports that one of Ian's female friends referred to Moo as "a cowering slave," which seems an exaggeration, yet clearly the relationship was unbalanced in Ian's favor.[22] Moo was eager to please, tolerated some frosty receptions at the Fleming family home of Joyce Grove, and also endured Ian's obvious pursuit of other women, especially the aristocratic, impeccably mannered Ann. Despite his attraction to Ann, Moo's tragic death in an air raid permanently engraved her as a figure of unattainable desire in Ian's imagination. Maud Russell clearly took Ian's mourning seriously, noting several days later that the "Muriel Wright business has affected me. I know what I[an] will be thinking and how he won't stop tormenting himself."[23]

Maud Russell was herself an important figure in Fleming's life, being not only a lover but a long-standing friend. Her home, Mottisfont Abbey in Hampshire, was a magnet for leading artists, thinkers, and politicians of the time, including Randolph Churchill, Peter Quennell, Cyril Connolly, and the Russian artist Boris Anrep, another of Maud's lovers. Being ten years older than Fleming, she took a supportive and protective role toward him. For example, it was Maud who got him the job at Cull & Co., the London merchant bankers, as her husband, Gilbert, was partner in the firm as well as being a cousin of the duke of Bedford.

The two became lovers in the 1930s, when Maud was married to Gilbert, who suffered from poor health, especially an acute form of asthma, meaning that much of Maud's life was devoted to looking after him, as she wrote in her diary for March 7, 1940: "I am always very sad when he isn't well. I dread the inevitable. And for 23 years I have thought about it. Where most women panic about their children, I panic, and always have, about G[ilbert]."[24] To distract herself from these troubles and find much-needed social interaction, Maud made frequent trips to London, often dining and lunching with Ian.

Maud's diary entries for this period provide fascinating insight into the progress of the war and her growing attachment to the handsome naval commander with whom she had been friends before the war. There is perhaps a note of envy in Maud's repeated comments about how "absorbed" Ian was by his wartime work—given that Maud herself was reduced to being a spectator for much of the war's duration, though she did work as a volunteer, and evacuees were billeted at Mottisfont.

More often, though, Maud expresses admiration for Ian's courage and heroism, presenting him as cool and effective in the face of danger. The secrecy and danger of Ian's job are also a source of tension between them. On Friday, November 1, 1940, Maud writes,

Figure 9.1. Maud and Gilbert Russell on a bench at Mottisfont, 1930s. ***Reproduced by permission of Maud Russell Estate.***

> Today lunched I. Coq d'Or. He has been on some dangerous job again. He cannot ever tell me what they are. A house in which he was dining was blown from under him. He and his friends were left marooned on the third floor, the staircase and most of the floors below were blown away. Eventually there was a tap on the window, a fireman's head appeared and they left the house by the fireman's ladder. The story was told as if there hadn't been any danger.[25]

Ian's story suggests that he is on the "front line" of World War II, despite being ensconced behind a desk in the Admiralty for much of the time. Maud's role appears to have been that of an avid listener to Ian's tales of wartime danger, for she relates another near-death experience of Ian's later the same month (November 28):

> He had a narrow escape at the Carlton a week or two ago sleeping on the third floor. The night was hellish, bombs dropping all round. Then one on the hotel. The place swayed, masonry started falling, the wall to the passage disappeared and I. was covered with cement, plaster and bricks but miraculously not hurt. Heard cries and moans. Rescued a waiter and a maid pinned down by debris. Finished the night in the hotel grill-room where other people were sleeping.[26]

The extensive damage to the Carlton Hotel during the Battle of Britain is a matter of historical record and led Ian to seek new accommodation at the Lansdowne Club. Yet, Maud's account of the episode places Ian in the heroic role of a prototype James Bond—under attack yet "miraculously" surviving and immediately turning his attention to protecting and saving others. Ian, in Maud's version, does all this with an impeccable, unruffled manner. Maud had the unique ability to present an image of Ian as he wanted to see himself—immersed in the cloak-and-dagger world of secret espionage yet able to enjoy elegant luncheons with beautiful women (the Coq d'Or in Mayfair was one of London's swankiest restaurants) and to react with instinctive courage in a crisis.[27]

There is ample evidence in Maud's diary of her romantic attachment to Ian Fleming. They were on lovers' terms, though she was married and had other affairs at the same time as Ian was deeply involved with both Muriel and Ann. In June 1940, Maud records how, during a dinner with Ian, he had immediately gone to stop a man talking and became so upset that "Ian's lovely face was white, or rather, turned white." This comment on Ian's physical appeal is more than that of a friend. In one entry, Maud relates that on October 6, 1940, the Russian artist Boris Anrep "told me he is in love with me. I am now nearly 49. The last time anyone said this to me was three years ago." This other admirer was almost certainly Ian Fleming.[28]

The impression that Ian and Maud were special intimates for each other—perhaps the most important people in each other's lives—comes across in her relating another remarkable fortuitous escape from death by Ian. Maud here seems to suggest an almost clairvoyant bond between her and Ian:

> Lunched with I. at the Coq d'Or. Has been touring the coastal defences. The house he was in at Dover was blown up and everyone killed soon after he'd left it. We discussed how either would know if the other was killed. Not knowing at once gives an empty blank feeling.[29]

After the death of her husband, Gilbert, in May 1942, Maud was distraught and often depressed. She sought solace in distraction with friends like Ian and Boris Anrep as well as through her war work. Maud's house in Hampshire was requisitioned by the US Army as a rest home for American servicemen, leaving her only a few rooms. Her focus, however, was socializing in London.

Later, Ian helped Maud get a job in the Naval Intelligence Division (NID), a role she desperately wanted, thus repaying the assistance Maud had given him finding a job in the City through Gilbert's influence. In August 1942, Maud writes,

> After dinner [at Prunier's] we walked across Green Park, mysterious and full of rustling shadows. I talked about getting a job and he said would I like the Admiralty—NID section. I said yes. He said he would get me fixed up four days a week, unpaid, to start early Oct.

Ian was as good as his word, helping Maud to secure a position at the Admiralty, where she joined NID 17Z, the propaganda unit in the basement of the building. Here she worked under Donald McLachlan, the head of the department, and alongside Charles Morgan, the journalist who was writing an official history of NID. She also kept Ian informed about the operations of the "section" as, she reports, "he likes hearing all about life in 17Z—the personalities, the jokes, the minor tragedies."[30]

Their work in Naval Intelligence was by no means the only subject Maud and Ian talked about, however. They seriously considered getting married, at least Ian suggested it while Maud demurred on the grounds that Ian was too young to be her husband. By an extraordinary coincidence, Maud's diary entry recording their conversation about marriage was written just a few days before the entry discussing the death of "Ian's girl" Muriel Wright in an air raid. Maud had reluctantly concluded that "it's no use a woman of 52 trying to keep pace with a man of 36," although "he is very good to me." Ian had "talked about marrying me, I had qualities he wants to find," yet Maud shows no jealousy toward Muriel Wright. Rather, she feels sympathy for Ian and worried about the fact that Ian refused to talk about Muriel after her death, remarking on March 27, 1944, "I left it to him if he wanted to but he said nothing and I didn't probe." Maud is clearly still concerned, on April 12, that "still we don't mention Muriel." After Muriel's death, Maud took over Muriel's role of "seeing about his rations," taking charge of Ian's ration card and making sure he got them.[31]

Maud was also Ian's chief confidante about his troubled relationship with Ann O'Neill, who had married Esmond Rothermere in 1945. Ian unfairly tries to blame Maud for his entanglement with Ann's aristocratic set, asking, "Why had I let him see such people, why hadn't I said what I thought about them?" Reading between the lines, it's apparent that Ian was fascinated by Ann O'Neill yet also repelled by the "frivolity" (Maud's word) of her and her circle. Maud severely judged that they are "people with little guts and very little sense of duty or obligation," yet she could not prevent Ian from being attracted by them like a moth to a flame. Maud had taken a dislike to Ann well before this, lunching with her in February 1942 when "Ann talked frivolous nonsense about us being unable to sink enemy ships and that they always sank ours. . . . I hate that sort of ill-considered talk."[32]

Ultimately, Ann represented an irresistible social prize or trophy to Ian, a woman who belonged to a powerful newspaper baron, Lord Rothermere, and was all the more desirable for being seemingly unattainable. Despite having assured Maud previously that he was not having an affair with Ann, Ian cannot help boasting about his conquest on July 3 1945, when "he talked about Ann O'Neill who has just married Esmond Rothermere and told me he'd slept with her a few times, though he'd always denied this before." Despite his misgivings about the "frivolity and the chatter" of her circle, Ian would marry Ann in 1952 in Jamaica, at which point, according to Emily Russell (who edited Maud's diaries), his friendship with Maud cooled off.[33]

Ian's relationship with Maud Russell was important for several reasons. She provided him with an entrée to an upper-class artistic milieu he relished, including important writers, artists, and bankers who visited the Russells at Mottisfont, in contrast to Ann's highbrow set. It is possible Maud, through her husband, Gilbert, helped Ian get the job in Naval Intelligence, as she noted in her diary for May 28, 1939,

> I think he [Ian] would like to do secret service work, or journalism, or both. He wrote a report about Russia and another about Germany after he'd been there this spring. . . . G[ilbert] read one of them, and had the idea of introducing him to the MI [Military Intelligence] which he did.[34]

For Ian, Maud was a happy combination of a lover, a patron, and a fairy godmother, one of the few people who understood his dreams and—no less important—had the means to make them come true.

Ian sometimes wrote to Maud as "M"—the initial he also used for his mother—and this may suggest a certain maternal role, given that she was seventeen years his senior. Certainly, her generosity and kindness to him, as well as her sympathetic attitude toward his various love affairs, were substitutes for the treatment he had hoped in vain to receive from his own mother. But their physical intimacy demonstrates that there was more than just friendship between them.

Their relationship is also important because it challenges the popular image of Ian Fleming as a rather selfish womanizer who pursued young and beautiful women that he clearly viewed as dispensable. John Pearson's biography at times portrays Ian as a cold-hearted selfish Lothario who was "totally amoral in sex" and reports that women "objected to his rudeness, his apparent insensitivity."[35] This portrayal of Ian was reinforced in the recent TV miniseries *Ian Fleming: The Man Who Would Be James Bond*. Ian's stepdaughter, Fionn Morgan, has stated her own disagreement with this position:

> If I concede that he was not always a perfect gentle knight I disagree profoundly with the opinion of Douglas Rae, executive producer of a "fantasy" biopic of Ian made for BBC America, that he "was cruel, particularly cruel to women. He was a very selfish man. He lived for himself." Nonsense.[36]

Pearson's description of Ian in his biography, as "something more than a philanderer, something less than a rake," places him firmly in the category of a self-absorbed womanizer. Most harshly, Pearson's portrait of Ian is that of a man incapable of friendship with women: "Real friendship," as Pearson alleges of Ian's views, "could exist only among men—women were there to be slept with and then forgotten" and then quotes from one of Ian's notebooks that "women . . . have their uses for the relief of tension and for giving a momentary relief from loneliness." However, Ian's long-enduring friendship with Maud Russell, as well as other women, is evidence against Pearson's claim that Ian had a "distrust of women who tried to mix intellect with sex."[37] On the contrary, Ian not only found Maud physically attractive but also saw her as an intellectual equal with whom he enjoyed many lengthy conversations about politics, literature, and intelligence matters.

Ian was an emotionally supportive and caring friend to Maud at times of great crisis in her life, especially during her worries about the fate of her youngest son, Raymond. A troubled young man and gifted harpsichordist who had difficulty getting settled in life, Raymond originally failed the entrance exam to King's College Cambridge but subsequently gained admission to Downing College.[38] This was followed by controversy when Raymond declared he was a conscientious objector during the war but then was called up for service because he was deemed medically fit. As Maud wrote, he was "posted for non-combatant duty which he resents and is going to appeal against." Maud herself was scornful about her son's pacifist opinions, commenting "what bunk COs talk." The result of Raymond's appeal was disastrous: it was "dismissed and he was ordered to do *any* duties in the Army so his position is worse than it was. . . . If, as he intends, R disregards call-up papers, he will get 3–12 months hard labour."[39]

Then, in a further crisis, Raymond was admitted to hospital in Cambridge, critically ill after a suicide attempt through an overdose of opium and Adalin—though a surgeon at the hospital believed that "there wasn't a serious intention to commit suicide." Maud—understandably fraught with anxiety about her son's state of mind—confided in Ian about Raymond's unhappiness. She felt Ian was especially sympathetic because of his own troubled youth, including his ignominious early exit from Sandhurst followed by his failure to gain admission to the Foreign Office. As she wrote, on March 10, 1942,

> Dined with I[an] at Boulestin's. Talked about my personal griefs and told him all about Raymond. Poor I. had a very troubled youth himself and understands this dreadful tangle better than anyone I know and better than I do. He understands it from R's point of view and from mine. He groaned as I told him. His heart is so good.[40]

Ian's willingness—despite his heavy burden of responsibility as assistant to the director of Naval Intelligence and head of the Naval Secret Service—to sympathize and identify with Raymond's sufferings made a deep impression on Maud. Maud's verdict about Ian's heart being "good" is evidence against the portrayals of him as a selfish exploiter of women, for she knew him as well as anyone at this time. Maud again asked Ian's advice about Raymond later that month:

> I rang up Ian who had such a stormy childhood himself, and lunched with him at the Carlton Grill. I told him the latest Raymond developments, asked his advice, and was prepared to follow it. It boiled down to this in the end: "Go on, make more sacrifices. You won't forgive yourself unless you do, unless you do your utmost. If you can, be emotional. Cry if you can."

In the end, Ian's advice proved superfluous as Raymond left Downing College voluntarily to report for noncombat duties after a visit from Maud to Cambridge. But she made clear how important Ian's emotional support had been by going directly from Cambridge "to I[an].'s flat to tell him how things had turned out. . . . He'd fortified me and strengthened me and, if it'd been necessary, I should have acted on his advice."[41] Ian's role as a supportive and emotionally generous friend has not been sufficiently recognized, and his capacity for close friendship with women is demonstrated by Maud's reliance on his support. Maud's granddaughter Emily Russell writes, "In 1973 there is a diary entry about Gilbert, Boris and Ian. About Ian she writes: 'Sometimes I think of Ian—mostly of his personality, his character & his innate kindness.'"[42]

Though he viewed her as his "comfort during the war," and she played a crucial role in the creation of James Bond, it is not easy to identify the presence of Maud in the Bond novels.[43] Her role was to make things happen for Ian behind the scenes without herself being in the limelight. Their meetings were often intimate tête-à-têtes between equals of a kind that aren't often recognized as occurring between Bond and women. However, the conversations between Vesper and Bond during his recuperation from his brutal beating by Le Chiffre capture some of this affectionate intimacy. There are also traces of Maud in Miss Moneypenny, to whom Bond is clearly attracted, yet there is an obvious taboo against their having a sexual relationship. Maud frequently worried about Ian's safety while on "dangerous jobs," much as Moneypenny worries about Bond when he is on a dangerous mission. Concerning Ian's missions in NID, Maud wrote, "It's all so dreadful and I have a feeling of nervousness and dread."[44]

While Monique, Muriel, Ann, and Blanche can all be linked fairly clearly with one or more of the "girls" that Bond becomes involved with, Maud belongs at the inner sanctum of power of Bond's professional world. If it might seem incongruous for a wealthy, aristocratic woman such as Maud to be embodied in the character of Secret Intelligence Service secretary, one should recognize that her role in 17Z during the war was that of support staff. Ian was an "important person" in NID, but she herself focused on gathering interrogation reports and fielding inquiries. Moreover, she was worried that she wouldn't get the job "because I hadn't diplomas or degrees," hence the gulf between Maud and Moneypenny is not so wide as it first appears.[45]

Muriel Wright's sudden death in 1944 poignantly raised her importance in Ian's emotional life, reflected in the fact that several of Bond's relationships with women end traumatically, even tragically. Like Muriel, Vesper Lynd dies in her sleep—though this is the result of a self-inflicted overdose of sleeping pills taken out of guilt at her betrayal of Bond and the Secret Service rather than masonry from a bomb blast. Bond's grief at losing the woman he hoped to marry replays Ian's guilt at not having proposed to Moo while he had the opportunity. There are other traces of Moo's tragic demise in Fleming's novels. In *Moonraker*, when Bond and Gala Brand narrowly escape death in the landslide at Saint Margaret's Bay, the episode was clearly influenced by the death of Moo, who was fatally struck by pieces of masonry. Whereas Bond, lying next to Gala on the beach, is able to protect her by throwing his body on top of hers and shielding her from the deadly rocks, Ian had not been with Moo in her bedroom to protect her from the bomb blast. In both cases, the damage was caused by German enemies attacking from above: from a Junker bomber flying over London in reality, and from Krebs's explosives detonated from the Kent clifftop in fiction.

Most dramatically of all, Moo's violent death prefigures and is replayed in the tragic fate of Tracy di Vicenzo—another beautiful, athletic blonde expert Alpine skier—whom Bond has just married. The sight of Tracy's corpse—"she was lying forward with her face buried in the ruins of the steering-wheel"—recaptures the haunting sight Fleming faced of Moo's dead body, which he had to identify in March 1944. Bond's final words to the Austrian patrolman also connects Tracy's death to Moo's: "It's quite all right. She's having a rest. . . . We've got all the time in the world."[46] It is as though Tracy, like Moo and Vesper, has died in her sleep, while Bond's bitter regret at her being snatched away mirrors Fleming's own remorse.

Apart from Maud, Ian's relationship with Phyllis Bottome is the most important example of his respect and affection for a woman of high intelligence and talent. It is hard to exaggerate the extent of Bottome's influence on

Ian's development at a formative period of his life when he was still reeling from the failures of humiliating exits from Eton and Sandhurst. In the Forbes Dennises, Ian found a couple who valued his own skills and characteristics and who, unlike most people, were not constantly comparing him (usually unfavorably) to Peter. Perhaps most important, this was Fleming's first close encounter with a successful novelist. He wrote his first story, "A Poor Man Escapes," under her tutelage, and Bottome's example planted the seed in Fleming's mind that he too could become a successful author. In a letter to Ernan Forbes Dennis, written after Phyllis died in August 1962, Ian wrote touchingly that "you and Phyllis were father and mother to me when I needed them most and I have always treasured the memory of those days at Kitzbühel."[47]

Of course, Fleming wrote a very different type of fiction than Bottome's. Where the Bond adventures reinvent the spy thriller tradition of Buchan, "Sapper," and Ambler, Bottome's novels are characterized by melodrama, focusing on moral and political themes, and are at times didactic about the issues important to the author. Moreover, Bottome's novels and characters are often a vehicle for the ideas of Alfred Adler, her mentor in psychology whose biography she published in 1939. As she makes clear in her memoir *The Goal*, Bottome saw her life's mission as the dissemination and popularization of Adler's ideas, and her fiction was the best means for accomplishing this.

Adler's theory of "social interest"—some form of external engagement—as the key to mature development and happiness was a pervasive theme of Bottome's fiction. Her leading characters—whether male or female—are redeemed and ennobled by making sacrifices for the social good, even at the cost of their own short-term happiness. Freya Roth, the heroine in *The Mortal Storm*, for example, pursues her love for Hans, a Communist peasant, despite the social and familial pressure on her to marry Fritz, the son of the local *graf* (lord), who repeatedly proposes to her. Her determination to transgress class and political boundaries with her love affair alienates her brothers (who have joined the Nazis) and ends in tragedy when Hans is shot and killed as he crosses the border between Austria and Switzerland. The party of Nazis that kill Hans is led by Fritz and Freya's brother. Yet, new life and hope emerge even from this tragedy, as Freya gives birth to the child she conceived with Hans and then goes off to the United States to become a doctor.

Freya's father, Professor Roth, is the clearest example in the novel of the Adlerian-type character. He refuses to join in the family's persecution of

Freya and urges his daughter to follow her love for Hans rather than marry for social advantage. Roth—a medical doctor and teacher—also refuses to bend to the Nazis' demands that he stop protecting Jews. Ultimately, Roth himself is banned from teaching and arrested, and he dies under torture in a Nazi cell. Bottome does not attempt to conceal the great cost of sticking to one's beliefs and principles, but her heroines and heroes are those who put the social good and their moral conscience before their own comfort and security.

Some have argued for a more direct literary influence of Bottome on Fleming, citing *The Lifeline*, published in 1946, as a revelatory work. This was the only spy novel Bottome published—though she did previously coauthor a mystery with Dorothy Thompson, *The Depths of Prosperity* (1925). The hero of *The Lifeline*, Mark Chalmers, is an Eton schoolmaster (an important Fleming connection) who enjoys his privileged life in an elite educational establishment, takes pleasure in his holidays spent mountaineering in the Austrian Alps, and tries to avoid romantic commitments. Both the protagonist's bachelor status and his somewhat selfish view of relationships may suggest that Ian was in Bottome's mind when she wrote the novel. Chalmers's recollection of a youthful love affair that ended badly may also allude to Fleming and Monique's failed engagement: "Only once before, when he had fallen wildly, hopelessly in love, and for a very short time, could he remember having this shaken feeling of uncontrollable dismay."[48]

Mark's selfish pursuits are disrupted when, as a favor to his friend Reggie, who works in the Foreign Office, he agrees to carry a message—while on one of his holidays—offering support to an Austrian resistance group struggling against Nazi control. Having delivered the message of support, Chalmers believes he has fulfilled his obligation and desires nothing more than to continue with his holiday. However, while staying with the resistance group, Mark is deeply influenced by meeting its leader, Ida, who he feels is judging him negatively for returning to his comfortable life. Ida urges Mark to take a more active role in the anti-Nazi resistance and to sacrifice his secure life in England in order to help their cause. Even before he meets Ida, however, Mark feels guilty about pursuing his pleasure trip through war-ravaged Europe: "His holiday seemed to have shrunk away from him, into a child's toy. He couldn't just purposelessly climb, in the clean mountain air—for the fun of the thing—with the whole of Europe rocking beneath him."[49] These are the early signs of Mark's awakening conscience and decision to commit himself to Ida's cause. He becomes, as a result, a secret agent for the anti-Nazi resistance.

The novel reflects Bottome's own dismay and anger at the ignorance, indifference, and complacency she found in England when she returned to her native country to live in 1935–1936. Having lived in Austria and France for many years, Bottome had witnessed the alarming rise to power of the Nazis and recognized Hitler as a megalomaniac and deeply anti-Semitic dictator who desired to conquer Britain as well as Europe. On her return to Britain, however, Bottome found that many were sympathetic to Hitler, and—under the leadership of Chamberlain—the country viewed appeasement of the Nazi Führer as the best policy. As Bottome recalls this period of her life in *The Goal*:

> It was the winter of 1935 to 1936. I had come from a Europe that was distraught and obsessed between Hitler and Mussolini, with Stalin waiting in the wings. I simply could not believe in the easy nonchalance of London. When I met Conservatives, they stared at me in frank bewilderment: "Oh, but we like Hitler!" they said.[50]

For Reggie, Mark is an ideal agent precisely because of his background and lack of attachments: "You've got a clean slate, your mother's dead, and you're not married. You've been brought up not to tell anybody anything. Chaps across the way would say 'ideal enemy agent.'" Mark agrees to assist Ida's group and, in order to maintain his cover, must pose as a lunatic in an asylum she runs in Austria. However, the key point is that Mark is inspired by Ida's zeal and commitment to take an active role in her mission to fight the tyranny of Nazism. Mark finds himself uncomfortable under the penetrating gaze of Ida: "But she did not really care if the material she had to work with was pleasant, or unpleasant to handle. The question her cold speculative eyes demanded was simply whether Mark could be useful or not." Ida can also be sarcastic and mocking toward Mark's proclaimed affection for Austria: "Herr Chalmers loves our country. I do not think he yet understands what this love involves. Nor, that this country is more than a country—it is a portrait of what is to happen to all helpless, free and harmless lands."[51]

As is evident from this summary, Bottome's novel is very different in style and structure to the Bond novels. Recently, however, it has been alleged that Bottome's contribution to Fleming's success was more than that of a literary role model. When the Forbes Dennises visited the Flemings at Goldeneye in 1947, Phyllis gave Ian a copy of *The Lifeline*, published the previous year, and evidently Ian was impressed by his mentor's versatility. However, the intelligence historian Nigel West has gone further, claiming that the relationship between Ian and Bottome is that of "thief and victim."[52]

Despite some superficial resemblances between Chalmers and James Bond, there is little solid evidence that Fleming used Bottome's character as a model for his own secret agent. Mark Chalmers belongs more in the category of "clubland heroes," upper-class gentlemen with privileged lifestyles who are definitely amateurs at espionage. Chalmers initially becomes a spy in order to help out an old friend and then continues as a covert agent to win the approval of the woman he falls in love with, Ida. Though Chalmers is at Eton (as Bond and Fleming were), he does not partake of the high-stakes gambling, luxury lifestyle, and jet-age travel beloved of Fleming's hero.

One can speculate that Bottome's writing a spy novel may have provided a spark for Ian by demonstrating that a respected novelist could indeed pen espionage fiction. Reading *The Lifeline* may even have stirred his competitive instincts and prompted him to start writing before other writers cornered the market. It is difficult, though, to imagine Fleming's Bond accepting a role as a lunatic in an asylum or offering such resistance to taking on a mission. Rather, Fleming's debt to Bottome was that of a grateful protégé who acknowledged her influence: "I remember clearly writing a rather bizarre short story for you which you criticized kindly and which was in fact the first thing I ever wrote."[53]

Bottome's politics, too, were very different from Fleming's. On arriving in Britain in 1935, she told a friend that she would not join the Conservative Party. Despite her support for Winston Churchill—one of Fleming's personal heroes (and a friend of his father's)—Bottome's political outlook was liberal. She was a feminist who saw the necessity of women taking a stand for their professional opportunities and sexual freedom and on crucial moral and political issues of her time. Bottome seems to have disapproved of Fleming's womanizing, and it is unlikely she would have appreciated some of the sexual antics in the Bond novels. And yet, Bottome's strong, multidimensional female characters furnished examples for Fleming of how to create complex, resolute, and in some cases emotionally damaged women in his novels.

Just as Bottome's heroines undergo personal and emotional traumas, the same can be said of Fleming's lead female characters. A surprising number of the women Bond becomes involved with have experienced sexual trauma, tragedy, and crisis in their past lives. Several of Bond's lovers have endured horrific rape and other forms of sexual abuse: Tiffany Case, Bond learns from Felix Leiter, was gang-raped as a teenager by some of the clients of her mother, a prostitute. Honey Rider was raped by the white overseer in her home of Beau Desert and took a deadly revenge on her violator. Pussy Galore confesses to Bond that she was raped as a girl by her uncle, adding incest to the already terrible sexual abuse. Tracy lost her only daughter to "that most terrible of all children's ailments, spinal meningitis."[54] Bond is deeply sympathetic to the traumas suffered by the women he's involved with.

Some might argue the traumas of Fleming's female characters are primarily used as an opportunity for Bond to demonstrate his heroic credentials and masculine prowess by saving them from their oppressors or even "curing" them of these past traumas. Fleming, this line of argument goes, constructs these damaged histories for his female characters only to highlight Bond's extraordinary powers of seduction, reclamation, and healing. Critics such as Bennett and Woollacott have argued that Bond is able to reclaim such resistant and refractory women for patriarchal society. As James Chapman argues, moreover, the more stereotypical elements of "Bond girls" has led "critics to suggest that women should be seen less as characters and more as functions of narrative."[55]

However, a close reading suggests a more complex and challenging role for women in Fleming's novels. We should take seriously the proposition that the "Bond girls" are not one-dimensional sex objects but essential characters in the novels as well as Bond's equals in intelligence and courage. Bond, as we know, tends to judge women at first by their physical appearance and behavior, reinforcing what Chapman calls "the *Playboy* ideal of sexuality."[56] In the course of the novels, however, Bond discovers—along with the reader—that there is a lot more to the leading woman than he has realized. They have vital secrets that he does not have access to, such as Vesper's role as a double agent, or private lives he knows nothing about, such as Tracy's tragic marriage and loss of her child. Although his first impression of Tiffany is of an almost-naked body splayed on a chair of her apartment, he will soon learn that she is an expert card player (and sharper) and a skilled professional smuggler. On his first encounter with Honey Rider on the beach of Crab Key, she is entirely naked apart from a knife on a belt, which leads Bond to objectify her. This knife, however, is a symbol of her own power and fighting spirit, a quality she elaborates on with her story of how she killed the man who broke her nose and raped her. In Fleming's novels, we are allowed to see the severe limitations of Bond's superficial evaluation of women and to appreciate their hidden depths, abilities, and powers.

The female characters in Ian's later work reveal his blossoming relationship with Blanche Blackwell, the Jamaican heiress with whom he began an affair in the 1950s. The Flemings' marriage, which had always been troubled and tempestuous, was falling apart by the late 1950s. Ann's affair with Britain's Labour Party leader Hugh Gaitskell (ironically, since she was a staunch Conservative) and Ian's affair with Blanche drove a deeper wedge between the couple, whose tastes, temperaments, and social circles were always, to some degree, pulling them apart. Ann protested that Ian's first act on their arrival in Jamaica was to telephone his "mistress" and arrange to meet her, a clear demonstration of his preference.

In his relationship with Blanche, Ian achieved a level of peace, companionship, and shared interests he could not find with Ann, especially during his trips to Jamaica. This might explain why Honey Rider—the character Fleming invented at the early stage of his romance with Blanche—is (despite her violent trauma) among the happiest, least agonized female characters Fleming created. She is capable of openness and affection and is notably direct in her questions and sexual propositions to Bond. Honey's final demand—and the final words of the novel—"Do as you're told"—place control in the woman's hands as she orders him to share her bed.[57]

The enhanced roles of women in the stories extends beyond the roles of women as characters to include Fleming's interest in writing from the female perspective. Such writing not only reveals added depth to female characters but also significantly shifts the focal point of the novel away from Bond. Early in his career, Fleming writes extensively from Gala Brand's perspective in *Moonraker*, first by relaying her impressions following her first meeting with Bond at Drax's missile base on the White Cliffs near Dover: "Commander Bond, James Bond. Clearly a conceited young man like so many of them in the Secret Service. And why had he been sent down instead of somebody she could work with, one of her friends from the Special Branch, or even somebody from MI5?"[58] Ironically, her reaction replays Bond's frustration when Vesper is sent to work with him in *Casino*. Gala's role in the novel expands as the plot progresses, and a crucial section of the story—in which Drax's true malevolent intentions toward Britain are revealed—is told from her perspective.

In 1961, at Goldeneye, Ian would write his most radical departure from the Bond formula by telling the story entirely from the woman's point of

Figure 9.2. Ian Fleming and Blanche Blackwell on the beach at Goldeneye, Jamaica. *The Times/News Licensing.*

view in *The Spy Who Loved Me*. Instead of the third-person narrator that usually presents events through Bond's perspective, Fleming switches to the first-person narrator and tells the story from Vivienne Michel's angle. The novel begins, "I was running away. I was running away from England, from my childhood, from the winter, from a sequence of untidy, unattractive love-affairs . . . and I was running away from drabness, fustiness, snobbery, the claustrophobia of close horizons."[59] This sentiment might sum up Fleming's state of mind going back to his departure from England for Kitzbühel in 1924 or indeed his feelings on leaving England for Jamaica each winter from 1946. But Viv's story is her own, and Bond is quite peripheral to the plot.

Remarkably, Fleming even included Viv Michel's name on the title page as his coauthor: "Ian Fleming, with Vivienne Michel." This gesture prompted an anxious query from Michael Howard at Cape, asking Fleming in a letter of June 12, 1961, "Does Vivienne Michel have to have her name on the jacket? I imagine that she does, but there is a body of opinion here which is against it."[60] Fleming's narrative experiment had the approval and support of other readers at Cape, however, including William Plomer, who wrote on April 28, "I am in the middle of being absorbed by the results of your collaboration with Mademoiselle Viv (Bimbo) Michel—your best she-character up to now." Fleming himself defended the novel in letters to his American publisher, Viking Press, assuring them the book possessed "special virtues."[61] These "virtues" were doubtless those of the charismatic and vivacious character of Viv Michel herself.

Ian endows Viv with some of his own personal memories and experiences: not only her relief at escaping the oppressiveness and cold climate of England but also her memories of her first sexual experience at a cinema in Windsor (where Eton College, as well as Windsor Castle, is located). The man who persuades her to have sex on the floor of the box at the cinema, Derek Mallaby, is a pupil at Eton as well as a skilled driver, which links the episode to Ian's own youthful adventures. The scene is remarkably graphic and also humiliating for Viv, as she describes the persistence of Derek's seduction and laments, "I had lost my virginity or some kind of virginity."[62] The couple is discovered *in flagrante delicto* by the cinema manager, who expels them from the movie house and brands Viv a whore.

Ian was deeply hurt by the public's and critics' hostile reaction to the publication of *The Spy Who Loved Me*, claiming he suffered "multiple contusions" from the critical outcry, as though he had been in the ring with a prizefighter.[63] Though Fleming tried to put a brave face on it, the novel's reception was a debacle, and Fleming decided to withdraw the book from paperback publication. For the rest of his life, as much as possible, Fleming disowned *The Spy Who Loved Me*.

James Chapman makes a persuasive case for including *The Spy Who Loved Me* in the Fleming Bond oeuvre, summing the novel up as "a flawed but genuine attempt to identify with the woman's point of view" while also claiming the novel's "attempt to present a woman's point of view is less than wholly successful" because "it was not well received and Fleming never wrote another one like it."[64] I submit, however, that the poor reception of the novel can suggest that it *was* successful in terms of what Fleming set out to do. The reason it failed with readers was that it broke with the formula and reduced James Bond to a secondary character, seen "at the other end of the gun barrel."[65]

Unsurprisingly chastened by this rejection of his experiment with narrative voice, Fleming returned to a more traditional Bond formula with his next novel, *On Her Majesty's Secret Service*. Though this was written before the publication of *The Spy Who Loved Me*, Fleming had already enough forewarnings—from the American publishers' reactions and reluctance to accept it—to conclude that the experiment was unlikely to be a popular triumph. Therefore, in *On Her Majesty's Secret Service*, Bond is present from the very beginning of the novel, and the reader's identification with him is strengthened by sharing Bond's flashback to childhood seaside holidays and his reflections about the "dirty dangerous memories" he has accumulated as a spy.

The influence of the female perspective of Viv Michel is evident, however, in that *On Her Majesty's Secret Service* features Fleming's most vividly imagined and complex female character, Tracy di Vicenzo. Not only does Tracy share the troubled history of other Bond women—in her case, a rebellious youth and marriage to an unfaithful Italian count who was killed in a car crash—but she entrances Bond as no other woman has since Vesper. Fleming does not need to tell the story from Tracy's perspective—as he had with Gala Brand or Viv Michel—to demonstrate she is Bond's equal and counterpart. Moreover, she is the only woman Bond chooses to marry—even willing to sacrifice his career in the Secret Service in order to build a new life with Tracy. *On Her Majesty's Secret Service* was a tremendous success both critically and commercially and launched a new era of promotion and marketing for James Bond novels that, as we will see in the next chapter, coincided with the release of the first Bond films.

Had it not been for the bold experiment of writing in the persona of Viv Michel, it is unlikely that Ian could have created such a deeply sympathetic, passionate, and complex female character as Tracy di Vicenzo, or (as she briefly became) Tracy Bond. Tracy's tragedy leads us back to the core of Ian's traumas, especially the wartime deaths of his father and of Muriel Wright, as well as his mixed feelings about his time in Kitzbühel. His novels are evidence that such painful episodes from his past continued to haunt him. Bond's girls, eroticized and objectified as they sometimes are, prove to be the multifaceted keys to understanding the women in Fleming's life.

Chapter Ten

Promoting Bond

Fleming, Mass Culture, and the Movies

On September 21, 1961, Michael Howard—Ian Fleming's chief editor at Jonathan Cape—wrote to the artist Richard Chopping, urging him to complete his cover design for Fleming's forthcoming novel, *The Spy Who Loved Me*, as soon as possible: "Now we have pushed Ian up into the top seller class, subscribing his new book is a major operation which takes a lot of time, and we shall really do him a great dis-service if we can't get his jacket out during the next month or two."[1]

Howard's letter reveals the publisher's purpose of creating a perpetual best seller with the Bond novels. In emphasizing the difficulty of achieving this feat, Howard notes the complex combination of factors required to maintain Fleming's status. Howard had initially been opposed to Cape publishing Fleming's first novel, *Casino Royale*, in 1953, feeling that a "literary" house like Cape should not be associated with thrillers. By the early 1960s, however, Howard was the first to admit that Fleming's books had become essential to Cape's financial solvency.

As it turned out, *The Spy Who Loved Me* would prove a disappointing setback to the Fleming "machine" of global popular success. The novel was banned in Australia and Canada for alleged "obscenity" (it was the most sexually explicit novel Fleming wrote, exacerbated at the time by the fact that the sexual intimacies were described in the voice of the female narrator). Critics were generally hostile toward Fleming's adoption of a female narrative persona, and his publishers had warned him about the likely negative response. Ultimately, the novel sold comparatively poorly, and Fleming withdrew the planned paperback issue of the novel. Despite the urging of Aubrey Forshaw, head of Pan Books, who wanted a paperback issue, Fleming insisted, “I think it was a bad book. I’d rather forget about it.”[2]

This disappointment, however, only added to the determination of Ian and Cape to launch an aggressive publicity campaign for its successor, *On Her Majesty’s Secret Service*. The novel, written at Goldeneye between January and March 1962, represented a triumphant return to the established Bond formula. As we have seen, the Tyrol region of Austria had a special personal significance for Fleming, and his decision to set his latest novel in that well-loved location was auspicious. The most encouraging development, however, was that EON Productions began filming the first Bond movie, *Dr. No*, in Jamaica while Fleming worked on his tenth novel. The new life of James Bond in cinema was launched.

Among the innovative promotional methods used by Cape to boost Fleming’s new novel and push it higher than ever before in publicity and sales was a revolving display unit designed for bookshop windows, intended to attract attention with props such as an imitation “dummy” pistol. Cape also introduced a contest between booksellers around the country for the best display. The final decision about the winner would be made by Ian Fleming himself, and the prize was priority discounts on future orders of Bond novels. Fleming awarded the prize to Boots the Chemist in Blackpool for its “irresistible eye at the centre” of the display. Cape had provided detailed instructions to booksellers for how to set up, design, and eventually return the display to the publisher: a letter from Cape to one branch of W. H. Smith states they will be receiving “direct from Messrs Cape one each of the turntables and dummy automatic pistols mentioned on Page 5. . . . The parcels will contain a Returns label and instructions on how to send both items back to Jonathan Cape immediately your display is finished.”[3]

Several booksellers wrote to thank Cape for the display, indicating that it had had a beneficial effect on sales of *On Her Majesty’s Secret Service*. Not everything went smoothly, however, which was hardly surprising given the complex design of the display: a letter from K. J. Bredon’s Bookshop, Brighton, April 17, 1963, apologized for some missing pieces: “We are returning, herewith, as much as we can of the revolving display unit for Ian Fleming’s OHMSS [*On Her Majesty’s Secret Service*]. Unfortunately, the gun was pinched from under our noses, and will not, we hope, be used in one of

Brighton's bank raids." Apparently, the temptation of possessing a replica of Bond's gun was too much for one Fleming fan.

Bennett and Woollacott have argued that "1957 . . . witnessed the first stage in the transformation of Bond from a character within a set of fictional texts into a household name," attributing this change to the popular serialization of *From Russia, with Love* in the *Daily Express* and ensuing comic strips. However, the sales figures suggest a later period for the transformation of Bond into a phenomenon of mass culture, coinciding with the launch of the EON films. The aggressive upswing for promotion of the Bond novels took off following the release of EON's *Dr. No* in October 1962. As Bennett and Woollacott note, there is "a marked lift in the sales for all the Bond novels over the period 1962 to 1967, a lift that was especially pronounced in 1963, 1964, and 1965." They conclude, correctly, that "the effect of the films in this period was to revivify the market for the Bond novels as a whole."[4] In order to capitalize on the popularity of the Bond films, Jonathan Cape—a quite traditional publishing house—had to adapt to popular methods of advertising, publicity, and promotion.

Fleming, of course, had devoted considerable effort for some years toward achieving a film deal for Bond to bring his spy hero to the big screen. After several false starts and aborted projects—the *Thunderball* fiasco being the most humiliating failure—the deal had finally been made. As Fergus Fleming notes, the first EON film production was accompanied by "an extraordinary amount of pre-production publicity that included far-fetched plans for new editions of *Dr. No* put forward by Harry Saltzman."[5] Ian, as he had been from the beginning of his career, was actively involved in the promotion of his novels as desirable commodities, eager to secure the most lucrative possible deals for overseas publishing rights.

As an intriguing example of how Fleming's publishers exploited the arrival of Bond in cinema to promote the literary work, the Bond party Jonathan Cape organized, together with EON Productions, deserves mention. Held at Pinewood Studios on April 1, 1963, the party was timed to celebrate both the publication date of *On Her Majesty's Secret Service* and the first day of filming of *From Russia, with Love*, the second EON Bond film. The party provides a fascinating glimpse at the collision of the two worlds of publishing and the film industry: special buses were hired to ferry Jonathan Cape staff and various literary personalities to Pinewood, where they would mingle with Sean Connery, Daniela Bianchi, and other stars of the new film. One person eager to attend was Geoffrey Boothroyd, who had become Fleming's unofficial armaments consultant since his letter of May 1956 pointing out faults with Bond's (or rather, Fleming's) choice of weapons.

Boothroyd—who received a personal invitation to the party from Michael Howard—eagerly looked forward to the chance to test his gunslinging skills against Connery and (a surprise addition to the invitation list) founding member of British radio comedy program *The Goon Show* Michael Bentine. Boothroyd wrote Howard on March 14, 1963, enthusiastically supporting the proposal of a shootout between Boothroyd, Sean Connery, Ian Fleming, and Bentine. Perhaps it was just as well that this proposed stunt of a shootout at Pinewood—for which Boothroyd had offered to provide both firearms and live ammunition!—came to nothing. Yet, this kind of theatrical tour de force reveals how the sober world of literary publishing—epitomized by the conservative firm of Jonathan Cape—had been invaded by the glamorous milieu of spy fiction and popular cinema.[6]

At this time, Michael Howard was increasingly eager to assuage Fleming's doubts about Cape's enthusiasm for promoting his work and especially anxious to prevent him leaving for another publisher. In order to conciliate their star author, Howard wrote to Fleming about the robust promotion campaign for *On Her Majesty's Secret Service*:

> I sincerely trust that even your exacting standards will be gratified by the degree to which sales will far outstrip all previous records. I doubt that we can surprise you but that is exactly our aim. We have mounted a terrific campaign with [W. H.] Smith's, who will be giving window displays all over the country and a whole arsenal [!] of promotional material is in preparation.[7]

Just as Howard had been skeptical about Cape agreeing to publish *Casino Royale*, he had also been doubtful at first about the likely success of bringing Bond to the big screen. Yet, he changed his mind on seeing the first Bond film, writing to Fleming on October 8, 1962, just days after the film's release,

> I have to confess to being astonished by that film of *Dr. No*. Judging only, I must admit, by the lamentable productions that have usually been made of most of my favourite thrillers I had become convinced that it was really impossible to translate that kind of book into visual terms. EON have certainly attacked the problem in the grand manner and, by pulling out all the stops, I rather think that they have got away with it.

Howard also praised Ian's own skills at self-promotion, adding, "I do congratulate you on the magnificent billing you have secured in all the publicity and in the credits in the film itself."[8]

Yet, Fleming did not rely solely on the production system and publicity machinery of Cape and EON to promote his novels. He also found ways to promote Bond in more direct ways, such as in his correspondence with his readers. One of Ian's chief assets as a writer of popular fiction was his enthusiasm for connecting with and responding to comments and criticisms from individual readers and fans. There is no better illustration of this than his responses to the dismay of readers following the apparent demise of James Bond at the end of *From Russia, with Love*. Ian received numerous letters protesting the ignominious way in which Bond had (apparently) been killed and objecting to the abrupt termination of the 007 series. He reassured readers that "in the next chapter of his life story, which will be published next March under the title of 'Doctor No,' James Bond will have benefited by the sharp lesson he learned on his previous case."[9] He also assured a South African reader that, despite his apparently fatal collapse to the floor at the end of *From Russia, with Love*, Bond had, in fact, survived Rosa Klebb's poison.

Such personal letters to readers might seem less efficient for promoting James Bond to the public than producing advertising copy or writing blurbs for the dust jackets of his books or giving interviews with the mainstream media. Ian, of course, also did all these things and did them well. But he also enjoyed the one-to-one interactions with his readers, feeling a sense of connection with his audience that transcended the relative isolation of the writer's profession. The letters he received were not always in praise of Fleming's work. Even in cases where they were critical and found fault with some aspect of his latest novel, Ian embraced such criticisms both as a way to help him improve his craft as a writer and as an easy means to acquire new knowledge and ideas for his books. One Scottish reader who declared his disapproval of novels in general nonetheless offered the criticism that Bond's vintage Bentley was old-fashioned, to which Ian replied that Bond was being reequipped with a more modern car (which turned out to be an Aston Martin). Whether such criticism came from the professional readers and critics at Cape, from the media, or from individuals, Ian handled the criticism graciously.

By referring to himself as James Bond's "biographer," and to the individual novels as "chapters" in Bond's "life story," Fleming also played up to the notion that Bond was an actual person rather than merely a fictional character. Of course, this suggestion of Bond's real existence was itself part of the fiction and might be written off as playfulness on Fleming's part, a way of creating a humorous dialogue with his readers. But, in some cases, the suggestion that Bond was a real person came from the letter writer, and Ian invariably played along with it. A Mrs. R. J. Frewin from Toronto, for example, pointed out inconsistencies in Bond's behavior as though he were a living individual with a will of his own. Ian found a way to explain these contradictions (such as Bond's use of cream in coffee) by essentially blaming Bond's own reticence, thus perpetuating the idea of Bond's reality: "In writing James Bond's biography I am entirely dependent on what he tells me, and if he is occasionally equivocal, particularly in the matter of dates, I assume that he has some sound security reason for confusing me."[10] Bond is not the only character in the novels that Fleming claims an actual existence for. He also refers to Felix Leiter as though he were a real person recovering from the shark bites he sustained in *Live and Let Die*. Fleming thus entertains the quirky notion that the world of his novels is based on fact rather than a fictional invention.

Ian's enthusiasm for the work of promoting Bond is apparent in some of the publicity materials he himself devised. Among these is a blurb for use in publicizing *On Her Majesty's Secret Service*, which Fleming enclosed in a letter to Howard on November 4, 1962. Enclosed with a note offering "a possible blurb for OHMSS," Fleming's blurb itself is dated August 30, 1962:

> It was one of those Septembers when it seemed that the Summer would never end. . . .
>
> But it did end and winter came in a lethal welter of mystery, bloodshed and multiple death amidst the snow.
>
> This, the eleventh chapter in the biography of James Bond, is one of the longest. It is also the most enthralling.
>
> Really the most? Really the most.[11]

This use of advertising-style slogans to hook his readers shows Ian's gift for anticipating the tastes and preferences of his audience.

As Ian's career progressed throughout the 1960s, it became increasingly difficult to distinguish aesthetic and critical assessments of James Bond as a character and Fleming as a writer from the commercial value of Bond as a "property." This was especially the case with the publicity boost accompanying the wave of "Bondmania" that swept Britain and the world in the early

1960s. This phenomenon has even been compared to Beatlemania, and Ann came up with a new nickname for Ian—"Beatlebird"—to reflect the growing scale of Bond's (and Fleming's) popularity. Sometimes critical judgments of Fleming's writing may have been influenced by the commercial success of Bond in film. For example, many at Cape assured Fleming that *On Her Majesty's Secret Service* was his best book so far when it appeared in April 1963. But this opinion was probably influenced by the success of the film of *Dr. No* and the consequent launch of Bond as a global popular icon. As Michael Denning points out, the popularity of Bond in the 1960s both dovetailed with and exploited the cultural fascination with espionage: "Spy stories proliferated in novels, on film, and on TV; in the daily newspapers, the sensational cases of George Blake and Kim Philby marked the spy fever of the 1960s."[12]

Ian had skillfully carved a niche for himself as a popular writer who was not attempting to mollify highbrow readers and critics. Eric Phillips wrote a favorable review of *On Her Majesty's Secret Service* in *The Writer* for July 1963, which praised Fleming for not attempting to join the avant-garde of literary arts while also recognizing that the author relied on a formula for success:

> The average reader . . . doesn't understand art or the high realms of literature. The average reader, in fact, wishes to be thrilled and entertained. It is good to aim high but it's useless to write for posterity unless you are a genius. Ian Fleming is a gifted story teller and a man of high intelligence and ability. Fortunately for us he has never tried to imitate Joyce. In the material sense it is also lucky for Mr Fleming—for whom James Bond has proved a money-spinner. The latest addition to the collection OHMSS [*On Her Majesty's Secret Service*] ranks with the best. I was enthralled. The story *has all the old ingredients* presented with that freshness Mr Fleming continually surprises us with.[13]

It was true that James Bond had become defined by a formula by the early 1960s. Indeed, the experiment of *The Spy Who Loved Me* was the exception that proved the rule of Bond's recipe for dominance of postwar espionage fiction. Certainly, Fleming's yearly routine was well established by the time he wrote *On Her Majesty's Secret Service* in 1962. He would spend January to March at Goldeneye in Jamaica producing the typescript of his latest Bond "opusculum." Fleming's notes, and the testimony of friends such as Ivar

Bryce, suggest that he wrote at a considerable pace, without stopping to critique or revise his work.

In his essay "How to Write a Thriller," published in 1962, Ian advised the aspiring writer to find a "mood that will . . . make you write fast and with application." In particular, the famous novelist recommended that would-be thriller authors not reflect too much on what they have written: after revealing that he wrote for three hours each morning, Ian insisted, "I never correct anything and I never go back to what I have written, except to the foot of the last page to see where I have got to. If you once look back you are lost. How could you have written this drivel?" Fleming explicitly refers to his writing method as a "formula" and claims, "By following my formula you write 2000 words a day and you aren't disgusted with them until the book is finished, which will be in about six weeks."[14] Of course, Ian plays down both his own literary skill and the dedicated labor he put into researching, writing, and revising his typescripts. But this essay does convey some of the "white heat" in which he wrote the original typescripts.

On his return to London each March, with new Bond typescript in hand, he would send the manuscript to the team he called the "Capeians" or the "Factory" at Bedford Square—consisting of Michael Howard, William Plomer, and Daniel George—and await their feedback and suggestions. He would then revise his newly composed manuscript and research ideas for his next installment. From 1959, when he lost his position as foreign manager at Kemsley House with the sale of *The Sunday Times* to Roy Thomson, Fleming worked at his private office in Mitre Court just off Fleet Street, revising the typescripts of his Bond novels, answering his correspondence, and occasionally spending the night.[15] This created a useful separation between the main burst of creative activity—carried out at Goldeneye—and the more reflective labors of revision, correspondence, and research necessary for the professional writer, which Fleming conducted at Mitre Court.

In effect, Ian would be working on three different novels—each at a different stage of composition, revision, or production—at the same time, following his return to London each spring. Even while in Jamaica, he had to deal with unexpected (and sometimes unwanted) intrusions into his creative "vacuum"—such as the arrival of a CBS TV crew to interview him about the US spy pilot Gary Powers, who had recently been captured by the Soviets after his U-2 spy plane crashed in Soviet territory. Ian wrote Michael Howard on February 28, 1962, from Goldeneye, "Fame is breathing down my neck. CBS flew a whole unit down to televise me about Powers, the Tatler has visited again & of course the Dr. No biz was a riot." Ian's amused reference to the ongoing film production of *Dr. No* suggests it was an entertaining distraction rather than a serious disruption of his writing schedule. He also noted with approval Harry Saltzman's promotional acumen: "Among other gimmicks he is turning out 5 million copies of a strip book on Dr. No."[16]

Like any successful writer, Fleming was protective of the time and space necessary for creative work. He referred to the need to "create a vacuum in my life which can only be satisfactorily filled by some form of creative work."[17] At the same time, Ian was one of the first modern writers to recognize that aggressive promotion and publicity were crucially important in establishing his reputation and—especially—generating high sales. Although this creative "vacuum" was necessary to write a novel, it was not going to make the novel successful without publicity. Through his persistence, Ian was able to convince a relatively conservative group of editors and managers at Cape that his American-style approach of "saturation" publicity, glitz, large print runs, and author interviews were essential for his books' success.

An important promotional and design feature of each new Bond novel published by Cape was the cover. Ian designed the early covers himself and always took a keen interest in the details of the artwork's appearance. For example, he wrote Jonathan Cape in October 1952 about his playing-card design for the cover of *Casino Royale*: "I think the idea is good, namely that the nine of hearts which plays such an important part in the book should provide the basic design."[18] From the outset of his Bond career, Fleming saw the importance of linking the design features of his covers to the key plot elements of the novel.

Despite Ian's initial involvement in the process, he came to realize the value of involving a professional artist in the cover design. And the visual quality and complexity of the cover art for Bond took a leap forward with the work of Richard Chopping, who Ian hired to design the covers starting with *From Russia, with Love* in 1957. Chopping's innovative and eye-catching trompe l'oeil designs were an essential contribution to the distinctiveness of Fleming's books. Just as James Bond was a unique spy hero, so Fleming wanted something that set his books apart from competitors in the spy thriller market. There was much correspondence between Fleming, Chopping, and Cape's editors about choosing the correct elements of each cover. Their goal was to use images that would at once capture the attention of readers, convey the ambience of James Bond, and reflect the unique themes of the novel's plot.

The amount of detail in these letters about the cover art is remarkable. For example, Howard wrote Ian about the cover for *The Spy Who Loved Me* in June 1961:

> I have been thinking hard about the prescription for Chopping, because I really must get him wound up very soon if I am to get a picture out of him in decent time. I roughed out a short list including a broken perfume bottle (of whatever flavour of Guerlain you mention; it slips my mind just now), a lengthy strand of ivy (poison for preference, but that is probably neither available nor readily identifiable over here) and a gun (can we borrow a current model from Boothroyd? Which ought it to be this time?) These might be disposed on a dressing table top which could be bird's eye maple.[19]

Howard was concerned about the precise details of the cover image, even down to the type of wood for the tabletop, both because he knew how important they were to the success of the book and because he knew how perfectionist (even obsessive) Ian was about such visual details.

Chopping's role in the success of the Bond novels has been unfortunately overlooked in the critical literature on Fleming's work.[20] Even at the time, Chopping felt that his contribution to Ian's—and Bond's—success was undervalued by Cape. Chopping began to be dissatisfied with the 200-guinea payment for each cover, and Ian—wanting to keep his prized artist happy—agreed to an increase to 250 guineas. However, Ian clearly believed that he therefore owned the cover art, writing Anthony Colwell (marketing director for Cape) in December 1961, "Should not the copyright line under 'Jacket design by Richard Chopping' be 'Ian Fleming'? As it was with the last book and since the picture is my property."[21]

Certain recurring images in the cover art—such as revolver pistols for *From Russia, with Love* and *The Man with the Golden Gun* or daggers in *Thunderball* and *The Spy Who Loved Me*—illustrate Chopping's clear grasp of the world of violence and danger that Bond inhabits. Another recurring motif is various flowers, and on the covers of *From Russia, with Love*, *Goldfinger*, and *You Only Live Twice* a flower (either a rose or a carnation) has a prominent place in the design. These are not only evocative of passion—given Bond's romantic adventures—but also show the importance of the natural environment and plants in the novels. Another significant recurring image in the cover art is a skull or skeleton, clearly a "memento mori" for James Bond with his license to kill, dangerous profession, and philosophy of "live and let die."

Chopping's distinctive artwork played an essential role in promoting James Bond as a classy literary product set apart from the mass-produced paperbacks, often with garish covers, that were often in vogue with the thriller market. At the same time, Fleming did not overlook the mass market for spy fiction, eagerly negotiating paperback rights deals with mass-market publishers such as Pan Books (in the United Kingdom) and New American Library (in the United States). Many of these Bond paperbacks would have far more sensational cover art than the Cape issues, and some would even have different titles for the US publication (*Moonraker*, for example, was published in the United States under the more sensational title *Too Hot to Handle*). But Chopping's work was important in establishing the aesthetic quality of Fleming's novels on their first appearance and was tailored to appeal to what Fleming termed the "A class of readers."[22]

By the early 1960s, Ian had carved out a niche for himself as the premier thriller writer in Britain, perhaps in the world. He had endorsements from such respected authors as Raymond Chandler and the even more valuable seal of approval from President John F. Kennedy, who included *From Russia, with Love* in the list of his ten favorite books of all time, published in *Life* magazine in March 1961. Yet, Ian recognized that there was a limit to how far Bond could go in literary form, however beautifully produced and aggressively promoted the initial publication or—in paperback issues—however large the print run.

Ian sometimes bemoaned the status of the writer in the postwar era, complaining that it was impossible, in his day, for an author to make substantial sums just from writing books. Fleming often compared his success—or desired success—with Somerset Maugham's, one of his literary idols as well as a close friend. He wrote Ann Marlow—with whom he had signed a makeshift contract at Sardi's Restaurant in New York in a desperate attempt to get a film deal—in June 1961, encouraging her to promote his work in the United States "in much the same way as you dealt with Willie Maugham."[23]

Perhaps Marlow should have been warned by the proviso that the agreement with her was "not . . . in perpetuity." Ian was not in his best health at that time, the letter to Marlow being written while he was still recovering from a serious heart attack, which occurred in April during an editorial meeting at *The Sunday Times*. Forbidden from using his typewriter because of his doctors' concern he would begin working on a new James Bond novel while in hospital, he evaded the prohibition by using pen and paper to write a story for children, *Chitty-Chitty-Bang-Bang*. Written for his son, Caspar, to whom

Ian had told earlier versions of the tales, *Chitty* would not be published until after Fleming's death (three volumes, between 1964 and 1965).[24] By this time, Ian was close to making the sought-after film deal with Harry Saltzman and Albert Broccoli and only two weeks later would write to Marlow requesting that she return his hastily signed contract. Effectively agreeing to cancel their deal, Marlow thereby cleared the way for Fleming to finalize his film deal with Saltzman and Broccoli, who named their new company EON Productions (Everything or Nothing).

This deal brought to fruition a plan that Ian had fantasized about and nurtured ever since he began writing the first James Bond novel in 1952. He mentioned in a letter to Jonathan Cape in 1952 that Paul Gallico, the American novelist, had borrowed a duplicate typescript of *Casino* to consider its suitability for Hollywood. Gallico's enthusiasm came to nothing, but Ian's next novel, *Live and Let Die*, was read in proof form by the legendary film producer Alexander Korda. Though impressed by the novel, Korda did not think his company could film it. Encouraged by Korda's interest, however, Fleming wrote his third novel, *Moonraker*, with a film adaptation specifically in mind. Yet, disappointingly, this project also came to nothing.

It is remarkable, though, how persistent Fleming was in his efforts to achieve cinematic success throughout his literary career. Graham Greene—another contemporary writer Fleming greatly admired—had been successful with film adaptations of his novels and stories, in particular *The Third Man* (1949) directed by Carol Reed. Greene also divided his work into two categories: "entertainments"—books intended for popular consumption—and more serious literary novels. Fleming, who began his literary career almost a quarter of a century after Greene despite being only four years younger, was not under the same burden of what Christopher Hitchens has called the "bifurcation" of Greene's work.[25] Fleming was more than happy for his novels to be read as entertainments, reaching as wide an audience as possible, and did not make claims to writing "serious" literature. He regularly pleaded with his publisher Cape to print enough copies of his works to satisfy demand, objecting that some booksellers had run out of copies of *Casino Royale*, for example.

Yet, as Fleming advised budding authors in "How to Write a Thriller," it was only through film and television rights that an author could hope to make serious money: "You don't make a great deal of money from royalties and translation rights and so forth . . . but if you sell the serial rights and the film rights, you do very well."[26] A film deal was an essential stage of the modern author's journey to financial success, and it increasingly became an obsession of Ian's. He wrote French film actress Claudette Colbert in April 1955 that he was unlikely to make another trip to Los Angeles, as "I have absolutely no excuse for another holiday unless Hollywood suddenly decides to film one of my books."[27]

In hindsight—with James Bond's global popularity today assured by each new Bond film and the novels still in print and selling—the adaptation of Fleming's novels for cinema seems to have been inevitable, a no-brainer. But for Ian himself, the film deal was far from an inevitability and appeared, on the contrary, a hopelessly desirable yet elusive fantasy. The power of this fantasy led Fleming into some of the most ill-advised decisions of his career, such as his collaboration with the Irish film producer Kevin McClory, who wanted to bring James Bond to the big screen. Having decided that none of Fleming's existing novels were suitable material, McClory launched a new collaboration with Ian, screenwriter Jack Whittingham, and Ivar Bryce to produce a Bond story specifically made for cinema. This was the film treatment and screenplay of *Thunderball.*

The key figure in the ill-fated collaboration between Fleming and McClory was Ivar Bryce. In order to understand how things went so wrong with the McClory-Fleming-Whittingham *Thunderball* project, we have to grasp the long-standing and eccentric friendship between Ian and Ivar. Ever since their days at Eton, the two friends had pursued adventures and escapades together, which included illicit trips to London on Bryce's motorbike and liaisons with local young women in Windsor. In later life, Fleming and Bryce had continued to enjoy outings and adventures together—sometimes quite spontaneously—and there was an unspoken pact between them not to let their friend down when called on. Bryce had struck it rich, marrying two wealthy heiresses in succession, the second being Jo Hartford—heiress of the Hartford Insurance Company and the A&P supermarket chain—whom he married in 1950. Seeking an investment for some of his newly acquired wealth, Bryce decided to join a group of investors who purchased the North American News Alliance in March 1951. This group included Ernest Cuneo, Bryce's friend and lawyer, who remained president of the company until 1963. Ian Fleming was appointed European vice president at an annual salary of £1,000.

However, the days of print news' dominance in the media were waning under competition from radio and television, and Bryce eventually sought other more profitable outlets for his financial assets. Ian saw his career at the

North American News Alliance suddenly come to an end with the takeover by a Canadian syndicate in 1957. Ivar then provided financial backing for Kevin McClory's film *The Boy and the Bridge*, released in 1959, which was critically well received but ended up losing money at the box office. Despite this disappointment, Bryce wanted to work with McClory again, and the two founded a production company, Xanadu Films. With financial backing from Jo Hartford and involvement from Ernie Cuneo, Xanadu decided to work on a film featuring Fleming's James Bond.

Ernie Cuneo wrote the first draft of the screenplay—named *Thunderball*—and sent it to Fleming, who used it as the basis for a sixty-seven-page film treatment. This treatment was developed further by McClory, who also hired a professional screenwriter, Jack Whittingham, to work on the screenplay. However, by the end of 1959, Bryce's interest in the project had waned, especially as he was now faced with financial losses from *The Boy and the Bridge*. McClory, however, remained enthusiastic and clearly expected the new project—*Thunderball*—to reach the big screen. Ian, meanwhile, had the additional distraction of his latest assignment for *The Sunday Times*: a trip around the "thrilling cities" of the world, writing a series of articles for publication in *The Sunday Times* (now owned by Roy Thomson) about his travel experiences in exotic locales, such as Tokyo, Macau, Hong Kong, and Honolulu. Eventually, the combined articles—together with pieces documenting Fleming's trip around Europe—would form Fleming's successful travelogue *Thrilling Cities*, published in 1963. When Fleming left on his trip in November 1959, the *Thunderball* project was still very much hanging in the balance.

Having completed his globe-trotting adventure, Fleming was back at Goldeneye in early 1960 to write his latest Bond adventure. In part due to the distraction of his extensive travels, he had not devoted as much time as usual to working up a new plot and creating the most important part of any Bond novel: the villain. Fleming was finding it increasingly difficult to come up with new ideas and villains for novels, hence the fact that his 1960 offering (written in winter 1959) was not a novel but a collection of short stories, *For Your Eyes Only*, in some of which (notably "Quantum of Solace") Bond plays a minor role. Struggling to find inspiration, Fleming decided to use the plot and characters of *Thunderball* for his latest novel.

Ian apparently believed that the film collaboration with McClory had been shelved and therefore felt free to use the material—for which he had written the original treatment—for his own purposes. McClory had insisted, before agreeing to make a Bond film with Xanadu, that their Bond film be based on an original screenplay and not be adapted from any of Ian's existing novels. Having tried and failed numerous times to secure a deal for one of his novels, Fleming resigned himself to accepting this condition. But it did mean that McClory, Whittingham, and Cuneo each had a legitimate creative and commercial stake in the new project, which had not originated exclusively with Fleming.

Unfortunately, in writing the new novel *Thunderball*, Ian failed to acknowledge the contributions of McClory and Whittingham to the plot and characters, including the new enemy organization SPECTRE (Special Executive for Counter-Intelligence, Terrorism, Revenge, and Extortion)—which replaced the earlier Soviet bête noire SMERSH—and its head, the master villain Ernst Stavro Blofeld. McClory, unlike more malleable individuals such as Ann Marlow, was not willing to let his agreement with Fleming go up in smoke. He took legal action against Fleming, Bryce, and Cape, attempting to stop the publication of *Thunderball*. The case was heard in March 1961, a few weeks before Ian had his heart attack in April.

Because the original print run was completed, the court did not prohibit the publication of the novel in April 1961. However, it did acknowledge McClory's right to sue for rights to *Thunderball*, and the case eventually went to court in 1963, where the verdict seemed likely to be in favor of McClory. Certainly, this was the view of Ivar Bryce, who decided to settle with the plaintiffs, fearing that a prolonged case would deplete his resources and also endanger Fleming's precarious health (this is the version Bryce tells in *You Only Live Once*). However, Ian believed that Jo Hartford Bryce was behind Ivar's capitulation, and Ann Fleming also saw matters in a more sinister light. Inside Ian's personal copy of *Diamonds Are Forever*, bound in green leather, is her handwritten note expressing bitterness about the outcome of the case: "dedicated to 'Ivar Bryce,' who afterwards betrayed Ian in the law suit concerning 'Thunderball'—the case undoubtedly caused Ian's coronary. A.F."

According to the judge's ruling, all future editions of the novel would have to acknowledge the contributions of McClory and Whittingham to the plot. More damagingly for Ian and EON, McClory was left in control of the film rights to the story. This allowed him not only to be credited as the producer of the 1965 film version of *Thunderball* but to produce a remake of the film based on the same plot after a period of ten years—an option he would eventually exercise with 1983's *Never Say Never Again*, in which Sean Connery returned to the role of 007.

It is ironic, with hindsight, that the acrimonious collapse of Ian's collaboration with McClory and Whittingham on *Thunderball* was followed so closely by the successful film deal he made with Saltzman and Broccoli in the summer of 1961. Had Fleming been more patient and waited for a more credible offer—which came relatively soon—the angst, expense, and public humiliation of the McClory court case might have been avoided. Even if one does not agree with Ann's claim that the *Thunderball* case was directly the cause of his death from a second heart attack in 1964, it is hard to deny that the stress, anger, and embarrassment caused by the case had a detrimental effect on his health. It also in some ways poisoned what should have been the happiest period of Fleming's life, when he was poised to enjoy the fruits of success and prosperity.

Though delighted at the film deal with Saltzman and Broccoli, Ian was at first unconvinced by their choice of actor to play James Bond. He had imagined his friend David Niven in the role, an English gentleman with the air of sophistication and upper-class panache that Ian admired. In fact, Niven's company attempted unsuccessfully to acquire the television rights to Bond in 1962. Later, in October 1962—the same month as *Dr. No*'s release—Niven suggested that Fleming come up with an idea for a "high class crook" for him to play in a forthcoming TV series.[28] Fleming declined, being preoccupied with working on the next Bond novel. At first Ian was concerned about the producers' selection of the young working-class Scottish actor Sean Connery to play Bond in the film of *Dr. No*. But he was soon won over, writing Blanche Blackwell on October 25, 1961, "the man they have chosen for Bond, Sean Connery, is a real charmer—fairly unknown but a good actor with the right looks and physique."[29] The ownership of James Bond was gradually being transferred from Fleming to the film industry.

Though Ian himself had no say in the choice of actor to play his famous character, he had now achieved his great dream of bringing Bond to life on the cinema screen. Fleming would also find a new lease on life for his writing in the excitement of film production. It was hardly a coincidence that *On Her Majesty's Secret Service*, the novel he wrote in winter 1962, while *Dr. No* was being filmed in Jamaica, was a great return to form for Fleming and one of his most masterful novels. Ian would also be influenced by the casting of the Scottish Connery in his decision to give James Bond a Scottish background in *On Her Majesty's Secret Service*, elaborated on in *You Only Live Twice*, where we learn his father, Andrew Bond, was born in Glencoe.[30]

Though Fleming, through his company Glidrose, continued to own Bond as a literary property, the screen version of 007—which would become far more famous and influential in popular culture—belonged to others. Ian would find it difficult to let go of James Bond, who had been his constant companion, arguably his alter ego, for over a decade. Toward the end of his life, Ian would comment mournfully on the fact that the movie tie-in paperback edition of *Goldfinger*—the third Bond film, released in the United Kingdom the month after Fleming's death—gave more prominence to Sean Connery's name than to Fleming's. After the euphoria of securing the film deals, Ian began to feel territorial about *his* character and *his* role as author.

Once the EON film series had been launched, it tended to strengthen rather than dissolve the connections between Fleming and his character. On the one hand, he lost a degree of creative control over James Bond, who was now freed in cinema to develop in other directions, some of them quite unintended or unforeseen by Fleming himself. On the other, Fleming's stock undoubtedly rose as a result of his connection with the internationally famous 007. Not only did each film credit "Ian Fleming's James Bond"—a fact pointed out admiringly by Michael Howard—but Ian was photographed or filmed in various poses that reinforce the idea of Fleming-as-Bond—sophisticated or thrilling portraits of Fleming half in shadow smoking a cigarette, wearing the tux and black bow tie often donned by his famous hero.

A fascinating example of how the identities of Bond and Fleming began to merge can be found in the invitation to the party following the premiere of *Dr. No* in October 1962:

Mr. Ian Fleming
has pleasure in inviting you
to meet
James Bond
at Supper
11.00 p.m. on Friday, 5th October 1962
At Les Ambassadeurs, 5 Hamilton Place,W.1[31]

There is an enigmatic quality to the invitation, suggesting either that Fleming has privileged access to James Bond, which the guest will be permitted to share, or that Ian Fleming *is* James Bond, whose dual "identity" with Fleming will be disclosed at the party.

Figure 10.1. Ian Fleming, smoking à la James Bond. *Horst Tappe/Contributor/ Getty Images.*

As the films grew in scale, budget, and popularity, capturing the imagination of people around the world, competition and disputes over the rights to Fleming's own lucrative literary property also escalated. For example, there was an acrimonious dispute between *Playboy* magazine and Jonathan Cape over licensing the US publication of *You Only Live Twice*. *Playboy*—which had published the Bond short story "The Hildebrand Rarity" in its March 1960 issue—had acquired the rights to serialize the novel in its April, May, and June issues of the magazine in 1964 (as it had done with *On Her Majesty's Secret Service* the previous year). Fleming was paid $35,000 by *Playboy* for the rights to serialize the novel on condition that this serialization appeared before the volume publication in the United States, demonstrating the high value of Fleming's name for selling the magazine. However, *Playboy* got wind of the intention of New American Library, Ian's US publisher, to publish the hardcover edition of the novel *before* August 21, 1964—the date stipulated in their contract with Cape. The magazine threatened legal action against Cape for breach of contract and demanded an assurance from the publisher that it would not allow an earlier publication date in the United States.[32]

While *Playboy* was understandably concerned that its sales would be harmed by an earlier publication of Fleming's novel, the caustic correspondence over his literary remains is a poignant reminder of how fragile and expendable Ian himself was in this scenario. By the time of the agreed-on book publication of *You Only Live Twice*—August 21, 1964—Fleming was dead, the victim of a second heart attack at his beloved Royal St George's golf club in Sandwich, Kent. Even after the premature death of the author, the bitter struggle to control the rights to publish, promote, adapt, and exploit James Bond would continue for decades afterward.[33]

Chapter Eleven

From Fleming, with Love

Travel Writings and Nonfiction

Even before the film deal that would bring him fame and wealth, Ian was growing weary of writing about James Bond. By 1957, he was so disenchanted by the yearly ritual of racking his brains for a new plot, unusual settings, and a memorable villain that he thought about killing Bond off. Fleming often complained of the labors of writing a new Bond, bemoaning to Plomer in March 1957 the burden of "having completed a further stint on the behalf of English literature"—this "stint" being *Dr. No.*[1] Fleming had even tried to free himself from Bond by killing off his hero at the conclusion of his previous novel, *From Russia, with Love*. The novel ended with Bond—having been stabbed by the poisoned shoe-blade of SMERSH colonel Rosa Klebb—collapsing to the floor, apparently never to rise again.

The one aspect of creating new Bond adventures that Ian most enjoyed was identifying, visiting, and researching the locations for his novels. This involved one of Ian's favorite pursuits, jet travel to exotic or unusual places, staying in (often) luxurious accommodations and experiencing local cuisine, culture, and customs. Fleming's job as foreign manager at Kemsley Newspapers had required much international travel and reporting, and his training as a journalist had given him the skills needed to write terse, action-packed, and evocative spy fiction. When *The Sunday Times* changed hands, being sold to Roy Thomson in 1959, the new owner wanted Ian to continue with his globetrotting.

Before this, in 1957, Ian was invited by his editor at *The Sunday Times* to travel to Tangiers to interview a man called John Collard, who was the chief agent appointed by Sir Percy Sillitoe, former director general of MI5, who had been hired by De Beers to head this investigation into diamond smuggling from its African mines. This opportunity combined Ian's love of travel with his long-standing interest in contemporary news stories involving treasure hunting, smuggling, and crime.[2] His fourth novel, *Diamonds Are Forever*, was based on Sillitoe's actual operation to shut down the smuggling operation from South African diamond mines. Therefore, *The Sunday Times* believed that he was the ideal person to bring Collard's manuscript, which it had acquired, to life. Collard shared this enthusiasm and requested Fleming as the author for his "story."

Fleming invented a romantic-sounding pseudonym for his protagonist, whom he called "John Blaize," using the same initials as his famous spy hero. Fleming also came up with an exciting title for his narrative to appeal to the thriller market—"The Diamond Spy"—but this was eventually replaced by *The Diamond Smugglers*. The serialized version appeared in *The Sunday Times* in September and October 1957, having been heavily censored due to the threat of legal action from De Beers.[3] Hence the final book—published in November 1957—was something of a disappointment compared to Fleming's expectations, and he complained that "it was a good story until all the possible libel was cut out." Yet, t-e book—probably due to Fleming's fame as the Bond author—proved a surprising success, and the Rank Organization purchased the film rights.[4] The book is significant because it demonstrates Fleming's ardent wish to be known as a writer beyond the scope of the James Bond novels.

JAMES BOND, MEET JOHN BLAIZE: FACT AND FICTION IN *DIAMONDS ARE FOREVER* AND *THE DIAMOND SMUGGLERS*

In discussing the formula used by Ian Fleming to create the Bond villains, Italian novelist and critic Umberto Eco notes one significant anomaly in the canon: "Only the evil characters in *Diamonds Are Forever* have no connections with Russia. In a certain sense the international gangsterism of the Spangs appears to be an earlier version of SPECTRE. For the rest, Jack and Seraffimo possess all the characteristics of the canon."[5] The name "Spectre" would become a bone of contention in the legal case pursued against Fleming by Irish film producer Kevin McClory, who alleged—in 1961—that Fleming had stolen this identity for his exclusive use in the novel *Thunderball*.[6]

Several of Ian's novels and stories involve Bond or his enemies assuming false cover identities (beginning with Bond posing as the son of a Jamaican plantocrat in *Casino Royale*). Yet, none of the other Bond novels feature identity theft as centrally as the fourth, *Diamonds Are Forever*. In trying to stop a diamond-smuggling pipeline that originates in Africa, M advises Bond that the most effective way to insert Bond into this pipeline is for him to assume the identity of a small-time crook and diamond smuggler, Peter Franks. In preparing for his role, Bond is given a makeover at Scotland Yard, after which "it all added up to someone who certainly wasn't James Bond."[7]

Posing as Franks, Bond works with Tiffany Case, an American smuggler who also sometimes travels using a false name and who readily accepts the counterfeit "Franks" (i.e., James Bond). When Bond admits to Case that his passport is in his own name, Case expresses concern about how he is to smuggle the diamonds into the United States. In Fleming's novel, Franks and Bond are seemingly interchangeable: the pictures of Franks showed a dark-haired, clean-cut man described by Vallance of Scotland Yard as "near enough like you to pass with someone who's only got his description."[8] Guy Hamilton's film version, by contrast, introduces an extended scene where the "real" Peter Franks escapes from the police and goes to his meeting with Tiffany Case (in Amsterdam), leading Bond into a fight to the death inside an elevator to determine who will keep the identity. As the victor, Bond then "switches" identity cards with the dead Franks, leading Tiffany Case (played by Jill St. John) to exclaim, "You've just killed James Bond!"[9]

The identity deceptions pile up in Fleming's novel, as Bond discovers that the man known as Rufus B. Saye, proprietor of the House of Diamonds in London, is also a fake: exposed by his failure to recognize that "Yellow Premier and Cape Unions" are not really types of diamond. Saye's deception goes deeper: he is really Jack Spang, one of the villainous brothers heading the Spangled Mob, the American end of the diamond-smuggling pipeline. Another of Spang's aliases is "ABC," the mysterious contact that all operatives within this smuggling network have to call in order to receive their instructions. Along with such colorful yet unlikely monikers as "Shady Tree," "Wint and Kidd," and "Tingaling Bell," the reader gets the impression that all identities in this novel are—like the "diamond" that Bond examines through an eyeglass in chapter 2—obvious counterfeits. Bond, having smuggled diamonds into the United States, travels to Saratoga, New York, in order to receive his payment by betting on a horse in a fixed race. But this horse, "Shy Smile," is also an imposter: Felix Leiter of the Central Intelligence Agency informs Bond that the real horse had been shot months ago.

As background for Bond's entrance into the diamond-smuggling pipeline, in *Diamonds Are Forever*, Fleming imports the details of the real-life operation to trace and close down diamond smuggling from the mines of Africa. This Sillitoe-led operation lends authenticity to Fleming's sometimes far-fetched plot: as M tells Bond, "our friend [Sir Percy] Sillitoe . . . [is] . . . out there now working in with the South African security people."[10] Onto this factual foundation, Fleming bolts a fantasy plot involving beautiful diamond smugglers, American gangsters, corrupt horseracing and Vegas casino operations, and the bizarre Wild Western town of Spectreville, where Seraffimo Spang lives out his own "pillow fantasy."[11]

Fleming's use of Sillitoe's real-life operation in his novel is an example of what intelligence historian Nigel West has described as "faction"—reflecting that "even what is purported to be copper-bottomed fact, from an ostensibly reliable source, can fall into the realms of fiction, or a potentially confusing mixture of the two, faction."[12] If Fleming's mixture of fact and fiction is potentially confusing in *Diamonds Are Forever*, it becomes even more so in the nonfiction book he published the following year, *The Diamond Smugglers* (1957).[13] Ian's original title for this work, "The Diamond Spy," highlighted his desire to make a seamless transition between his Bond thrillers and the nonfictional narrative. This link is also made by including the titles of Fleming's fourth and fifth Bond novels on the cover blurb of *The Diamond Smugglers*: "By the author of *Diamonds Are Forever*, *From Russia, with Love*, etc."

Despite having achieved some commercial and critical success with James Bond, Fleming aspired to write at a "higher" level—that is, to attempt more "serious" genres than spy fiction. As he admitted in a letter to Raymond Chandler, "if one has a grain of intelligence it is difficult to go on being serious about a character like James Bond."[14] In *Diamond Smugglers*, Fleming recycled the diamond smuggling plot in a "serious" format that broke free of Bond while returning the story to the context of the Cold War. Whereas in *Diamonds Are Forever*, the Soviet Union and the Cold War had played no significant part, in *The Diamond Smugglers*, Fleming makes clear that the diamond-smuggling operation has implications for the Cold War due to Soviet use of smuggled diamonds for industrial and military purposes.

The Diamond Smugglers was based on Fleming's extensive interviews with "John Blaize," which took place in Tangiers, a North African city Fleming disliked intensely, describing it as "a pretty dreadful place and the weather has been ghastly." From the outset, the project was shrouded in secrecy: as he wrote melodramatically to his wife, Ann, "my brains have been boiling over. . . . It has been very exciting and the story is sensational. . . . Please don't say a word about it or we may be stopped publishing."[15] This stress on the "sensational" elements of the story places it in the same category as his thrilling novels but with the added intrigue that the story was based on fact: as he told his editor William Plomer—whom he also swore to secrecy—"it is all absolutely true with the exception of the man's name."[16]

"John Blaize's" own preface to the book—written under the pseudonym rather than his actual name—brings a cautionary note into the proceedings, stating, "It was [my] notes and my memories which [Fleming] has most skillfully *forged into a connected narrative*." Identifying Fleming's role as a "forger," Blaize reminds us that Fleming is first and foremost a fabricator of fiction, a teller of adventure tales. Beyond the practical purpose of concealing the true identity of the agent—that is, John Collard—Fleming's use of a pseudonym allows him to take creative license with the character, partially fictionalizing him and enhancing his role in the story. "Blaize" also cautions the reader, modestly, that "Fleming has adopted the convenient literary device of making one individual, myself, the chief and omniscient operator for IDSO [International Diamond Security Organisation]," whereas in actuality the organization "was a team whose success, such as it was, should be credited to Sir Percy Sillitoe."[17]

Fleming was just as keen to highlight Blaize's status as a "secret agent" working with the "Diamond Detectives branch of the South African Police": "like all Britain's best secret agents . . . he had common sense, a passion for accuracy and a knowledge of men and how to use them." Inventing other Bond-like escapades for his hero, Fleming describes how "Blaize had a very unfortunate time at Monte Carlo. I gave him an infallible system which nearly broke him"—an apparent allusion to *Casino Royale*, in which James Bond's gambling system was nearly broken by Le Chiffre.[18]

The blurring between novel and nonfiction account increases as "John Blaize" shows his awareness of the fictional hero whom he was designed to supplant. "Blaize" notes, specifically, that his role in Sillitoe's operation mirrored the plot of *Diamonds Are Forever*: "Putting a spy in at one end [of the pipeline] in the hopes that he'd work his way up it till he got to the top. . . . Rather like that book you wrote last year, but the girls don't come quite so pretty around the diamond fields."[19] Several years before EON Productions began the official Bond film series in 1962, "John Blaize" also offered the tantalizing prospect of a cinematic coup.

Fleming also takes the opportunity availed by nonfiction to reflect critically on the methods and limits of spy fiction, noting, "Even in fiction there is very little good spy literature. There is something in the subject that leads to exaggeration. . . . Perhaps only Somerset Maugham and Graham Greene and Eric Ambler have caught the squalor and greyness of the Secret Service." Hoping to join this distinguished company, Fleming felt he had to abandon the romance and "exaggeration" of the Bond novels and attempt a grittier portrait of the "squalor" of spies. *The Diamond Smugglers* differs from the Bond novels in jettisoning 007's luxurious, hedonistic lifestyle. For example, the book eschews the kind of sexual adventure that Fleming made a hallmark of the Bond novels, Blaize's comment that "the girls don't come so pretty" in the real diamond-smuggling racket illustrating the lack of sexual exploits in the story. Even so, Ian attempted to lure his new hero Blaize into making confessions of amorous adventure: a risqué anecdote about his exploits in a nightclub "was my cue to ask Blaize if he had come across many women in the smuggling racket—beautiful couriers, glamorous shills in the mining towns, and so on. Blaize said sadly that the only beautiful girls he had come across had been on the side of the angels." Fleming's ardor for Blaize's adventures to match Bond's womanizing is further dampened by the agent's anticlimactic admission that "in general diamond smugglers didn't trust women. They had found that the stones were too much of a temptation."[20]

But if *Diamond Smugglers* was conspicuously lacking in "Bond girls," it could hardly sacrifice the presence of a larger-than-life villain. Here, in fact, Fleming sought to improve on the unconventional villains of the Spangled Mob in *Diamonds Are Forever*. Bond has a hard time taking the American gangsters seriously despite the fact that M views "American gangs" as a comparable threat to Chinese opium rings and SMERSH. According to Bond, "They're not Americans. Mostly a lot of Italian bums with monogrammed shirts who spend the day eating spaghetti and meat-balls and squirting scent over themselves."[21]

In his preface, Blaize notes that the real-life smuggling case is far from closed, as "there are still dotted round the world powerful criminals living beneath a cloak or sunny respectability in an affluence which still comes from diamonds smuggled out of Africa." Ian's job was to condense these anonymous criminals into a single, memorable villain. Fleming tasks Blaize with introducing the authentic villain of the plot, "the biggest [operator] of all, whom I'll call 'Monsieur Diamant.' Of course, this isn't his real name, but it's the name, or rather title, we gave him." Diamant is named for the precious commodity he covets, hoards, and smuggles. M. Diamant *is* diamonds just as Goldfinger *is* gold. Blaize suggests that even Fleming's notorious fictional villains like Mr. Big and Drax pale by comparison to the real thing: "You've written about some pretty good villains in your books, but truth is stranger, etc, and none of your villains stands up to Monsieur Diamant. I should say he's the biggest crook in Europe, if not in the world." Adding a spice of danger, Blaize then warns Fleming that, were he to publish the whole truth and real identity of Monsieur Diamant, "he'd have you bumped off."[22]

Like the best Bond villains, Monsieur Diamant has a respectable front for his criminal activity, having run a legitimate diamond business. Diamant also has vast wealth and excessive appetites, including "endless champagne and caviar and half a dozen girls that some agent used to procure for him." Diamant's predatory use of girls who "always had to be young and . . . were paid fifty pounds a night each" is reminiscent of Bond villains like Le Chiffre (a "flagellant" who runs a chain of brothels in France) and Goldfinger (who pays women to be painted gold before having sex with them).[23] Yet Blaize, in common with Bond, realizes the most potent passion is the lust for diamonds themselves. After studying an authentic jewel at the beginning of *Diamonds Are Forever*, Bond "could understand the passion that diamonds had inspired through the centuries."[24] Various characters in both the novel and nonfiction book fall victim to this "passion"; even Sillitoe was "dazzled" by the thousands of stones set out for his inspection, as he felt "some of the sinister fascination which has always surrounded these coldest of all gems."[25]

Diamond Smugglers also makes use of the Cold War conflict, revealing that the diamonds are sought by the hostile power of the Soviet Union, which provides large suns to fund illicit diamond buying. On the other hand, Blaize tells Fleming that the British proposal to buy illicit diamonds in Liberia with government money is approved by Whitehall, who wanted to prevent diamonds falling into the hands of "the Russian armaments industry."[26]

Blaize, like Bond, is an agent "on Her Majesty's Secret Service," a hero fashioned by Fleming to help Britain's economy hold its own in a postimperial age. Like Fleming, he is dismayed at the global decline of the British

Empire. Blaize shares one other surprising quality with James Bond: his disenchantment with the life of a spy. Bond, in *From Russia, with Love* (published in the same year), was "disgusted to find that he was thoroughly bored with the prospect of the day ahead."[27] Though one might find it hard to imagine Bond in a "nice quiet job," he does often express disdain for his profession. In a similar vein, Blaize complains, "I'm sick of crooks and sick of spying on them. All I want is a nice quiet job as a country lawyer or administrator." Similarly, Blaize ends the book by quoting back Fleming's own words: "As you said in the last sentence of one of your books: 'It reads better than it lives.'"[28] There are no glittering prizes for identifying the Fleming novel whose concluding words Blaize quotes: it is, of course, the coda uttered by Tiffany Case in *Diamonds Are Forever*.

KEEPING UP WITH MY HERO: IAN FLEMING AS JAMES BOND'S FELLOW TRAVELER IN *THRILLING CITIES*

In 1959, Ian accepted an assignment from *The Sunday Times* to travel to cities around the world and write a series of articles from these exciting places to be published in the newspaper. Ian's first trip around the world took in the Far East and North America, in November and December 1959, and was followed by a second expedition around the cities of Europe in the spring of 1960. The resulting articles would eventually be collected together and published, in 1963, under the collective title *Thrilling Cities*.

Ian clearly enjoyed his international travels—especially as his expenses were paid for by *The Sunday Times*—and seized with relish the opportunity to take center stage as both narrator and main character of the travelogue. One inducement for writing the series—suggested by Leonard Russell, the editor of *The Sunday Times* leisure and travel section, who gave him the assignment—was that it would provide Fleming with new material for the "exotic backgrounds" of his Bond novels. Indeed, Fleming would later set a Bond novel in Japan—which he visited for the *Thrilling Cities* articles—and also used Macau and Hong Kong as locations.

The Bond novels are themselves a variety of travel writing, in which the locations—including the natural environments and landscapes, the luxurious accommodations, the unusual cuisine, and the local culture—are as important as the espionage plots. This key role played by travel and location in the novels has not escaped the notice of critics. For example, in writing about Fleming's "taste for the exotic," Umberto Eco has noted that in the Bond novels, "the islands of Dream are reached by jet."[29] Also, as Michael Denning notes, "Travel and tourism make up much of the interest and action of a Bond thriller . . . and in almost all the novels some space is given to narrating Bond's travels by plane and train."[30]

Fleming's travel writing was an important aspect of his literary portfolio, but these works are far less well known than the Bond novels. In addition to *The Diamond Smugglers*, both *Thrilling Cities* and *State of Excitement*—the unpublished work he wrote about the oil-rich nation of Kuwait—also deserve closer attention.

In 1959, Ian was recruited on this special mission to travel to the "thrilling cities" of the world and write reports of his travels for publication in *The Sunday Times*. Formerly owned by Lord Kemsley, *The Sunday Times* had been sold—along with the rest of Kemsley Newspapers—to the Canadian media mogul Roy Thomson in 1959. As a result, Fleming's cozy arrangement as foreign manager, allowing him a two-month vacation in Jamaica each winter, came to an end.

Ian's fame as author of the James Bond novels (the most recent, *Goldfinger*, had been published in April 1959) was, of course, the key factor in his being commissioned to "make a round trip of the most exciting cities of the world and describe them in beautiful, beautiful prose. This could be accomplished, they said, within a month."[31] But also, as his "Author's Note" explains, Ian believed he was ideally suited by temperament and background for such an assignment: "All my life I have been interested in adventure and, abroad, I have enjoyed the frisson of leaving the wide, well-lit streets and venturing up back alleys in search of the hidden, authentic pulse of towns. It was perhaps this habit that turned me into a writer of thrillers."[32]

Leonard Russell offered an incentive to Fleming to live up to the example set by 007 in the form of new material for fiction, noting that the readers of his James Bond novels "seem to like the exotic backgrounds. Surely you want to pick up some more material for your stories?" When Ian reminded Russell that his novels were fiction, not real life, Russell responded with a dismissive retort: "Rot!"[33] With this spurning of Fleming's chief objection—and perhaps a veiled threat of consequences if Fleming refused the assignment—Russell, like a martinet M, demanded that Ian assume the international jet-setting mantle of Bond.

Russell's "invitation" would launch Fleming into an intriguing, self-conscious rivalry with his own fictional creation. This rivalry was in some ways a continuation of Ian's youthful competitiveness with his older brother, Peter, who had achieved academic excellence at Eton and Oxford University before going on to become a successful adventurer, travel writer, and novelist. Peter had also served in British intelligence during World War II, another challenge to his younger brother. Ivar Bryce, who knew both Fleming brothers at Eton, told John Pearson (Fleming's first biographer) that Ian was never as good a scholar as Peter. Their mutual friend Cyril Connolly told Pearson that the fraternal rivalry intensified when, after their father Val's death in World War I, "Peter became the father figure, but also something far more. Something very fierce. A competitor more than an ordinary father." Connolly went so far as to compare the Fleming brothers' rivalry to "the situation of Cain and Abel."[34]

This spirit of rivalry between Fleming and Bond is apparent in the Tokyo chapter (chapter 3) from *Thrilling Cities*, in which the author tries to imitate his hero's carefree attitude to air travel. On discovering that his flight to Hawaii with Japan Air Lines would require him to fly on Friday the thirteenth, Fleming quotes a passage from *From Russia, with Love*, in which Bond defies superstition and flies to Istanbul on Friday the thirteenth, ignoring the misgivings of his secretary. Invoking his hero's cavalier attitude of courage and immunity to superstition, Ian is under pressure to imitate it: "I felt I must try and keep up with my hero." Indeed, Ian goes Bond one better: for as his Australian friend Dick Hughes points out, Ian will actually be crossing the international date line and therefore flying on *two* Friday the thirteenths. Ian then seeks an unheroic reassurance by visiting a fortune-teller, who reassures him, "the next ten years was going to be quite splendid for me. I would live happily until I was eighty."[35]

In *Thrilling Cities*, Ian conveys the pleasure, excitement, and—in the 1950s—novelty and glamor of air travel with a relish that recalls the jet-setting experiences of Bond. In *Diamonds Are Forever*, where Bond flies by Stratocruiser to New York, we get the bird's-eye view from the jet plane: "Twenty-thousand feet below, the houses began to show like grains of sugar spilt across a brown carpet. Nothing moved on the earth's surface except a thin worm of smoke from a train."[36] Fleming again uses this "bird's-eye" technique in describing his long-haul flight to Hong Kong: "Below us Venice was an irregular brown biscuit surrounded by the crumbs of her island. A straggling crack in the biscuit was the Grand Canal" and then, as they approach the Middle East, a description of Beirut as "a sprawl of twinkling hundreds-and-thousands under an Arabian Nights new moon that dived down into the oil lands as the Comet banked to make her landing." Even the reading preferences of author and character while traveling are similar: where Bond reads Eric Ambler's *Coffin for Dimitrios* on his journey to Istanbul in *From Russia, with Love*, Fleming chose Ambler's latest thriller, *Passage of Arms*.[37]

Ian's long-standing fascination with treasure hunting and smuggling, which feature in many Bond plots, is on display in the Macao chapter of *Thrilling Cities*, where he meets "the gold King of the Orient . . . the internal Geiger-counter of a writer of thrillers ticking furiously," offering potential inspiration for future Bond villains. If this "gold king" is reminiscent of Auric Goldfinger, other Bond villains are evoked by Fleming's meeting with "Our Man in Macao" when he learns about the "four Mr. Bigs" who control the territory. While visiting the gambling palaces of Macao, Fleming points out that all his expenses, including gambling losses, are covered, as Bond's are, by his generous employer. Fleming's losses are more modest than Bond's: he plays a game called hi-lo and even tries to compete with Bond's sexual prowess, embracing what he discreetly terms "Oriental ladies' . . . almost inexhaustible desire to please."[38]

The casino, of course, holds a special place in Bond lore. Seeking to re-create Bond-like suspense and drama in his travelogue, Fleming uses the gambling setting in several locations in *Thrilling Cities*, resulting in a curious merging of Ian's identity with Bond's. The standout episode occurs in the Monte Carlo chapter, as he describes (in what he admits is a "slightly fictionalized account") how he is approached by an (unnamed) English woman who refuses to recognize any distinction between the author and his fictional hero. When Fleming explains that the gambler he has been observing evidently has a system, the woman replies, "I suppose James Bond's got an infallible system. . . . Why don't you let other people in on his secret? Tell me, or I'll never speak to you again."[39]

At this flattering moment of actually being *addressed* as James Bond, Ian accepts the challenge and simply explains his "system" or what he modestly calls the best way to win the price of a good dinner. When Fleming meets the woman again later that evening, it appears that "James Bond's" advice has yielded success: "Her eyes were shining. 'I've won a fortune' she said. 'Come and have a drink.'" Fleming proudly gloats about the success of his system, but the woman brings him back down to earth: "Your system's just another way of losing money. . . . Typical of James Bond to dream it up." She explains that she won a fortune not by following James Bond's elaborate system but by impulsively placing her final thousand francs on her own birthday number: "'What had clever Mister James Bond got to say to that?' she said scornfully."[40] In this sarcastic manner, she is asking Fleming to speak not *for* James Bond but rather *as* James Bond.

The blurring of roles between Bond and Fleming in *Thrilling Cities* plays on a similar idea to that developed in the next Bond novel, *You Only Live Twice* (1964)—namely, that Bond's adventures are a "fictionalized account" of Fleming's own intelligence operations. By flaunting his "license" to fictionalize, however, Fleming risks undermining the reader's belief in the travelogue as a nonfictional narrative. The reader, of course, *understands* that the James Bond novels are fictional narratives and that this is not the same as *believing* in them as accurate representations of real espionage missions or actual travels.

But the reader's expectations of the travelogue are different, and Ian's playing with the boundaries of fact and fiction may backfire. One's belief in the book's veracity may influence the reader's actual travel experiences in the world. Fleming even encourages this belief by providing sections at the end of each chapter called "Incidental Intelligence," containing information about the best places to stay, eat, and be entertained in the various cities he visits. Fleming states in his "Author's Note," "since they were provided for the most part by foreign correspondents of *The Sunday Times*, [they should] be of value to the traveller of today." Yet, Ian cannot resist the temptation of merging his own identity with that of his fictional hero, calling into question the realism (if not the authenticity) of his travelogue. For example, when Ian declares his special pleasure in "the smoke-filled drama of the casino and the momentary fever of the game," the phrasing clearly echoes the famous opening of *Casino Royale*.[41]

The overlapping of identities between author and character is most extreme in the New York chapter of *Thrilling Cities*. Ian here expresses his disappointment with a city that once enchanted and excited him. Throughout the book, there are signs of nostalgia and regret at the symptoms of global cultural decline. At the beginning of *Thrilling Cities*, Fleming stated his urge "to see the world, however rapidly, while it was still there to see"—an urgency that derives from fear that the "old world" is disappearing, being supplanted by the new. In New York, Fleming is already too late to record the city at its vibrant best, as he had known it during and shortly after World War II: "Each time I come back (and I have revisited the city every year since the war) I feel that it has lost more of its heart."[42]

Doubtless anticipating a hostile reaction from readers in the United States to this diatribe against the Big Apple, Fleming included a short story—"007 in New York"—in the 1964 American edition of *Thrilling Cities*, ostensibly to make amends for the negative descriptions in his New York chapter: Fleming introduces "a friend of mine with the dull name of James Bond, whose tastes and responses are not always my own and whose recent minor adventure in New York . . . may prove more cheerful in the reading."[43] Fleming not only attributes Bond a reality but also makes himself a fictional character in his narrative, the equivalent of Bond's role as protagonist in the novels.[44]

At first it seems that Bond, in "007 in New York," is charmed by the very features of the city that appall Fleming: "Bond liked the Times Square jungle—the hideous souvenir shops, the sharp clothiers, the giant feedomats, the hypnotic neon sign. . . . Here was the guts of New York, the living entrails." Yet, on further inspection, Bond's role is to amplify Fleming's negative views of New York rather than contrast them: he complains "that flavor had gone from all American food. Except the Italian. Everything tasted the same—a sort of neutral food taste." Like Ian, James Bond laments the passing of the "real" New York, staying at the Astor because "his other favourite quarters had gone. . . . What fun it had been in the old days! . . . Ah me! Yes, the Astor would do as well as another."[45] By the end of the story, 007 has become little more than a mouthpiece for Ian Fleming's lament for a lost New York.

This leads into the strongest lament in *Thrilling Cities* for another lost realm: the British Empire. Following the "incidental intelligence" about New York, Fleming notes his "constant depression to observe how little of our own influence was left in that great half of the world where we did so much of the pioneering. I cannot remember meeting a single Briton all the way from Hong Kong to New York." Ian further draws a depressing lesson from his trip around the world, about "the fantastically rapid contraction of our influence, commercial and cultural, over half the globe, and our apparent lack of interest in what can broadly be described as the Orient." Fleming suggests that renewal is possible only if "the spirit of adventure which opened the Orient to us can be rekindled [in] our youth."[46] With James Bond as his fellow traveler in *Thrilling Cities*, Ian invites the reader to share his "spirit of adventure" as well as his belief, however wishful, that Britain is still a global force to be reckoned with.

OFFENDING THE SHEIKS: *STATE OF EXCITEMENT*

Scholars who visit the Lilly Library, Indiana University at Bloomington, to research the Ian Fleming papers are delighted at being granted access to the precious original manuscripts of some of the most iconic works of fiction of the twentieth century. Of course, "manuscript" may be a misleading term, for Ian Fleming typed each new novel between January and March at Goldeneye, and so the original versions of the Bond novels are typescripts. Yet, many of the significant revisions and expansions of the typescripts are in holograph, adding a distinctly personal touch to the Fleming archive. The visiting scholar may pore to her heart's content over the typed and corrected pages of *Casino Royale*—the first Bond novel—and then delve into the fascinating leaves of *Goldfinger* (original title: "The Richest Man in the World"). We may make notes, of course, and, with the permission of the library staff, take photographs of these unique and groundbreaking novels. Only in one case are we instructed—politely but firmly—by a library staff member that there must be no photographs taken of the manuscript and no direct quotation of its contents: this is for *State of Excitement*, Ian Fleming's unpublished 1962 book about the oil-rich state of Kuwait.

The reasons for the ban on publishing, copying, or directly citing this manuscript are complex, but in effect the Kuwaiti royal family vetoed the project after Fleming had completed and delivered the book. The manuscript was reviewed by the Kuwait Oil Company—which had commissioned it—and they did not approve it due to objections by the Kuwaiti royal family. The sheiks felt that Fleming's narrative dwelt too much on the outlawry and romantic aspects of the country's colorful history—such as smuggling, banditry, and other illicit activities. Instead, the Kuwaiti royals wanted the book to emphasize the dramatic postwar transformation of Kuwait, made possible by the vast riches from the country's oil reserves, into a modern state, civilized in every respect, and boasting state-of-the-art transportation, technology, construction of modern skyscrapers, and advanced medicine. In Fleming's words, therefore, the book was "stillborn." *State of Excitement* still remains an anomaly as the only unpublished book by the creator of James Bond.

Even the title of the book demonstrates that Fleming was attracted to the romantic aspects of Kuwait's history rather than its modern civilization. From Ian's perspective, this presented the best story and also tied in with his lifelong fascination with buried treasure, smuggling, piracy, and crime. As the plots of novels such as *Live and Let Die*, *Diamonds Are Forever*, and *Goldfinger* demonstrate, Fleming had exploited the popular appeal of precious metals and stones and their illicit export to the most valuable markets or to fund SMERSH activities. In *State of Excitement*, the precious commodity that interests Fleming is oil, and the bonanza for the country was even greater.

The theme that most engages Ian's interest is Kuwait's dramatic transformation from one of the poorest countries in the world, before World War II, into one of the richest—in terms of per capita revenue—in the postwar era. The discovery of vast oil reserves in Kuwait has all the romance and drama of finding buried treasure at the end of a hunt—as the adventurers do in Robert Louis Stevenson's *Treasure Island* and H. Rider Haggard's *King Solomon's Mines*, two of Fleming's favorite adventure stories as a boy. But in this case, the treasure hunters are not a group of mercenary individuals or pirates but an entire nation that is thus able to use its newfound wealth to transform a medieval society into a modern state.

Throughout his narrative, Fleming develops a comparison between the discovery of oil wealth by Kuwait and a hypothetical English family who win the football pools and suddenly strike it rich beyond their wildest dreams. Fleming's use of this device has the obvious advantage of translating the thrills, opportunities, and challenges of sudden riches into a context the typical English reader could grasp. However, the somewhat undignified analogy—suggesting the sheiks were no better than an ordinary English family who struck lucky with a form of gambling—may have been part of the reason for their veto of the manuscript.

Fleming, of course, makes no claims to be writing as a scholar of indigenous cultures—such as his friend Patrick Leigh Fermor, whose book *The Traveller's Tree* (1950) was an essential source for the voodoo background in *Live and Let Die*. Nor was Ian an Arabist, equipped with knowledge of Islamic languages, culture, and history to understand the complexities of Kuwait's transformation. Fleming had originally hoped to include Kuwait on his first tour of the "thrilling cities of the world," but it was too far off his route for that journey, as well as the fact that Kuwait was a difficult place to access without the official support of the Kuwait Oil Company.

For Ian, Kuwait is—because of its oil—like a bank overflowing with riches that is likely to attract predatory criminals. Like a kind of Arabian Fort Knox, the country is a tempting target for villains as ambitious as Goldfinger. Although the oil reserves were originally exploited by a joint British-

American partnership, which combined to form the Kuwait Oil Company, Fleming points to the canny arrangements that prevent any non-Kuwaiti subject from owning land in the state and require foreign investors to form a fifty-fifty partnership with a Kuwaiti concern. This policy was designed to prevent the hemorrhaging of the state's resources overseas. Fleming is quite complimentary, even flattering, toward the Kuwaiti royals, showing how wisely the sheiks have managed their nation's immense fortune, singling out the present ruler, His Highness Shaikh Sir Abdullah al Salim al Sabah, for praise.

The provision of water for the population is perhaps the greatest benefit that the oil riches have bestowed on Kuwait, providing the resources for modern hydro-engineering. Those engineers, doctors, lawyers, and other professionals who came out from Europe to work in Kuwait to build the country's infrastructure are the unsung heroes of the book. They have those qualities that Fleming had lamented, in *Thrilling Cities*, were missing in the younger generation, primarily a sense of adventure, an embrace of risky ventures, and a love of distant travel. These are the qualities that Ian assigned to James Bond, of course, but which he feared were dying out in modern Britain. In Fleming's view, the creation of Kuwait as a modern state brought out the best of postwar human ambition, adventure, ingenuity, and cooperation. Not only does the economic opportunity offered by Kuwait attract the most adventurous and ambitious individuals, but it also produces cooperation between former wartime enemies—thus the Germans built the sewage system, while the British designed and constructed a new international airport.

Like the best travel writing, *State of Excitement* does not just record a set of information or facts about another country. Rather, it describes the writer's personal impressions of a new place and the different perspective brought about under the influence of contact with a location and culture dramatically different from his own. Fleming writes of being depressed by his first impressions of Kuwait, which included apparently barren desert as far as the eye could see; the proliferation of oil rigs, engineering works, and motor cars; and the ubiquitous smell of oil. Yet, Fleming comes to realize that the "lack" is in his own perception rather than the environment and that he has to adapt to his new surroundings in order to assess and appreciate them. In particular, Fleming is self-critical of his jaded European perspective, which eventually adjusted itself to a new landscape. If Kuwait presents more of a challenge to Fleming's powers as a writer than the cities he visited in *Thrilling Cities*, this is because of its profound difference from his familiar surroundings and the lack of amenities he normally expected on his travels. He describes, for example, how he began to perceive beauty in a landscape he had initially found desiccated and featureless.

Fleming also deploys humor to engage with and appeal to the Western reader in describing an unfamiliar place. Even the ongoing comparison of the Kuwaiti government with an English family winning the football pools was perhaps intended to be a kind of running gag designed to amuse the reader. But the humor can also function as a kind of social satire, especially concerning the alarming standard of driving and ignorance about auto mechanics that Fleming—always an enthusiastic motorist—found in Kuwait. For example, Fleming explains the reasons for frequent car breakdowns in Kuwait as due to the *bedu* (i.e., Bedouin) treating his automobile like his camel, capable of traveling for days without water. Consequently, the *bedu* neglects to put oil, gas, or water into his vehicle. The tone seems condescending toward the *bedu*'s primitive ignorance of modern transportation, but the analogy is intended to engage the British or American reader in a foreign culture.

Despite such occasional mirth at the expense of the *bedu* and their lack of familiarity with modern technologies, Fleming displays great respect for the nomadic tribesmen and also regret that they will be forced to adapt to modern "civilization." For example, he laments the idea that the *bedu* tribesmen will have to take "modern" jobs as taxi drivers or hotel workers. We see here the high value placed on "primitive" cultures and peoples that characterizes the Bond novels, leading Bond to idealize the Cayman Islander, Quarrel, in *Live and Let Die* and to prefer Darko Kerim's traditional ways to the modern Turks in *From Russia, with Love*.

Fleming even goes on to suggest a kind of modern conspiracy by the Kuwaiti authorities to censor the thrilling history of the Bedouin. If Fleming is right about this, then it is hardly surprising that the modern Kuwaiti rulers wished also to censor Fleming's book, in which he gives the *bedu* generally such positive representation. Perhaps like the Smiths—Fleming's imaginary English football pool–winning family—the sheiks had become embarrassed by their impoverished yet colorful ancestry and so wished it to be suppressed.

Ian also appeals to modern treasure hunters by telling a tale of a Royal Air Force jet laden with treasure—including perhaps Crown jewels—that crashed into the sea just off the Kuwaiti island of Failaka. Fleming suggests that modern dredging equipment—such as that used by his friend Jacques Cousteau, the famous oceanographer and explorer, on his expeditions—could be used to retrieve the mysterious treasure from the waters of the

Persian Gulf. With this anecdote, Fleming implies that the spirit of treasure hunting is still alive in modern times and that Kuwait offers a possibly unique trove.

Fleming's accounts of the history of smuggling and piracy in Kuwait form the most romantic and exciting parts of the book and are also the likely reason it was disliked by the sheiks. Doubtless, his accounts of rampant gold smuggling into India (where greater profits could be made) using gold parts for motor cars, airplanes, and the like to conceal the illicit hoard may be the stuff of adventure fiction, but they did not impress the Kuwaiti royals. Fleming's excited claims about the success of nineteenth-century pirates in Kuwait, for example, would surely not impress the modern leaders who wished to establish the legality, authority, and, above all, modernity of their state.

Yet another drawback to Fleming's manuscript is that, for all its fascination with the thrilling acquisition of wealth and valuable commodities such as gold, diamonds, and opium, it has little interest in the actual business of extracting oil. In acknowledging his lack of enthusiasm for the oil business, Fleming contrasts the extraction of oil unfavorably with the discovery of gold and diamonds. But it is implicitly insulting to the Kuwait Oil Company and the sheiks to suggest that they are involved in such a sordid business.

Fleming is acutely aware throughout of the strategic and economic importance of Kuwait and its oil to the West. He is especially impressed by the spirit of cooperation between Britain and the United States in Kuwait and compares it to the Anglo-American forces of Supreme Headquarters Allied Powers Europe under US General Eisenhower (who was just completing his second term as American president while Fleming was in Kuwait) during World War II. Fleming points out that Kuwait supplies Britain alone with 50 percent of its oil requirements and that therefore the protection of the country by the Western powers is essential to Britain's national security interests. In this context, Fleming raises the specter of Soviet bloc aggression toward Kuwait in order to steal its oil reserves.[47]

In Fleming's Bond novels, of course, the gold, diamond, and drug smuggler villains are usually working for the Soviet Union—SMERSH—and plundering Western-owned resources (such as the British and American gold reserves) in order to fund Soviet espionage operations and fifth-column activities in NATO countries. As a prime example, M speculates that Goldfinger with his gold-smuggling operation might "turn out to be the foreign banker, the treasurer so to speak, of SMERSH."[48] Fleming's innovative method of suggesting the potential role of Kuwait in future Cold War conflicts between East and West is apparent in an anecdote late in the book involving a scorpion.

At the beginning of *Diamonds Are Forever*, Fleming had used the scorpion as a powerful symbol of a predator (attacking and consuming a beetle) that then becomes prey to a more powerful creature—a man. Fleming again uses the scorpion, in this case as analogous to a Cold War confrontation, in *State of Excitement*. While in Kuwait, Fleming's host gives him a jar containing a scorpion and another jar containing a viper, and his first idea is to put the two creatures together and witness the violent struggle between them—an example of Ian as the cold observer fascinated by Darwinian struggle for existence and life-and-death battle between rivals.

However, in the end, the two creatures are placed on separate parts of the table, and Fleming ruminates on their apparent reluctance to fight. He suggests that the two creatures ignored each other because to attack might be suicidal. Fleming thus uses the natural analogy to illustrate the "mutually assured destruction" scenario in which each superpower (the United States and the Soviet Union) knows that an attack by one might well result in the nuclear annihilation of the entire world.

At the same time, the way in which each creature preserves its own territory, not risking an attack or invasion of the other's domain, is suggestive of the strategy of containment of Soviet influence that characterized US foreign policy under Truman (the "Truman doctrine") and Eisenhower. The United States and NATO (after its foundation in 1949) would tolerate the existence of Communism in the Soviet-controlled Eastern bloc but would seek to contain any expansion of its sphere of influence in Western Europe or Southeast Asia. To do so, the United States offered economic and military support for Greece, Turkey, and other nations it believed were threatened by Soviet Communism. This strategy provided a solution—if a potentially fragile one—to the threat of nuclear war.

Finally, the analogy of the scorpion also suggests that Kuwait's security—despite being an attractive target for robbers and invaders—will be protected by its strategic position between East and West. As long as it provides oil to the Western nations, Kuwait will be defended by these powerful allies against aggression from the East. The Soviet bloc would not risk attacking the small and wealthy country for fear of leading to military conflict and possible nuclear war. Lacking the military means to defend itself, Kuwait is as safe as a bank guarded by its powerful and fully armed security guards.

As with his other travel and nonfiction works, *The Diamond Smugglers* and *Thrilling Cities*, Fleming's title conveys a sense of danger, adventure, and exhilaration concerning a subject that might otherwise seem somewhat dry. Given Ian's own lack of interest in the oil business, this infusion of "excitement" was essential. In the case of *State of Excitement*, the title was worthy of a Bond novel or other spy thriller, but it conveyed disturbing connotations for the Kuwaiti sheiks. They wanted Kuwait to be perceived internationally as a model of transformation from poverty, rural nomadism, and "backwardness" in terms of technology to a marvel of modern civilization, technocracy, and wealth. Fleming's interest in the romantic, piratical, and scandalous aspects of Kuwait's history did not sit well with those who wanted Kuwait to be portrayed as a state not of excitement but of order, productivity, and prosperity. It therefore remains the only unpublished book written by Ian, a pity given its stirring depictions of Kuwait's dramatic history.

Taken as a whole, Ian Fleming's travel writings—a category that includes *The Diamond Smugglers*—reveal an important group of themes that fascinated his imagination throughout his career, indeed throughout his life. Travel—as an end in itself, pursued in a spirit of adventure—was a source of pleasure and excitement for Ian. It provided a "way of escape" from the dull office routine of working life in London as well as a respite from the dreary climate of his native country and, increasingly, the tensions of his marriage. Of course, Ian's annual working winter holidays at Goldeneye offered an important relief from the monotony of his regular job, but this had itself become part of his working routine as a novelist. Besides, that still left ten months remaining each year to find other sources of excitement. One reason Fleming took the Kuwait assignment, he tells us, is that it provided him with an opportunity to get out of Britain in November, one of his least favorite months.

Fleming was a gifted and patient observer of landscape, environment, wildlife, and behavior—both human and nonhuman—and he conveys to a remarkable extent the sights, sounds, smells, and atmosphere of the various foreign locations he visits. As a journalist, Fleming felt it his role to provide a faithful rendition of what he sees, hears, and experiences. At the same time—and as the titles of his books suggest—the real world was not enough for Fleming, either as a travel writer or as a novelist. He could not accept the mundane or predictable reality of his regular life but sought adventure, distraction, and, above all, fantasy on his travels overseas. To keep himself entertained and to enthrall his readers, Ian would at times embellish, magnify, or distort what he saw in the furnace of his own vivid and powerful imagination. In the Bond novels, Fleming had the advantage of creating a fictional persona who possessed glamor, courage, sex appeal, gadgets, and a flair for international adventure. When traveling without Bond, Ian needed to find other sources of excitement, and he discovered these in the exotic locations, intriguing histories, and unusual sights he encountered on his travels.

Thrilling themes and motifs such as smuggling, piracy, drug trafficking, organized crime, sexual adventure, high-stakes gambling, luxurious living, espionage, and intrigue feature in Fleming's travel writing just as they do in his fiction. What Kingsley Amis dubbed the "Fleming effect"—the use of meticulous detail, factual information (such as technical specs and brand names), and precise locations to lend a sense of realism to sometimes far-fetched plots—helped shape Fleming's fiction as not only entertainment but also a guide to the real world.[49] And so, too, with the nonfiction. If the actual world he encountered in his travels was not enough for Ian, he made up for it by penning a series of colorful, exuberant, original, and vivid picture postcards from various parts of the globe—each one signed, with a flourish, "From Fleming, with Love."

Chapter Twelve

The Iron Crab

No one could argue that Ian hadn't seen the end coming. In fact, the Bond novels provide evidence that he had been contemplating his own mortality for years. In *From Russia, with Love* (1957), Ian gave voice to these misgivings using one of Bond's key allies, Darko Kerim, who speculates on the likely end of his life after an existence defined by excess: "I drink and smoke too much. . . . Too many tensions and too much thinking. . . . Suddenly one day my heart will fail. The Iron Crab will get me as it got my father. But I am not afraid of The Crab. At least I shall have died from an honourable disease."[1] In this passage, Ian describes what he called the "iron crab," a threat that would haunt him in the 1960s despite the various successes of these years.

Characteristically, Ian tries to romanticize his health problems by making them essential to Kerim's bold, fearless personality. By describing the "iron crab" as an honorable death, Kerim makes his self-destructive excesses appear a form of heroism comparable to a soldier being killed in action. Ian's own father had died in battle, but the son was more likely to fall victim to his own destructive habits. In *Thunderball*, the symptoms of Fleming's malaise are given to Bond and treated more matter-of-factly through the critical gaze of M, who cites the medical officer's report: "Despite many previous warnings, he admits to smoking sixty cigarettes a day. . . . The officer's average daily consumption of alcohol is in the region of half a bottle of spirits of between sixty and seventy proof." Though the medical officer finds little evidence of deterioration in Bond's physical condition, M clearly thinks otherwise. Unlike M, Bond had not heeded the warning that the result of taking medicines "is a more highly poisoned condition which may become chronic disease."[2] Therefore, M sends Bond off to Shrublands for a health treatment.

It is ironic that Fleming's physical decline is represented in *Thunderball*, the novel that did more than any other to accelerate his deterioration. The draft of *Thunderball* was completed in March 1960, and although Fleming was dissatisfied with the manuscript, it received enthusiastic praise from his editors at Cape. Michael Howard wrote encouragingly that not only did Cape want to publish *Thunderball*, "but more than that, may I assure you that . . . I mean to sell just twice as many as before and I shall not rest until we do."[3]

But, unfortunately, not all readers of the novel were similarly enthusiastic. In March 1961, after McClory read an advance copy of *Thunderball*, he and Jack Whittingham petitioned the High Court to issue an injunction to stop publication, claiming that it plagiarized the screenplay they had collaborated on with Fleming along with Ernie Cuneo. The plagiarism case was heard in March 24, 1961, and although the court allowed the book to be published (given that copies had already been printed), the court's judgment explicitly left the way open for McClory to pursue further legal action. This he would eventually do in November 1963.

Thunderball was published by Cape on March 27, 1961. Two weeks later, Ian suffered a major heart attack at an editors' meeting of *The Sunday Times*. He was rushed to hospital and survived but was then confined to the London Clinic and the Dudley Hotel in Hove for several months while he recuperated. He was warned by his doctors, including his old friend Jack Beal, that unless he dramatically cut back his consumption of cigarettes and alcohol, he was likely to suffer another, possibly fatal, coronary. Ian's reaction to these warnings was in some ways typical: he wrote to Christopher Soames at the Ministry of Agricultural and Fisheries to ask Soames's advice "on the purest and finest liquor obtainable in England" due to the fact that "I am condemned for the rest of my life to three ounces of hard liquor per day."[4] Ian was also amused to learn that *The Times* had prepared his obituary, and he was determined to get hold of it.

Ian suffered acutely from boredom during this period of convalescence and chafed against the restrictions placed on his writing. He was forbidden the use of a typewriter lest he overexert himself by trying to write a new Bond novel. Even his correspondence had to be dictated. Ian found a way around this prohibition by requesting paper and pens, then setting to work on a children's story for his son, Caspar, about a magical car with special powers of transformation. His name for the car—and the book—was Chitty-Chitty-Bang-Bang.

Writing the story was intended to take Ian's mind off the perils to his health, but it served another purpose as well. It gave Ian the chance to explore a different side to his writing, creating a story for children rather than the "warm-blooded heterosexuals in railway trains, airplanes and beds" that he claimed he wrote for.[5] *Chitty* allowed the lighter, more playful side to Ian's character to find expression as well as giving an outlet for his parental affections for Caspar. The story is told with enjoyment and whimsy, describing the lovable Pott family—Caractacus, Mimsie, Jemima, and Jeremy—as they acquire and enjoy the extraordinary car.

The car was based on a series of aero-engined racing cars called "Chitty Bang Bang" built by Count Louis Zborowski in the 1920s. The fantasy car, which can transform into an airplane and a hovercraft as well as a high-speed road vehicle, reflected Ian's lifelong fascination with unique and exotic automobiles. In some respects, the "magical car" Ian invented is related to the high-tech Aston Martin DB-III he gives Bond to drive in *Goldfinger*. But it is more significant as an inspiration for the far more elaborate vehicles in the Bond films, including cars with ejector seats, cars that can fly, and amphibious cars that can travel underwater.

Significantly, Ian endows the "machine" Chitty with human characteristics. At one point the car is referred to as "by now . . . really a member of the family too," and when the Pott family members congratulate Chitty after it takes them to the Goodwin Sands, away from the crowds at the beach at Dover, Ian writes, "her big gleaming headlights seemed to dip slightly in modesty and shyness just as Jemima's do when she's complimented on doing particularly well at her lessons."[6]

The magical car is the product of Ian's enduring interest in nonhuman characters and the hybrid of human and machine. As we have seen, Ian often attributed personalities and feelings to birds, trees, plants, and flowers in the Bond novels. Yet, his passion for mechanical life is just as strong as his love of nature, as illustrated by the numerous weapons, advanced vehicles, and ingenious gadgets that populate the Bond novels. As we recall, Bond was described as a "wonderful machine" by Mathis in *Casino Royale*. In *Chitty*, Fleming invents another "wonderful machine" with human characteristics, a humanoid car that is the stuff of fairy tales and children's fantasies.

The story is told in a voice designed to appeal to the youthful reader—doubtless with Caspar in mind—and Fleming often addresses the child's experience and perspective, as when he writes, "being marooned on the Goodwin Sands in the middle of the English Channel is enough to frighten you." He compares the Potts' act of setting a fuse to detonate the secret cache of weapons and explosives to the child reader trying to light a firework. Later, Ian playfully quizzes the child reader on the coded meaning of Chitty's registration number, "GEN II," which "could be read in two ways? Do you see what they saw in the letters and numbers?"[7]

But the story is also an homage to the engineering brilliance of Commander Pott—who significantly has the same rank in the navy as James Bond and Ian Fleming. Caractacus's first name is also derived from an English hero, "the British chieftain who was a sort of Robin Hood in AD48 and led an English army against the Roman invaders."[8] Like Bond and Fleming, Caractacus has served his country in the armed forces, while his eminent namesake defended the country against foreign invaders. Fleming depicts the modern hero as an engineer, explorer, and inventor, a man who devotes his life to technology and gadgets and is part of a worldwide craze for invention in the postwar era, when "everything is being invented or improved all the time . . . whether by teams of scientists in huge factories and laboratories or by lonely men sitting and just thinking in tiny workshops." Fleming unsurprisingly sympathizes with the "lonely man" Pott, who eventually sells the rights to his invention, the "toot sweet," and uses the proceeds to purchase an old neglected but beautiful car, a "twelve-cylinder, eight-litre, supercharged Paragon Panther."[9]

Although written for children, *Chitty* has a number of parallels and echoes of the James Bond novels. It is as though Ian, unable or unwilling to work on a Bond novel while convalescing, uses his children's story to reflect back on his literary career and showcase some of the highlights of the James Bond adventures. The story also parallels episodes from his own life and travels in England and France.

Notably, the Potts' journey to the Kent coast replays Fleming's frequent journeys between London and Saint Margaret's Bay or Sandwich, when he also took the A20 Dover road. The trip also recalls Bond's drive in his Bentley on the A20 toward Maidstone, in *Moonraker*, on his way to Drax's base on the coast between Dover and Deal. Bond had noticed the Goodwin Sands at low tide in *Moonraker*, describing them as "golden and tender in the sparkling blue of the Straits," and this is where the Potts finally alight for their picnic.[10] There are other echoes of *Moonraker* in *Chitty*, such as the hidden cache of weapons and explosives buried under a French cliff. This concealed armory brings to mind the Moonraker rocket itself, a deadly weapon lurking beneath the White Cliffs of Kent.

However, the most direct allusion to Bond's adventures in *Chitty*—aside from the gadget-laden car itself—occurs after the Potts have escaped from Joe the Monster's gang in the aero-car (after the car magically sprouts wings and flies). The family takes refuge in the Hotel Splendide in Calais, which is, of course, the name of Bond's hotel in *Casino Royale*. The seaside resort of Royale-les-Eaux, based on Le Touquet, is not far from Calais, and the Potts thus follow in Bond's footsteps. They celebrate their victory over the villain (having destroyed Joe's cache of weapons) by enjoying "a delicious dinner in the bright and cheerful dining room" of the Splendide—echoing Bond's triumphant meal with Vesper after defeating Le Chiffre at baccarat.[11] Unfortunately, while the parents are asleep, their two children are kidnapped from the Splendide by Joe's gang, mimicking Vesper's kidnapping from the hotel by Le Chiffre. Both abductions are acts of revenge by the enraged villain and occur due to the negligence of their assigned protectors—the adult Potts and James Bond, respectively. While the children are eventually rescued unscathed, Bond endures a savage beating at the hands of his enemy.

Ian is writing for at least two audiences in *Chitty*. He explicitly addresses the child reader who probably knows nothing of Bond but is enthralled by the adventures of the Pott family and its "magical car." However, he is also writing for the adult reader, who probably has read at least some of the Bond novels and will note the frequent allusions to the adventures, locations, cars, and villains of 007. As so often in his career, Ian demonstrates his mastery of his audience—or audiences—by being able to write engaging stories that will appeal to a wide range of readers. Had Ian lived longer, it is quite possible he would have continued to write children's fiction and thereby established a third dimension to his literary career—building on his spy novels and travel writing.

Having received a note of good wishes from Michael Howard while in residence at the clinic, Ian replied (in a playful allusion to his magical car), "I shall be firing on all cylinders again before too long. Meanwhile I am writing a children's book, so you will see that there is never a moment, even on the edge of the tomb, when I am not slaving for you." Ian was greatly encouraged by the enthusiastic response from the "Factory" at Cape, Howard writing enthusiastically about Ian's "invention of genius" and encouraging him to write more episodes.[12] While praising Ian's creativity, Howard clearly had one eye firmly on Cape's likely profits from the venture, expecting (or at least hoping for) a future series of lucrative children's stories. Ian's complaints about "slaving" for Cape while at death's door were only half joking. Ian, too, was aware of the potential commercial appeal of the story and offered to write a book a year. Sadly, this plan was not to be realized, for he did not live to see the publication of *Chitty-Chitty-Bang-Bang: The Magical Car* in three volumes, issued between 1964 and 1965.

Meanwhile, Ian's literary stock had been boosted by *Life* magazine's issue for March 17, 1961, which contained an article titled "The President's Voracious Reading Habits" by Hugh Sidey, listing President John F. Kennedy's ten favorite books of all time. The selection included Fleming's *From Russia, with Love* at number nine, further distinguished by being the only work of fiction on the list. This gave a significant boost to Fleming's popularity and presence in the United States, which was, of course, a necessary market for any film version of Bond. According to Christopher Booker, the revelation "that one of the most fervent Bond readers was President Kennedy" meant that "in 1961 and 1962, the sales of Bond books on both sides of the Atlantic had soared."[13]

John Cork has questioned this narrative about the impact of Kennedy's endorsement on Fleming's book sales in the United States, arguing that there were not enough copies of Fleming's novels in circulation stateside to meet an increased demand:

> In March 1961 no ready supply of James Bond books existed on the shelves of American bookstores. Macmillan published the hardback of *From Russia, with Love*—the title cited by JFK—nearly four years earlier. Signet published the paperback in September 1958. It was still in its first printing with no serious plans for a second. Without hardbacks and paperbacks available, the brief mention [of Kennedy's choice of *From Russia, with Love*] in *Life* could not translate into legions of new readers, and it did not.[14]

However, Fleming was taking steps to amend this shortfall by negotiating a paperback deal with New American Library, who would begin publishing his novels in the early 1960s. Readers in the United States could obtain *From Russia, with Love* as part of the *Gilt-Edged Bond* omnibus (for which Graham Greene had backed out of his agreement to write a preface, much to Ian's chagrin), released in July 1961, and the US paperback of *For Your Eyes Only* was released in June of that year.[15] Unfortunately, Ian's current US publisher, Viking—with whom he had signed after moving from Macmillan in 1959—was expressing doubts about Ian's latest offering, *The Spy Who*

Loved Me. Thomas Guinzberg, head of Viking, was concerned that this novel, "while it is certainly acceptable Fleming, is not quite top-grade Fleming."[16] He pointed out that unlike Cape in the United Kingdom, Viking had not yet established the market for Bond and therefore needed a more conventional, Bond-focused Fleming novel to consolidate its readership. Fleming refused to concede, saying he had nothing to offer as a replacement for *The Spy Who Loved Me*.

There was more encouraging news in the form of the film deal Ian made with Harry Saltzman and "Cubby" Broccoli's EON Productions. Given the legal controversy surrounding *Thunderball*—the obvious candidate for film treatment, having originally begun as a screenplay—EON's choice of *Dr. No* as the first Bond novel to be filmed was fortuitous. The deal was signed in June 1961, giving EON a six-month option on all the novels except *Casino Royale* (the rights to which had been sold separately). As filming of *Dr. No* in Jamaica began in the winter of 1962, Ian was busily writing his tenth Bond novel, *On Her Majesty's Secret Service*. Fleming was quite involved in the production, his role including securing a position for Christopher Blackwell—the son of his Jamaican lover Blanche—as recruiter for local musical talent.

In addition to the anxieties of the *Thunderball* legal saga, Ian's severe heart attack and long recuperation, and the humiliating reception of *The Spy Who Loved Me*, this period involved another new anxiety: the Flemings were again moving house. Due to Ann's unhappiness at White Cliffs at Saint Margaret's Bay, Ian had agreed to a move inland to the Old Palace at Bekesbourne, near Canterbury. This had seemed a promising compromise, being a grander house but still in Ian's favorite county of Kent, with access to Ian's beloved Royal St George's golf course. Ann had also lost interest in visiting Goldeneye and tried to convince Ian to sell the Jamaican house in order to buy something bigger in England. Ian had no intention of relinquishing his Jamaican paradise but realized that he needed to compromise with Ann's wishes if their marriage was to survive.

When Ann discovered Warneford Place, a Grade II–listed eighteenth-century mansion in Sevenhampton, Wiltshire, she fell in love with it. Ian was not convinced and balked at the expense and delay of the extensive renovations—effectively, rebuilding—proposed by Ann. But he wanted to please Ann and, as he wrote to his mother, "I am not happy about it [Sevenhampton Place] myself but it's quite impossible being married unless you are prepared to compromise."[17] They purchased the property in 1959, but the renovations were so extensive and costly that they didn't fully move in until June 1963, the year before Ian's death.

In truth, Ian never grew to love their new home. It was too large, even ostentatious, for his taste, a far cry from the Spartan bungalow at Goldeneye or the modest coastal property at White Cliffs. It was remote from the locations he preferred, where he felt at home, such as the Kent coast and London, where he was born, spent his war years, and had always worked (currently, at his office in Mitre Court, Fleet Street, which he had leased in 1959). Warneford Place—also known as Sevenhampton Place—was, unlike White Cliffs, a long drive from Ian's favorite golfing venue of Royal St George's at Sandwich. As a consolation, Huntercombe golf course—one of Ian's haunts from his Nettlebed days—could be reached by car in an hour or so.

Ian's misgivings about the move were social as well as environmental. He dreaded the prospect of having Ann's highbrow Oxford don friends over to tea and of filling long hours with dreary walks along country lanes. It was too far from the sea, Ian's personal lifeline and the most important stimulus for his imagination. Because Ann was not content with the existing house—Warneford Place, a forty-bedroomed manor house that at least had some history and character—the Flemings were involved in a vast expense of construction. However, Ann insisted it was the house in the country she had always wanted—in beautiful Sevenhampton, Wiltshire, within striking distance of her friends in Oxford but offering the tranquility of rural life. Sevenhampton was, therefore, Ann's choice from the very beginning. And Ian agreed to invest in the renovations because he wanted to repair not just the house but their damaged and frayed relationship.

However, Ian complained to Amherst Villiers, the engineer who built the supercharger for his (and Bond's) 4.5-liter Bentley, that he spent his time in Wiltshire cutting nettles and removing mushrooms from his suits due to the dampness caused by the nearby lake. Villiers had also recently completed a portrait of Ian to be included in the special edition of his tenth Bond novel, *On Her Majesty's Secret Service*. With this proof of Villiers's artistic gifts in hand, Ian then had the brainwave of asking for Villiers's help with the illustrations of *Chitty-Chitty-Bang-Bang*. Although he was happy with the general illustrations by John Burningham, he realized that Cape's regular illustrators lacked the necessary technical knowledge to produce a convincing drawing of his "magical car." He asked Villiers to produce illustrations that were "really snazzy looking to excite the imagination of children between about 7 and 10."[18]

There were some compensations in the move to Wiltshire. Not only was Fleming thinking of Caspar in writing *Chitty*, but the relocation to rural Sevenhampton also had the advantage of being ideal for Caspar to run about. In order to make Sevenhampton, a vast property in its extensive grounds, feel more like his home as well as Ann's, Ian installed a set of expensive custom-made bookshelves for his collection of rare first editions of landmark works, including Darwin's *On the Origin of Species* and Marx and Engels's *Communist Manifesto*. Ian had assembled the collection over many years, using the expertise and thriftiness of his rare book dealer Percy Muir, also a key figure in *The Book Collector*, which Ian took over from Kemsley in 1952. Ian contributed forty-four volumes to Muir's exhibition "Printing and the Mind of Man" held in July 1963 at Earl's Court and the British Museum, but the majority of his collection had remained in storage for years. He now arranged his outstanding display of rare first editions at Sevenhampton, each in its own black box embossed with the family crest, in the newly built shelves.

Ironically, on moving to their new home in Wiltshire, Ian became an honorary "Moonraker"—the local term for the natives of the county. The term—which apparently has no connection with the title of Ian's 1955 novel—derives from a bit of local lore involving some rural smugglers in Wiltshire, at the time when the county was on the smuggling route between the south coast and the center of England. As the legend goes, one bright moonlit night, these smugglers were trying to retrieve a cache of contraband kegs of French brandy from the village pond with rakes, when they were discovered by excisemen (revenue officers). To avoid being prosecuted, they assumed the roles of simple "yokels" and told the officer that they were "raking the moon." The excisemen, dismissing them as backward "country folk," rode off and left them to recover their booty. Ian no doubt relished this ruse of deception that left these smugglers with their trove of contraband and enabled them to escape the law. He himself enjoyed adopting a similar deception, that of a simple writer of pulp fiction who dashed off his novels in a white heat in Jamaica, did not take them very seriously, and never went over them again.

The reality was that Ian was a dedicated professional author who worked hard on his craft and took his writing seriously indeed. He was also deeply hurt by the savage attacks on his works in publications such as *The Twentieth-Century*, *The Manchester Guardian*, and *The Spectator*.[19] Ian's typescripts, housed in the Lilly Library, provide ample evidence of his painstaking craft, involving research, revision, and rewriting of each of his novels. In his own way, Ian was a literary "moonraker"—using a pose of simplicity and diffidence to deceive readers and critics about the true extent and purpose of his labors. Likewise, Sir Hugo Drax, the villain of his third novel, is also a type of "moonraker"—he has deceived the British people into thinking that he is a benevolent, generous "national hero" donating his personal fortune to furnish Britain with an atomic weapon. Ian—who had become such a master of deception during his years in Naval Intelligence in World War II—always had a fascination for those who could outwit the law and the critics, even when they were branded as villains.

With these complex personal and professional factors affecting Ian's life, a great deal was at stake when he began his tenth James Bond novel, *On Her Majesty's Secret Service*, in January 1962 at Goldeneye. With the new and very expensive property at Sevenhampton to restore and maintain, he and Ann could not rely on the hoped-for success of the film of *Dr. No* to finance this project. Ian also had his health to consider, realizing that nothing would be the same after his heart attack the previous April. Ian was the first to realize that he was living—and writing—on borrowed time.

Given his health problems, Ian also had to make financial provision for the future of Caspar, whom he had signed up for Eton at his birth. With an expensive private education in prospect and other expenses of raising a son, Ian knew he had to deliver a book that would impress readers and—above all—sell many copies and provide the basis for a future film. The production of *Dr. No* underway in Jamaica proved to be an inspiration rather than a distraction to his creativity, because Ian produced one of his strongest novels, one that would eventually form the basis of one of the most impressive Bond films.

Even as his own marriage to Ann was deteriorating—worsened by the extramarital affairs of both partners—Ian boldly offered Bond the prospect of a happy wedded future in *On Her Majesty's Secret Service*. James's passionate feelings for Tracy lead him to take a decisive step further than he did with Vesper in *Casino Royale*, where he had been on the "brink" of proposing marriage. In *On Her Majesty's Secret Service*, he finally proposes with the simple yet heartfelt words, "Tracy. I love you. Will you marry me?" Her joyful acceptance seems to offer Bond a way out of the "dirty, dangerous" past of espionage, as he promises not to get hurt in finishing the Blofeld business: "For once I'll run away if someone starts any shooting."[20] In Peter Hunt's remarkably faithful 1969 adaptation of *On Her Majesty's Secret Service*, starring George Lazenby and Diana Rigg, Bond's proposal takes place in the romantic setting of a barn during a blizzard, after his escape from Piz Gloria, as the couple hide from Blofeld's men. In the film, Bond makes clear that his marriage to Tracy means he will give up his profession as a secret agent and pledge himself to a wedded future: "I'll have to find something else to do."[21]

Ian's own misgivings about the hazards of marriage nonetheless make an appearance in *On Her Majesty's Secret Service* when Bond has a nightmare in which he has become a domesticated social husband, a kind of trophy for Tracy. On waking, though, Bond reassures himself, "it wouldn't be like that! Definitely not. He would still have his tough, exciting life, but now there would be Tracy to come home to." In Ian's novel, Bond evidently wants the best of both worlds: he still needs his personal freedom and professional identity but believes he can find a balance with domestic happiness. The locations for Bond and Tracy's marriage ceremony and honeymoon also seem auspicious in light of Ian's history. The couple are wed in Munich, the city where Ian studied German as a young man in preparation for his Foreign Office exam. Under the influence of heady nostalgia, Ian decides to send Bond and Tracy for their honeymoon in Kitzbühel, because—as Bond tells Tracy's father—"I love that place. So does she." Given Ian's recollection of his time in Kitzbühel as "the time when the sun always shone," the choice of honeymoon location seems benign.[22]

The prospect of the drive to Kitzbühel incites Bond to take the roof of their car down, fatally exposing them to Blofeld's attack from his and Irma Bunt's Maserati. Fleming's reference to the warlike past of the Tyrol region, "where blood had been shed between warring armies for centuries," is another omen of impending doom. Even Bond's uncharacteristically patient gesture of asking Tracy (who is driving) to let Blofeld's car pass theirs—believing that "we've got all the time in the world"—is a moment of folly that has tragic consequences, for it allows the hail of bullets that ends Tracy's life.[23] Had Bond agreed to Tracy's offer to "lose him," by racing ahead of Blofeld's Maserati, it would have saved her life.

If Bond's past belonged to Ian Fleming, his future increasingly became the property of EON Productions. In the spring of 1963, Ian visited the on-location film production of *From Russia with Love*, the second Bond novel filmed by EON, in Istanbul, marking his return to the city where he had witnessed the chaos of ethnic riots by Turks against Greeks in 1955. Like other visits to places he had been to in his prime, this was a poignant reminder of his physical decline. Also present on the set, as one of the screenwriters, was Len Deighton, who had published his debut novel *The Ipcress File* the previous year. Heralded as a fresh approach to spy fiction, *Ipcress* was also recognized as being "anti-Bond" in its rejection of the glamor, romance, and upper-class trappings of Fleming's hero. As Donald McCormick writes, "*The Ipcress File* was an instant success. 'Better than Fleming,' said some critics, though it must be admitted this was more due to their dislike of Fleming than their love of Deighton."[24]

Deighton had been hired to write a draft of the screenplay for *From Russia with Love*, though he soon left the production team, and his contributions were not credited in the final film. But Deighton's success as a novelist was a reminder of the new competitors emerging in the field of espionage fiction, challengers to Bond's supremacy as the world's most famous spy. Ian was critical of Deighton's writing, protesting in a letter to William Plomer in May 1964, "I simply can't be bothered with his kitchen sink writing & all this Nescafé. . . . I think Capes should send him to Tahiti or somewhere & get him to 'tell a story.'"[25] The fact that a large section of *Ipcress* was set at a US military base on Taiwe Atol, an exotic fictional location in the South Pacific, was apparently lost on Ian.

Many of the letters Ian wrote in the last year of his life begin by admitting his precarious health. The extent of his physical decline was on display during the party he threw after the premiere of EON's *From Russia with Love* on October 10, 1963. Accompanied by his doctor, he attended the premiere at the Odeon Leicester Square and had purchased large amounts of caviar and champagne for the party following the film at their elegant home in Victoria Square. But, finding the social occasion overwhelming, Ian went to bed early, leaving his guests to wonder what had happened to their generous but elusive host. For Ian, the pleasures of fame and wealth had come too late. When his friend Selby Armitage asked him, near the end of his life, if he enjoyed being famous, Ian replied despondently, "Ashes, old boy. Just ashes. You've no idea how bored one gets with the whole silly business."[26]

Ian returned to Jamaica in January 1964 to write his latest novel in the Bond series: the book that, Fergus Fleming notes, "he had decided would be the last Bond novel."[27] *The Man with the Golden Gun* returned Bond to Jamaica for a decisive showdown with the Spanish hitman Francisco Scaramanga. Yet, despite the familiar setting, the novel makes it clear that both Bond and Jamaica have changed, and not for the better. Bond is sent on the job as a kind of suicide mission, having attempted to assassinate M under the effect of brainwashing by the Soviets. As in *From Russia, with Love*, Bond is almost killed at the end of the novel by a poisoned weapon wielded by his antagonist, demonstrating the loss of his killer instincts.

Like previous Bond villains, Scaramanga discloses his evil intentions by an act of violence against birds. Two "kling kling" birds, with a "metallic clangour of song unlike the song of any other bird in the world," are being fed by Tiffy, who runs the bordello at 3½ Love Lane. Scaramanga's brutal act of shooting the birds—which "disintegrated against the violet backdrop of the dusk, the scraps of feathers and pink flesh blasting out of the yellow light of the café into the limbo of the deserted street like shrapnel"—recalls the avian atrocities committed by the villains in "For Your Eyes Only" as well as by the "Robber" in *Live and Let Die.*[28] At the end of his career, Ian's love of natural beauty and bird life in particular is just as intense, reflected in his villainizing of those who are cruel to defenseless creatures.

Jamaica, in *The Man with the Golden Gun*, is no longer the island of idyllic natural beauty as it appeared in *Live and Let Die* but is now an ugly tourist trap colonized by American money and visitors. Bond's mission takes him to the south coast, which Ian states "is not as beautiful as the north" (where Ian, of course, lived). Bond's arrival at Kingston is dystopian as, rather than experiencing the island's natural beauty, Bond is confronted with the trappings of tourism like the crassly commercial Kingston airport shop with "piles of over-decorated native ware." Instead of the refreshing breezes of the mountains, Bond suffers as, through "the slatted jalousies a small breeze, reeking of the mangrove swamps, briefly stirred the dead air and then was gone."[29] It is sadly apparent that, for Ian, the thrill even of Jamaica had eroded.

In 1964, Ian's health continued to decline, worsened by a bout of pleurisy that followed a reckless game of golf at Easter in the rain, followed by a drive home in wet clothes. Ian was again confined to hospital, then sent to recuperate at the Hove, where, as he had done while living at White Cliffs, he spent many hours gazing out to sea. A devastating emotional blow came with the death of Ian's mother on July 27, 1964. Their relationship had been troubled from his early ignominious exits from Eton and Sandhurst and failure to gain a place in the Foreign Office. The most stressful point in their mother-child bond had undoubtedly come with their conflict over Monique, but there were more recent humiliations, such as the lawsuit against Eve filed by Bapsy Pavry over the affections of the octogenarian Marquis of Winchester. Yet, Eve had generally been supportive and caring toward her second son, and the affection in Ian's letters to her, addressed to "Darling Mama," is palpable. With the loss of his only remaining parent, combined with the disintegration of his marriage, Ian felt that he was alone and vulnerable in a hostile world.

Aside from his writing, Ian's chief pleasure in life remained golf, although following his heart attack he could no longer compete on the links as strenuously as in the past. Despite their move to Sevenhampton, a long drive from the Kent coast, Ian still returned, as though by homing instinct, to the Royal St George's golf course. In the summer of 1964, Ian learned that he was to be elected captain of the Royal St George's. Deeply touched by this honor, he and Ann drove down to Sandwich for the celebratory dinner at the club. After the dinner on August 11, at the very pinnacle of his personal triumph, Ian suffered a major heart attack. He was rushed to hospital in Canterbury, the same route Bond had followed in *Moonraker*. But this time there was to be no hero to save the day and no miraculous recovery. He died in the early hours of August 12, 1964, on his son, Caspar's, twelfth birthday. He was buried in Saint James Churchyard, Sevenhampton, in Wiltshire—ironically the location that he had enjoyed least of his various homes.

At the memorial service organized for Ian by his half sister Amaryllis Fleming at Saint Bartholomew's Church on September 15, 1964, Ian's friend and mentor William Plomer gave the memorial address. Plomer declared that Ian had, in James Bond, created a "romantic myth" for the modern age, a necessary source of escape and hope for the postwar generation battered by years of austerity. He also defended Ian against those who criticized his popularity—noting that some claimed Fleming was "not their cup of tea," Plomer points out that Fleming's works are not "cups of tea" but something much more stimulating. He also emphasized Ian's wartime service as a vital part of his life's work, pointing out that it was the dedicated service and brilliant administrative efforts of those like Fleming that "allows us to sit in judgement on him today."[30]

In a deeply personal address, Plomer further memorialized Ian as "an entertainer of millions and for us a friend never to be forgotten." Quoting Admiral John Godfrey's high opinion of his former assistant in the Naval Intelligence Division, Plomer described Ian as a "war-winner" and referred insightfully to the "several different Ians" who were "quite separate."[31] It is hard to dispute the claim that Ian was a multifaceted personality or that he liked to compartmentalize his life by keeping his various friends, lovers, and pursuits separate. Yet, however distinct and complex these identities or lives may have been, they had all been confined to—and dependent on—the single body that now lay buried in Saint James Churchyard. Ian Fleming had passed from the world at the age of fifty-six. Like the scorpion preying on the beetle in the opening chapter of *Diamonds Are Forever*, the iron crab had finally claimed its victim.

Notes

PROLOGUE

1. Wikipedia, s.v. "The Carlton Hotel, London," last updated June 30, 2020, 22:13, https://en.wikipedia.org/wiki/Carlton_Hotel,_London.

2. Schwerin, who had been sent by a former chief of the German General Staff, also recommended that a squadron of Royal Navy battleships be sent to the Baltic and that Royal Air Force bombers should be stationed in France. These suggestions were passed to Chamberlain, who considered them "provocative." The Foreign Office commented that the German army seemed to want the British to save them from the Nazis.

1. SPYWAY

1. Thomas Pellatt, *Boys in the Making* (London: Methuen, 1936), 227.

2. Paul Ferguson, "Fleming. Valentine Fleming," The Pipes of War Production Blog, October 5, 2012, http://thepipesofwar.com/production-blog/?p=1205.

3. Ferguson, "Fleming. Valentine Fleming."

4. "Over by Christmas," The National WWI Museum and Memorial, accessed November 24, 2020, https://www.theworldwar.org/explore/exhibitions/past-exhibitions/over-christmas.

5. John Pearson, *Ian Fleming: The Notes* (London: Queen Anne Press, 2020), 140.

6. Amaryllis Fleming—Ian's half sister—had a less harsh assessment of Val's will, which she revealed to John Pearson: "I don't think that Ian's father thought of it [the will] as punitive at all. He would have assumed that his wife would marry again and that she would marry someone with so much money that she would not need his" (Pearson, *Notes*, 163). Amaryllis also referred to Val as "a sort of saint" (162).

7. Cited in Frank McClynn, *Robert Louis Stevenson* (London: Pimlico, 1994), 408.

8. Gary Giblin, *James Bond's London: A Reference Guide to Locations* (London: Daleon, 2001), 14.

9. Giblin, *James Bond's London*, 117.

10. Giblin, *James Bond's London*, 23.

11. Ian Fleming, *Moonraker* (Las Vegas: Thomas and Mercer, 2012), 7.

12. Fleming, *Moonraker*, 7.

13. Andrew Lycett, *Ian Fleming* (London: Phoenix, 1996), 10.

14. Ben Macintyre, *For Your Eyes Only: Ian Fleming + James Bond* (London: Bloomsbury, 2008), 15.

15. "Spyway School," Spyway School (blog), accessed November 24, 2020, http://spywayschool.blogspot.com.

16. Pearson, *Notes*, 186.

17. Pearson, *Notes*, 322.

18. Pellatt, *Boys in the Making*, 271.

19. Pellatt, *Boys in the Making*, 195.

20. Pellatt, *Boys in the Making*, 196.

21. Pearson, *Notes*, 321–22.

22. Pellatt, *Boys in the Making*, 240.

23. Pellatt, *Boys in the Making*, 211.

24. Pearson, *Notes*, 322.

25. Pellatt, *Boys in the Making*, 199.

26. Pearson, *Notes*, 322.

27. Pearson, *Notes*, 186.

28. Pellatt, *Boys in the Making*, 133.

29. Macintyre, *For Your Eyes Only*, 15.

30. Pellatt, *Boys in the Making*, 133.

31. Pellatt, *Boys in the Making*, 213, 214.

32. Pellatt, *Boys in the Making*, 226–27.

33. Pellatt, *Boys in the Making*, 228, 227.

34. Pellatt, *Boys in the Making*, 227.

35. Pearson, *Notes*, 323.

36. Pearson, *Notes*, 186.

37. Letter from Ian Fleming to his mother, Ian Fleming Publications, https://www.ianfleming.com/ian-fleming/.

38. Lycett, *Ian Fleming*, 10.

39. Maud Russell, *A Constant Heart: The War Diaries of Maud Russell 1938–1945*, ed. Emily Russell (Stanbridge, Dorset: Dovecote, 2017), 80.

40. "Spyway School."

41. Pearson, *Notes*, 322.

42. Lycett, *Ian Fleming*, 10–11.

43. Pearson, *Notes*, 324.

44. Pellatt, *Boys in the Making*, 36.

45. Pellatt, *Boys in the Making*, 47, 39, 49.

46. Pearson, *Notes*, 323. *Moonfleet* (1898), an adventure story of smuggling, treasure, and seafaring, is the second novel published by English author John Meade Falkner (1858–1932). The novel is largely set on the Dorset coast, close to the location of Durnford School.

47. Pearson, *Notes*, 162.

48. Lycett, *Ian Fleming*, 10.

49. Lycett, *Ian Fleming*, 10.

50. One of Hester's novels, *Ever Thine*, was set in a boys' prep school based on Durnford. Coincidentally, it was published by Jonathan Cape in 1951, two years before Ian published *Casino Royale* with the same house.

51. Ian Fleming, *On Her Majesty's Secret Service* (Las Vegas: Thomas and Mercer, 2012), 59.

52. Nick Britten, "Ian Fleming 'Used 16th Century Spy as Inspiration for James Bond,' *Telegraph*, October 30, 2008, https://www.telegraph.co.uk/news/uknews/3285886/Ian-Fleming-used-16th-century-spy-as-inspiration-for-James-Bond.html .

53. Pearson, *Notes*, 187.

54. John Pearson, *The Life of Ian Fleming* (London: Bloomsbury, 2003), 13.

55. Pearson, *Notes*, 187.

56. Ivar Bryce, *You Only Live Once*: *Memories of Ian Fleming* (London: Weidenfield & Nicholson, 1984), 1, 3.

57. Bryce, *You Only Live Once*, 39, 40–41.

58. Bryce, *You Only Live Once*, 16.

59. Lycett, *Ian Fleming*, 17.

60. Ian Fleming, *The Spy Who Loved Me* (Las Vegas: Thomas and Mercer, 2012), 46.

61. Bryce, *You Only Live Once*, 204.

62. Bryce, *You Only Live Once*, 5–6.

63. Bryce, *You Only Live Once*, 15.

64. Pearson, *Notes*, 147.

65. Bryce, *You Only Live Once*, 6.

66. Alfred Adler, *The Practice and Theory of Individual Psychology*, trans P. Radi (Mansfield Center, CT: Martino, 2011), 60.

67. Adler, *Individual Psychology*, 62.

68. Pearson, *Notes*, 359.

69. Pearson, *Notes*, 100. This claim was also alleged by Jacob Stallworthy, "Ian Fleming—The Real James Bond," *Telegraph*, August 12, 2014.

70. National Archives, Kew, "Fleming, Ian Lancaster" (CSC 11/98).

71. National Archives, Kew, "Fleming, Ian Lancaster" (CSC 11/98).

72. Adler, *Individual Psychology*, 93.

73. Adler, *Individual Psychology*, 94.

2. ESCAPE IN THE ALPS

1. Pam Hirsch, *The Constant Liberal: The Life and Work of Phyllis Bottome* (London: Quartet, 2010), 350.

2. Pearson, *Notes*, 191.

3. Pearson, *Notes*, 333.

4. Hirsch, *Constant Liberal*, 154, 152.

5. Hirsch, *Constant Liberal*, 210.

6. Fergus Fleming, ed., *The Man with the Golden Typewriter: Ian Fleming's James Bond Letters* (London: Bloomsbury, 2015), 326.

7. Hirsch, *Constant Liberal*, 148.

8. Pearson, *Notes*, 194.

9. Hirsch, *Constant Liberal*, 167.

10. Hirsch, *Constant Liberal*, 330.

11. Intelligence historian Nigel West has recently accused Ian Fleming of taking ideas and characters from *The Life Line* and using them in his first Bond novel. An article in the *Radio*

Times stated, "But the similarities between Chalmers and Bond are so great that the spy writer Nigel West describes the relationship between the two novelists as 'thief and victim': '1946 is the moment when Phyllis Bottome writes a James Bond book. He's not called James Bond, he's called Mark Chalmers'" ("Could This Woman Have Invented James Bond?," *Radio Times*, December 10, 2016, https://www.radiotimes.com/news/2016-12-10/could-this-woman-have-invented-james-bond). This seems on balance a dubious charge given the long delay between publication of *The Life Line* and *Casino Royale*.

12. Hirsch, *Constant Liberal*, 346.

13. In the same letter to Bottome, Fleming alluded to his forthcoming installment of Bond's adventures, suggesting a connection between them: "Anyway, I loved the book, and above all I was delighted to be reminded of what really beautiful English you write. It is quite brilliantly good and clear and true. I am off to Jamaica next week to try and write another book myself" (Hirsch, *Constant Liberal*, 346; Phyllis Bottome Papers, British Library).

14. Pearson, *Notes*, 336.

15. Pearson, *Life*, 38.

16. Pearson, *Life*, 38.

17. Pearson, *Notes*, 195.

18. Lycett, *Ian Fleming*, 48.

19. Pearson, *Notes*, 325.

20. Pearson, *Notes*, 264.

21. Pearson, *Life*, 70.

22. Mark Amory, ed., *The Letters of Ann Fleming* (London: Collins, 1985), 221.

23. Amory, *Letters*, 277.

24. Ihsan Amanatullah ["Revelator"], "Was Ian Fleming's 'Octopussy' Autobiographical?" *Artistic Licence Renewed*, February 24, 2014, https://literary007.com/2014/02/24/was-octopussy-autobiographical (original emphasis).

25. Jon Gilbert, *Ian Fleming: The Bibliography* (London: Queen Anne Press, 2017), 440.

26. Gilbert, *Ian Fleming*, 441.

27. JamesBondBrasilTV, "Ian Fleming—The CBC Interview (Legendado)," YouTube, December 4, 2013, https://www.youtube.com/watch?v=fKtO34YNcFw.

28. Ian Fleming, *Octopussy and the Living Daylights* (Las Vegas: Thomas and Mercer, 2012), 11.

29. Fleming, *Moonraker*, 189; Ian Fleming, *Diamonds Are Forever* (Las Vegas: Thomas and Mercer, 2012), 95. My thanks to Matthew B. Sherman for drawing my attention to the quote from *Diamonds Are Forever*.

30. Fleming, *Octopussy*, 14, 18, 19, 19, 20.

31. Fleming, *Octopussy*, 20, 22, 22.

32. Fleming, *Octopussy*, 24, 26.

33. Pearson, *Notes*, 51.

34. Fleming, *On Her Majesty's Secret Service*, 2.

35. Fleming, *On Her Majesty's Secret Service*, 26.

36. Fleming, *On Her Majesty's Secret Service*, 220.

37. Fleming, *On Her Majesty's Secret Service*, 256.

38. Fleming, *On Her Majesty's Secret Service*, 257–58. There is one possible interpretation of the end of *On Her Majesty's Secret Service*, that Bond and Tracy are *both* killed in the serious car crash. We know that Bond hit the windscreen of the Lancia and lost consciousness. We also know that he "came to" and discovered Tracy dead beside him. But we don't know for certain how serious Bond's injuries are. The perspective then shifts to the Autobahn patrolman, who asks, terrified, in German, "What has happened?" Bond is able to answer him, but the final

reference to Bond and Tracy is "the young patrolman took a last scared look at the motionless couple" (258). That Bond and Tracy are both "motionless" may mean they have both died. Of course, Bond's return the following year in *You Only Live Twice* shows that, if Fleming intended to kill Bond off at the end of *On Her Majesty's Secret Service*, he subsequently changed his mind.

39. Smythe, as discussed above, is a disillusioned portrayal of Fleming in late-life decline, living in Jamaica and destroying himself with smoking, drink, and rich food. Blofeld—besides sharing Fleming's own birthday of May 28, 1908—shows symptoms of venereal disease. Fleming had, it has been alleged, contracted gonorrhea while at Sandhurst, less serious than syphilis but nonetheless an embarrassing consequence of his risky sex life.

40. Pearson, *Notes*, 190.

41. Ian Fleming Publications, "Time in Europe," https://www.ianfleming.com/ian-fleming.

42. Amory, *Letters*, 277.

43. Fleming, *Man with the Golden Typewriter*, 274, 343.

44. Pearson, *Notes*, 192.

45. Phyllis Bottome Papers, British Library.

46. Pearson, *Notes*, 212.

47. Russell, *Constant Heart*, 239.

48. Lycett, *Ian Fleming*, 152.

49. Hirsch, *Constant Liberal*, 330.

50. Ian Fleming, *Casino Royale* (Las Vegas: Thomas and Mercer, 2012), 178.

51. Fleming, *On Her Majesty's Secret Service*, 255.

52. Ian Fleming, *You Only Live Twice* (Las Vegas: Thomas and Mercer, 2012), 13. Ian's brother Peter, oddly, found fault with this image. Peter's "correction" suggests his hostility, and perhaps envy, toward Ian's fame, as he "seemed to treat the success quite separately from the books. 'Which, frankly, I don't all that much care for.' But the success he was clearly in awe of" (Pearson, *Notes*, 188–89).

53. Fleming, *You Only Live Twice*, 13.

54. Richard Troughton, director of W. H. Smith, recalled, "I liked Ian because I thought that he was a person the world misjudged, and that far from being a tough, ruthless man, he was a soft rather kind one" (Pearson, *Notes*, 220).

55. Fleming, *Octopussy*, 164.

56. Ian Fleming, *Thrilling Cities* (Las Vegas: Thomas and Mercer, 2013), 162–63.

57. Fleming, *Thrilling Cities*, 163.

3. FROM MOSCOW TO EBURY STREET

1. However, Duff Cooper later served as minister of information under Winston Churchill, who came to power in May 1940.

2. Russell, *Constant Heart*, 43.

3. Hirsch, *Constant Liberal*, 206.

4. Hirsch, *Constant Liberal*, 211.

5. Eric Ambler, *Cause for Alarm* (New York: Vintage, 2002), 7.

6. Graham Greene, *The Confidential Agent* (Harmondsworth, UK: Penguin, 1971), 38.

7. Robert Harling, *Ian Fleming: A Personal Memoir* (London: Robson/Biteback, 2015), 354.

8. Lycett, *Ian Fleming*, 57.
9. Pearson, *Notes*, 325.
10. Michael Smith, *Six: The Real James Bonds, 1909–1939* (London: Biteback, 2011), 338.
11. Smith, *Six*, 338, 339.
12. Pearson, *Notes*, 325.
13. Lycett, *Ian Fleming*, 62.
14. Pearson, *Notes*, 239.
15. Russell, *Constant Heart*, illus. 13. See figure 4.1 in the present work.
16. See Lycett, *Ian Fleming*, 62.
17. Jonathan Conlin, *Mr Five Percent: The Many Lives of Calouste Gulbenkian, the World's Richest Man* (London: Profile, 2019), 245.
18. Andrew Lycett, *From Diamond Sculls to Golden Handcuffs: A History of Rowe & Pitman* (London: Robert Hale, 1998), 19–20.
19. Lycett, *Diamond Sculls*, 59–60.
20. Officially, Ian was the personal assistant to the DNI, not the deputy director. But in practice his role was that of Godfrey's deputy, as Godfrey himself admitted (see chapter 4).
21. Lycett, *Diamond Sculls*, 24, 36.
22. Lycett, *Diamond Sculls*, 45.
23. Lycett, *Diamond Sculls*, 46.
24. Lycett, *Diamond Sculls*, 59.
25. Pearson, *Notes*, 229.
26. Lycett, *Diamond Sculls*, 59.
27. Lycett, *Diamond Sculls*, 63.
28. Fleming, *Moonraker*, 7.
29. Ian Fleming, *Goldfinger* (Las Vegas: Thomas and Mercer, 2012), 58–59.
30. Amory, *Letters*, 35, 35, 36.
31. Amory, *Letters*, 35, 36.
32. Amory, *Letters*, 35, 36, 36.
33. Giblin, *James Bond's London*, 21, 21.
34. Pearson, *Notes*, 128.
35. Lycett, *Ian Fleming*, 82.
36. Before Connery's first appearance on screen in *Dr. No*, we see a representative of the SIS arrive late at night at a London club called Le Cercle and ask the concierge if Mr. James Bond is present. The concierge's first words are "Excuse me Sir, are you a member?" In this way the idea of Bond's privileged access to an exclusive club in which only "members" are allowed is established before we even see Bond on screen.
37. Pearson, *Notes*, 91.
38. Amory, *Letters*, 13.
39. Peter Fleming, *Brazilian Adventure* (Evanston, IL: Northwestern University Press, 1999), 258, 255.
40. Pearson, *Notes*, 210.
41. *Brief Encounter* was based on the 1936 play *Still Life*, by Noël Coward, who also wrote the screenplay for the film. Indeed, the theatrical film release poster advertised the film as Noël Coward's *Brief Encounter*. Coward would become one of Ian Fleming's closest friends when they became neighbors both at Saint Margaret's Bay, Kent, and on the coast of Jamaica near Oracabessa after the war.
42. Russell, *Constant Heart*, 56.
43. Most of this book collection of rare first editions of landmark publications in science, history, and the social sciences is held in the Lilly Library, Indiana University. A prominent

photograph in the apartment showed Ian wearing a Russian shirt, a reminder of his visits to Moscow and love of Russia.

44. Russell, *Constant Heart*, 62, 57.

45. Ian Fleming, Letter to *The Times*, September 28, 1938, https://thetimes.co.uk/letterarchive/Ian_Fleming.html#collapse.

46. Fleming would keep a copy of this obituary, inscribed by WC, on his bedroom wall throughout his life.

47. While working in NID, Fleming would also travel back and forth between Britain, Europe, and the United States to coordinate with the British Security Co-ordination (BSC, William Stephenson's organization), the OSS (Donovan's, forerunner to CIA), all with the ultimate purpose of bringing in the United States to the war and defeating the Nazis.

48. Fleming, "Letter to *The Times*."

49. Eric Ambler, *A Coffin for Dimitrios* (New York: Vintage, 2001), 10.

50. Pearson, *Notes*, 125.

51. Ian Fleming, "Russia's Strength," British Library, RP 7369. Reproduced by permission of Ian Fleming Estate.

52. Fleming, "Russia's Strength."

53. Fleming, "Russia's Strength."

54. Russell, *Constant Heart*, 50.

55. Lycett, *Ian Fleming*, 90.

56. Russell, *Constant Heart*, 56.

4. MY MAN GODFREY

1. See Pearson, *Notes*, 85.

2. Ben Macintyre, *Operation Mincemeat: How a Dead Man and a Bizarre Plan Fooled the Nazis and Assured an Allied Victory* (New York: Harmony, 2010), 12.

3. Fleming's younger brother Michael would also be killed in World War II in 1940, adding to the family's tragic losses. Fleming would make this connection in *Thrilling Cities*, writing of Berlin in 1960, "I left Berlin without regret. From this grim capital went forth the orders that in 1917 killed my father and in 1940 my youngest brother" (153).

4. Admiral John Godfrey, "The Naval Memoirs of Admiral J. H. Godfrey," Churchill Archive Center (© Estate of Admiral John Godfrey).

5. Only in Fleming's last and posthumously published Bond novel, *The Man with the Golden Gun*, is M's full identity finally revealed, along with his naval rank. When Bond, returning to SIS headquarters, is asked to identify "this man Mr Em you want to talk to," Bond replies, "'Admiral Sir Miles Messervy. He is head of a department in your Ministry'" (Ian Fleming, *The Man with the Golden Gun* [Las Vegas: Thomas and Mercer, 2012], 3).

6. Harling, *Ian Fleming*, 354.

7. Pearson, *Notes*, 281.

8. Godfrey, "Naval Memoirs," 9–10.

9. Harling, "Where Bond Began," in Godfrey, "Naval Memoirs," 388.

10. Harling, *Ian Fleming*, 36.

11. Harling, "Where Bond Began," in Godfrey, "Naval Memoirs," 390. This essay is reprinted, with slightly different wording, in Harling's memoir *Ian Fleming*, 353–59.

12. Lycett, *Ian Fleming*, 102.

13. Godfrey, "Naval Memoirs," 57, 37–38.

14. Harling, *Ian Fleming*, 14.

15. Harling, *Ian Fleming*, 354.

16. Harling, *Ian Fleming*, 45, 195, 129.

17. Pearson, *Notes*, 132.

18. Pearson, *Notes*, 164.

19. Harling, "Where Bond Began," in Godfrey, "Naval Memoirs," 391.

20. "History of AU30," National Archives, Kew (ADM 223/480).

21. Christopher Moran and Trevor McCrisken, "The Secret Life of Ian Fleming: Spies, Lies and Social Ties," *Contemporary British History* 33, no. 3 (2019): 342.

22. Harling, *Ian Fleming*, 188, 191.

23. Lycett, *Ian Fleming*, 121–22.

24. Charles Morgan, "History of Naval Intelligence 1939–42" (National Archives ADM 223/464).

25. William Somerset Maugham, *Ashenden: Or, The British Agent*, "Preface" (OTB Ebook, Kindle).

26. Maugham, *Ashenden*, "Preface."

27. Macintyre, *For Your Eyes Only*, 36.

28. Fleming, *Casino Royale*, 56, 131. In the 2006 EON film of *Casino Royale*, directed by Martin Campbell, the opening pretitle scene deals with Bond's requirement of "two kills" to become a 00, one of which is the double agent Dryden (Malcom Sinclair), the Prague section chief, whom Bond kills for selling government secrets (Martin Campbell, dir., *Casino Royale* [Eon Productions, 2006]).

29. Papers of H. Montgomery Hyde, Churchill Archive Center.

30. Bryce, *You Only Live Once*, 54.

31. Bryce, *You Only Live Once*, 66.

32. Pearson, *Notes*, 300.

33. Bryce, *You Only Live Once*, 53.

34. Bryce, *You Only Live Once*, 54.

35. Pearson, *Life*, 159.

36. Fleming, *Thrilling Cities*, 225.

37. Pearson, *Life*, 160.

38. Pearson, *Life*, 161.

39. Oliver Sachgau, "The Name's Bond, Maybe St. James Bond: Ian Fleming's Toronto Inspirations," *Toronto Star*, November 7, 2015, https://www.thestar.com/news/gta/2015/11/07/the-names-bond-maybe-st-james-bond-ian-flemings-toronto-inspirations.html.

40. David Stafford, *Camp X: SOE School for Spies* (London: Thistle, 2013), 294.

41. Stafford, *Camp X*, "Introduction."

42. Pearson, *Notes*, 278. The name of the Commandant at Camp X was Bill Brooker, according to Stafford.

43. Pearson, *Life*, 163.

44. Pearson, *Notes*, 279.

45. Pearson, *Life*, 153.

46. Fleming, *Casino Royale*, 77.

47. Ian Fleming, *Live and Let Die* (Las Vegas: Thomas and Mercer, 2012), 1.

48. Ian Fleming, *From Russia, with Love* (Las Vegas: Thomas and Mercer, 2012), 111.

49. George Blake, *No Other Choice: An Autobiography* (New York: Simon & Schuster, 1990), 23.

50. Pearson, *Notes*, 84.

51. Godfrey, "Naval Memoirs," 259.

52. Russell, *Constant Heart*, 72, 114.

53. Russell, *Constant Heart*, 299.

54. "Progress Report on Goldeneye," National Archives, UK (NA DDNI 3).

55. Sir Anthony and Clarissa Eden would later stay at Fleming's Jamaica home, Goldeneye, in order to recover from the debacle of the Suez crisis in November 1956.

56. The influence of Operation Goldeneye is arguably seen more clearly in the Bond films rather than the novels. The name was used for the title of the seventeenth Bond film, in 1995—the first to star Pierce Brosnan as 007—although the plot had nothing to do with Fleming's wartime operation or his Jamaican home. However, the debut of Timothy Dalton in the fifteenth film—*The Living Daylights* (1987)—does open with a "war game" invasion by SIS agents (including Bond) of Gibraltar in order to test the security and defenses of the "Rock."

57. Mark Simmons, *Ian Fleming and Operation Golden Eye: Keeping Spain out of World War II* (Oxford: Casemate, 2018), ch. 9, Kindle.

58. Fleming, *On Her Majesty's Secret Service*, 62.

59. Stella Rimington, "Introduction," in *The Spy's Bedside Book*, ed. Hugh Greene and Graham Greene (London: Hutchinson, 2007), xii.

60. Ian Fleming, *For Your Eyes Only* (Las Vegas: Thomas and Mercer, 2012), 26; *Octopussy*, 89.

61. Fleming, *From Russia, with Love*, 108.

62. Fleming, *Casino Royale*, 14.

63. Fleming, *Thrilling Cities*, 126.

64. Fleming, *You Only Live Twice*, 48. MAGIC 44 also draws on the extraordinary intelligence-gathering and codebreaking expertise of Bletchley Park during the war.

65. Fleming, *You Only Live Twice*, 80.

66. Fleming, *You Only Live Twice*, 81.

67. In *Dr. No*, Fleming imagined the enemy attacks on the colonial bastion of the Queen's Club: "One day Queen's Club will have its windows smashed and perhaps be burned to the ground" (2). Might the same fate have been imagined by Fleming for Goldeneye? It was an embattled "retreat" from the real world, where the fantasy of James Bond could take root. Of course, Fleming took the precaution of not installing glass windows in Goldeneye, but its clifftop position made it a landmark of British presence in the Caribbean.

68. Fleming, *You Only Live Twice*, 203, 205. This can be seen as a way to evade prosecution under the Official Secrets Act—or at least censure from NID (bearing in mind how much trouble H. Montgomery Hyde went through in trying to publish *Quiet Canadian* about wartime ops).

69. Moran and McCrisken, "Secret Life," 337.

70. Russell, *Constant Heart*, 143.

71. Pearson, *Notes*, 279–80.

72. Macintyre, *Mincemeat*, 10.

73. The original nonfiction narrative about Mincemeat is Ewen Montagu's *The Man Who Never Was* (1953), which was adapted into a film of the same name directed by Ronald Neame in 1956. Prior to this, Duff Cooper—a former Cabinet minister—had published a novel, *Operation Heartbreak* (1950), based on the plot of Mincemeat. Detailed accounts are also contained in Charles Morgan's "History of Naval Intelligence 1939–42" (in the National Archives) and, more recently, Nicholas Rankin's *A Genius for Deception: How Cunning Helped the British Win Two World Wars* (New York: Oxford University Press, 2008), esp. ch. 25; and Ben Macintyre's *Operation Mincemeat.*

74. Macintyre, *Mincemeat*, 64.

75. Morgan, "History," 265.

76. Morgan, "History," 265.

77. Simmons, *Ian Fleming and Golden Eye*, ch. 1 (Kindle).

78. Fleming, *From Russia, with Love*, 253.

79. Pearson, *Life*, 407.

80. Fleming, *Moonraker*, 87.

81. Bray later recalled, "During the war there was a premium on crazy ideas round the NID. . . . Ian fitted into this sort of atmosphere perfectly" (Pearson, *Notes*, 229).

82. Fleming, *On Her Majesty's Secret Service*, 71, 72.

83. Fleming, *On Her Majesty's Secret Service*, 143. Peter Hunt's film of *On Her Majesty's Secret Service* (1969)—very close to Fleming's novel in most respects—further emphasizes the risks of Bond's sexual adventuring. Bond is caught and captured by Irma Bunt when he secretly enters Ruby's room, believing the woman in the bed to be Ruby, whereas it is in fact Bunt. As Blofeld (Telly Savalas) points out to the captive Bond (George Lazenby), "Employees of the College of Arms do not go around seducing female patients."

84. Fleming, *On Her Majesty's Secret Service*, 144, 146 (original emphasis), 153.

85. Fleming, *On Her Majesty's Secret Service*, 167.

86. Fleming, *You Only Live Twice*, 202.

87. Fleming, *You Only Live Twice*, 211.

88. Lewis Gilbert, dir., *You Only Live Twice* (EON Productions, 1967).

89. Godfrey, "Naval Memoirs," 275–76.

90. Mark Simmons writes about one such secret mission in which Ian Fleming travels to France in summer 1940, following the fall of France to the Nazis, in an effort to persuade the French naval head Admiral Darlan to send the French fleet to Britain to avoid its capture by the Germans. See *Ian Fleming and Golden Eye*, chapter 2.

91. Godfrey, "Naval Memoirs," 388.

92. Godfrey, "Naval Memoirs," 387.

93. Godfrey, "Naval Memoirs," 85, 277.

94. See Macintyre, *Mincemeat*, 15.

95. Godfrey, "Naval Memoirs," x.

96. Ian Fleming, *From Russia, with Love*, 134.

97. Macintyre, *Mincemeat*, 18.

98. Peter Hennessy, *The Secret State: Preparing for the Worst 1945–2010*, 2nd ed. (London: Penguin, 2010), 50. Bevin's actual words were less reasoned and more M-like, conveying the desperation he felt: "No Prime Minister, that won't do at all. We've got to have this. . . . I don't want any other Foreign Secretary of this country to be talked at, or to, by the Secretary of State in the United States as I just have in my discussions with Mr Byrnes. We've got to have this thing over here, whatever it costs. We've got to have the bloody Union Jack on top of it" (Hennessy, *Secret State*, 50–51).

99. Rankin, *Genius*, xiii.

100. John 8:44. Cf Proverbs 6:16–19: "These six things the Lord hates, yes, seven are an abomination to Him: A proud look, a lying tongue, hands that shed innocent blood, a heart that devises wicked plans, feet that are swift in running to evil, a false witness who speaks lies, and one who sows discord among brethren."

101. Rankin, *Genius*, 420.

102. Fleming, *Man with the Golden Typewriter*, 121.

103. William Stevenson, *A Man Called Intrepid: The Secret War* (New York: Ballantine, 1977), 97.

104. Godfrey, "Naval Memoirs," 279, 280 (emphasis added).

105. Pearson, *Notes*, 256.
106. Cited in Godfrey, "Naval Memoirs," 398.
107. Lee Richards, *The Black Art: British Clandestine Psychological Warfare against the Third Reich* (Peacehaven, Sussex: Psywar, 2010), 25–26.
108. Richards, *Black Art*, 26, 26n.
109. Russell, *Constant Heart*, 89.
110. Macintyre, *Mincemeat*, 63.
111. Cited in Godfrey, "Naval Memoirs," 392.
112. Pearson, *Life*, 379.
113. This shared investment in deception of novelist, spy, con man is the theme par excellence of John le Carré's *The Perfect Spy*. For all Magnus Pym's contempt for his father, Rick's, crimes, cons, and scams, he is forced to recognize—after Rick's death—that his father provided the ideal training for the world of espionage, made him into the "perfect spy."
114. Fleming, *You Only Live Twice*, 205.
115. "Ian Fleming Timeline," Ian Fleming Publications, accessed December 15, 2020, http://www.ianfleming.com/ian-fleming.
116. Godfrey, "Naval Memoirs," 278.
117. Moran and McCrisken, "Secret Life," 350.
118. Godfrey, "Naval Memoirs," 278.
119. Pearson, *Notes*, 282.

5. AFTER THE WAR WAS OVER

1. Pearson, *Notes*, 332.
2. Pearson, *Notes*, 208.
3. Fleming, *From Russia, with Love*, 67.
4. Bryce, *You Only Live Once*, 28.
5. Russell, *Constant Heart*, 69.
6. Christopher Andrew, *The Defence of the Realm: The Authorized History of MI5* (London: Penguin, 2010), 253.
7. Bryce, *You Only Live Once*, 69–70.
8. Bryce, *You Only Live Once*, 70–73.
9. Bryce, *You Only Live Once*, 74.
10. Pearson, *Notes*, 294.
11. Russell, *Constant Heart*, 291.
12. Russell, *Constant Heart*, 276.
13. Russell, *Constant Heart*, 294, 297, 299. As Emily Russell writes, "Goldeneye was an outright gift. On 23 July 1958, Ian came to tea. Among other comments she writes in her diary: 'He talked about Goldeneye and what a wonderful present it had been and that he spent two months there every year.' She gave him GBP2,000 to buy the land and GBP3,000 to build the house in 1946" (provided to the author by Emily Russell from the private diaries of Maud Russell).
14. Bryce, *You Only Live Once*, 82.
15. Bryce, *You Only Live Once*, 80, 79.
16. Bryce, *You Only Live Once*, 81.
17. Harling, *Ian Fleming*, 196.

18. Harling, *Ian Fleming*, 196.
19. Bryce, *You Only Live Once*, 82.
20. Bryce, *You Only Live Once*, 74.
21. Harling, *Ian Fleming*, 197.
22. Emily Temple, "Ian Fleming Explains How to Write a Thriller," *Literary Hub*, May 28, 2019, https://lithub.com/ian-fleming-explains-how-to-write-a-thriller.
23. Russell, *Constant Heart*, 293.
24. Russell, *Constant Heart*, 294.
25. Russell, *Constant Heart*, 196.
26. Fleming, *The Spy Who Loved Me*, 92.
27. Fleming, *The Spy Who Loved Me*, 86.
28. Gilbert, *Ian Fleming: The Bibliography*, 661.
29. Harling, *Ian Fleming*, 196.
30. Mark Edmonds, "My Secret Life at the *Sunday Times*," *Sunday Times*, October 14, 2012.
31. Pearson, *Notes*, 282.
32. Macintyre, *For Your Eyes Only*, 41.
33. Edmonds, "My Secret Life."
34. Fleming, *Moonraker*, 7.
35. Amory, *Letters*, 37, 41.
36. Amory, *Letters*, 42.
37. Peter Lewis, *Eric Ambler: A Literary Biography* (New York: Odyssey Press, 2014), 140.
38. "Nöel Coward and Ian Fleming," Dover Museum, https://www.dovermuseum.co.uk/Information-Resources/Articles--Factsheets/Coward--Flemming.aspx.
39. Fleming, *Man with the Golden Typewriter*, 15.
40. Fleming, *Goldfinger*, 91.
41. Gilbert, *Ian Fleming: The Bibliography*, 661.
42. Matthew Parker, *Goldeneye: Where Bond Was Born: Ian Fleming's Jamaica* (New York: Pegasus, 2015), 71, 69.
43. Parker, *Goldeneye*, 73.
44. Parker, *Goldeneye*, 113.
45. Amory, *Letters*, 37.
46. Jonathan Cape Archive, University of Reading Special Collections. Reproduced by permission of Ian Fleming Estate.
47. Jonathan Cape Archive, University of Reading Special Collections. Reproduced by permission of Ian Fleming Estate.
48. Macintyre, *For Your Eyes Only*, 57.
49. Gilbert, *Ian Fleming: The Bibliography*, 663.
50. Fleming, *Man with the Golden Typewriter*, 35–36 (original emphasis).
51. Amory, *Letters*, 115.
52. Gilbert, *Ian Fleming: The Bibliography*, 662.
53. Pearson, *Notes*, 92.
54. Ian Fleming, *Thunderball* (Las Vegas: Thomas and Mercer, 2012), 3.
55. Amory, *Letters*, 97.
56. Hirsch, *Constant Liberal*, 307, 291.
57. Hirsch, *Constant Liberal*, 288, 289.
58. George Orwell had previously used the phrase "cold war" as a general term in his essay "You and the Atomic Bomb," published on October 19, 1945, in *Tribune*. Baruch was the first to use the term specifically to refer to the US-Soviet confrontation in the postwar era.

59. Macintyre, *For Your Eyes Only*, 52.

60. Peter Fleming, *The Sixth Column* (Hornchurch, Essex: Ian Henry, 1975), 9, 11, 15–16.

61. Fleming, *Thrilling Cities*, 126.

62. Fleming, *Sixth Column*, 11–12.

63. Fleming, *Sixth Column*, 16. There are also certain intriguing parallels between *The Sixth Column* and the first of the so-called anti-Bond spy novels, Len Deighton's *The Ipcress File* (1962) in which the spy mastermind known as "Jay" seeks to kidnap and brainwash leading British scientists and politicians prior to selling them to the highest bidder, which is probably the Soviet Union. In the words of Jean, the assistant to the unnamed narrator, Jay has attempted "a plan to brain-wash the entire framework of a nation" (Len Deighton, *The Ipcress File* [London: Harper, 2015], 228).

64. Ross Kenneth Urken, "How James Bond's Legacy Is Saving Jamaica," *Bloomberg*, July 23, 2018, https://www.bloomberg.com/news/features/2018-07-23/how-the-birthplace-of-james-bond-is-helping-save-the-caribbean.

65. Fleming, *Sixth Column*, 16. The fortune of Ivar Bryce's father had also been made in guano.

66. Steve Vogel, *Betrayal in Berlin: The True Story of the Cold War's Most Audacious Espionage Operation* (New York: Custom House, 2019), 230.

67. See Ben Macintyre, *A Spy among Friends: Kim Philby and the Great Betrayal* (London: Bloomsbury, 2014), 157–64.

68. Macintyre, *Spy among Friends*, 161.

69. Michael Smith, *The Anatomy of a Traitor: A History of Espionage and Betrayal* (London: Aurum, 2017), 14, 243, 243, 244.

70. This phrase was used on several occasions in the 1940s to characterize the close military, economic, and intelligence-sharing cooperation between Britain and the United States. Most famously, Churchill used the phrase in his "Sinews of Peace" address at Fulton, Missouri, on March 5, 1946.

71. Pearson, *Notes*, 143.

72. Fleming, *You Only Live Twice*, 204. M's obituary of Bond in *You Only Live Twice* states that his early education "was entirely abroad" (203) and that he passed from Eton to Fettes and thence to "the Ministry of Defence" during World War II (204).

73. Patrick Leigh Fermor describes an election party at Warwick House on October 26, 1951, noting that "when Conservative victories began to predominate there were outbursts of cheering largely led by Ann [Rothermere] waving a glass and shouting 'Hooray!' as though at a boat-race, occasionally changing her note when some Labour member who was a friend lost his seat" (Amory, *Letters*, 100).

74. Fleming, *Man with the Golden Typewriter*, 18.

75. James Chapman, *Licence to Thrill: A Cultural History of the James Bond Films*, 2nd ed. (London: I. B. Tauris, 2007), 16.

76. When Ian's housekeeper at Goldeneye, Violet, was told by Lady Foot, the wife of the governor in chief, that she had to leave the house when Prime Minister Sir Anthony Eden and his wife, Clarissa, arrived in 1956, she responded defiantly, "No, I obey the Commander" (Pearson, *Notes*, 157).

77. Edmonds, "My Secret Life."

78. Russell, *Constant Heart*, 294, 297.

79. Edmonds, "My Secret Life."

6. THE SPY STORY TO END ALL SPY STORIES

1. Harling, *Ian Fleming*, 97. Harling 's reaction to Ian's plan, according to his memoir, was hardly encouraging, considering Ian's proposal "a programme of preposterous grandeur and ambition" (97).

2. Ian's final novel was *The Man with the Golden Gun*, written at Goldeneye in January and February 1964. The manuscript was "tidied up" (in Fergus Fleming's phrase)—in other words, not substantially revised—by Kingsley Amis, who went on to pen the first Bond continuation novel, *Colonel Sun*, under the pseudonym Robert Markham (Fleming, *Man with the Golden Typewriter*, 364).

3. Jeremy Duns, *A Spy Is Born: Dennis Wheatley and the Secret Roots of Ian Fleming's James Bond* (Norwich, UK: Skerry, 2019), 29. David Salter has suggested Carbourg as an alternative inspiration for Royale-les-Eaux ("Was Cabourg an Inspiration for Royale-les-Eaux?" The James Bond Dossier [blog], September 25, 2013, https://www.thejamesbonddossier.com/content/cabourg-inspiration-royale-les-eaux.htm).

4. Blake, *No Other Choice*, 100.

5. Fleming, *Moonraker*, 7.

6. Fleming, *Casino Royale*, 6.

7. Fleming, *Casino Royale*, 1.

8. Pearson, *Notes*, 234.

9. Fleming, *Casino Royale*, 1.

10. Fleming, *Casino Royale*, 3.

11. Fleming, *Casino Royale*, 9, 13.

12. Fleming, *Casino Royale*, 45.

13. Fleming, *Casino Royale*, 177.

14. Fleming, *From Russia, with Love*, 61.

15. Fleming, *Casino Royale*, 25, 27.

16. Pearson, *Life*, 49.

17. Fleming, *On Her Majesty's Secret Service*, 30.

18. According to Bryce, Ian got the idea for the "Vesper" cocktail from an old couple he visited living in the hills near Kingston, Jamaica. During his visit, a butler appeared and announced "Time for Vespers, sir"—referring to evening cocktails (Pearson, *Notes*, 235). This suggests that the name of the cocktail came to Ian before the idea of naming his first female character Vesper.

19. Fleming, *Casino Royale*, 178.

20. Arguably, Le Chiffre's psychological moves and manipulative acts during the baccarat game are an extreme form of the "gamesmanship" discussed at length by Ian and his golfing friend Stephen Potter, author of *The Theory and Practice of Gamesmanship, or the Art of Winning Games Without Actually Cheating*, which was published by Rupert Hart-Davis in 1947 (Pearson, *Notes*, 351).

21. Fleming, *Casino Royale*, 136.

22. Fleming, *Casino Royale*, 1.

23. Fleming, *Casino Royale*, 77.

24. Fleming, *Casino Royale*, 84.

25. Fleming, *Casino Royale*, 115.

26. Fleming, *Casino Royale*, 41.

27. Lycett, *Ian Fleming*, 85. As Lycett describes the plot, the group of friends "abandon their narrow political prejudices and . . . establish a fellowship dedicated to nobility and honour and opposed to nationalism and mass culture" (85).

28. Fleming, *Moonraker*, 27.

29. Fleming, *Casino Royale*, 52.

30. Geoffrey Household, *The Third Hour* (New York: Open Road, 2015), "Appendix," ch. 12.

31. With typical class consciousness, Fleming grouped his readers into categories; thus he originally wrote for the "A class" of readers but felt his novels could also appeal to the "B and C classes" of readers—who were, of course, necessary for Fleming to achieve the level of popular success he desired (Fleming, *Man with the Golden Typewriter*, 97).

32. Fleming, *Live and Let Die*, 1

33. Psalm 23:4.

34. Fleming, *Casino Royale*, 110.

35. Fleming, *Man with the Golden Typewriter*, 12.

36. Fleming, *Casino Royale*, 114–15.

37. Tony Bennett and Janet Woollacott, "The Moments of Bond," in *The James Bond Phenomenon: A Critical Reader*, 2nd ed., ed. Christoph Lindner (Manchester: Manchester University Press, 2009), 24.

38. Fleming, *Casino Royale*, 111.

39. Lycett, *Ian Fleming*, 82.

40. Fleming, *Casino Royale*, 113.

41. Bennett and Woollacott identified the "most notable exception" to the pattern of the villainesses being ugly and relatively marginal as "Vesper Lynd in *Casino Royale*, a part in which the roles of 'the girl' and the villainess are completely fused" ("Moments of Bond," 30).

42. Fleming, *Casino Royale*, 120.

43. Fleming, *Casino Royale*, 124, 155 (emphasis added).

44. Amory, *Letters*, 118.

45. Gilbert, *Ian Fleming: The Bibliography*, 126.

46. Gilbert, *Ian Fleming: The Bibliography*, 24.

47. Blake, *No Other Choice*, 156, 157.

7. THE EDGE OF DANGER

1. JBond007, "Remembering Ian Fleming: 28th May 1908–12th Aug 1964," YouTube, August 13, 2014, https://www.youtube.com/watch?v=5E7HBjafG7M.

2. Fleming, *On Her Majesty's Secret Service*, 58.

3. JamesBondBrasilTV, "Ian Fleming—The CBC Interview (Legendado)," YouTube, December 4, 2013, https://www.youtube.com/watch?v=fKtO34YNcFw.

4. Robert Markham [Kingsley Amis], *Colonel Sun* (London: Ian Fleming Publications, 1968), "Introduction."

5. Fleming, *Casino Royale*, 35–37.

6. Bryce, *You Only Live Once*, 80.

7. Bridport Museum, "WW2: People' s War," BBC, April 24, 2005, http://www.bbc.co.uk/history/ww2peopleswar/stories/22/a3943622.shtml.

8. Bridport Museum, "WW2: People's War."

9. Fleming, *On Her Majesty's Secret Service*, 204.
10. Fleming, *On Her Majesty's Secret Service*, 198, 203.
11. Fleming, *On Her Majesty's Secret Service*, 204, 207.
12. Kingsley Amis, *The James Bond Dossier* (London: Jonathan Cape, 1965), 111.
13. Fleming, *On Her Majesty's Secret Service*, 208.
14. Fleming, *Thunderball*, 110, 50.
15. Fleming, *On Her Majesty's Secret Service*, 214.
16. Fleming, *Man with the Golden Typewriter*, 345.
17. Fleming, *You Only Live Twice*, 12, 13.
18. Fleming, *Thrilling Cities*, 44.
19. Fleming, *You Only Live Twice*, 48.
20. Fleming, *You Only Live Twice*, 63, 65.
21. Fleming, *You Only Live Twice*, 67, 71.
22. Fleming, *Thrilling Cities*, 44.
23. Fleming, *You Only Live Twice*, 76.
24. Fleming, *You Only Live Twice*, 81.
25. Fleming, *You Only Live Twice*, 126.
26. Fleming, *You Only Live Twice*, 50.
27. Fleming, *You Only Live Twice*, 82.
28. Fleming, *You Only Live Twice*, 127.
29. Fleming, *You Only Live Twice*, 162.
30. Fleming, *Brazilian Adventure*, 233–34.
31. Fleming, *You Only Live Twice*, 163–64.
32. Fleming, *You Only Live Twice*, 165.
33. Sue Matheson argues persuasively that Bond's instincts lie in his "stomach" and ensure his survival: "Throughout the series, Fleming assigns appetites, instincts, and intuition to the stomach. . . . The stomach, not the heart or the head, governs the state of man: gut responses, the primitive instincts of fear and intuition, ultimately determine the well-being of the secret agent: in *Dr. No*, for example, Bond's body recognizes the danger that the giant centipede represents before his brain does—once the danger is past, Bond's reaction is to vomit; in *Thunderball* the 'crawling sensation' that Bond knows so well, the signal that he has 'made a dangerous and silly mistake,' is located explicitly in 'the pit of his stomach.'" In Fleming's world, Matheson argues, "only the master animals like Bond enjoy the fruits of victory" (Sue Matheson, "Primitive Masculinity/'Sophisticated' Stomach: Gender, Appetite, and Power in the Novels of Ian Fleming," *CEA Critic* 67, no. 1 [Fall 2004]: 27, 23).
34. Fleming, *You Only Live Twice*, 200.
35. Fleming, *Casino Royale*, 134.
36. Fleming, *You Only Live Twice*, 196–97.
37. Pearson, *Notes*, 230.
38. This was the title of a notebook Fleming took with him to Goldeneye each winter, which he titled "Sea Fauna or the Finny Tribe of Goldeneye." See Urken, "How James Bond's Legacy Is Saving Jamaica."
39. Amory, *Letters*, 238.
40. Fleming, *For Your Eyes Only*, 11.
41. Fleming, *For Your Eyes Only*, 13–14.
42. Charles Darwin, *On the Origin of Species by Means of Natural Selection* 1859 (Project Gutenberg, http://www.gutenberg.org/files/1228/1228-h/1228-h.htm#chap14 (emphasis added). A first edition of Darwin's classic work formed one of the rare books in Ian Fleming's collection.

43. Amory, *Letters*, 301, 335, 336.

44. The property is now on the New York state side of the border with Vermont. A Realtor's advertisement for the property boasts that "it is Fleming who may linger as the presiding spirit of Black Hole Hollow Farm. It was here that he wrote the Bond novels *Diamonds Are Forever* and *Goldfinger*." ("Saratoga Country Estate, Black Hole Hollow Farm," Christie's International Real Estate, accessed November 24, 2020, https://www.christiesrealestate.com/sales/detail/170-l-775-1606241201487809/saratoga-country-estate-black-hole-hollow-farm-cambridge-ny).

45. "Saratoga Country Estate."

46. See Fleming, *Man with the Golden Typewriter*, 83.

47. Pearson, *Notes*, 155.

48. Fleming, *For Your Eyes Only*, 29.

49. Fleming, *Live and Let Die*, 5.

50. Fleming, *For Your Eyes Only*, 32, 34.

51. Fleming, *For Your Eyes Only*, 38, 40.

52. Fleming, *The Spy Who Loved Me*, 6.

53. Fleming, *Thrilling Cities*, 154.

54. Fleming, *Thrilling Cities*, 153.

55. The Colour Section derived from Fleming's success in persuading his friend Somerset Maugham to serialize his latest book, revealing his views of the ten best novels in the world, in *The Sunday Times*. As Jon Gilbert writes, "Its popularity encouraged Lord Kemsley to consider publishing a separate magazine section, often leading with a popular book serial. Fleming's coup therefore influenced a new direction for the British newspaper industry" (Gilbert, *Ian Fleming: The Bibliography*, 443).

56. Gilbert, *Ian Fleming: The Bibliography*, 440.

57. Fleming, *Octopussy*, 68, 69, 70. In his letter of April 5, 1958, to the *Manchester Guardian*, which had published an attack on the Bond novels, Fleming wrote of Bond: "Exotic things would happen to and around him but he would be a neutral figure—an anonymous blunt instrument wielded by a Government Department" (Fleming, *Man with the Golden Typewriter*, 185).

58. Fleming, *Octopussy*, 73, 75, 76.

59. Fleming, *Octopussy*, 74.

60. Fleming, *Octopussy*, 73, 74, 77.

61. Fleming, *Octopussy*, 82, 86.

62. Fleming, *Thunderball*, 178.

63. An apt example of this occurs in the first post-Fleming Bond novel, *Colonel Sun*, written by Robert Markham (Kingsley Amis). When Bond arrives at M's home of Quarterdeck, from Sunningdale golf course, he notices the absence of the normal "background" noises of the household. This alerts him that something is seriously wrong, and that M is in danger, "when his trained senses warned him of the total absence of any such noise" (Markham, *Colonel Sun*, 15).

64. Fleming, *For Your Eyes Only*, 87.

65. See Jim Wright, *The Real James Bond: A True Story of Identity Theft, Avian Intrigue and Ian Fleming* (Atglen, PA: Schiffer, 2020), 7.

8. "SUCH STUBBORN RETREATS"

1. Bryce, *You Only Live Once*, 83. As Emily Russell, Maud's granddaughter, writes, "Maud and Ian remained close friends up until Ian's marriage to Ann Charteris in 1952. In 1946 Maud gave Ian £5,000 to buy a home in Jamaica; he bought the 15-acre property for £2,000 and budgeted £3,000 to build a house. He originally thought of calling it Shadylady after a sensitive plant that grew profusely on the land but decided on Goldeneye, the codename for a wartime operation" (Russell, *Constant Heart*, 299–300). Bryce records that the name he proposed for the house was "Shame Lady."

2. Fleming, *Live and Let Die*, 34.

3. Vivian Halloran, "Tropical Bond," in *Ian Fleming and James Bond: The Cultural Politics of 007*, ed. Edward P. Comentale, Stephen Watt, and Skip Willman (Bloomington: Indiana University Press, 2005), 168.

4. Fleming, *Live and Let Die*, 34.

5. Fleming, *Dr. No* (Las Vegas: Thomas and Mercer, 2012), 3.

6. Fleming, *From Russia, with Love*, 123, 161. Because of the difference in sequence order between the Bond novels and films, Quarrel is replaced in the 1973 film of *Live and Let Die*, directed by Guy Hamilton, by "Quarrel Jr." (played by Jamaican actor Roy Stewart). The original Quarrel (played by John Kitzmiller) had been killed in 1962's *Dr. No*.

7. Fleming, *Man with the Golden Typewriter*, 109.

8. Fleming, *Man with the Golden Typewriter*, 110.

9. Fleming, *Moonraker*, 150.

10. Fleming, *Live and Let Die*, 113, 126.

11. Fleming, *You Only Live Twice*, 206.

12. This phrase is taken from *On the Nature of Things (De rerum natura)*, a six-book didactic poem written in honor of the Greek philosopher Epicurus by the Roman writer Lucretius, who lived during the first half of the first century BCE. The line comes from book three (*DRN* 3.955-62), which in part explores the fear of death and physical decline.

13. Fleming, *Live and Let Die*, 169, 168.

14. Gilbert, *Ian Fleming: The Bibliography*, 619.

15. Patrick Leigh Fermor, *The Traveller's Tree: A Journey through the Caribbean Islands* (New York: New York Review Books, 2011), 290.

16. Fleming, *Live and Let Die*, 170.

17. Pearson, *Life*, 161.

18. The concept of an innate "nobility" that transcends class and ethnic identities is an important theme of Geoffrey Household's *The Third Hour* (1937)—a novel that Fleming admired and, according to Andrew Lycett, distributed copies of to his friends (Lycett, *Ian Fleming*, 85).

19. In the original typescript in the Lilly Library, the original title is written in red pen, "The Undertaker' s Wind," but has been crossed out and "Live and Let Die" written above it.

20. Fleming, *Live and Let Die*, 173.

21. Fleming, *Live and Let Die*, 34–35.

22. Fleming, *Live and Let Die*, 158.

23. Ironically, Ian took the name Trueblood from his secretary, Una Trueblood, who typed up the manuscript of *Dr. No* (as she had typed up the film screenplay *Commander Gunn*) (cf. Mark Edmonds, "I Finished Off Bond in a Flash," *The Sunday Times*, October 14, 2012).

24. Jon Gilbert gives this title, while Lycett refers to the series as "James Gunn—Secret Agent" (Lycett, *Ian Fleming*, 298). See Gilbert, *Ian Fleming: The Bibliography*, 196.

25. Fleming, *Dr. No*, 29, 27, 31.

26. Fleming, *Dr. No*, 5. The term *chigro* was Fleming's own invention. His friend, the Jamaican author Maurice Cargill, observes, "Chigro just is not a Jamaican term. We would call them Chinese Royals" (Pearson, *Notes*, 276).

27. Fleming, *Dr. No*, 19.

28. Fleming, *Dr. No*, 20. Jim Wright notes, "The first hint that Fleming might have based his protagonist on a real person came with the publication of *Dr. No* in 1958. Toward the end of the book, after 007 is apprehended by Dr. No's henchmen, Bond claims he's an ornithologist" (Wright, *Real James Bond*, 66).

29. Fleming, *Dr. No*, 56.

30. Halloran, "Tropical Bond," 164.

31. Fleming, *Dr. No*, 28, 30.

32. Christoph Lindner, "Criminal Vision and the Ideology of Detection in Fleming's 007 Series," in *The James Bond Phenomenon: A Critical Reader*, 2nd ed., ed. Christoph Lindner (Manchester: Manchester University Press, 2009), 79–80. Likewise, in discussing the villain Lindner highlights the grand scale of his operations: "Simply put, large-scale international crime requires an equally large-scale base of operations. . . . Dr. No's Caribbean island, for example, houses 'the most valuable technical intelligence centre in the world,' hidden appropriately under a mountain of guano" (82).

33. Fleming, *Dr. No*, 128.

34. Fleming, *Dr. No*, 131, 132.

35. Gilbert, *Ian Fleming: The Bibliography*, 198.

36. Fleming, *Dr. No*, 32, 52.

37. Fleming, *Dr. No*, 86.

38. In the film of *On Her Majesty's Secret Service*, Blofeld (Telly Savalas) plots a biological warfare against the entire world, represented by the "angels of death" from various countries. In Fleming's novel, however, Britain alone is the target of Blofeld's virus of sterility.

39. Cynthia Baron, "*Dr. No*: Bonding Britishness to Racial Sovereignty," in *The James Bond Phenomenon: A Critical Reader*, 2nd ed., ed. Christoph Lindner (Manchester: Manchester University Press, 2009), 164.

40. Fleming, *Dr. No*, 127.

41. Halloran, "Tropical Bond," 161.

42. Fleming, *You Only Live Twice*, 204.

43. "Noël Coward and Ian Fleming," Dover Museum, https://www.dovermuseum.co.uk/Information-Resources/Articles--Factsheets/Coward--Flemming.aspx.

44. Fleming, *Man with the Golden Typewriter*, 12.

45. Public Signage at Saint Margaret's Bay, Kent.

46. Bob Cromwell, "Military Tunnels in the White Cliffs of Dover," Cromwell-Intl (blog), accessed November 24, 2020, https://cromwell-intl.com/travel/uk/dover.

47. "Noël Coward and Ian Fleming in Kent."

48. Pearson, *Notes*, 199.

49. Amory, *Letters*, 270.

50. As Ann wrote to Waugh in November 1954, "The annual journey to Jamaica is always a horrible problem to me though it appears to present few difficulties to rational human beings. I want to bring the baby and I thought we could all travel together, but Ian is appalled at the prospect" (Amory, *Letters*, 146).

51. Amory, *Letters*, 214–15.

52. Fleming, *Moonraker*, 21.

53. Fleming, *Moonraker*, 81–82, 88.

54. Fleming, *Moonraker*, 94, 99.
55. Fleming, *Moonraker*, 99.
56. Fleming, *Moonraker*, 143–44.
57. Fleming, *Moonraker*, 144.
58. Matthew Hall, *Plants as Persons: A Philosophical Botany* (Albany: State University of New York Press, 2011), 5. Hall argues that the human tendency to dismiss plants from moral consideration as sentient "persons" contributes to our current environmental crisis: "Our general Western view of plants as passive resources certainly plays a significant role in our ecological plight" (4).
59. Fleming, *Moonraker*, 144.
60. Fleming, *Moonraker*, 265.
61. Fleming, *Moonraker*, 144
62. "The Granville, St Margaret's Bay," Fleming's Bond, March 24, 2014, https://flemingsbond.com/the-granville-st-margarets-bay. An article in the *East Kent Mercury* for November 4, 1994, advertising the auction for the contents of the soon-to-be-demolished Granville noted, "The Granville Hotel, at St Margaret 's, had welcomed many notable guests in its heyday, Noël Coward and James Bond author Ian Fleming among them. They had stayed in its bedrooms, eaten in its dining room, sipped at its bar and relaxed on its balcony" ("Granville Arms Hotel," Dover Kent Archives, updated November 7, 2020, http://www.dover-kent.com/Granville-Arms-Hotel-St-Margarets.html).
63. Fleming, *Moonraker*, 142.
64. Fleming, *Moonraker*, 143.
65. Fleming, *Moonraker*, 145.
66. Fleming, *Moonraker*, 152.
67. Fleming, *Moonraker*, 108.
68. Fleming, *Moonraker*, 159.
69. Fleming, *Moonraker*, 167, 168. It may be another warning of Drax's true allegiances that this model of Mercedes contains the initials of the Nazi security police, Schutzstaffel, which was responsible for controlling the concentration camps during World War II.
70. Fleming, *Moonraker*, 175.
71. Fleming, *Moonraker*, 177.
72. Fleming, *Moonraker*, 209–10.
73. Fleming, *Moonraker*, 231, 234. The BBC reporter states, of Drax, "He's out on the jetty. He looked back and raised his arm in the air" (231), clearly suggesting the "Heil Hitler" salute. The scene directly recalls the climax of an earlier spy novel, John Buchan's *The Thirty-Nine Steps*, in which Bond prototype Richard Hannay captures the German spies of Black Stone as they attempt to flee the country by ship, the *Ariadne*, from the Kent coast: "As the handcuffs clinked on his wrists I said my last word to him. 'I hope Franz will bear his triumph well. I ought to tell you that the *Ariadne* for the last hour has been in our hands'" (John Buchan, *The Complete Richard Hannay* [London: Penguin, 1992], 103).
74. Fleming, *Goldfinger*, 72.
75. Fleming, *Goldfinger*, 75.
76. Fleming, *Goldfinger*, 117.
77. Fleming, *Goldfinger*, 75.
78. Fleming, *Goldfinger*, 102.
79. Fleming, *Goldfinger*, 89, 118.
80. Fleming, *Goldfinger*, 118, 120.
81. Fleming, *Goldfinger*, 115, 134.

82. A German Junkers plane was shot down over Kent while returning from a raid on London, leading to the last action between British and foreign military forces on British soil.

9. FLEMING'S WOMEN, BOND'S "GIRLS"

1. Lisa Funnell, ed., *For His Eyes Only: The Women of James Bond* (New York: Wallflower, 2015), 1.
2. Fleming, *Casino Royale*, 27.
3. Fleming, *Man with the Golden Typewriter*, 127.
4. Fleming, *Moonraker*, 104.
5. Claire Hines emphasizes the role of Sean Connery's Bond in representing the *Playboy* ideal, describing Connery as "an iconic embodiment of the playboy fantasy ideal that was being readily imagined" (*The Playboy and James Bond: 007, Ian Fleming, and* Playboy *Magazine* [Manchester: Manchester University Press, 2018], 58). Hines further points to the role of consumerism in this masculine fantasy, noting that both Bond and *Playboy* "celebrated a sophisticated, playful, consumerist lifestyle and offered a fantasy ideal" (117). By contrast, Fleming's wife, Ann, referred dismissively to *Playboy* as "an obscene America publication" (Amory, *Letters*, 338) and commented of the Playboy Bunnies on Jamaica: "The Bunnies are girls wearing Bunny headdresses but . . . untouchable. A vulgar Western version of geishas" (338).
6. For an interesting discussion of the variants and possible origins of this phrase, see Edward Biddulph, "Women Want to Be with Him, Men Want to Be Him—and Other Phrases," James Bond Memes: Exploring Bondian Ideas and Influences, April 29, 2012, http://jamesbondmemes.blogspot.com/2012/04/women-want-to-be-with-him-men-want-to.html.
7. Fleming, *Goldfinger*, 237.
8. Fleming, *For Your Eyes Only*, 42, 43.
9. Fleming, *For Your Eyes Only*, 49.
10. The story was first published in the United Kingdom in *Modern Woman* magazine in November 1959 under the title "A Choice of Love and Hate" before appearing as part of the first Bond short story collection *For Your Eyes Only: Five Secret Occasions in the Life of James Bond*, published by Cape in April 1960. Jon Gilbert relates, "The story was inspired by his friend Blanche Blackwell, who related the experiences of a police inspector involved in a similar decline" (Gilbert, *Ian Fleming: The Bibliography*, 264).
11. Amory, *Letters*, 296–97.
12. Fleming, *Goldfinger*, 257.
13. Fleming, *From Russia, with Love*, 98.
14. Temple, "Ian Fleming Explains How to Write a Thriller."
15. Fleming, *Diamonds Are Forever*, 145.
16. Fleming, *Moonraker*, 243.
17. Amory, *Letters*, 78, 81. Interestingly, Lisl Popper reported of Ian, "He always used to say to me that there was no reason for him to get married because he never had the urge to reproduce" (Pearson, *Notes*, 129).
18. Amory, *Letters*, 81, 93. Ann's phrase alludes to Dickens's *David Copperfield* (1851), in which the cart driver Barkis passively courts Clara Peggotty, David's childhood nurse, repeatedly saying, "Barkis is willing," but will not directly propose marriage.

19. Amory, *Letters*, 337. Interestingly, Ann links Ian's fantasy of being James Bond to her husband's apparent preference for exclusively male company. Hilary Bray's name had been used by Fleming for the "alter ego" of James Bond in *On Her Majesty's Secret Service*, posing as a senior researcher at the College of Arms.

20. Amory, *Letters*, 197, 278.

21. Fleming, *Man with the Golden Typewriter*, 168.

22. Lycett, *Ian Fleming*, 84.

23. Russell, *Constant Heart*, 239.

24. Russell, *Constant Heart*, 86.

25. Russell, *Constant Heart*, 114.

26. Russell, *Constant Heart*, 115.

27. The restaurant on Stratton Street in Mayfair is now the site of the Langan Brasserie, opened in 1977 by the Irish entrepreneur Peter Langan in partnership with Michael Caine, the British actor who became famous for playing Harry Palmer, Len Deighton's spy hero.

28. Russell, *Constant Heart*, 96, 112. According to Maud's granddaughter and editor Emily Russell, "It is likely they became lovers in the 1930s and the affair continued intermittently over the next decade or so. . . . To me the most telling evidence is a small envelope with a black lock of hair inside that I found among her papers. On the envelope, Maud has written a simple 'I.'s' in pencil" (*Constant Heart*, 16). Also of interest is the photograph of Ian in naval uniform during the war that "takes up almost an entire page of Maud's photo album" (*Constant Heart*, illus p13). Emily relates that Ian wrote Maud from Colombo, Ceylon (the former name of Sri Lanka), in 1945, "You're the one reason I want to see London again. I have missed you very much" (16).

29. Russell, *Constant Heart*, 111.

30. Russell, *Constant Heart*, 175, 225.

31. Russell, *Constant Heart*, 239, 241, 242.

32. Russell, *Constant Heart*, 279, 150.

33. Russell, *Constant Heart*, 290, 279. Emily Russell writes it was Maud who "gave Ian £5,000 to buy a home in Jamaica; he bought the 15-acre property for £2,000 and budgeted £3,000 to build a house" (299).

34. Russell, *Constant Heart*, 56.

35. Pearson, *Life*, 48, 105.

36. Fionn Morgan, "Ian Fleming: Cruel? Selfish? Misogynistic? Nonsense, Says His Stepdaughter," *Spectator*, August 23, 2014.

37. Pearson, *Life*, 103, 106.

38. As Maud related in her diary, "On Friday G[ilbert] had a long letter from Beves [vice provost of King's] saying he'd failed, work superficial, appeared to have a dislike for learning and for authority. . . . It's too disappointing. R. thought he'd passed" (*Constant Heart*, 87–88).

39. Russell, *Constant Heart*, 137, 141.

40. Russell, *Constant Heart*, 150, 153.

41. Russell, *Constant Heart*, 156, 157.

42. Provided by Emily Russell from the private diaries of Maud Russell.

43. Russell, *Constant Heart*, 16.

44. Russell, *Constant Heart*, 172.

45. Russell, *Constant Heart*, 203.

46. Fleming, *On Her Majesty's Secret Service*, 258.

47. Hirsch, *Constant Liberal*, 350.

48. Phyllis Bottome, *The Life Line* (Boston: Little, Brown, 1946), 15.

49. Bottome, *Life Line*, 13.

50. Phyllis Bottome, *The Goal* (London: Faber, 1962), 58.
51. Bottome, *Life Line*, 39, 27, 29.
52. "Could This Woman Have Invented James Bond?"
53. Hirsch, *Constant Liberal*, 346.
54. Fleming, *On Her Majesty's Secret Service*, 44.
55. James Chapman, "'Women Were for Recreation': The Gender Politics of Ian Fleming's James Bond," in *For His Eyes Only: The Women of James Bond*, ed. Lisa Funnell (New York: Wallflower, 2015), 14.
56. Chapman, "Women Were for Recreation," 13.
57. Fleming, *Dr. No*, 246.
58. Fleming, *Moonraker*, 128.
59. Fleming, *The Spy Who Loved Me*, 1.
60. Letter from Michael Howard, Cape Archive. Reproduced by permission of The Random House Group Ltd.
61. Fleming, *Man with the Golden Typewriter*, 271–72, 277.
62. Fleming, *The Spy Who Loved Me*, 38.
63. Fleming, *Man with the Golden Typewriter*, 296.
64. Chapman, "Women Were for Recreation," 16.
65. Fleming, *Man with the Golden Typewriter*, 296.

10. PROMOTING BOND

1. Letter from Michael Howard, Cape Archive. Reproduced by permission of The Random House Group Ltd.
2. Pearson, *Notes*, 51.
3. Cape Archive. Reproduced by permission of The Random House Group Ltd.
4. Bennett and Woollacott, "Moments of Bond," 16, 21.
5. Fleming, *Man with the Golden Typewriter*, 264.
6. The formal invitation to the Pinewood party ran as follows:

The Directors of Eon Productions Limited
Harry Saltzman & Albert R. Broccoli
And
The Directors of Jonathan Cape Limited
Invite you to a party at Pinewood Studios at 5.15pm on April 1 1963
To celebrate the publication of
ON HER MAJESTY'S SECRET SERVICE
By
IAN FLEMING
On the first day of shooting of
FROM RUSSIA, WITH LOVE

Cape Archive. Reproduced by permission of The Random House Group Ltd.

7. Cape Archive. Reproduced by permission of The Random House Group Ltd.
8. Cape Archive. Reproduced by permission of The Random House Group Ltd.

9. Fleming, *Man with the Golden Typewriter*, 136.

10. Fleming, *Man with the Golden Typewriter*, 246.

11. Cape Archive. Reproduced by permission of Ian Fleming Estate.

12. Michael Denning, "Licensed to Look: James Bond and the Heroism of Consumption," in *The James Bond Phenomenon*, 2nd ed., ed. Christoph Lindner (Manchester: Manchester University Press, 2009), 56.

13. Cape Archive. Reproduced by permission (emphasis added).

14. Temple, "Ian Fleming Explains How to Write a Thriller."

15. Giblin, *James Bond's London*, 34.

16. Cape Archive. Reproduced by permission of Ian Fleming Estate. Fleming, *Man with the Golden Typewriter*, 319.

17. Temple, "Ian Fleming Explains How to Write a Thriller."

18. Fleming, *Man with the Golden Typewriter*, 22.

19. Cape Archive. Reproduced by permission of The Random House Group Ltd.

20. An important exception is Tom Cull's website *Artistic Licence Renewed*, https://literary007.com, which gives extensive coverage, illustration, and discussion of Chopping's artwork.

21. Fleming, *Man with the Golden Typewriter*, 294.

22. Bennett and Woollacott, "Moments of Bond," 13. Bennett and Woollacott note, "The jacket designs for the first hardback editions of the early Bond novels thus typically consisted of a collection of objects associated with either espionage or luxurious living, or both, and connoted the category of superior quality, 'literary' spy fiction" ("Moments of Bond," 13–14).

23. Fleming, *Man with the Golden Typewriter*, 251.

24. Like James Bond, *Chitty* was more successful in cinematic incarnation, when Albert R. Broccoli produced the film musical *Chitty Chitty Bang Bang*, in 1968. The film was directed by Ken Hughes, whose previous assignment was directing the Berlin scenes of the 1967 spoof version of *Casino Royale*. Another Bond connection was Roald Dahl—who had formally worked with William Stephenson's British Security Co-ordination during World War II—who penned the screenplay for *You Only Live Twice* (1967) and was also one of the screenwriters for *Chitty*.

25. Christopher Hitchens, "Introduction," in *Orient Express* by Graham Greene (New York: Penguin, 2004), vii.

26. Temple, "Ian Fleming Explains How to Write a Thriller."

27. Fleming, *Man with the Golden Typewriter*, 97.

28. Fleming, *Man with the Golden Typewriter*, 259. One can here see the origins of the hugely successful film series that began with Blake Edwards's *The Pink Panther* starring Niven, and Claudia Cardinale, in 1963. Niven would, ironically, go on to play James Bond in the spoof adaptation of *Casino Royale* in 1967. Niven would also be referred to by name in Fleming's 1964 novel *You Only Live Twice*. Here the Japanese diver and former film star Kissy Suzuki—who ends up becoming Bond's lover following his amnesia—tells Bond about her time in Hollywood where the only person who treated her kindly was David Niven. In recognition of Niven's kindness, she has named her diving cormorant—who accompanies her on her dives—"David."

29. Fleming, *Man with the Golden Typewriter*, 257.

30. This provides another link between Bond and Fleming, whose father, Valentine, was also Scottish born.

31. British Library, Add MS 81057. Reproduced by permission of Ian Fleming Estate.

32. Cape Archive. Reproduced by permission of The Random House Group Ltd.

33. *Playboy* would accuse Cape of having allowed the NAL publication of *Man with the Golden Gun*—Fleming's last and posthumously published novel—before the agreed-upon date of August 21, 1965. Fleming's death, far from resolving such disputes, seemed to exacerbate them for he was no longer there to act as a go-between for different publishers and interests (Cape Archive. Reproduced by permission of The Random House Group Ltd.).

11. FROM FLEMING, WITH LOVE

1. Fleming, *Man with the Golden Typewriter*, 171.

2. As Mark Simmons has noted, Fleming had always been fascinated by treasure hunts since boyhood, and many of his novels incorporated themes of hidden or buried treasure (*Ian Fleming and Operation Golden Eye*, ch. 10). Among other adventures, Fleming joined in treasure-hunting expeditions at Creake Abbey, Norfolk, in 1953, and the Seychelles in April 1958. Neither expedition brought him personal enrichment, but he enjoyed the experiences and they gave him material for the Bond novels and stories.

3. Fleming was concerned about the "libel points" of the manuscript and told Plomer, "We will go into [them] very carefully" (Fleming, *Man with the Golden Typewriter*, 172).

4. Ian Fleming, *The Diamond Smugglers* (Las Vegas: Thomas and Mercer, 2013), viii.

5. Umberto Eco, "Narrative Structures in Fleming," in *The James Bond Phenomenon*, 2nd ed., ed. Christoph Lindner (Manchester: Manchester University Press, 2009), 43.

6. Might this "earlier version of Spectre" be indicated by the name of Seraffimo Spang's fantastic recreation of a wild west frontier town, "Spectreville"? According to Andrew Lycett, "McClory remained adamant that SPECTRE was a 'cumulative idea,' the product of their joint endeavours" (Lycett, *Ian Fleming*, 354).

7. Fleming, *Diamonds Are Forever*, 26.

8. Fleming, *Diamonds Are Forever*, 21.

9. Guy Hamilton, dir., *Diamonds Are Forever* (EON Productions, 1971).

10. Fleming, *Diamonds Are Forever*, 15.

11. Fleming uses the name of the real Specter mountain range in Nevada as the basis for his fictional wild west town. The spelling of this town's name, "Spectreville," demonstrates that Fleming had changed the spelling long before his collaboration with Kevin McClory on *Thunderball*. I am grateful to Matthew B. Sherman for drawing my attention to this point.

12. Nigel West, "Fiction, Faction, and Intelligence," *Intelligence and National Security* 19, no. 2 (2004): 276.

13. This confusion in *Diamonds Are Forever* is due to the jarring between the "realism" of the smuggling framework and the flagrant fantasy of the American gangster plot.

14. Fleming, *Man with the Golden Typewriter*, 228.

15. Amory, *Letters*, 196–97. In his introduction, "John Blaize" advises the reader that "some interesting names and details had to be withheld altogether" (Fleming, *Diamond Smugglers*, xi).

16. Fleming, *Man with the Golden Typewriter*, 172.

17. Fleming, *Diamond Smugglers*, xi, xvi (emphasis added).

18. Fleming, *Diamond Smugglers*, xiii, 27, 172.

19. Fleming, *Diamond Smugglers*, 28.

20. Fleming, *Diamond Smugglers*, 13, 59, 60.

21. Fleming, *Diamonds Are Forever*, 19.

22. Fleming, *Diamond Smugglers*, xvi, 93.
23. Fleming, *Diamond Smugglers*, 94.
24. Fleming, *Diamonds Are Forever*, 11.
25. Fleming, *Diamond Smugglers*, xiii.
26. Fleming, *Diamond Smugglers*, 67.
27. Fleming, *From Russia, with Love*, 95.
28. Fleming, *Diamond Smugglers*, 100.
29. Eco, "Narrative Structures," 54.
30. Denning, "Licensed to Look," 64.
31. Fleming, *Thrilling Cities*, 3.
32. Fleming, *Thrilling Cities*, ix. Ian returns to this connection between adventurous travel and writing thrillers at the beginning of the first chapter on Hong Kong: "If you write thrillers, people think that you must live a thrilling life and enjoy doing thrilling things" (1).
33. Fleming, *Thrilling Cities*, 4.
34. Pearson, *Notes*, 101.
35. Fleming, *Thrilling Cities*, 50, 52. In fact, Fleming died of a heart attack in 1964—the year after *Thrilling Cities* was published—at the age of fifty-six.
36. Fleming, *Diamonds Are Forever*, 51.
37. Fleming, *Thrilling Cities*, 5. Ambler's *Passage of Arms* (1959)—which won the Gold Dagger Award from the Crime Writers Association—deals, appropriately, with a conspiracy to smuggle a cache of arms abroad for profit.
38. Fleming, *Thrilling Cities*, 23, 25, 31. Mr. Big is the Haitian-born villain in *Live and Let Die*. His name refers to his physical size and is an acronym for his full name: Buonaparte Ignace Gallia.
39. Fleming, *Thrilling Cities*, 229, 226.
40. Fleming, *Thrilling Cities*, 228–29.
41. Fleming, *Thrilling Cities*, viii, 229.
42. Fleming, *Thrilling Cities*, 2, 115.
43. Fleming, *Octopussy and the Living Daylights* (New York: Penguin, 2004), 112. This story, as Peter Janson-Smith notes in a foreword to this edition of the story, "was first published in the USA in October 1963 in the *New York Herald Tribune* under the title 'Agent 007 in New York' and was included in the 1964 US edition of *Thrilling Cities* to placate 'the hostile reaction of many Americans (not only New Yorkers) to the original piece'" (111–12).
44. Fleming here perpetuates the myth of James Bond's actual existence—indeed, of his friendship with Fleming—which provided John Pearson with such good material in his *Authorized Biography of James Bond*, published in 1973.
45. Fleming, *Octopussy and the Living Daylights*, 116, 119.
46. Fleming, *Thrilling Cities*, 126. Clearly the implication is that American influence has usurped the British, adding bitterness to his (and Bond's) critical portrayal of American culture.
47. In fact, it was only after the Soviet Union had collapsed and the Cold War had ended—in 1990—that the oil riches of Kuwait proved too tempting for one of its powerful neighbors to resist, resulting in the Iraqi invasion of Kuwait and the first Gulf War of 1990–1991.
48. Fleming, *Goldfinger*, 71.
49. Amis, *James Bond Dossier*, 111.

12. THE IRON CRAB

1. Fleming, *From Russia, with Love*, 143.
2. Fleming, *Thunderball*, 3, 4.
3. Fleming, *Man with the Golden Typewriter*, 243.
4. Fleming, *Man with the Golden Typewriter*, 269.
5. Temple, "Ian Fleming Explains How to Write a Thriller."
6. Ian Fleming, *Chitty-Chitty-Bang-Bang: The Magical Car* (Somerville, MA: Candlewick, 2013), 56, 52.
7. Fleming, *Chitty-Chitty-Bang-Bang*, 57, 83.
8. Fleming, *Chitty-Chitty-Bang-Bang*, 2. Caractacus was also the name of the horse that won Britain's Epson Derby in 1862.
9. Fleming, *Chitty-Chitty-Bang-Bang*, 4, 16. Ian, of course, had used the proceeds of selling the film rights to his own "invention," *Casino Royale*, to purchase his own favorite car, a Ford Thunderbird.
10. Fleming, *Moonraker*, 142.
11. Fleming, *Chitty-Chitty-Bang-Bang*, 110.
12. Fleming, *Man with the Golden Typewriter*, 270, 275.
13. Cited in Denning, "Licensed to Look," 56.
14. John Cork, "James Bond Invades America," in "Ian Fleming and Book Collecting," ed. James Fergusson, special issue, *Book Collector* 66, no. 1 (Spring 2017): 169–70.
15. Cork, "James Bond Invades America," 178.
16. Fleming, *Man with the Golden Typewriter*, 277.
17. Fleming, *Man with the Golden Typewriter*, 274.
18. Fleming, *Man with the Golden Typewriter*, 328.
19. For an in-depth discussion of these attacks on Fleming's works—which were ad hominem rather than literary in nature—see Jeremy Duns, *Enemy Action: The Literary Assassination of Ian Fleming* (Norwich, UK: Skerry, 2020). Of Paul Johnson's 1959 essay "Sex, Snobbery, and Sadism," published in *The Spectator*, Duns comments, "It ranks as one of the most vitriolic and unprofessional literary pieces published in Britain in the 20th century" (*Enemy Action*).
20. Fleming, *On Her Majesty's Secret Service*, 183, 184.
21. Peter Hunt, dir., *On Her Majesty 's Secret Service* (EON Productions, 1969).
22. Fleming, *On Her Majesty's Secret Service*, 187, 220. Even Marc-Ange's threat to join them on their honeymoon—"You will have a time keeping me away from Kitzbühel" (220)—cannot dampen Bond's optimism.
23. Fleming, *On Her Majesty's Secret Service*, 257.
24. Donald McCormick, *Who's Who in Spy Fiction* (New York: Taplinger, 1977), 61.
25. Fleming, *Man with the Golden Typewriter*, 373.
26. Pearson, *Notes*, 309–10.
27. Fleming, *Man with the Golden Typewriter*, 362.
28. Fleming, *Man with the Golden Gun*, 50, 53.
29. Fleming, *Man with the Golden Gun*, 45, 32, 33.
30. William Plomer, "Address Given at the Memorial Service for Ian Fleming by William Plomer on September 15th 1964" (St. Ives, UK: Westerham Press, 1964).
31. Plomer, "Address Given at the Memorial Service for Ian Fleming."

Bibliography

ARCHIVES

Churchill Archive Center, Churchill College, University of Cambridge, UK.
Ian Fleming Papers, Lilly Library, Indiana University, Bloomington.
John Pearson Papers, Lilly Library, Indiana University, Bloomington.
Jonathan Cape Archive, University of Reading Special Collections, UK.
National Archives, Kew, UK.
Phyllis Bottome Papers, British Library, London.

BOOKS, ARTICLES, FILMS, WEBSITES

Adler, Alfred. *The Practice and Theory of Individual Psychology*. Translated by P. Radi. Mansfield Center, CT: Martino, 2011.

Amanatullah, Ihsan ["Revelator"]. "Was Ian Fleming's 'Octopussy' Autobiographical?" Artistic Licence Renewed, February 24, 2014. https://literary007.com/2014/02/24/wasoctopussy-autobiographical.

Ambler, Eric. *Cause for Alarm*. New York: Vintage, 2002.

Ambler, Eric. *A Coffin for Dimitrios*. New York: Vintage, 2001.

Amis, Kingsley. *The James Bond Dossier*. London: Jonathan Cape, 1965.

Amory, Mark, ed. *The Letters of Ann Fleming*. London: Collins, 1985.

Andrew, Christopher. *The Defence of the Realm: The Authorized History of MI5*. London: Penguin, 2010.

Baron, Cynthia. "*Dr. No*: Bonding Britishness to Racial Sovereignty." In *The James Bond Phenomenon: A Critical Reader*, 2nd ed., edited by Christoph Lindner, 153–68. Manchester: Manchester University Press, 2009.

Bennett, Tony, and Janet Woollacott. "The Moments of Bond." In *The James Bond Phenomenon: A Critical Reader*, 2nd ed., edited by Christoph Lindner, 13–33. Manchester: Manchester University Press, 2009.

Biddulph, Edward. "Women Want to Be with Him, Men Want to Be Him—and Other Phrases." James Bond Memes: Exploring Bondian Ideas and Influences, April 29, 2012.

http://jamesbondmemes.blogspot.com/2012/04/women-want-to-be-with-him-men-want-to.html.

Blake, George. *No Other Choice: An Autobiography*. New York: Simon & Schuster, 1990.

Bottome, Phyllis. *The Goal*. London: Faber, 1962.

Bottome, Phyllis. *The Life Line*. Boston: Little, Brown, 1946.

Bottome, Phyllis. *The Mortal Storm*. Foreword by Phyllis Lassner and Marilyn Hoder-Salmon. Evanston, IL: Northwestern University Press, 1998.

Bridport Museum. "WW2: People's War." BBC, April 24, 2005. http://www.bbc.co.uk/history/ww2peopleswar/stories/22/a3943622.shtml.

Britten, Nick. "Ian Fleming 'Used 16th Century Spy as Inspiration for James Bond.'" *Telegraph*, October 30, 2008. https://www.telegraph.co.uk/news/uknews/3285886/Ian-Fleming-used-16th-century-spy-as-inspiration-for-James-Bond.html.

Bryce, Ivar. *You Only Live Once: Memories of Ian Fleming*. London: Weidenfeld & Nicolson, 1984.

Buchan, John. *The Complete Richard Hannay*. London: Penguin, 1992.

Campbell, Martin, dir. *Casino Royale*. EON Productions, 2006.

Campbell, Martin, dir. *Goldeneye*. EON Productions, 1995.

Chapman, James. *Licence to Thrill: A Cultural History of the James Bond Films*. 2nd ed. London: I. B. Tauris, 2007.

Chapman, James. "'Women Were for Recreation': The Gender Politics of Ian Fleming's James Bond." In *For His Eyes Only: The Women of James Bond*, edited by Lisa Funnell, 9–17. New York: Wallflower, 2015.

Comentale, Edward P., Stephen Watt, and Skip Willman, eds. *Ian Fleming and James Bond: The Cultural Politics of 007*. Bloomington: Indiana University Press, 2005.

Conlin, Jonathan. *Mr Five Percent: The Many Lives of Calouste Gulbenkian, the World's Richest Man*. London: Profile, 2019.

Cork, John. "James Bond Invades America." In "Ian Fleming and Book Collecting," edited by James Fergusson. Special issue, *Book Collector* 66, no. 1 (Spring 2017): 169–81.

"Could This Woman Have Invented James Bond?" *Radio Times*, December 10, 2016. https://www.radiotimes.com/news/2016-12-10/could-this-woman-have-invented-james-bond.

Cromwell, Bob. "Military Tunnels in the White Cliffs of Dover." Cromwell-Intl (blog). Accessed November 24, 2020. https://cromwell-intl.com/travel/uk/dover.

Darwin, Charles. *On the Origin of Species by Means of Natural Selection*. 1859. Project Gutenberg. http://www.gutenberg.org/files/1228/1228-h/1228-h.htm#chap14.

Deighton, Len. *The Ipcress File*. London: Harper, 2015.

Denning, Michael. "Licensed to Look: James Bond and the Heroism of Consumption." In *The James Bond Phenomenon*, 2nd ed., edited by Christoph Lindner, 56–75. Manchester: Manchester University Press, 2009.

Duns, Jeremy. *Enemy Action: The Literary Assassination of Ian Fleming*. Norwich, UK: Skerry, 2020.

Duns, Jeremy. *A Spy Is Born: Dennis Wheatley and the Secret Roots of Ian Fleming's James Bond*. Norwich, UK: Skerry, 2019.

Eco, Umberto. "Narrative Structures in Fleming." In *The James Bond Phenomenon*, 2nd ed., edited by Christoph Lindner, 36–55. Manchester: Manchester University Press, 2009.

Edmonds, Mark. "I Finished Off Bond in a Flash." *The Sunday Times*, October 14, 2012.

Edmonds, Mark. "My Secret Life at the *Sunday Times*." *The Sunday Times*, October 14, 2012.

Ferguson, Paul. "Fleming. Valentine Fleming." The Pipes of War Production Blog, October 5, 2012. http://thepipesofwar.com/production-blog/?p=1205.

Fleming, Fergus, ed. *The Man with the Golden Typewriter: Ian Fleming's James Bond Letters.* London: Bloomsbury, 2015.

Fleming, Ian. *Casino Royale*. Las Vegas: Thomas and Mercer, 2012.

Fleming, Ian. *Chitty Chitty Bang Bang: The Magical Car*. Somerville, MA: Candlewick, 2013.

Fleming, Ian. *The Diamond Smugglers*. Las Vegas: Thomas and Mercer, 2013.

Fleming, Ian. *Diamonds Are Forever*. Las Vegas: Thomas and Mercer, 2012.

Fleming, Ian. *Dr. No*. Las Vegas: Thomas and Mercer, 2012.

Fleming, Ian. *For Your Eyes Only*. Las Vegas: Thomas and Mercer, 2012.

Fleming, Ian. *From Russia, with Love*. Las Vegas: Thomas and Mercer, 2012.

Fleming, Ian. *Goldfinger*. Las Vegas: Thomas and Mercer, 2012.

Fleming, Ian. Letter to *The Times*, September 28, 1938. https://thetimes.co.uk/letterarchive/Ian_Fleming.html#collapse.

Fleming, Ian. *Live and Let Die*. Las Vegas: Thomas and Mercer, 2012.

Fleming, Ian. *The Man with the Golden Gun*. Las Vegas: Thomas and Mercer, 2012.

Fleming, Ian. *Moonraker*. Las Vegas: Thomas and Mercer, 2012.

Fleming, Ian. *Octopussy and the Living Daylights*. New York: Penguin, 2004.

Fleming, Ian. *Octopussy and the Living Daylights*. Las Vegas: Thomas and Mercer, 2012.

Fleming, Ian. *On Her Majesty's Secret Service*. Las Vegas: Thomas and Mercer, 2012.

Fleming, Ian. "Russia's Strength." British Library. RP 7369.

Fleming, Ian. *The Spy Who Loved Me*. Las Vegas: Thomas and Mercer, 2012.

Fleming, Ian. *Thrilling Cities*. Las Vegas: Thomas and Mercer, 2013.

Fleming, Ian. *Thunderball*. Las Vegas: Thomas and Mercer, 2012.

Fleming, Ian. *You Only Live Twice*. Las Vegas: Thomas and Mercer, 2012.

Fleming, Peter. *Brazilian Adventure*. Evanston, IL: Northwestern University Press, 1999.

Fleming, Peter. *The Sixth Column*. Hornchurch, Essex: Ian Henry, 1975.

Funnell, Lisa, ed. *For His Eyes Only: The Women of James Bond*. New York: Wallflower, 2015.

Giblin, Gary. *James Bond's London: A Reference Guide to Locations*. London: Daleon, 2001.

Gilbert, Jon. *Ian Fleming: The Bibliography*. London: Queen Anne Press, 2017.

Gilbert, Lewis, dir. *You Only Live Twice*. EON Productions, 1967.

Glen, John, dir. *The Living Daylights*. EON Productions, 1987.

Godfrey, John. "The Naval Memoirs of Admiral J. H. Godfrey." Churchill Archive Center. Estate of Admiral John Godfrey.

Greene, Graham. *The Confidential Agent*. Harmondsworth, UK: Penguin, 1971.

Hall, Matthew. *Plants as Persons: A Philosophical Botany*. Albany: State University of New York Press, 2011.

Halloran, Vivian. "Tropical Bond." In *Ian Fleming and James Bond: The Cultural Politics of 007*, edited by Edward P. Comentale, Stephen Watt, and Skip Willman, 158–77. Bloomington: Indiana University Press, 2005.

Hamilton, Guy, dir. *Diamonds Are Forever*. EON Productions, 1971.

Hamilton, Guy, dir. *Goldfinger*. EON Productions, 1964.

Hamilton, Guy, dir. *Live and Let Die*. EON Productions, 1973.

Harling, Robert. *Ian Fleming: A Personal Memoir*. London: Robson/Biteback, 2015.

Hennessy, Peter. *The Secret State: Preparing for the Worst 1945–2010*. 2nd ed. London: Penguin, 2010.

Hines, Claire. *The Playboy and James Bond: 007, Ian Fleming, and* Playboy *Magazine*. Manchester: Manchester University Press, 2018.

Hirsch, Pam. *The Constant Liberal: The Life and Work of Phyllis Bottome*. London: Quartet, 2010.

"History of AU30." National Archives, Kew. ADM 223/480.

Hitchens, Christopher. "Introduction." In *Orient Express* by Graham Greene, vii–xiv. New York: Penguin, 2004.

Household, Geoffrey. *The Third Hour*. New York: Open Road, 2015.

Hughes, Ken, dir. *Chitty Chitty Bang Bang*. United Artists, 1968.

Hunt, Peter, dir. *On Her Majesty's Secret Service*. EON Productions, 1969.

Ian Fleming Publications. Accessed November 2, 2020. http://www.ianfleming.com/ian-fleming.

JamesBondBrasilTV. "Ian Fleming: The CBC Interview (Legendado)." YouTube, December 4, 2013. https://www.youtube.com/watch?v=fKtO34YNcFw.

JBond007. "Remembering Ian Fleming: 28th May 1908–12th Aug 1964." YouTube, August 13, 2014. https://www.youtube.com/watch?v=5E7HBjafG7M.

Leigh Fermor, Patrick. *The Traveller's Tree: A Journey through the Caribbean Islands*. New York: New York Review Books, 2011.

Lewis, Peter. *Eric Ambler: A Literary Biography*. New York: Odyssey Press, 2014.

Lindner, Christoph. "Criminal Vision and the Ideology of Detection in Fleming's 007 Series." In *The James Bond Phenomenon: A Critical Reader*, 2nd ed., edited by Christoph Lindner, 76–88. Manchester: Manchester University Press, 2009.

Lindner, Christoph, ed. *The James Bond Phenomenon: A Critical Reader*. 2nd ed. Manchester: Manchester University Press, 2009.

Lycett, Andrew. *From Diamond Sculls to Golden Handcuffs: A History of Rowe & Pitman*. London: Robert Hale, 1998.

Lycett, Andrew. *Ian Fleming*. London: Phoenix, 1996.

Macintyre, Ben. *For Your Eyes Only: Ian Fleming + James Bond*. London: Bloomsbury, 2008.

Macintyre, Ben. *Operation Mincemeat: How a Dead Man and a Bizarre Plan Fooled the Nazis and Assured an Allied Victory*. New York: Harmony, 2010.

Macintyre, Ben. *A Spy among Friends: Kim Philby and the Great Betrayal*. London: Bloomsbury, 2014.

Markham, Robert [Kingsley Amis]. *Colonel Sun*. London: Ian Fleming Publications, 1968.

Matheson, Sue. "Primitive Masculinity/'Sophisticated' Stomach: Gender, Appetite, and Power in the Novels of Ian Fleming." *CEA Critic* 67, no. 1 (Fall 2004): 15–24.

Maugham, William Somerset. *Ashenden: Or, The British Agent*. OTB Ebook, 2020. Kindle.

McClynn, Frank. *Robert Louis Stevenson*. London: Pimlico, 1994.

McCormick, Donald. *Who's Who in Spy Fiction*. New York: Taplinger, 1977.

Moran, Christopher, and Trevor McCrisken. "The Secret Life of Ian Fleming: Spies, Lies and Social Ties." *Contemporary British History* 33, no. 3 (2019): 336–56.

Morgan, Charles. "History of Naval Intelligence 1939–42." National Archives, Kew. ADM 223/464.

Morgan, Fionn. "Ian Fleming: Cruel? Selfish? Misogynistic? Nonsense, Says His Step-daughter." *Spectator*, August 23, 2014.

"Noël Coward and Ian Fleming." Dover Museum. Accessed November 24, 2020. https://www.dovermuseum.co.uk/Information-Resources/Articles--Factsheets/Coward--Flemming.aspx.

"Over by Christmas." The National WWI Museum and Memorial. Accessed November 24, 2020. https://www.theworldwar.org/explore/exhibitions/past-exhibitions/over-christmas.

Parker, Matthew. *Goldeneye: Where Bond Was Born: Ian Fleming's Jamaica*. New York: Pegasus, 2015.

Pearson, John. *Ian Fleming: The Notes*. London: Queen Anne Press, 2020.

Pearson, John. *The Life of Ian Fleming*. London: Bloomsbury, 2003.

Pellatt, Thomas. *Boys in the Making*. London: Methuen, 1936.

Plomer, William. "Address Given at the Memorial Service for Ian Fleming by William Plomer on September 15th, 1964." St. Ives, UK: Westerham Press, 1964.

Rankin, Nicholas. *A Genius for Deception: How Cunning Helped the British Win Two World Wars.* New York: Oxford University Press, 2008.

Richards, Lee. *The Black Art: British Clandestine Psychological Warfare against the Third Reich*. Peacehaven, Sussex: Psywar, 2010.

Rimington, Stella. "Introduction." In *The Spy's Bedside Book*, edited by Hugh Greene and Graham Greene, xi–xx. London: Hutchinson, 2007.

Russell, Maud. *A Constant Heart: The War Diaries of Maud Russell 1938–1945.* Edited by Emily Russell. Stanbridge, UK: Dovecote, 2017.

Sachgau, Oliver. "The Name's Bond, Maybe St. James Bond: Ian Fleming's Toronto Inspirations." *Toronto Star*, November 7, 2015. https://www.thestar.com/news/gta/2015/11/07/the-names-bond-maybe-st-james-bond-ian-flemings-toronto-inspirations.html.

Salter, David. "Was Cabourg an Inspiration for Royale-les-Eaux?" The James Bond Dossier (blog), September 25, 2013. https://www.thejamesbonddossier.com/content/cabourg-inspiration-royale-les-eaux.htm.

"Saratoga Country Estate, Black Hole Hollow Farm." Christie's International Real Estate. Accessed November 24, 2020. https://www.christiesrealestate.com/sales/detail/170-l-775-1606241201487809/saratoga-country-estate-black-hole-hollow-farm-cambridge-ny.

Simmons, Mark. *Ian Fleming and Operation Golden Eye: Keeping Spain Out of World War II.* Oxford: Casemate, 2018.

Smith, Michael. *The Anatomy of a Traitor: A History of Espionage and Betrayal.* London: Aurum, 2017.

Smith, Michael. *Six: The Real James Bonds, 1909–1939.* London: Biteback, 2011.

"Spyway School." Spyway School (blog). Accessed November 24, 2020. http://spywayschool.blogspot.com.

Stafford, David. *Camp X: SOE School for Spies*. London: Thistle, 2013.

Stallworthy, Jacob. "Ian Fleming—The Real James Bond." *Telegraph*, August 12, 2014.

Stevenson, William. *A Man Called Intrepid: The Secret War*. New York: Ballantine, 1977.

Temple, Emily. "Ian Fleming Explains How to Write a Thriller." *Literary Hub*, May 2, 2019. https://lithub.com/ian-fleming-explains-how-to-write-a-thriller.

Urken, Ross Kenneth. "How James Bond's Legacy Is Saving Jamaica." *Bloomberg*, July 23, 2018. https://www.bloomberg.com/news/features/2018-07-23/how-the-birthplace-of-james-bond-is-helping-save-the-caribbean.

Vogel, Steve. *Betrayal in Berlin: The True Story of the Cold War's Most Audacious Espionage Operation*. New York: Custom House, 2019.

West, Nigel. "Fiction, Faction, and Intelligence." *Intelligence and National Security* 19, no. 2 (2004): 275–89.

Wikipedia, s.v. "The Carlton Hotel, London." Last edited June 30, 2020, 22:13. https://en.wikipedia.org/wiki/Carlton_Hotel,_London.

Wright, Jim. *The Real James Bond: A True Story of Identity Theft, Avian Intrigue and Ian Fleming*. Atglen, PA: Schiffer, 2020.

Young, Terence, dir. *Dr. No*. EON Productions, 1962.

Young, Terence, dir. *From Russia with Lo*ve. EON Productions, 1963.

Young, Terence, dir. *Thunderball*. EON Productions, 1965.

Index

About the Author

Oliver Buckton is the author of four books and numerous articles on Victorian and modern British literature, spy fiction and film, and travel writing. He published *Espionage in British Fiction and Film since 1900: The Changing Enemy* with Lexington Books in 2015 (paperback 2017), which included substantial discussion of Ian Fleming and James Bond. He published the edited collection *The Many Facets of* Diamonds Are Forever*: James Bond on Page and Screen* with Lexington in 2019—the first full-volume treatment of Ian Fleming's fourth Bond novel and Guy Hamilton's famed film adaptation. He has received visiting research fellowships at Yale University, Cambridge University, Indiana University, and the Huntington Library and has given lectures and presentations on Ian Fleming; James Bond; and spy fiction in Britain, Europe, and North America. A native of London, England, Oliver Buckton has lived with his wife in South Florida for over twenty-five years. He is presently professor and chair of English at Florida Atlantic University, Boca Raton.